EARLY CHILDHOOD CURRICULUM

A CONSTRUCTIVIST PERSPECTIVE (2ND EDITION)

Through its unique integration of curriculum and learning principles, *Early Childhood Curriculum: A Constructivist Perspective, 2nd Edition* fosters authentic, developmentally appropriate practice for both preschool and early elementary classrooms. The constructivist format of this book encourages active involvement on the part of readers by asking them to observe, question, reflect, research, and analyze, thus allowing readers to create their own knowledge through their responses and actions.

Early Childhood Curriculum examines curricular goals such as autonomy, development, and problem solving and links those goals with constructivist principles of learning. It explores ways teachers can create meaningful learning environments and choose curriculum tasks appropriately—in all content areas—that are linked to the learning and development needs of young children. The text provides a wealth of practical detail about implementing constructivist curriculum as the authors discuss classroom climate and management, room design, play, and cooperative learning, among other topics. The book also includes information about how teachers can meet required mandates and national and state standards in appropriate ways as they plan their curriculum, and examines the early childhood educator's role with community agencies, reform and legal mandates, and public relations.

Special Features

- "Curriculum Strategies" highlight models for developing curriculum, including projects, curricular alignment, integration of various subject matter areas, and types of knowledge.
- "Constructions" promote problem solving by allowing students to explore, revisit, examine, and learn from first-hand experience.
- "Multiple Perspectives from the Field" provide interviews with teachers and other early childhood professionals, offering students a realistic look at the profession from a diverse group of educators.

- "Teacher Dialogues" explore a wide range of student concerns, including curriculum, learning environments, assessment, and documentation, representing a collaborative support group for pre-service teachers and readers.

Nancy Amanda Branscombe is Associate Professor of Early Childhood Education at Athens State University.

Jan Gunnels Burcham is Professor of Early Childhood Education and Moselle W. Fletcher Distinguished Chair of Teacher Education at Columbus State University in Columbus, Georgia.

Kathryn Castle is Professor and Chuck & Kim Watson Endowed Chair in Education and Graduate Coordinator at Oklahoma State University.

Elaine Surbeck is Professor Emeritus of Educational Leadership and Innovation at Arizona State University.

EARLY CHILDHOOD CURRICULUM

A CONSTRUCTIVIST PERSPECTIVE (2nd edition)

N. Amanda Branscombe
Athens State University

Jan Gunnels Burcham
Columbus State University

Kathryn Castle
Oklahoma State University

Elaine Surbeck
Arizona State University, Emerita

with

Anne G. Dorsey
University of Cincinnati, Emerita

Janet B. Taylor
Auburn University, Emerita

Routledge
Taylor & Francis Group

NEW YORK AND LONDON

9-26-13
LB
$ 59.95

First published 2014
by Routledge
711 Third Avenue, New York, NY 10017

Simultaneously published in the UK
by Routledge
2 Park Square, Milton Park, Abingdon, Oxon OX14 4RN

Routledge is an imprint of the Taylor & Francis Group, an informa business

Library of Congress Cataloguing-in-Publication Data

Branscombe, N. Amanda, author.
  Early childhood curriculum : a constructivist perspective/Nancy Amanda Branscombe,
Jan Gunnels Burcham, Kathryn Castle, and Elaine Surbeck with Anne G. Dorsey and
Janet B. Taylor. — 2nd edition.
    pages cm
  Earlier edition entered under title.
  1. Early childhood education—Curricula—United States. 2. Constructivism (Education)—
United States. I. Title.
LB1139.4.E164 2014
372.21—dc23   2013004164

ISBN: 978-0-415-89526-2 (hbk)
ISBN: 978-0-415-89527-9 (pbk)
ISBN: 978-0-203-80884-9 (ebk)

Typeset in New Baskerville
by Apex CoVantage, LLC

Printed and bound in the United States of America by Publishers Graphics,
LLC on sustainably sourced paper.

This book is dedicated to

My mentors in NAECTE and to Priscilla, Kenneth, Gaines, and George McMillan;

My loving daughters, Kara Layne Taylor and Michelle Pendergraph;

Robert W. Dorsey;

Loren Thomas;

My husband, Douglas B. Aichele;

My wonderful husband, Andy Burcham;

The original authors of the first edition of this book, N. Amanda Branscombe, Kathryn Castle, Anne G. Dorsey, Elaine Surbeck, and especially, Janet B. Taylor: Thank you for sharing your knowledge and friendship, and thank you for allowing me to be a part of this second edition;

The teachers and students who taught us about teaching and learning; and

To all children who may eventually benefit from this work.

CONTENTS

PREFACE

The principal goal of education is to create men [and women] who are capable of doing new things, not simply of repeating what other generations have done—men [and women] who are creative, inventive, and discoverers. The second goal of education is to form minds which can be critical, can verify, and not accept everything they are offered. We need pupils who are active, who learn early to find out by themselves, partly by their own spontaneous activity and partly through materials we set up for them: who learn early to tell what is verifiable and what is simply the first idea to come to them.

—Jean Piaget, 1964

Early Childhood Curriculum: A Constructivist Perspective (2nd ed.) is intended for use in teacher preparation programs that are educating preservice teachers to teach young children from birth through third grade. Its content is grounded in constructivist understandings of how young children learn and the kinds of classroom environments that facilitate this learning. The text involves readers in active participation with others to explore the various aspects of a constructivist curriculum.

We designed the text from a constructivist perspective to help readers address key questions–for example,

- What are the aims of constructivist curriculum?
- What are the guiding principles on which constructivist curriculum is based?
- What are some of the key components of constructivist curriculum?
- Are there established models of constructivist curricula?
- How do you evaluate constructivist curriculum?

New in This Second Edition

This second edition includes updated information, research, and resources related to constructivist curriculum. Additionally, it includes

- information about how constructivist teachers can address required national and state standards, such as the Common Core Standards, in appropriate ways as they plan their curriculum;
- a revisiting of the importance of practitioners using theory to guide their practice and curriculum;
- ideas for teachers and teacher educators to use constructivist principles, practices, and tenets in a standards- and assessment-driven world while maintaining focus on the learner and the processes the learner is using;
- discussion and ideas for using constructivist curriculum practices with all learners, including children with disabilities or special needs;
- additional content, examples, and up-to-date research on the benefits of play and projects and the importance of play in the curriculum; and
- a revisiting of the importance of teachers and teacher educators developing their own autonomy and becoming strong advocates for curriculum and teaching based on scientifically proven, constructivist principles.

Authors' Backgrounds and Ideas About the Book

We, the authors of the book, share similar ideas about how children construct knowledge and have had similar experiences in using constructivist principles in our work with college students as well as with children. These shared experiences, ideas, and interests brought us together and helped us build strong professional relationships as we interacted with each other. Our colleagues' interest in how we were using constructivist principles in the design of our university classes and programs led us to collaborate on many presentations, this text, and the publication *Early Childhood Education: A Constructivist Perspective* (Houghton Mifflin, 2000). *Early Childhood Education: A Constructivist Perspective* was written for those considering early childhood education as a career and for those already preparing to work with young children. It can be used as a stand-alone text in an introductory course in early childhood education or as a supplemental text for other courses requiring more expanded course work. It is divided into parts that discuss the early childhood professional community, the world of children and their families, the settings for various early childhood programs, and early childhood professionals. This edition of the book continues many of the features introduced in *Early Childhood Education: A Constructivist Perspective.*

All of us agreed that our book should not simply present ideas about constructivist curriculum, but should actively engage readers in the construction of knowledge about curriculum design and implementation. We designed the book so that readers are invited into the text as active learners. We use six teacher characters to portray a variety of teacher types we have encountered in our work in the field. We suspect that you may find aspects of yourself or other early childhood teachers you know in these simulations.

Each of us entered the field of early childhood at different stages in our lives and from different experiential backgrounds. That we write from our perspectives as university professors, classroom teachers, relatives of young children, parents, and grandparents adds a dimension of thoughtfulness and experience not found in all other texts. We work at different universities and live in various cities around the country, and working together on the book was quite a challenge. Nevertheless, it was well worth the effort in that it produced a text that is balanced by our diverse work experiences. Elaine Surbeck summed up the experience of working as a team: "I would like to thank my coauthors for their friendship and for their ability to always further my thinking. It has been a rich and varied experience that we have shared as we wrote the two books together, and I appreciate their collective and individual knowledge and warmth." Our collaborative interactions in designing the text have strengthened the book beyond what a single-authored text could provide. The authors all contributed to this edition and are represented by the alphabetical, nonhierarchical listing of authors. Kathryn Castle and Jan Burcham filled the role of liaison with the publisher, in addition to their writing responsibilities.

Uniqueness of the Book

The many interactive and unique features found in the first edition are continued throughout this second edition. We begin by introducing six teachers who teach in programs that range from infancy through the primary grades. They meet on a regular basis to discuss their diverse positions on theoretical and practical issues related to constructivist curriculum. These teachers appear in each chapter and express their own questions and ideas as they struggle to make sense of a constructivist curriculum. Readers will identify with some of these teachers and their concerns, and they will become colearners with these teachers as they explore how constructivist curriculum is designed and implemented. Each chapter is designed to prompt thinking about curriculum topics and includes perspectives of authentic voices in the field—that is, actual constructivist teachers.

The book provides a range of content that one might expect in a curriculum text, along with challenging "constructions" (tasks that ask the reader to research a topic, observe children, reflect in a journal, analyze ideas, and implement an approach) to help readers examine all aspects of using theory to guide curriculum practice. The content of this book reflects our goal of providing material that is sensitive to diversity and other issues important in curriculum today, such as incorporating required standards, inclusion, evaluation, and use of technology in the classroom. We also provide substantial resources for exploring an early childhood curriculum from a constructivist perspective.

Content and Organization

The book is organized into three parts. Part 1, "What Are Constructivist Aims and Assumptions?," consists of three chapters that provide the theoretical rationale for the curriculum. Chapter 1, "The Aims of a Constructivist Curriculum," welcomes readers to an examination of constructivist theory in an early childhood classroom. Students are introduced to Jennifer, Kenisha, Matt, Parul, Ron, and Sheila, teachers in programs that serve children from infancy through the primary grades. Readers follow these teachers throughout the text as they discuss how to implement a constructivist approach in their classrooms. Chapter 2, "How Constructivist Assumptions Guide Practice," presents the view of curriculum as a series of dynamic decisions and assumptions teachers make about children and how they learn. Readers are offered significant constructivist principles that can be used to guide their decision-making process in all classroom settings. Chapter 3, "Learning and the Three Kinds of Knowledge," invites readers to reflect on learning and how learning takes place. It provides meaningful information about the processes that all learners use to construct knowledge, the three kinds of knowledge to be constructed, and the role of representation in externalizing thought.

Part 2, "What Are Key Components of Constructivist Curriculum?," consists of four chapters that invite readers to consider practices that are vital to a constructivist curriculum. Chapter 4, "Authentic Tasks, Choice, and Decision Making," helps readers construct a deeper understanding of three of the key components and provides examples of how these components are used with developmentally diverse children. Additionally, this chapter explains and demonstrates how these components promote the reasoning and autonomy of learners, as well as meets the teacher's curriculum standards. Chapter 5, "Social Interaction, Play, and Projects," helps readers expand their understanding of three additional components of the curriculum and provides many examples and explanations of the importance of social interaction, play, and project work in children's construction of knowledge. Chapter 6, "Problem Posing, Problem Solving, and Reflection," explains how these elements help children, families, and teachers become lifelong learners. It addresses the importance of respecting and responding to the thinking of children and provides suggestions for developing curriculum related to their interests and needs even in the current environment of standards- and assessment-driven requirements. It also discusses the dynamic processes of awareness, reflection, and disequilibration and their role in cognitive development. Chapter 7, "The Role of Community," presents a constructivist perspective on community and provides numerous examples that distinguish it from other perspectives. Included are suggestions that help readers create a community where children learn mutual respect and can develop a sense of belonging in a caring environment. Additionally, readers learn how to expand this perspective of community so that it includes families and others.

Part 3, "What Are Constructivist Practices?," consists of three chapters related to established curriculum models, methods, and evaluation procedures that have been proven to be effective, and helps readers think about ways they might begin to implement their own curriculum. Chapter 8, "Building a Constructivist Curriculum," helps readers use knowledge considered in earlier chapters to plan various ways to get started in their own classrooms and to address standards as they make changes. It assists readers with practical examples and assurance that a gradual approach is a reasonable way to begin. Readers also learn about working with a broad range of students and consider ways to help principals and families understand how children are learning. Chapter 9, "Constructivist Models of Instruction," summarizes the components of several constructivist models that started in the preschool and have been extended into the primary grades. Readers will construct the necessity for such models, explore how these models interpret and apply theory, and use that information to compare other models. Chapter 10, "Constructivist Evaluation: Assessment and Documentation," offers readers different processes that can be used to evaluate the effectiveness of their teaching and the curriculum. It provides a strong rationale for consistency between the goals of the program and the processes used to gather the data on which to base evaluation. This chapter gives numerous examples of authentic assessment and documentation techniques for evaluating a constructivist curriculum.

Throughout the text, we note curriculum guidelines suggested by professional associations, such as the National Association for the Education of Young Children, the National Council of Teachers of Mathematics, and the National Council of Teachers of English, representing best practices arrived at through consensus among early childhood and content-area professionals. Additionally, the text is designed to foster the reader's autonomy and development through the use of multiple perspectives, individual and group constructions, and reflective questioning. The goals of autonomy and development are continuous through every chapter in the book.

Using Constructivist Learning Strategies and Features

Holding an active conversation with our readers as they construct their understandings of constructivist curriculum was a goal we had for this book. Continued in this edition are interactive devices (which we maintain are constructivist) to encourage ongoing conversations. The devices, interspersed throughout each chapter, ask readers to observe, reflect, research, analyze, and question. Each device has been developed and placed at a specific point in the chapter to help readers make sense of constructivist curriculum.

Teacher Dialogues

Students are introduced to six teacher characters—Jennifer, Kenisha, Matt, Parul, Ron, and Sheila—who represent a group of teachers in programs for children from infancy through primary grades. They represent teachers at varying levels of understanding of constructivist curriculum and teaching strategies. They appear in each chapter so that readers will recognize that, as these teacher characters begin to teach and apply what they have learned in their teacher preparation programs, they will continue to question and learn. The teacher characters wonder about children, curriculum, learning environments, assessment and documentation, theory, and their understandings of constructivism. As they question their roles and constructivism, they are candid and straightforward. They represent a collaborative support group for preservice teachers and other readers as all develop understandings of constructivist curriculum.

Multiple Perspectives From the Field

Interviews with a diverse group of teachers and other early childhood professionals offer realistic looks at the profession through their stories and perspectives on various issues. These professionals speak directly to readers so that the readers can understand constructivist curriculum from the perspectives of practitioners currently in the field.

Curriculum Strategies

Each chapter offers constructivist curriculum strategies that readers can use as considerations when they begin to teach. Because we know that each teacher has to construct curriculum practices and strategies individually, we view these strategies as guidelines, not dogma.

Constructions

We designed these features to have readers apply what they are learning. Just as with the other features, they are intended to encourage interaction and co-ordination of perspectives with other readers. The constructions might ask the reader to use Analysis/Synthesis, Reflections, Interviews, Research, Observations, Collaborations, and Writings. Readers and instructors may want to use this feature as a form of self-assessment or assessment for the course. We prefer features like this for assessment because they document students' thinking.

End-of-Chapter Summaries and Constructions

Each chapter offers an end-of-chapter summary that highlights major concepts introduced in the chapter. The end-of-chapter constructions encourage students to revisit the chapter, reflect on what they have learned, and apply it. They also create a need for students to coordinate what they expected to read and what they actually read in that chapter with their beliefs before reading the next chapter.

Resources

An annotated list of resources—including books, articles, children's literature, Web sites, and videos—is provided at the end of each chapter. We have selected these resources carefully so that students will have additional information for their own resource files and portfolios.

Glossary

Key terms that may not be familiar to the reader are printed in boldface type the first time they appear in the text and are concisely defined in the Glossary at the end of the book.

Acknowledgments

We acknowledge and thank many people who have helped us write this book. First, we acknowledge our own teachers, who inspired us to think beyond the status quo, raise questions, and then construct answers to those questions through reading, reflecting, discussing, observing, and researching children's thinking and learning. Rheta DeVries, Eleanor Duckworth, George Forman, Catherine Twomey Fosnot, Constance Kamii, Hermina Sinclair, and Janet B. Taylor have been mentors and role models who have challenged us to question and advance our thinking about constructivist curriculum.

Our students have been our teachers as well. Whether the students were children in our classrooms and preschool sites, graduate and undergraduate university students, or teachers in the field who were attending workshops, they have taught us through their questions, their attempts to apply what we taught them, and their efforts to go beyond our knowing. These students and teachers include Pamela U. Brown, Angela Carr, Kristi Dickey, Beth Fuqua, Mary Glover, Anna Hall, Ulli Land, Sandy Little, Julia Lorenz, Jamie Lynch, Katherine McNaughton, Eun-hye Park, Debra Pierce, Kathy Preusse, Karen Rogers, Brenda Sharman, Nancy Simpson, Linda Skinner, Jeff Smith, Barbara Thompson, Ronda P. Ware, Pamela Wetherington, and Heidi Weber.

We recognize the social and interactive nature of learning, which provokes transformations in our own thinking. We also recognize that such social interaction with our colleagues has contributed to furthering our thinking. Those colleagues include Christine Chaille, Deirdre Greer, Marjorie Fields, Joan Isenberg, Cynthia Lumpkin, Joan Moyer, Deborah Burk Rodgers, Frances Rust, Steve Silvern, and Peter Williamson.

We thank those who helped us with the actual preparation of this book. This includes each of the students and teachers who allowed us to interview them and use their materials, expertise, and insights. We also thank Alex Masulis and the team at Routledge/Taylor and Francis for their efforts in assisting us in completing this book.

PART 1

WHAT ARE CONSTRUCTIVIST AIMS AND ASSUMPTIONS?

The aims and guiding principles of a constructivist curriculum are based on constructivist explanations of how children learn and the nature of the knowledge to be learned. The work of Jean Piaget and his followers provides the theory and research for those explanations. The three chapters in Part 1 of this book offer perspectives on the aims of a constructivist curriculum and the theory and research that support those aims. Chapter 1 introduces the aims of a constructivist curriculum. Chapter 2 provides an overview of how constructivist assumptions guide practice and introduces the constructivist components that will be detailed in later chapters. Chapter 3 explains the theoretical tenets of constructivist teaching and details how learning takes place. All three chapters provide a constructivist foundation for the constructivist teacher so that decisions about curriculum are based on theory and research rather than personal opinion.

1

THE AIMS OF CONSTRUCTIVIST CURRICULUM

Chapter 1 is designed to help you understand the basic concepts and aims of constructivist curriculum. When you finish reading and discussing the material in this chapter, you should have a better understanding of the following topics and be able to explain them to others:

- What is meant by *curriculum*
- Curriculum sources
- What constructivism means
- Some basic principles of constructivist practice
- How constructivist curriculum differs from other curricula

Because Chapter 1 is an introductory chapter, these topics will be addressed only briefly. Subsequent chapters and your own reflections and constructions will help you understand each topic more thoroughly.

First, let's meet six teachers who are interested in learning more about constructivist theory and how it may apply to curriculum in their classrooms. They are composites of real teachers in real schools and were once in teacher preparation programs such as yours. Like you, they continue to learn in order to provide the best education possible for children. Although they are already licensed to teach, they continue to create new understandings for themselves. You will follow them throughout this book as they learn from others and as the result of their own reflections and risk taking. We hope you will join them by sharing your thinking with your classmates and by listening to their ideas.

Introduction

Six teachers have gathered in the teachers' lounge of an elementary school at 3:30 on a September afternoon. The building is fairly quiet now, and the teachers are seated around a table, looking somewhat tentative.

Kenisha: Well, I guess I'll start, since this was my idea. I invited each of you to my school today so that we can consider whether we can help each other. Although I've been teaching kindergarten for such a long time that one of my former pupils is now a teacher, I still feel the need to keep modifying what I do in the classroom. New issues are facing our children and families and—well, I'll stop there. Let's hear from the rest of you.

Jennifer: I need help, but I don't see how I'm going to get it by sitting around talking. I teach third grade in an inner-city school. I practically have to force them to learn, but they've got to learn; I'll see to that. What I need is an assistant to drill them on math facts and sight words.

Matt: I teach in a first- and second-grade multiage class in the suburbs, and our kids probably are different from yours in some ways, Jennifer. But don't think they don't have problems, too. I grew up in the inner city with a single mom who worked two jobs so my three brothers and I could eat. But when I look at some of my students, I know my life was better than their lives. We didn't have any money, but we were always there for each other—still are, as a matter of fact.

Ron: I guess in a way I'm the one who really needs this group. You all seem like you know what you're doing. I don't. I thought I did, but it's obvious I don't. Last year at this time, I was a student teacher with a wonderful mentor, Ms. Gleason. Children in her class did all kinds of projects. They worked independently, and they learned so much. I'm now a first-grade teacher, and I'm wondering if all the constructivist theory and principles I learned in college have anything to do with teaching. But then, I remember that in Ms. Gleason's room, those constructivist ideas guided her. Why doesn't it work for me? When Ms. Williams—Kenisha, I mean—called me, I didn't even want to come. She's the reason I became a teacher. I loved being in her kindergarten all those years ago. And now . . .

Parul: It's sometimes overwhelming at first.

Kenisha: Sheila, we haven't heard from you. Tell us where you teach.

Sheila: Oh, I'm just a Head Start teacher in the next county. It's pretty rural out there. I probably shouldn't be here.

Jennifer: Most of my kids went to Head Start, and I'd like to hear more about it.

Parul: Sheila, my children are even younger than yours. I have infants and toddlers in a child-care center. So, we're really all in early childhood education.

Kenisha: Absolutely! But let's take some time to figure out whether we can all benefit from meetings like this one. I met each of you at various workshops and conferences, and we talked a little bit about our teaching on those occasions, but why don't we just talk informally about how we could support one another. I brought some snacks, and there's coffee and a vending machine here in our lounge.

What Is Curriculum?

Curriculum is defined in a variety of ways. Since you started school, you have been taught according to a curriculum of some sort. You may have realized some time ago that a curriculum has something to do with what you are supposed to learn in school. Box 1.1 provides sample definitions of curriculum.

BOX 1.1 SAMPLE DEFINITIONS OF CURRICULUM

"The set of courses offered by an educational institution; A set of courses constituting an area of specialization" (*Merriam-Webster Dictionary*, www.Merriam-webster.com).

"All the organized and intended experiences of the student for which the school accepts responsibility" (Ryan & Cooper, 2000, p. 308).

"Educational objectives that are applicable to a specific academic area or area of study" (Spafford, Pesce, & Grosser, 1998, p. 67).

"The organized experiences designed to provide formal and informal opportunities for learning to children in a school setting" (Spodek & Saracho, 1994).

"A definition of what is to be learned. The origins of the word are from the Latin *curriculum*, a racing chariot, from which is derived a racetrack, or a course to be run, and from this, a course of study" (Ross, 2000, p. 8).

"An organized framework that delineates the content children are to learn, the processes through which children achieve the identified curricular goals, what teachers do to help children achieve these goals, and the context in which teaching and learning occur" (Bredekamp & Rosegrant, 1992, p. 10).

Notice that the last definition in the box, provided by the National Association for the Education of Young Children (NAEYC), is broader than most others in that it goes well beyond content. Our approach, too, goes well beyond content.

Teachers Plan Curriculum

Good teachers recognize that an appropriate, worthwhile curriculum involves much time and thought on their part. They think first about their overall objectives for children. Some objectives that relate to constructivist theory have been developed by Kamii and DeVries (1993). (See Box 1.2.) They think about large chunks of time and then move down to smaller periods. Teachers plan what they want to help children learn during the year, the semester, several weeks, a day, and even a particular time period. Even if teachers are provided with curriculum books or predetermined curriculum, they must plan how they will use these materials and what, when, and how they will help their students learn. They know that most worthwhile learning is constructed over time rather than in one class period.

BOX 1.2 CONSTRUCTIVIST TEACHING OBJECTIVES

Socioemotional Objectives

For the child to

1. become increasingly more autonomous within a context of generally noncoercive relationships with adults.
2. respect the feelings and rights of others and begin to cooperate (through decentering and coordinating different points of view).
3. be alert and curious and use initiative in pursuing curiosities, to have confidence in his ability to figure things out for himself, and to speak his mind with conviction.

Cognitive Objectives

For the child to

1. come up with a variety of ideas, problems, and questions.
2. put objects and events into relationships and notice similarities and differences (Kamii & DeVries, 1993).

Curriculum Development Is a Shared Enterprise

Teaching can be an isolated profession, particularly when teachers work alone in their own classrooms with few opportunities to discuss issues of substance with other teachers. Even when teachers work in teams, the focus often tends to be on planning the curriculum, troubleshooting, and taking care of administrative details rather than larger issues. You might ask yourself, "How do I feel about working with other teachers? Am I open-minded about sharing and accepting ideas? What examples can I provide from my experiences?"

When there are opportunities to discuss substantive issues, to work through and clarify new thinking, then teachers grow and change. In the same way, children need many opportunities to discuss their thinking and to support one another as they work out their understandings. Skilled teachers know how to arrange and sustain such a supportive environment for their students and for themselves. Teachers grow and change when they discuss issues with other teachers.

CONSTRUCTIONS

1. Research

Find out what standards your college or university must meet. Who imposes those standards? Who determines whether the standards are met? How? What would happen if the standards were not met?

2. Research

What standards will you have to meet in order to be a licensed teacher? Who determines these standards?

3. Writing

Write a paper on standards in education. Use either the research questions here, or relate your paper to standards in a particular content area.

Curriculum Is Based on Standards

In designing curriculum, teachers think about the **content** that children are expected to know. Those expectations may come from a governmental body such as a local board of education, from state and/or national standards, from professional organizations, from textbooks, and certainly from teachers' understandings of children, their interests, and their current and emerging abilities. Teachers must be familiar with and knowledgeable about a variety of standards.

Teachers need an organized framework as they develop day-to-day curriculum. Such a framework differs from a prepackaged curriculum, which delineates what is to be done in classrooms all over the country in a fair amount of detail and in a particular sequence. Teachers consider the context, as well as the content, as they design curriculum. As teachers refer to standards, they must be aware of their value and of the possibility of misusing them as day-to-day teaching guides. Standards are not intended to give teachers a specific teaching plan. Rather, they provide guides for considering areas to be addressed within the curriculum that knowledgeable teachers design for the children in their own classes.

The work by the National Science Teachers Association (NSTA) and the National Research Council (NRC) is a good example of professional organization standards. In 2011, after completing in-depth study and research, the NRC released *A Framework for K–12 Science Education: Practices, Crosscutting Concepts, and Core Ideas.* This document, which outlines the key scientific ideas and practices all students should learn from kindergarten through twelfth grade, became the foundation for the development of new K–12 education standards: Next Generation Science Standards (www. nsta.org). The development of these standards, as with most national organization standards, occurs through extensive review by experts in the field as well as open, public review.

Beginning in 2010, the National Governors Association and Council of Chief State School Officers led the development of the Common Core State Standards. The effort led to the development of a "single set of clear educational standards for kindergarten through 12th grade in English language arts and mathematics that states voluntarily adopt" (www.corestandards.org). As of 2013, 45 states, the District of Columbia, four territories, and the Department of Defense Education Activity have adopted the Common Core Standards. The widespread adoption of the Common Core Standards is leading many professional organizations and educational systems to look at ways to appropriately implement and meet the intended outcomes of these standards.

With all of these standards and expectations being imposed on teachers and educational systems, teachers, themselves, must first develop their own understandings. Teachers will still find themselves reaching new thinking about scientific or mathematical principles as they exchange ideas with their students, even when their students are quite young. The curriculum strategies listed below suggest ways to incorporate one Common Core State Standard (CCSS) in math, the measurement and data category, at the kindergarten level.

CURRICULUM STRATEGIES: USING STANDARDS

Standard: (CCSS.Math.Content.K.MD.B.3) Classify objects into given categories; count the numbers of objects in each category and sort the categories by count.
Strategy:

- Help individual children develop questions to research.
  Example: Do you have a pet? If so, what animal is your pet?
- Provide a child with a clipboard and encourage the child to ask the question of each child in the class and to record responses.
- Guide the child to demonstrate the results using the interactive white board or pencil and paper.
- Encourage the class to analyze the whole data set and components of the set.

Following the lead of early standards development, many professional organizations have developed standards for teaching and learning. A list of some of the curricular standards appears in Box 1.3. Some of these standards are well researched, while others appear to have been hastily put together (Bredekamp & Rosegrant, 1995).

**BOX 1.3 SELECTED LIST OF ORGANIZATIONS
AND THE STANDARDS THEY PROVIDE**

- International Reading Association and the National Council of Teachers of English: Standards for the English Language Arts (1996) http://www.reading.org/Libraries/reports-and-standards/bk889.pdf
- International Society for Technology in Education: NETS for Students (2007) http://www.iste.org/standards/nets-for-students
- Joint Committee on National Health Education Standards: National Health Education Standards: Achieving Health Literacy (1995) http://www.cdc.gov/HealthyYouth/SHER/standards/index.htm
- National Association for Music Education: National Standards for MusicEducation (1994) http://musiced.nafme.org/resources/national-standards-for-music-education
- National Association for Sport and Physical Education: Moving into the Future: National Physical Education Standards: A Guide to Content and Assessment, 2nd ed. (2004) http://www.aahperd.org/naspe/standards/nationalStandards/PEstandards.cfm
- National Council for the Social Studies: NCSS National Standards for Social Studies Teachers (2002) http://www.socialstudies.org/standards/teacherstandards

---

The theory that guides curriculum decision making will determine, to a large extent, how teachers teach. Theory also has an impact on what is taught. As you read this textbook, you will learn about constructivist theory and how that theory relates to curriculum development and implementation.

What Does Constructivism Mean?

Constructivism is a theory of knowing that emphasizes the role each person plays in constructing his or her own knowledge rather than absorbing knowledge directly from the environment. The focus is on children's creation of knowledge rather than on their repeating what others consider important. This occurs as the individual mentally, and often physically, acts on the environment (see Kamii & DeVries, 1993).

Each individual uses knowledge she has already constructed and relates new information to that knowledge. In the process, she creates knowledge for herself. For example, a child's idea about fruit juice may be that it is something sweet to drink. Then she encounters tomato juice for the first time. What happens is described next: Jaime's mother is seated at the kitchen table drinking tomato juice. Jaime loves apple juice and orange juice, and when her mom says,

"Want some juice?" she quickly nods yes. One taste and she spits it out. "No juice, Mommy!" "Yes, Jaime, it's tomato juice," her mother replies.

For Jaime, the process of **disequilibration** is operating. Disequilibration refers to "a mental sense of imbalance that occurs when incoming information does not fit into the individual's existing cognitive structures" (Branscombe, Castle, Dorsey, Surbeck, & Taylor, 2000, p. 465). What Jaime understood before is not in balance with the new information she just obtained about juice. She had an understanding of juice that she constructed earlier from her experiences with apple and orange juices. Now she encounters something that her mother calls juice. It looks pretty to her and it is in a glass, but, she thinks, it doesn't taste like juice. For her, at this point, it can't be juice because it doesn't fit her understanding of juice. To achieve equilibrium, or cognitive balance, Jaime creates a new category, tomato juice, and does not relate it to apple or orange juice.

After additional experiences, perhaps with cranberry juice and pineapple juice, Jaime may create new categories that relate all five juices. Perhaps she will create for herself mental subcategories: juices that are sweet and those that are not. Or she may construct other mental categories: juices I like and juices I don't like. Another child might mentally group juices by consistency, categorizing tomato juice and pineapple juice as thick, and orange, apple, and cranberry as not thick.

With more opportunities to explore her environment, Jaime may learn about onion juice, beet juice, and carrot juice. Perhaps you have never considered those three juices. You may be thinking, "Whoever heard of carrot juice?" while others in your class may have blended carrots and other vegetables in a juicer to produce a delicious beverage or may have visited a store that sold such juices. Even after you see or bravely taste them, you may not relate them to the kinds of juices that you enjoy, or you may become a vegetable juice advocate. Several principles common to constructivist theory may help you understand the theory a little better. We will discuss them here and expand on these and additional concepts in other chapters.

Learners Revise Their Thinking

As people construct knowledge, they often go through levels of disagreement with others, particularly with more experienced learners who have encountered the same or a similar kind of content. You might ask yourself, "When was the last time I engaged in meaningful discussion with a classmate about a topic on which we held different views? Did explaining my views help me clarify them? Did listening to my classmate's views help me to understand? Did either of us modify our understanding?" Constructivists strongly support the notion of changing one's thinking as the knower considers the opinions and ideas of others and encounters conflicting evidence. Acceptance of revised thinking provides many opportunities for learners to advance their knowledge and refine their thinking. Read the information in Box 1.4 for an example of revision of thinking.

BOX 1.4 CHILDREN REVISE THEIR THINKING

The child who has never seen an apple tree may firmly believe that apples grow underground. Another child may relate apples to a display in a store and be unable to consider that they originate from somewhere other than the store. This child, like those who do understand where apples come from, is using what she knows at the time. Gradually she may revise her thinking. She may reason that some apples grow on trees and others come from stores. As she begins to classify apples as something that grows, she will be able to construct the knowledge that the apples in stores are not growing and that they, therefore, grew somewhere else.

When teachers try to force children to revise their thinking by responding to an answer with "Think again," the child will often learn to use the words the teacher requires but will probably not have constructed the knowledge that is related to the words. A better response would be for the teacher to continue providing opportunities for the child to interact with others and/or with materials (perhaps books or Internet sites) that will present differing perspectives and make it more likely that the child will reconsider her own thinking. The key is that we cannot force children to revise their own thinking. Instead, we must provide opportunities that will challenge children's present thinking so that they, themselves, will revise their own thinking

---

Learning as a Community Activity

Kenisha and the other teachers in the opening scenario are about to embark on a community activity. They are thinking about how they can get the kind of support each of them needs, while at the same time supporting one another. The group members' needs differ based on each teacher's current situation and past experiences.

Even before you begin teaching, you will benefit from sharing ideas and resources with your classmates, instructors, and mentor teachers; these resources will be quite helpful in the future as well as now. You will have opportunities to share your thinking and become open to new ideas so that you can consider what others have to offer. Considering the points of view that others present helps you rethink your own ideas. Sometimes your thinking will become more solidified, and sometimes you will continue to think in a particular way for the moment, changing your thinking only later with additional experience and consideration.

Let's go back to the teachers' lounge and see this principle in action. Kenisha has just asked the group to indicate whether they want to focus on curriculum since that seems to have been the topic that elicited the most response during the discussion.

Matt: I'm just about to start a master's of education at the university. It's a constructivist program, so I want to discuss that here too. Maybe you all can help me with some of my assignments.

Jennifer: Well, be prepared. I'm halfway through that program, and it's not the real world at all. You can't just let kids run wild and decide what they want to do all the time. I say, keep control; be in charge.

Ron: But actually all last year, it was clear to Ms. Gleason's children that she was the teacher. They were making a lot of decisions, but the limits were pretty clear.

Parul: Even the babies I work with make a lot of decisions. They let me know when I haven't understood what they need. But I would like to talk with all of you about whether there is a curriculum for toddlers and infants.

Sheila: I don't really know anything about constructivism. What I have to find out is whether I am harming my children. They learn all about animals and things that grow. We explore the creek and take care of class pets. Lots of parents come to school and tell the children stories. We visit the local businesses and the cannery. Our community is small, so everybody knows everybody else. We also take three or four trips to the city. But I found out that my children aren't really ready for kindergarten. Our children go to a consolidated school, and the teachers told me that they come to school not knowing the sounds letters make, so the teachers say they are not ready for kindergarten. Some of them know the names of all the letters, and some of them don't. I really want to talk about curriculum. If constructivism will help my children get ready for kindergarten, that's what I want to talk about too.

CONSTRUCTIONS

1. Research

Find out what "ready for kindergarten" means. Who decides? How are individual differences accounted for? Make a journal entry and be sure to cite your sources.

2. Research

Check your library and the Internet for information about infant-toddler curriculum. Report your findings to your classmates.

Learners Support One Another

The six teachers you met earlier have come together to discuss educational issues. Based on their discussions so far, it appears that they are seeking support from one another. Constructivists believe that learning occurs through interactions with one another and with the rest of the environment. (After all, we are all part of the environment.) The thinking that we share supports others by giving them confirmation of their own ideas or by countering their ideas with a different way of looking at a situation or problem. They, then, must reconsider and decide whether to change their thinking or continue to uphold it. This sharing is important both as you go through your teacher education program and as you work in educational settings as a teacher. Learners support one another and discuss education issues at every phase of their education and careers.

Individuals Are Responsible for Their Own Learning

Individuals act on their environment and relate what they notice to what they already know. Thus, each person's knowledge is uniquely developed. The person sitting next to you in class has had experiences that differ from yours. Therefore, when you each experience reading this chapter, you each bring to it different ways of thinking, and you each construct from it different knowledge to apply to the classroom.

CONSTRUCTIONS

Interview

Interview two classmates. Find out what they know about constructivism. Ask whether their early schooling seems to have been based on constructivist theory. If so, what are the indicators? If not, what was the theory that seemed to undergird the program? Report your findings to your class.

Back in the teachers' lounge, the six teachers seem to be about ready to wrap up their study group for this session.

Matt: I really do need help to get through this master's degree. I never even heard of constructivism until I took my first master's-level class. When I was an undergrad, no one mentioned it. I don't need to talk about curriculum. I do that every day.

Jennifer: Matt, you've got it all wrong. Constructivism seems to have a lot to do with curriculum—or maybe it's the other way around.

Sheila: I do want to talk about curriculum, but it does sound as if maybe my Head Start children are kind of in a constructivist program. Can you be a constructivist and still help children learn what they have to know?

Parul: Maybe that would be something we could talk about. Are constructivist teachers teaching content?

Ron: Yeah, and how do I get to be one—a constructivist teacher, I mean? I've seen it work. Maybe I'll send an e-mail to Ms. Gleason and find out how she became a constructivist.

Kenisha: Great idea. That's your homework, Ron! I'd like to keep on talking, but I'd also like to bring in some other ideas so we don't just create a gripe session. Would everyone be willing to read something about constructivism? Bringing in new ideas helps clarify thinking.

Parul: That would help me. Maybe Jennifer or Matt has some ideas from their classes.

Kenisha: If you want to give me your e-mail addresses, I'll set up a listserv, and we can make reading suggestions and try to come to an agreement that way. Shall we meet again in two weeks?

Constructivist Curriculum

When teachers espouse constructivist theory, they use their understandings of the theory to bring together their beliefs about learning and about curriculum. Their knowledge and belief systems guide their planning and implementation of curriculum. Children's learning, in turn, guides teachers' revisions of curriculum planning and teaching.

Teachers Consider the Processes Through Which Children Learn

All teachers must examine their beliefs about learning because the curriculum they plan must be closely tied to the ways in which children learn. Children learn in a variety of ways and their learning styles vary, so this topic is complex.

Constructivist teachers understand that learning occurs as children interact with the environment, including classroom materials, the people in the environment, and the ideas of those people and of the teacher. Constructivist teachers understand that children need time and space to explore and examine their own thinking.

An Example: Learning to Read

Consider learning to read. Many schools expect children to have the ability to read certain types of books by the end of first grade. Some schools are trying to accomplish this at kindergarten. Perhaps you have heard of a child who taught herself to read when she was four years old. And you may know a child who is just becoming interested in reading at age seven. Each child learns at her own pace. Learning to read occurs as the child's interest in reading develops. But children can't really learn to read unless they have been exposed to books. This experience gives children something to relate to, and it often occurs in a socio-emotional context that is quite comfortable for the child, such as sitting on an adult's lap, turning the pages together. For very young children, even infants, the reading curriculum, whether at school or home, starts with hearing someone read, then holding a book, figuring out how to turn the pages, remembering what happened on each page, and all the while learning that reading is interesting, enjoyable, and something to be continued.

Think about the young children you know who want you to read to them, maybe even the same story over and over again. They have constructed for themselves an interest in reading and a beginning understanding of what it is all about. They are doing it not so they can pass a test but because they enjoy reading. Perhaps it is because they appreciate doing something with an adult or older child; perhaps it is the fascination with finding out that the story is always the same no matter who reads it or how many times they hear it. Maybe it's the delight of identifying the dog and the cow and the horse, or predicting that, yes indeed, that carrot in *The Carrot Seed* (Krauss, 1945) certainly can grow. Yet some of these same children may be those who can't read when they are in the third grade. Teachers have to think about curriculum that meets each child's needs, interests, and current knowledge and abilities.

Constructing Curriculum

Even when teachers just pick up a teachers' manual on the first day of school and follow it page by page until the end of the school year, they are basing their curriculum on their beliefs about how children learn. When someone who knows nothing about the particular group of children plans the curriculum, he or she does not take into account the individual differences and needs of those children. This teacher does not view these individual differences and needs as being important in learning. When the curriculum is predesigned and followed in a lockstep manner, the assumption is that the goal is to internalize a body of information in a particular order and often in a particular form. Teachers who use this approach are likely to believe that learning is a process of taking something from the environment and memorizing it rather than constructing it based on the individual's own actions and interactions.

Many current curricula are based on behaviorist theories. Behaviorist teachers see their role as transmitting information to children to be remembered. Constructivist teachers see their role as providing opportunities for children to experience ideas related to content, guiding them to consider the content, and working with individuals and groups in discussion and questioning to clarify thinking.

Although behaviorism can be subsumed under constructivism, it is not a substitute. That is, within a constructivist curriculum there are instances when independent thinking or **autonomy** could be dangerous, in part because the child does not yet have the ability to take his or her own needs or the needs of others into account. For example, when the fire alarm is sounded, children have been taught through direct instruction and repeated practice to get in line immediately and follow the teacher silently. This approach is essential because a potentially life-threatening emergency is not the time for a young child to think independently and creatively (although there could be exceptions). Similarly, the contractor working on an office building is expected to follow the drawings and specifications provided by the architect rather than independently choosing to build the building in the way she or he prefers. Therefore, constructivist teachers consider the context, what is to be learned, and the needs and abilities of the children when constructing curriculum, and they match what they know about learning to what and how they teach.

Constructivist Teachers Address Problem Solving

Constructivist teachers focus on desired outcomes rather than on breaking learning into small, meaningless pieces. The third-grade classroom discussed in the case study contains an example.

The third graders in Ismelda Evans's class found it more interesting and engaging to plan an end-of-the-year primary school picnic than to begin by calculating the number of ounces of soda five children would consume if each drank one 12-ounce can. They soon discovered they needed that information, but at the start, they focused on the outcome: planning a successful picnic. Along the way, they considered others' points of view. Would kindergartners want to play softball? How much time would they need for eating? Would there be enough time for games? How many hot dogs would each child get? Does everybody eat hot dogs? Would there be enough money to get ice cream? How would they keep the ice cream cold?

Ms. Evans looked at this project from a long-term perspective. She used the project to involve students in reading, writing, and calculating as they planned the event and recorded and modified their plans. When they considered the needs of other children and when they debated among themselves, they were developing skills involved in considering others' points of view, a component of the social studies curriculum. Mathematical thinking was enhanced as they gathered information about prices, considered quantities needed, and related that information to the amount of time and money available. When her children considered how to keep ice cream cold, Ms. Evans encouraged them to research freezing and melting in science references. She also considered the areas of curriculum that were integrated and the specific outcomes the school or district had set forth.

Good teachers recognize that learning is not always fun. It is work for children and teachers, but it can be enjoyable and intriguing. You will read more about how curriculum is developed throughout this textbook.

Teachers Organize Materials

Teachers are responsible for obtaining appropriate materials from the school, sometimes from contributors and often from their own salaries or resources. For example, one teacher called furniture stores and asked if there was a floor model sofa available to be donated to her inner-city school classroom when the new styles came in. Before anyone believed it would happen, a delivery truck with a new green sofa arrived and became a favorite reading area for the children. On a smaller scale, teachers gather manipulative materials for children who choose to use them to help them understand a math concept. They make interactive charts for preschoolers who can insert their own names or those of friends as they sing the words to a favorite song. Teachers select books at the library, buy several types of paper for the writing center, and search dollar stores for pawns for math games.

Once teachers have gathered materials, they organize the classroom so that it is easy for everyone to use. Teachers consider routines. Where will children put their belongings when they arrive? When they need paper and pencils, where will they get those? Where does completed work belong? Then they stand back and consider the aesthetic appeal of the room. Is it too cluttered? Too busy? Welcoming? Child oriented but not cartoony? Teachers use their classroom organization as a way to help children learn.

Teachers Take an Active Role Throughout the Day

Good teachers focus on helping children construct knowledge. They recognize that they can't give children knowledge and can't force children to acquire it. Therefore, they hold high expectations for all children, but these expectations are realistic and filled with encouragement, and these teachers are never punitive. They observe, ask questions, make suggestions to extend thinking, and encourage.

Teachers understand children's mistakes. If they don't, they ask the child to explain his thinking. Teachers accept what seem to be errors, recognizing that, at that moment, the child has constructed a particular understanding. They understand that the child will soon move to a higher level of understanding. As teachers gather information about children's thinking, they record their observations mentally and in print. They then use these observations not only to plan future curriculum, but also to help them work with the child in that moment. For example, when a child is expected to write about an event, the constructivist teacher might read the child's description and comment, "I wonder how your grandmother got from Denver to your house in Sioux Falls," rather than, "You have to have at least four sentences." The teacher might say, "You wrote that your aunt lives near a beach. What are some things that children there can do that you can't do here in Columbus?"

Constructivist teachers avoid sitting at a desk monitoring the children and doing paperwork while requiring children to sit at their desks doing paperwork. They set up a range of centers for children's use or help children prepare the centers. They set aside reasonable amounts of time for children to use the centers, and they encourage children to choose centers that interest them rather than limiting each child to one 15-minute turn per week at each center or rotating through all the centers. Constructivist teachers realize that children may need to work at a center for a number of days in a row as they clarify their understandings of a concept. Certainly, teachers recognize that centers are an integral part of the curriculum rather than a reward for finishing "work."

Curriculum Relates to Context

Teachers consider the context as well as the content in planning curriculum. Each teacher encounters a different context for teaching. Context includes geography, community values, required standards, and developmental levels and interests of children and teachers. Personal knowledge and beliefs all play roles. Even more important are the specific children in the class. Each of them brings his or her own culture, needs, and interests. This is the case even when the entire class is composed of children with disabilities, children of poverty or wealth, children from an ethnic group or race, or any relatively homogeneous group. Context includes children of divorce, single parents, blended families, and lesbian and gay parents. The children, as well as their families, form the context.

Although the context provides a major planning framework, it is not an indication to lower standards because of a teacher's personal beliefs about a group. In fact, individuals who hold any group or child as less important than others should not be teaching. Context does mean, however, that teachers consider it their responsibility to learn about the particular context and, insofar as possible, to become informed about a wide variety of cultures. Teachers must also have an understanding of child development and the many variations in development. Teachers use all this information to help children grow in understanding content. Serious attention must be given to the society in which our children will continue to grow. You will read more about the importance of context in the chapters that follow.

Multiple Perspectives: From a Teacher and Researcher

Brenda Hieronymus is a constructivist teacher who has been working with young children for more than twenty years. She has coauthored multiple books on constructivist curriculum and has been a speaker at many local, regional, and national conferences. When we interviewed Brenda, she was in the midst of conducting a week-long workshop on art and music for current teachers.

Brenda hasn't always been a constructivist teacher. When she began her career, there was little information and attention directed to the theory in the United States. But after completing her master's degree, Brenda continued to pursue learning about her role. She began to read books on constructivist theory and to talk with professors and fellow teachers about the theory and what it might mean for classroom teachers. Most important, she began to reflect on her own teaching and how she might apply what she was learning.

Brenda began by using approaches that had been researched, such as the questioning strategies described by Kamii and DeVries (1993). For example, she might ask a child who requests more water for his work with clay, "What do you think will happen if you add more water to your clay?" Within reason, she lets children try their ideas. When presenting materials that are new to a child, she might ask, "What could you do with these?" For example, she prepared a tray with a pint-sized fruit basket filled with artificial strawberries. Also on the tray were a pair of tongs and another small basket. The child began by taking one berry at a time and lining them up near the tray. When he finished, Brenda asked, "How could you use these tongs?" as she touched the tongs. The child began to pick up each berry with the tongs and return each to the fruit basket. Handling the tongs was challenging for him, and he soon reverted to using his fingers. Brenda noted that on ensuing days, the child returned repeatedly to the strawberries, working with the tongs until he seemed to need to go back to using his hands. The next week she added a die with one, two, or three dots on each face. Some of the children began to use the die to determine how many berries they would put in the basket at one time. This extension offered an additional math component to a fine-motor activity, which already had opportunities for some mathematical thinking.

Brenda told us that one of the hallmarks of constructivist teachers is that they are careful planners. "I pay close attention to what children are doing and try to figure out how they are thinking. Then, as I ask questions, I try to focus on that child's thinking rather than just using any open-ended question." She commented that she looks at curriculum in a long-term fashion, thinking first of a semester and then a three- to four-week period as she makes decisions. She considers the needs of the group as well as of individual children. She selects materials that many children can use but each in a different way.

Brenda is aware of how the classroom looks. She believes that aesthetics are important and help determine what children will use. Her room is never cluttered, and everything that is selected for the classroom has a purpose. When too many choices are available, children may become overwhelmed. Each item that is on one of the shelves is available to children, who can easily see and select items. All the materials they need are on trays or in baskets. Often, duplicate sets are available to encourage children to play together and exchange ideas. Brenda has found that management is easier when two baskets of large, colorful, interlocking bricks, each with identical pieces, are placed side by side on a shelf. If the children who are using them decide to put them together or to trade pieces, that works well. However, when it is time to return them to the shelf, Brenda explains that each basket should contain the same pieces and she helps the children work this out if necessary. What a great lesson in division!

Every Friday, Brenda considers which items she will remove from the classroom, which she will retain, and which new items she will add. Her decisions are based on how the current items are being used. Themes are not used as the major framework. Rather than deciding that several children's interest in their pet dogs will be the theme and bringing in everything that she can find related to dogs (books, puzzles, games, charts, and so forth), Brenda instead picks up on children's interests in a concept or idea—a ramp, for example. Perhaps they have been exploring what will roll down a small wooden ramp. She may extend that exploration by providing large ramps that children themselves can roll down. She might help them construct a safe ramp for tricycle riding or take them to see the ramp that the truck driver sets up when unloading cartons of groceries for the child-care center. She considers the possibilities for learning math, science, and language, as well as opportunities for small-motor development, social skills development, and creativity. A dancer herself, Brenda is also studying the harp. She brings her appreciation of the arts to the classroom, and her quiet calm as she moves gracefully about the classroom sets the tone.

Despite the positive tone, some children struggle with learning behaviors that are appropriate in a classroom of 16 children. Child tempers flare, and children choose their own most effective tools to vent their anger; angry words, physical attacks, and tears are not unknown in this classroom. Brenda usually senses what is brewing. Her room is arranged so that she can observe easily and be aware at all times of what is happening in each area. Brenda moves to the child or children who need her, stops any dangerous behavior, listens to what children have to say, and then explains her expectations.

When another child is involved, she helps that child express her feelings too. All the while, she is helping each child construct knowledge of what is required to be an effective member of a group.

Brenda's class always contains children from a wide range of cultures. At the beginning of the year, there are usually several who speak no English. Half the children in the class are funded through Head Start, while other families pay tuition. Several children have disabilities. Brenda sees this diversity as a great opportunity for herself and for all the children and families. She enlists the support of all families in helping her understand each child's needs and interests and in finding ways to bridge transitions between home and school. For example, one family provided a quilt, a product of their Appalachian culture; others may teach all the children words in their own languages or bring picture books to share.

A study by Elgas and others (personal communication, 2000) demonstrated that children began to learn English during group time as they sang together. Brenda described an incident in which a non-English-speaking child, Yomi, went to the area where group time was held. All the other children were playing throughout the classroom. Yomi picked up the name cards of the members of the class. As she selected a name card, she looked around the classroom until she spotted that child, and then she returned the card to the basket and continued with the next name card. From across the classroom, Brenda smiled as she observed this significant example of construction of knowledge.

Constructivist Curriculum Focuses on the Development of Autonomy

Teachers must understand constructivist theory and know how to develop curriculum based on learning and teaching principles. They must value and respect the context in which learning is to occur. When these components are in place, teachers will be able to help children develop autonomy.

As children move from **heteronomy** (being governed by others), they begin to be able to think for themselves. If you have spent time with 2-year-olds, you have seen children who do think for themselves, running when an adult says, "Wait," saying "No" when an adult says, "Time for nap," and grabbing a toy from a playmate even though an identical toy is nearby.

Later, children make decisions about what to play and with whom, and within reason, what to wear and what and how much to eat. As their self-help skills and ability to make judgments improve, children become increasingly independent. In some cultures, very young children assume a great deal of responsibility, while in others, real responsibility does not come until college graduation.

Being able to speak for oneself, make decisions, and live independently are only parts of autonomy. An important component is consideration of the needs and desires of others. Young children usually believe the world revolves around their own desires. As they develop, they can begin to take others' points of view or at least recognize that other points of view do exist. The young child who observes family members helping one another and perhaps helping neighbors is likely to begin to relate that outlook as part of his own way of being. When parents and teachers take time to listen to children's points of view, those children are more likely to begin to listen to the points of view of the adults as well as of other children.

Constructivist teachers recognize that they must support the development of autonomy in their children not only in the social or interpersonal realm, but also in the moral and cognitive realms. Just as teachers must have courage to teach in the way they understand to be more appropriate for the context and content, so too must they help children have the courage to do what they believe is right even when other children may be choosing other paths. For example, when children with disabilities enter the class, some children may shun them. Autonomous teachers help children form their own opinions by getting to know the new children rather than making assumptions out of fear or as a result of following someone else's thinking.

Similarly, in the area of academic content, teachers must support children as they express their thinking, whether or not it is in agreement with the point of view of other children. Most of the class may think chocolate chip ice cream is better than any other flavor the teacher has listed on a graph. The autonomous child will be able to choose strawberry if that is what she prefers. Note, however, that many 4-year-olds will choose chocolate chip to be on what they perceive as the "winning side." In effect, many adults also take that path.

The autonomous child will be able to explain his understanding of what an author is trying to convey in a story the class is reading. Autonomous children will think of and try new ways to solve a problem that involves several mathematical steps. If, as they explain their solutions, they come to the realization that their method is incorrect, autonomous children will acknowledge the error and consider another approach. When other children present methods they view as incorrect, autonomous children will ask for further explanation, point out where they think an error is occurring, and respect the feelings of discouragement that doing so may be engendered.

Identifying One's Own Developing Autonomy

You might ask yourself, "How autonomous am I when it comes to stating a political opinion? What do I do when my friends make fun of another person? Would I be willing to ask my professor a question about constructivism if I just don't think the theory makes sense?" These kinds of questions help you consider your own developing autonomy. It is important for teachers and students to reflect on their own level of autonomy. Jasmine, a third grader, wrote in her journal, "When we are supposed to be writing in our journals, a lot of my friends are talking to each other and laughing. I want to talk to them too, but I know I have to get my work done. When I was younger, I was always talking. They might not like me if I didn't. But now they do."

Teachers must recognize that some cultures do not value thinking for one-self, but rather emphasize the importance of following the designated author-ity. Although in all cultures, all individuals have the responsibility to follow authority to an extent in order to maintain an orderly society, the way in which autonomy is expressed varies based on the context. Teachers must be sensitive to family and community values regarding this aspect of development. Teachers who help children establish the broad-based autonomy described earlier have provided them with the tools to understand content and context. These tools apply across a lifetime.

If you find that you are usually unwilling to state your ideas because oth-ers may think they are wrong, remind yourself that you have constructed your ideas based on what you know right now. As you get more information, you may change those ideas, and you must be open to new information. You must also be willing to take risks. As a teacher, you must help your students learn to agree and disagree with others politely, state reasons to support their ideas, and remain open to new ideas.

Doing What One Believes Takes Courage

When you take time to examine your beliefs carefully, you may find that your thinking has moved away from that of some of your peers. For example, when teachers find that they are in a nonconstructivist environment, one in which others follow the teacher's manual in lockstep fashion, those who have decided that the lockstep approach is inappropriate for the children in their classes may be cautioned that they are taking things too seriously. They may be encouraged to follow what everyone else is doing. Teachers who have constructed an under-standing of how children learn know that they must allow each child to develop within his or her own framework. They understand that a one-size-fits-all cur-riculum won't be in the children's best interests. They also know that merely transmitting or telling information to children does not provide the rich op-portunities for learning to which children are entitled. In the face of ridicule, criticism, and lack of understanding on the part of others, it takes courage for constructivist teachers to teach according to their conscience.

SUMMARY

- Constructivist teachers are interested in their own learning and let children know that they are continuing to learn.
- The curriculum reflects the teacher's belief that each child is responsible for his or her own learning.

- Learning occurs in community. Therefore, the curriculum provides opportunities to work in pairs or groups and to have whole-class discussions, while still providing opportunities for children to assume responsibility for their own learning.
- Teachers discuss with children and guide them as they construct ways to support one another, particularly in situations requiring risk taking.
- Teachers base their curriculum on knowledge of child development with emphasis on how learning occurs. They use theory and content as the basis of their planning and are courageous when people in power disagree with their points of view.
- Teachers focus on the broad outcome of the development of autonomy in the children they teach.

CONSTRUCTIONS

1. OBSERVATION

Visit an early childhood classroom and observe how it is arranged. Are there any indications that the teacher's decisions are based on children's needs and interests?

Spend an hour observing the teacher. Note examples of the teacher's use of constructivist principles discussed in this chapter.

Record your observations in your journal and bring it to class to share with your classmates. Keep in mind that the goal is to learn from the teachers you observe rather than to critique their teaching.

2. RESEARCH

Locate at least two Web sites that address constructivist theory. Record the sites in your Resource File and write a review of the site. If you have not already established a Resource File, begin developing one now. You will need to establish a system for collecting and filing, in an organized manner, the many tools you will use as a teacher. In addition to Web sites, you may want to include stories and songs; activities for various curricular areas; copies of relevant articles; bibliographic data on books that have been helpful; and DVDs, CDs, and videos that you may want to use in your classroom.

Many states have posted state standards on their Web sites. You may find them on your state's department of education Web page. Select a grade range such as pre-K–K or primary, and locate your state's standards. Review the standards and write a report on the pros and cons of the standards.

Select a curricular area that particularly interests you. Check the Web or contact the professional organization for a copy of standards for that area of curriculum. Some of the more thorough standards are in book form, on CDs, or online and may be available at your library, in your college's resource center, or online.

Resources

Books

Branscombe, N.A., Castle, K., Dorsey, A. G., Surbeck, E., & Taylor, J. (2000). *Early childhood education: A constructivist perspective.* New York, NY: Houghton Mifflin.

The first version by the five authors of the original edition of this curriculum textbook, this book serves as an orientation to early childhood education (ECE). The text provides a strong introduction to constructivist principles in early childhood education.

DeVries, R., & Kohlberg, L. (1987b). *Constructivist early education: Overview and comparison with other programs.* Washington, DC: National Association for the Education of Young Children.

Provides a scholarly study of Piagetian curriculum approaches and compares and contrasts them with other early childhood approaches.

Kafai, Y. B., & Resnick, M. (2011). *Constructivism in practice: Designing, thinking, and learning in a digital world.* New York, NY: Routledge.

Offers an explanation of constructionism and how it converges with constructivism to coordinate design and learning theory.

Kamii, C., & DeVries, R. (1993). *Physical knowledge in preschool education: Implications of Piaget's theory.* (Reissued with a new introduction). New York, NY: Teachers College Press.

An easy-to-read text that explains and provides detailed examples of physical knowledge.

Web Sites

Association of Constructivist Teaching https://sites.google.com/site/assocfor constructteaching

This website introduces you to the Association for Constructivist Teaching. It provides you with additional information about conferences, current news, a journal, and blogs on constructivism.

Jean Piaget Society http://www.piaget.org/index.html

This Web site is an overview of the Jean Piaget Society and its work. The Web site contains a students' page, recent publications, conference information, and news. It's an excellent resource.

2

HOW CONSTRUCTIVIST ASSUMPTIONS GUIDE PRACTICE

Although the principles of constructivist practices and their roles in children's learning are the focus of this chapter, the children and their thinking are at the heart of that focus. As constructivist teachers, we study, make decisions, and reflect on the nature of the learner and what the learner can do rather than beginning with the curriculum or content within that curriculum. Because of this perspective, we view curriculum as a series of dynamic decisions and assumptions we make about children, their day-to-day learning, and the content they are studying. We continually test these assumptions and decisions through the learning environments and experiences that we design for children. If we define ourselves as constructivist teachers, then we recognize that learning is an internal process that begins with the study of the child and his or her interactions with objects. Teachers can be constructivists no matter what expectations, curriculum, philosophy, or standards a school system or program places on them.

This chapter introduces you to some constructivist assumptions about the nature of the learner. Each of these assumptions will be discussed in detail in other chapters within this book. We hope that the assumptions help guide you in your efforts to make sense of your curriculum decisions. These assumptions are beginnings for you, not a recipe for constructivist teaching. They do not teach children to get the correct answer on Piagetian tasks or move from one cognitive stage to another. Rather, they arise from the overall aims of education that we believe are essential to constructivism: autonomy, development, and community.

After reading this chapter, you will have a beginning understanding of

- the nature of knowledge;
- the assumptions that constructivists hold for how children learn;
- what it means for children to be actively engaged in their own learning;
- the assumptions we (the authors) hold for ways that children use a learning environment; and
- an understanding of constructivist teaching assumptions.

Introduction

The teachers you met in Chapter 1 have visited Ron's classroom to observe and are now sitting in a coffee shop discussing their notions of what it means to be a constructivist teacher.

Ron:　　　I would like to hear everyone talk about constructivist principles for teaching. So many teachers say they are constructivists, but no one really says what they do in their classroom.

Jennifer:　My school system said that I had to use direct instruction teaching and the core curriculum standards. You know, I have to drill with worksheets so that the children have memorized the material. I also have to follow this prescribed curriculum that dictates what I do when. I'm not interested in doing that. I mean, I'd like to teach using constructivist principles, but I have to teach and document that I taught phonetics thirty minutes each day. I just don't have time to add anything.

Kenisha:　Well, I'm a constructivist. I use themes and activities within those themes. I just love what I do. In fact, one thing I just love to do is talk to a group of teachers and get new ideas for activities and themes. The more I have, the better.

Matt:　　 I must say that I have a problem with the word *principles*. I would use *assumptions*. Principles mean a code of law. I think of constructivist teaching as anything but dogma. To me, you can use constructivist assumptions even when you do direct teaching. I also think you can use themes without being a constructivist. I learned that assumptions are different from an approach to curriculum or activities.

Sheila:　 What do you mean? I thought aims had to let the kids do their own thing to be a constructivist! I thought you just let them construct and invent!

Parul:　　They can't construct and invent in a vacuum.

Kenisha:　Sheila, my kids just do their own thing. You should see some of the ideas those kids come up with. Of course, I do my activities with them each day.

Parul:　　Let's go back to what you were saying. What did you mean when you said that assumptions are different from activities and approaches?

Matt:　　 Well, to me, assumptions are the underpinnings of what you are doing with curriculum. So it really doesn't matter whether you do direct teaching or thematic teaching. What matters is whether you allow children to have choices about their learning, whether you have authentic tasks for the children to do, and whether those choices and tasks are based on theory—in other words, whether you consider the nature of the learner.

Parul: I totally disagree with you! You just don't understand constructivism, and you claim to have graduated from a constructivist program. In order to be a constructivist, you have to use certain approaches.

Matt: I did graduate from a constructivist program! It's not the themes, activities, and approaches that make a teacher constructivist; it's the teacher's way of thinking about how children learn. For example, a constructivist teacher focuses on the learner and the learning process.

Jennifer: What? Now you're really confusing me. I thought if I used the practices that the constructivist teachers used, I would have a constructivist classroom. When you go to those workshops or national conferences, you can attend sessions where constructivist teachers tell you how to do themes and daily activities. Some even give handouts of themes they've done.

Matt: But, Jennifer, you have to think about the information from the workshops and conferences and decide what that information means to you and the children in your classroom. You can use those themes from the handouts. The question you have to ask yourself is whether the projects and activities within those themes are truly integrated or just associated with the themes. Next, you have to ask yourself whether you are imposing this theme on the children or whether they are making choices about the tasks and activities within the theme. You also have to think about whether the tasks and activities are authentic. Finally, you have to ask how this theme addresses the child's needs.

Jennifer: Oh! So I have no assurance that a theme done by teachers who call themselves constructivists is constructivist? I have to study that theme to make sure its tasks, projects, and activities are integrated and authentic rather than just collected to go with a topic.

Matt: Right! Once I really studied themes and how children learn within theme work, I began to make a distinction between correlating and integrating activities, projects, and tasks within the themes. I also began to understand that the child is the learner. When I did that, I really began to understand how important it is to study children and how they learn.

Kenisha: I know I began to have a better understanding of constructivist teaching when I realized that thematic teaching is one way to organize curriculum and facilitate the child's learning rather than a topic and lots of activities that go along with that topic. I am now beginning to think and read about how important authentic tasks are for children. Let's talk some more about this.

As we mentioned earlier, this chapter is designed to introduce you to constructivist assumptions about how children's learning guides practice. It is a preview of what's to come in this book, and so it offers glimpses through vignettes and brief discussions. Just as previews at the movies capture your attention but don't spoil the story by telling everything, we plan to capture your attention and then tell more later. We begin the preview with a look at ways children learn. Box 2.1 summarizes constructivist assumptions that we will cover in this chapter and shows how you can supply constructivist assumptions in your classroom.

BOX 2.1 USING CONSTRUCTIVIST ASSUMPTIONS

- Begin your curriculum, planning with what you know about the nature of the learner and the nature of what is to be learned.
- Plan learning environments that are authentic and allow for children to engage in their learning actively.
- Remember that a constructivist teacher begins with what is known about the child and the child's ways of knowing rather than with the curriculum or national standards.
- Being a constructivist teacher relates more to how the teacher thinks about teaching and learning than how she uses a specific set of methods, materials, or approaches.
- A constructivist teacher can apply constructivist tenets to any curriculum.

Children Learn as They Engage in Authentic Tasks They Have Chosen

Children are constantly engaged in learning. As they experience their daily routines, they make decisions about when, where, and how they learn. As they engage in real or **authentic tasks,** defined as tasks that they have a genuine need to accomplish, they experience being the one who makes (that is, designs, creates, writes, builds) or decides something. For example, as they pour milk on their cereal, they construct hypotheses about solids and liquids, as well as about quantity. As they wait for a bus, they construct notions of time, distance, sequences of events, and speed. Once they arrive at school, they continue to make decisions about their learning, and they continue to seek the kinds of authentic tasks that they experience at home and on their way to school.

The constructivist teacher builds on the knowledge of children's cognitive and emotional growth to shape the curriculum. Because constructivist teachers know that children are internally motivated to learn and to construct knowledge, these teachers design the classroom environment so that it provides children with tasks that are authentic and meaningful.

There are several ways to accomplish authenticity in a classroom. One way is for the teacher to provide children with "real" or "natural" materials, equipment, and supplies: woodworking tools that are child-sized tools (not toy tools), scissors that actually cut, and real feathers or leaves. When children are provided with real or natural materials, equipment, and supplies, they recognize that the teacher trusts them and values their ability to invent and complete meaningful projects. For example, when the teacher offers a child-sized saw to the children so that they can use it to make a curtain rod for their puppet stage, the children know that their puppet stage is equivalent to a stage made by adults. They value their own stage as much as the one built by an adult. When children are provided with children's scissors that actually cut, they are excited that they can focus on creating their design.

Another way to achieve authenticity is through daily routines—predictable events that occur in the classroom each day. These routines can relate to the management of the classroom or to curriculum events. Children learn to expect and rely on those routines as they provide order, predictability, and security. In addition, the ordering of events allows children to construct relationships about time. For example, the children know that providing the attendance report occurs before recess. Because daily routines are predictable, they provide security and help with classroom management. For example, the children may select chores or jobs (e.g., door holder, snack helper, line leader) from the Community Helper Chart so that they have a role in the management of their classroom. The children can create and use sign-in charts, attendance charts, and lunch preference charts to record information that others need. When the daily routines are part of the curriculum, the children know that each day, they will have a time for math and reading, as well as science and writing. Some teachers use daily routines as part of their math curriculum. They know that having the children count for the attendance report and lunch report is authentic and necessary each day. In addition, they may use daily math experiences like math journals (journals that children use to record math problems and their process for solving the problems) as part of their curriculum.

Project work—tasks that children identify and have an interest in doing—can also provide authenticity in the classroom. Teachers have used project work with children for over fifty years. John Dewey, one of the early champions of project work, believed that children need the opportunity to learn through doing. The projects could be problems that need solutions, models that need to be designed and made, objects that need to be made, and topics of interest that need to be studied and written about. **Projects** can be short term, in that they can be completed in a few hours, or long term, in that they may be completed in four or five weeks. Projects may be part of a theme or a separate event in the classroom. Projects are inquiry based so they meet curriculum standards such as the Common Core Standards.

Project work can provide authenticity in the classroom. The following example illustrates a short-term project that met the needs of the classroom community. Although the project was not part of a theme, it had meaning and an authentic purpose.

The 4- and 5-year-olds excitedly discussed a problem that they had observed: Birds were flying against their classroom windows and breaking their necks. The children had found four dead birds on their playground. They hypothesized that the berries on the tree close to the windows were poison. When the birds ate those berries, they became disoriented and crashed into the windows. The teacher asked if anyone had any thoughts about a solution for their problem. Several children suggested that they cut down the tree. Others didn't like that idea because they enjoyed playing under the tree. One child suggested that they use the Internet to learn more about birds. The teacher agreed that that was a good idea. When the teacher told a parent about the children's new project, that parent said that she subscribed to a bird magazine and offered a solution. She explained that a recent article described how to make a reflective tube from an empty toilet paper roll and aluminum foil. The tube was then hung on the window, and when the birds flew toward it, they would see their reflections, become frightened, and fly away from the window. When the teacher introduced this information to the children, they gathered materials quickly and made enough reflective tubes to have two for each of the eight windows. All were excited that they had solved their problem in less than a week.

This *Save the Birds* project had a real purpose for the classroom community. The children and teacher were distraught over watching the birds fly against the windows and needed to do something about it. They were pleased when they could quickly and easily make the reflective tubes and solve their problem. Not all authentic tasks are as dramatic as the example or as easy to accomplish in as short a time.

Organizing activities, tasks, and projects around themes can provide for authenticity for children. Thematic teaching is an integrated approach to studying a topic of interest. It helps the teacher organize the content and strategies for learning that content so that it is supported by theory, has authenticity, is of interest to the child, and has the child as its focus. Because children view learning as holistic rather than as separate subject matter areas, themes provide the teacher with a way to relate reading, writing, math, science, social studies, art, and other areas of the curriculum to each other so that children learn them from a holistic perspective. Themes should include projects as well as field trips, information books that the children have written, activities, books that document the steps of the project, and a host of other tasks.

Some teachers have year-long themes, while others have themes that last a month to 6 weeks. The length of the theme is not as important as the authenticity of the topic for the theme. For example, themes that concern the children's community and events within that community allow children to study where they live. Such themes serve as a vehicle for children to study the community's history as well as present-day events. For example, third graders in a small town in northwest Georgia began their school year by studying their community for six weeks.

As a result of their study, the children developed a new pride in and understanding of their community and the people who lived there. They also learned how to do research. As a result of their study, they produced and gave the local historical society museum pamphlets they had written, oral history interviews, and artifacts that people had given them during the study.

Projects within a theme can also provide authenticity. For example, one second-grade class decided to do a theme on the ocean, and one of their projects was to find sites on the Internet about the ocean. The teacher and children found sites that provided them with daily opportunities to follow the travels of conservationists, scientists, explorers, and whales. Those interactive Internet sites provided the children with the opportunity to e-mail scientists and explorers questions about the ocean and solutions to problems that are being encountered. Then the children documented the journeys through various kinds of media.

Often approaches from different curricular areas, such as language arts and social studies, generate authentic tasks. These approaches may be used every day and be separate and apart from the thematic work. For example, children often do authentic tasks as an extension of the shared journal experience, a daily approach that integrates reading, writing, speaking, and listening. Because the children tell true stories from their lives, they are often moved to action.

The children in Jeff Smith's kindergarten classroom were moved to action when a child told the story of a cousin who had cancer and was going to the hospital for treatments. The children wanted to do something more than send get-well cards. One noted that she had a favorite blanket that helped her feel safe when she was scared. Another child suggested that they make a blanket and send it to the child with cancer. With Mr. Smith's help, the children planned and made squares for a quilt, and Mr. Smith had someone help them sew the squares together. When they finished, they sent the quilt to the ill child so that she could feel safe. This project also led to a study of quilts, quilt patterns, and quilt making.

> **CONSTRUCTIONS**
>
> **Reflection**
>
> As you think about the importance of authenticity in the classroom, recall memorable experiences you had when you were in preschool, kindergarten, or first, second, or third grade. Were they inquiry based? Were they authentic and meaningful? If so, what caused you to think that they were? As a teacher, how would you design similar experiences for your own classroom? Once you have identified an experience, what will be your role in shaping it?

As we return to the conversation the teachers are having, we find them sitting at the same table in the coffee shop. All are so intent about their conversation that they don't realize they've been there for over an hour. Let's listen to them again.

Kenisha: We have talked a lot about authenticity as a constructivist assumption. Are there other assumptions that constructivists use to guide their practice?

Matt: Yes. I think children learn as they act on objects and interact with others.

Parul: In other words, children are active learners. They actively engage in their own learning.

Matt: Right. But they also learn as they talk with others about those actions.

Kenisha: That's easy enough to understand. It's even easy to do.

Sheila: I don't think it's easy to do. That's where you have to put all of those things in your classroom—lofts, pulleys, dress-up clothes, dolls, clay, building and construction materials, light tables, interlocking blocks, puzzles, and on and on. I could name a hundred different things. Then every day you have to pick them up and keep them organized and neat. On top of all of that, you have to make sure that you are addressing health and safety issues with the room design and the stuff the children are using. I'm like the custodian. I just hate a constructivist classroom!

Matt: It's true that a constructivist classroom is more complex than the classrooms that are organized around tables or desks, chairs, a teacher's desk, and a few supply shelves.

Parul: You just have to have a plan that helps you organize and clean your room as quickly as possible.

Kenisha: Yeah! I take the first three weeks of each school year and teach the children how to organize, clean, and manage their centers. They do the work. I just monitor and help when unexpected events happen, like the pep rally last week. But, Matt, you said that a teacher could use back-to-basics or direct teaching and still be a constructivist. How?

Matt: Children act on objects to construct knowledge. Because of this, an ideal constructivist classroom would have objects for children to use. It would be a more interactive classroom. A back-to-basics teacher could have a more traditional classroom but would also have to provide opportunities for the children to act on objects and interact with others.

Ron: The learning environment is one of the most important aspects of the constructivist teacher's roles. Because of this, I would not recommend having a classroom with desks in straight rows, the teacher in the front of the room, and rules that say, "No talking!" Children need interaction and objects to construct knowledge.

Children Learn as They Act on Objects and Interact With Others

Most students of early childhood education have read numerous articles and textbooks that state that children learn by doing. Children are active learners. As constructivists, we know this is true. Jean Piaget and his colleagues and other constructivist researchers have documented that children are active learners. In this section, we discuss the assumptions that children learn as they act on objects and interact with others. Through examples, we show how children do this. We begin the discussion by explaining the importance of the learning environment. Then we describe how children use that environment to construct **knowledge** for themselves. We explain the theoretical aspects of constructivist theory in Chapter 3.

In constructivist learning environments, teachers design a safe space to accommodate the children's need for movement, work surfaces, materials, and equipment. This space serves two functions. First, it provides the teacher with a place to observe, hypothesize, talk about, and create theories about children's learning. Based on those observations and hypotheses, the teacher can test certain ideas about what needs to be included in that space. Second, this area allows children a place to act on and interact with objects of their choosing. Furthermore, just as it allows teachers the opportunity to hypothesize and test those hypotheses, it allows children an opportunity to interact with others by asking questions, sharing ideas and feelings, touching and using materials, and testing their thinking.

Encouraging Children to Act on Objects

The following examples provide illustrations of children as they act on objects and interact with others. One example documents how a teacher introduced a loft as a place for children to act on objects. The second example recounts how a teacher used literature to introduce an object for the children's use. The third example recounts how children learn about objects through their errors.

In this first example, Jackson, a 2-year-old, studied the new classroom loft in the exercise room of his preschool. Because he lived in the Midwest, his preschool had a room designed for play during snowy winter days. He walked down steps every day to get to his preschool room, but those cement steps had a metal foot guard and had railings and a wall on both sides. This loft had steps up to a platform and then more steps to another platform. He could even see the platforms from where he was standing. He reached down to touch the first step. With a surprised look, he stood up and looked at his teacher. The teacher hypothesized that he remembered that the steps to his classroom were a different material (cement and metal) from the ones (wooden) for the loft. She remarked that these steps were wooden and the ones he used each day to get to his dad's car were cold cement and metal.

Jackson reached back to touch the step. As he reached for the loft's rail, he stepped on the first step, then the second, and so on until he reached the first platform. Again, he touched the surface of the platform, traced the railing with his fingers, and then smiled at his teacher. Quickly, he walked up the next three steps to the top platform, which was encased with clear plastic. He knelt down and peered through the plastic. A bit frightened, Jackson stepped back. The teacher sensed his realization that he was no longer on the actual floor because he could look down at her. She told him that he was safe and that he could look at the toys from "way up high." He moved back to the railing and laughed. Jackson spent most of his day walking up and down the steps to the platform, looking through the clear plastic, gesturing, and babbling about his experience. He acted on objects (the new classroom loft) and then interacted with others (through his babbling, gestures, and actions). The teacher set up this opportunity for Jackson by designing her classroom so that it included a loft. She did this so that the children could act on and use the loft to experience climbing as well as having different perspectives (provided by the loft's varying heights) within the room.

The following classroom vignette is a second example of children acting on objects that the teacher provided to guide their learning and her teaching practice. The teacher planned a 3-week study of one of the children's favorite authors. After a discussion and vote, the children decided to study Dr. Seuss. One of the books the teacher wanted to use was *Bartholomew and the Oobleck*. She knew that after they read that book, they would want to make *oobleck* (known also as ooze or slime, and made with cornstarch, water, and food coloring). She gave the children the recipe and observed their actions and interactions. As the children acted on the oobleck, they constructed hypotheses about the properties of solids and liquids, transformations, shape changes, as well as mixing and pouring.

A third vignette offers another kind of example. This time, a child acts on an object and learns through error. An error is a decision that on reflection is viewed as not the best choice. A student teacher made putty from starch and glue with the 5-year-old prekindergarten class and gave each child a small container of it. Katie began to investigate its properties. Yes, it poured. It would break. It would stick to her fingers. When placed on the table, it would spread.

Suddenly, Katie giggled and said to her friend, Kayla, "Watch what happens when I put it in my hair." The teacher rushed to stop her, but it was too late. Katie had her entire glob of putty in her long, brown hair. The student teacher tried to pull it from Katie's hair, but to no avail. Both teachers tried washing the hair with water, wiping it with a cloth, and combing it. Finally, the teacher held out Katie's strands of hair, rubbed ice on each strand, and then pulled the putty from the strand. After an hour, most of the putty was out of Katie's hair. Katie said to her teacher, "I guess this wasn't such a good idea! You don't have to punish me. I think I got the picture. I won't do this again!"

Children Learn When They Are Surprised and Intrigued About Phenomena

When children experience a situation or objects that offer choices or attributes that they didn't expect or that conflict with what they expected, they are actively engaged in learning. Because children are internally motivated, they want to understand, figure out, or resolve the conflict so that they can reconcile their internal conflict (Forman & Kuschner, 1983) or **cognitive conflict**. For example, when the children in the pre-K class played with the putty, they experienced an object that contradicted what they expected.

Teachers can provide situations to create surprise and intrigue for children in several ways (discussed in detail in Chapter 4). Questioning and designing experiences that surprise or create cognitive conflict for children are the two that we will mention in this chapter. A constructivist teacher can use questioning and experiences that create cognitive conflict regardless of the curriculum or program being used by the school or child-care center. The following examples show the use of questioning in a classroom where children are experiencing cognitive conflict.

Teachers trained in the **Reggio Emilia approach,** a northern Italian approach to teaching preschool children that focuses on helping the children understand perspective taking, community building, and aesthetics through questioning and challenging their assumptions, often create surprise and intrigue for children. The light table is one of the ways they do this. Because the surface of the table is covered with clear Plexiglas and lit, children are often surprised and intrigued by the way the light shines through the materials that they are using. For example, when the teacher suggests that the children place leathers, leaves, textured paper, and fabrics made from silk or cotton on the light table, the children are surprised and curious about the way the materials look. In addition, if the teacher introduces the use of multicolored Plexiglas, plastic bricks, or building materials, the children become intrigued with the shades of color. The teacher can use questioning as the children work with their materials at the light table or can allow the materials and the table to generate children's internal questions that may be answered by the child or shared with the group. Thus, through the use of a light table, teachers are able to create intrigue, questioning, and surprise for the children.

In addition to the light table, teachers can use butterfly farms, substances such as oobleck and putty, tadpoles that turn into frogs, goldfish, and class pets. Each of these generates a myriad of questions from children.

In addition to creating and providing experiences for children to have cognitive conflict, the teacher can use questioning to guide a child to an awareness or resolution of a contradiction. The teacher's questioning is guided by his or her observations of the child.

Once you have raised questions (e.g., "How has the child acted on the object?" "What does such action mean?"), then you think of a related question for the child. At times, the question may be in the form of an action. For example, a 4-year-old child has built a solid wall of unit blocks. Next to it, you build a wall with open spaces like windows. When he looks at your structure, he questions, "How did you do that? Make those windows?" Or you might add a second small wooden engine to the train track that a child has built and is using in her play. You place the engine so that it faces her engine. Such action may anger the child and cause her to move your engine. It may cause the child to puzzle over your actions and think of ways to respond to your invitation to elaborate her play.

At other times, the teacher's question provokes the child so that he or she thinks about an action or object in a new way. For example, when the child is pouring water through the water wheel, the teacher might give him blue-colored water in a cup and ask, "What will happen when you pour this water through your water wheel?"

Let's return to the teachers one more time in this chapter.

The teachers were thinking about finishing their group session, but because of Parul's question about ways children refine what they know, Sheila poured everyone a little more coffee from their common pot. She knew that that question would lead to several more. Sure enough, it did.

Parul: How do children refine their old ways of thinking? You know, we just accept that as constructivists, we will advance children's thinking by causing them to question, reflect, act on objects, and interact with others. We don't really know how that happens, do we?

Ron: All of the questioning, reflecting, interacting, and acting on objects are necessary for children to refine their old ways of thinking. They are like scientists in that they consistently observe, hypothesize, experiment, and draw conclusions. Through this process, they coordinate their old ways of thinking with the new ones. As a result, they create new structures.

Sheila: Well, that sounds pretty academic to me!

Ron: Yes, but when you watch children, you can almost see that happening.

Kenisha: You really can. I know that when my children solve a problem, they will use that process in the future.

Sheila: Well, don't other people teach children anything? And how do we know what those kids really know?

Matt: Children use writing, drawing, symbolic play, acting, making models, dance, music, as well as several other ways of showing or representing what they know.

Parul: It's wonderful to see them when they begin to represent what they know. It really means that they want to reach out to others.

Sheila: Don't the children learn anything from their culture?

Ron: Yes! They learn to read, play games, write, appreciate their cultural heritage, and understand what expectations their culture has for them. If they didn't have someone teach them about Thanksgiving and tell them when it's celebrated in the United States, how else would they know when to celebrate it?

Matt: Before we leave, I want to remind you to read the interviews with Piaget in Bringuier's book for our next conversation.

Children Learn as They Refine and Coordinate Old Ways of Thinking

Children are like scientists who consistently observe objects and the changes within those objects, pose questions, and then test out those questions by acting on the objects. Within this process, children refine and coordinate their old ways of thinking, which allows them to create mental transformations and constructions that lead to new or more elaborated cognitive structures. This section will help you think about your assumptions about children's thinking. It should cause you to think of curriculum approaches that might encourage children to use coordination and cognitive conflict to refine their thinking.

Two classroom experiences that allow children to refine and coordinate their cognitive structures are daily math activities and discussions about project work.

One daily math experience that children use to refine their ways of thinking can occur as they talk with their teachers about snacks. Kamii (2000) describes how a teacher, Linda Joseph, uses such an opportunity for children to refine their schemes about quantity. Joseph asks the children how many small pieces of candy each child can have if the large bag she bought for them has a given number of pieces in it. Once the children have had an opportunity to solve the problem for themselves, Joseph has them explain their solutions to their classmates. As they talk, they raise questions and clarify their thinking.

As children talk about project work, they also refine and coordinate their old ways of thinking. For example, the children in a kindergarten class decided to build a car that they could ride. Their teacher explained that she would buy the materials that they requested. Their first list included cardboard for the base, paint, wooden dowels, and glue. When they began to assemble the car, they discovered that if they sat on the cardboard, it wouldn't support their weight. They then requested lumber for the base.

Once they had a frame, they discovered that the wooden dowels were not strong enough to hold their weight and the wooden frame. They again revised their plans because of their new understanding of weight. Throughout the next few weeks, the children continued to work on their car, constantly revising and refining their plans. By the end of the school year, they had a wooden frame for a base, metal dowels and lawn mower wheels, a steering wheel, and a rope to pull the car. As a result of their project work, the children refined and coordinated various ways of thinking so that their car would hold the weight of a driver and passenger, roll, steer left and right, and be able to be pulled.

CONSTRUCTIONS

Observation

Visit a classroom, and observe three groups of children as they play a game or work on a project. Record how they refine their old ways of knowing. Some may do this through actions and others through social interaction. Share your observations with classmates.

Children Represent What They Know to Others

Children represent what they know through their behavior, mental imagery, and language. Those representations may be in the form of movements and gestures, as well as drawings, writing, and talking. Such representational competence helps them control and apply the relationships they've constructed. It also allows them to connect two actions, two discontinuous events, and two emotions at different times or even at the same time. Most classrooms provide children with a myriad of experiences and opportunities to show others what they know. Examples are performing puppet shows, playing in the dramatic play area, writing, drawing, painting, building, talking to others, and using the computer. Following are three examples to help you think about the role of representation in children's thinking. The examples also suggest ways you could provide opportunities for the children to develop and elaborate their representational competence.

Examples of Representation

Maria, a 5-year-old, sat at the writing center making a book she had titled *Bugs*. Her teacher had talked about butterflies during group time and had shown the child a live butterfly in the bug box. Maria loved the butterfly. She had even taken the magnifying glass to try to see it from a different perspective. As she looked at the butterfly, she decided to make a book about all of the bugs she had seen. She sat at the table and began to draw a bug that looked like a centipede. When the teacher looked surprised, Maria said, "But my book is about all of the bugs I know, not just your butterfly." Maria was representing her knowledge of bugs through the drawings in her book.

Another way children represent what they know is through the use of the computer. They make representations by writing stories using the word processing component of the computer, programming robotics constructions that they have made, making graphic designs and drawings, and playing games. For example, Larry, a developmentally delayed kindergartner, was using the computer for the first time. He held up the mouse and moved it in the air in his efforts to make the cursor move on the screen. His movement and gestures helped the teacher and other children realize what he knew about the way to operate the computer and its mouse.

Another example documents how a typically developing 4-year-old demonstrates his representation of his knowledge of the computer. George sat at the computer and decided he no longer wanted to do the games. He found one of his favorite story CDs and reloaded it. As he clicked on the icons and objects within the story, he demonstrated what he knew about using the computer as well as playing within the story. Next, he decided to try a word game. The game offered empty spaces representing letters in the name of the dinosaur that was pictured. George said, "That's a brontosaurus. It starts with a B." Then he began to drag letters from the list to the empty spaces.

One final example of children's representational competence occurred in a kindergarten classroom. During their shared journal time, a child told about a wedding he had attended. He said that the bride wore a long white dress, danced with a lot of people, and smashed cake into the groom's mouth. One child asked if the bride kissed the groom. He said, "Of course, 'cause that's what they do at weddings." Once the sharing was over, some of the children wrote about his story. Later in the day during free play, several turned the dramatic play area into a wedding. They used scraps of fabric for the veil, a cape for the long skirt, and a chair for the altar. The children were representing what they knew through talking, writing, and reenacting the wedding.

Children Learn From Other People in Their Culture and Society

People within a culture or society teach children by their actions and by direct teaching of facts such as through games, songs, rules, vocabulary, and moral expectations: the cultural heritage of the society. Because of the arbitrary nature of these actions and facts, children cannot construct them. But they are important for the child, as well as the community in which he or she lives, because they help the child understand how to communicate within that culture, what is valued by that society, and how to process factual information. Piaget called this kind of knowledge **social knowledge**.

A constructivist teacher recognizes the importance of such knowledge but questions what factual information and what imitations the child needs rather than embracing social knowledge as the total curriculum. The kindergartners in the shared journal example were learning about the culture of weddings and their society's expectations for weddings. As a result of their discussions, play, and writing, they were beginning to learn how to behave, dress, and act at weddings.

Here is an example that documents how children learn from people within their culture and society. A third grader, Drew, told a college curriculum class about his social studies theme on Japan. He explained that they made their own passports and plane tickets. He noted that their teacher had brought in a sample passport and sample tickets so that they could make their own creations "look like the real thing." He also pointed out that he and his friend had decided to be the pilots of the plane. He elaborated by saying that he and his friend had found caps that looked like pilots' caps and had made an instrument panel for their class's plane. When someone asked him how he knew what a pilot did, he explained that he had seen pilots on television and at the local airport, and he had seen them when he and his family flew on vacation.

Through the use of a theme on Japan, Drew's teacher created an opportunity for Drew and his classmates to imitate travelers, pretend, and make documents that society uses for monitoring people and their movement from one place to another. Although the children constructed physical and **logico-mathematical** knowledge as they used this theme, social knowledge was an important component.

Multiple Perspectives: From Graduate Students

Two former Auburn University graduate students wrote the following perspectives about their assumptions of constructivist teaching. First, Carol Ensminger described how her knowledge of constructivist theory and assumptions helped her define herself as a constructivist teacher. Then Barry Jurgens explained his understandings of constructivist theory that he observed in a classroom.

Carol Ensminger

When young children enter my classroom, they are abounding with curiosity and excitement about the world around them. As a teacher, I hold that I must build on the experiences that these children bring into my classroom and capture the enthusiasm and excitement they have for learning. My beliefs are grounded in my knowledge that young children learn by constructing knowledge from within, rather than externally, and they do this through the creation and coordination of relationships. In essence, children learn by expounding on the experiences they have already had and the knowledge they have previously constructed. Children take incoming information and try to incorporate it into what they already know. When this doesn't work, they must accommodate and form new relationships. Children learn in this fashion across the three realms of knowledge: social, physical, and logico-mathematical. These three types of knowledge are interrelated; none of them can be constructed in isolation.

I have established my beliefs about how children learn and discussed why we know this to be true. Now I must take this knowledge and ascertain how I can become a more effective teacher. I hope to provide numerous occasions for children to blossom in their construction of knowledge while they are in my classroom. Because children learn from experiences, my classroom will provide a plethora of opportunities for students to engage in hands-on activities using a variety of media.

Choice is an element that will saturate my curriculum and my classroom as well. Providing choices fulfills one of the fundamental personal needs that children have, and it is also a necessary means of fostering a child's intellectual and moral autonomy. I will encourage social interaction on a daily basis in my classroom. In their attempts to build meaning and knowledge, children can construct understandings through interactions with other children and adults. The possibilities for creating opportunities for young children to construct their own knowledge are endless. It is truly motivating and excit-ing to know that I will serve as a facilitator in helping children to construct meaning for themselves.

Barry Jurgens

Children learn through hands-on experiences with their world. Through investigations of their own world, children develop problem-solving strategies and self-confidence. Chil-dren must be accountable for their own learning. Instead of coming to the teacher for the right answer, they must learn to reflect and look inside themselves for the solu-tions. This emphasis on children's self-regulation fosters the self-confidence that will lead them to question their world. Through that questioning, they develop hypotheses that they then test by asking questions, formulating answers, and reflecting on their answers.

Providing free choice centers is an excellent way to encourage children's indepen-dence and exploration of their ideas. By allowing children to choose a center, I am en-couraging their exploration of thought. When they are able to test different hypotheses, whether it is in a building center, a home living center, or a water center, they depend on themselves to find the answers. They learn to construct new knowledge and modify old ideas by manipulating the things in front of them.

One example of how children learn through their own exploration of centers oc-curred this semester. I observed a child go to the choice board and choose the build-ing center, where he worked by himself for an hour. An observer might have decided that he was just playing with blocks, but when I asked him, "What are you learning?" he told me that the more blocks he stacked, the more the tower would fall. He also said that if he used five rectangle blocks, he couldn't make a square. As I listened to him explain more of his reasoning, I realized he had critically thought out numerous relationships. He was given the opportunity to choose a center, and he chose to go where he was interested. This interest led to the questioning of and reasoning about his own answers. Through my questioning, I knew he had learned from his experience with blocks.

Thematic units are also an important part of fostering children's interest. The the-matic unit for my internship was Jamaica. We asked the children to write a question about a topic relating to Jamaica that they would like to learn about. Each child would then work on researching and finding the answers to his or her question. One child asked a question about the Jamaican market. I worked with her as she did research using books and the Internet to find out what items are sold at the Jamaican market. When the child was satisfied with our findings, she and another child presented the findings to the class. They built a market stand, complete with everything they learned about the market. The children measured, added, compared, discussed, and negotiated to build our final market stand. These experiences were authentic ways of representing what the children knew.

I know that children learn through meaningful learning experiences. Therefore, I must provide a positive learning environment that encourages them to explore these experi-ences. I can do this by having a choice board, free choice centers, thematic units, shared reading, and shared journals. I must also display the children's work so that they will value their work and have ownership of the room.

SUMMARY

- Children are the center of a constructivist curriculum.
- Six basic assumptions about children guide teachers with their practice:

  1. Children learn as they engage in authentic tasks they have chosen and as they make decisions about their learning.
  2. Children learn as they act on objects and interact with others.
  3. Children learn when they are surprised or intrigued about phenomena they can't explain.
  4. Children learn as they refine and coordinate old ways of thinking.
  5. Children show others what they know through their behavior and by developing representations of their knowledge.
  6. Children learn from other people in their culture and society.

- Constructivist teachers do not have a recipe for success. They study the child and his or her attempts to construct knowledge. They read and study Piagetian and constructivist research. Based on their observations and readings, they design their curriculum.
- Teachers can apply constructivist tenets with any approach to curriculum and when using standards like the Common Core.

CONSTRUCTIONS

1. OBSERVATION AND ANALYSIS

Visit two different kinds of educational settings (e.g., a science center, a hands-on museum, an art gallery) and observe the people in the setting. Do they use any of the constructivist assumptions as they observe and interact with the displays in the settings? Analyze how they are using those assumptions.

2. REFLECTION

Reflect on the assumptions that a constructivist teacher holds. Add any of your own. Then list ten classroom experiences, projects, or tasks that show those assumptions in action. Make a chart that shows how each idea supports constructivist teaching.

Resources

Books

DeVries, R., & Kohlberg, L. (1987b). *Constructivist early education: Overview and comparison with other programs.* Washington, DC: National Association for the Education of Young Children.

Provides a scholarly study of Piagetian curriculum approaches and compares and contrasts them with other early childhood approaches.

Edwards, C., Gandini, L., & Forman, G. (2011). *The hundred languages of children: The Reggio Emilia approach to early childhood education* (3rd ed.). Santa Barbara, CA: Praeger.

Provides a comprehensive look at the origins, philosophy, teaching methods, and policy implications for the early childhood programs of Reggio Emilia, Italy.

Forman, G., & Landry, C. (2000). The constructivist perspective on early education: Applications to children's museums. In J. L. Roopnarine & J. E. Johnson (Eds.), *Approaches to early childhood education* (3rd ed., pp. 149–174). Upper Saddle River, NJ: Merrill.

Provides an overview of ways constructivist education is used outside of school settings.

Kafai, Y. B., & Resnick, M. (2011). *Constructivism in practice: Designing, thinking, and learning in a digital world.* New York, NY: Routledge.

Offers an explanation of constructionism and how it converges with constructivism to coordinate design and learning theory.

Kamii, C., & DeVries, R. (1980). *Group games in early education: Implications of Piaget's theory.* Washington, DC: National Association for the Education of Young Children.

Discusses the value of board games, card games, and physical action games that advance children's thinking.

Kamii, C., & DeVries, R. (1993). *Physical knowledge in preschool education: Implications of Piaget's theory.* (Reissued with a new introduction). New York, NY: Teachers College Press.

An easy-to-read text that explains and provides detailed examples of physical knowledge.

Papert, S. (1993). *The children's machine: Rethinking school in the age of the computer.* New York, NY: Basic Books.

Helps advance one's understanding of the cultural and historical implications of new technologies for education. Discusses the use of computers in schools.

Videos

Kamii, C. (1989). *Double-column addition: A teacher uses Piaget's theory.* New York, NY: Teachers College Press.

Kamii, C. (1990a). *Multiplication of two-digit numbers: Two teachers using Piaget's theory.* New York, NY: Teachers College Press.

Kamii, C. (1990b). *Multidigit division: Two teachers using Piaget's theory.* New York, NY: Teachers College Press.

All three videos describe Kamii's constructivist approach to math. They include theory as well as show teachers using her approaches.

Web Sites

Association for Constructivist Teaching https://sites.google.com/site/assocforconstructteaching

This Web site introduces you to the Association for Constructivist Teaching. It provides additional information about conferences, current news, a journal, and blogs on constructivism.

Early Childhood News http://www.earlychildhoodnews.com

This Web site is for students, practitioners and families. It offers a variety of helpful articles. One example is Huber's (2008) article on woodworking (see next source).

Early Childhood News http://www.earlychildhoodnews.com/earlychildhood/article_view.aspx?ArticleID=181

Huber, L. K. (2008). Woodworking in my classroom? You bet! *Early Childhood News.*

L'Atelier School www.latelier.org

This Web site introduces one of the Reggio Emilia preschools. It offers detailed information about the philosophy and curriculum.

MIT Media Lab www.media.mit.edu

This Web site offers the opportunity to explore basic research and applications for how children learn through computational projects. Click on the Research link and the Centers link to find information about projects with young children. University of Sydney http://sydney.edu.au/education_social_work/learning_teaching/ict/theory/constructivism.shtml

This Web site provides a series of Web quests that provide an extensive overview of constructivism and constructivist teaching. Because it's from the University of Sydney, it offers an international view of constructivist teaching.

Workshop 5: Idea Making www.learner.org/channel/workshops/lala/lalaprint5.pdf

This Web site is from Annenberg Learner, which has as its goal the advancement of teaching excellence. It provides interactive workshops with Eleanor Duckworth, Constance Kamii, Mitchel Resnick, and others.

3

LEARNING AND THE THREE KINDS OF KNOWLEDGE

In this chapter, you will read about how learning takes place. Because you are preparing to be an early childhood educator, it is essential that you understand the learning process so that you can base your teaching on theory and research. It is also important for you to be able to explain it to colleagues, parents, and members of the community.

After reading this chapter, you will have a beginning understanding of

- how learning occurs;
- the development of mental structures;
- the processes of assimilation, accommodation, and equilibration;
- physical, logico-mathematical, and social kinds of knowledge; and
- representational thought.

Introduction

The teachers who have formed the study group have gathered in the library at Ron's school. They have just toured Ron's first-grade classroom and are enjoying the brownies that Sheila brought.

Kenisha: Ron, your block area looks great. I hope your first graders enjoy building as much as my kindergartners do. I took some pictures of the city they built last week. You wouldn't believe how well they worked together so early in the year.

Matt: Wait a minute, Kenisha. That might be accepted in kindergarten, but in first grade—no offense, Ron—they're supposed to be learning, and that takes work.

Ron: Well, I'm still not sure this is the right thing to do. None of the other teachers here have blocks, but I think the children are learning in all the areas in my classroom. At least, that's how I think about learning.

Jennifer: Since it's my turn to be group leader, let's use that as a starting point. I suggest we each give a brief idea about what we believe learning to mean. Parul, would you start?

Parul: I'm surprised every day. I don't know how it happens, but every day I see children doing something that I haven't seen them do before. This morning I got out a brand-new ball, and one of the toddlers said "lelow." She was right. It was yellow.

Matt: Well, of course, someone just told her the word yellow, and after she heard it enough times . . .

Kenisha: Sorry to interrupt, Matt, but Sheila, go ahead and tell us your thoughts on learning.

Sheila: I guess I just think children hear things from their families, and then they know them.

Kenisha: Hey, I've watched kids for 20 years. They just have a look when they're thinking about something. After a while you just know. And then, WOW! They run up and say, "Ms. Williams, guess what?" and they tell me that there were three baby hamsters yesterday and now there are only two—or something amazing like that.

Ron: I know that last year I learned that children construct their own knowledge, but I guess I didn't learn it very well, because now I can't remember how it works. I did pass the course, though!

Using Theory and Research

Because the field of education is about teaching and learning, educators look for a scientific theory about how children develop knowledge, study the research that supports that theory, and then use that information to make decisions as they plan and implement their day-to-day work. Many educators, including the authors of this text, have studied **constructivist theory** and have found it to be a solidly researched theory that provides documentation about how knowledge is constructed. They also recognize that just as in other professions such as medicine, researchers continue to study and develop new understanding.

Constructivist theory does not directly address how teachers teach. Because constructivist teachers understand that, they use the theory to plan their curriculum. They do not expect to find a predesigned package to fit all children in all classrooms; they depend on their own knowledge of the children in their group or classroom to guide their teaching interactions.

In this book, you will read about areas to consider as you learn about planning a curriculum for a class of young children. You will be challenged to consider constructivist theory and to use it in learning about curriculum. Because the theorist most closely associated with constructivist theory is Jean Piaget, we will begin with a brief description of his extensive body of work.

Jean Piaget's Work

Constructivist theory is a solidly researched theory that documents how knowledge is constructed. Jean Piaget and his colleagues at the International Center for Genetic Epistemology in Geneva, Switzerland, studied hundreds of children. These researchers' interests centered on learning and the ways in which it occurs. You may have learned that Piaget was a genetic **epistemologist** who published hundreds of books and articles. (An epistemologist is a person who studies how knowledge develops.) Information for Piaget's publications came from children's responses in interviews. As Piaget observed children, he often found responses that intrigued him. He and his colleagues discussed these and developed a plan for gathering data. Piaget pursued ideas and often reexamined them years later as his own thinking continued to develop. The central issue was always "How do we construct new knowledge and how do these constructions develop?" (Vuyk, 1981).

Typically, at least a year was spent on one research idea, and then the results of the child interviews were examined for similarities and patterns. These patterns or progressions in cognitive development enabled Piaget to write about what we can generally expect as children develop knowledge through interaction with their environments.

Piaget was adamant in explaining that his work did not involve testing children. In a discussion with Bringuier (1980), Piaget commented, "A test is related to performance, to results. We're interested in how the child reasons and how he discovers new tools, so we use direct conversation, informal conversation" (quoted in Bringuier, p. 24). Although Piaget died in 1980, his work of studying how children come to know continues in Geneva and in many other locations. Although even now the Genevan interviewers typically ask children several initial questions, which are common to all the interviews on a topic, the interviewer is expected to craft questions based on children's responses.

Skilled interviewers are required so that the children are not led to say something they don't really believe. The interviewer must also relate well to children, ensuring that children are comfortable enough to participate freely. Developing a model for teachers was never Piaget's purpose, but in reading transcripts of interviews, we can pick up cues for ways to understand the thinking of children whom we are trying to teach. See Box 3.1 for a listing of some of the books written by Jean Piaget.

BOX 3.1 A FEW OF THE BOOKS WRITTEN BY JEAN PIAGET

Piaget, J. (1962). *Play, dreams and imitation in childhood.* New York, NY: Norton.
Piaget, J. (1965). *The child's conception of number.* New York, NY: Norton.
   (Original work published 1941)

Piaget, J. (1941/1965). *The child's conception of time*. New York, NY: Ballantine.

Piaget, J. (1976). *The grasp of consciousness: Action and concept in the young child*. (S. Wedgewood, Trans.) Cambridge, MA: Harvard University Press. (Original work published 1974)

Piaget, J., & Inhelder, B. (1967). *The child's conception of space*. (F. J. Langdon & J. L. Lunzer, Trans.). New York, NY: Norton. (Original work published 1948)

Piaget, J., & Inhelder, B. (1969). *The early growth of logic in the child*. (E. A. Lunzer & D. Papert, Trans.). New York, NY: Norton. (Original work published 1964)

CONSTRUCTIONS

Reflection

Read sections of several of Piaget's books that include partial transcripts of child interviews (some of them are listed in the box). Note patterns and variations in the interviewers' questions. Record your findings and your thoughts about the interviews in your journal.

Constructivist Theory

Although Piaget is probably the best known and most widely published constructivist theorist, many other researchers have contributed to our understanding of this important theory. Were Piaget alive today, it is likely that he would continue to revise his thinking, as all good researchers do. As you study, you too will continue to revise your thinking.

Constructivist theory is based on the premise that it is the child's interaction with the environment that enables the child to use the **mental structures** she has developed and continues to develop. Using mental structures allows a child or an adult to create or construct new knowledge or to modify previously constructed knowledge and to modify and construct new structures. You will read about the notion of structures shortly. However, next we consider how biology and cognition are both involved.

One way in which biology affects the development of knowledge relates to the fact that children begin to develop knowledge immediately after birth by using reflexes such as sucking. They then build on that sensory structure, perhaps combining sucking on a rattle with shaking it. Based on the physical makeup of the human body, most children are able to perform a wide variety of actions on objects. For example, they can push and pull things, throw them, drop them, smell them, taste them, squeeze them, and kick them. You can probably think of many more actions in which you have seen young children engaging. As the child uses his body to interact with objects, he extracts properties of those objects. A 1-year-old might find that a rubber ball's properties include that it can be squeezed, rolled, dropped, or chewed, and is wet or dry depending on whether he has been chewing on it. Generally, he will pay attention to one property at a time as he explores an object. The golfer's construct differs dramatically from that of the 1-year-old, yet both of them use the same **functions**; that is, they both use organization and adaptation.

Piaget viewed knowledge as both biological and cognitive. In terms of cognition, the child is mentally considering what he does and what he observes as he pushes, pulls, squeezes, and sucks. The child's thought continually interacts with his environment. For example, a child may roll a toy car down a wooden ramp. He extracts from this action a property of the car: It rolls. Then the child may find a second car and try to compare the two cars. Which one goes down the ramp faster? In the first case, he finds that toy cars roll on ramps. In the second case, he mentally sets up a relationship as he observes the reaction of the two cars on the ramp and compares their performance.

The child's environment includes objects such as toys, dishes, soap, and a whole host of others. It also includes people (those she knows and those she doesn't know) and experiences, such as falling and getting a scraped knee, going to the zoo, and snuggling up on a parent's lap to hear a story. In each situation, the child is constructing knowledge, but she is not starting over every time she encounters a situation. She uses what she has already constructed for herself, and her functions enable her to organize each new idea. As Piaget studied children, he noticed that the child builds or constructs knowledge himself. He is not producing a mental copy of exactly what is "out there" in the environment, as some theorists have proposed. Piaget's studies showed children making and remaking "the basic concepts and logical thought forms that constitute . . . intelligence" (Gruber & Voneche, 1995, p. xxxviii). As you work with children and pay attention to what they do and say, you will begin to get an idea of how they are thinking. That is, you will begin to understand that the child constructs a mental structure that is then used to build new structures.

Constructivist theory has three major components—content, function, and structure—and each has subcomponents. The following paragraphs briefly introduce you to them.

Content

Content refers to the topics about which the child is constructing knowledge. It might be friendship or how bicycles work, or, for you, Piaget's theory. The content for each child differs from that of every other child, even if they are best friends, sit next to each other in school, and play together as soon as they get home. That is because each child constructs her own knowledge, and knowledge is not a copy of the external world.

Function

Function is an aspect of constructivist theory that refers to two major ideas: organization and adaptation. Individuals organize and reorganize what they know as they continue to increase their knowledge and understanding. Imagine that in every course you take, every sentence you read or hear in class is completely unrelated in any way to any other sentence. You would have millions of unorganized ideas every time you finish a course and probably would not be able to use any of them. On a more concrete level, assume that your friend collects CDs. He has hundreds of them and stacks them around wherever he can find a space. When he wants to play one, he has no organizational plan for finding it.

A second aspect of function is adaptation. Each of us is constantly adapting to circumstances we encounter; that is, we work out ways to adjust to new situations. One definition of intelligence is the ability to adapt to new situations through reasoning and understanding. Piaget's research led him and his colleagues to write about two parts of adaptation: assimilation and accommodation.

Assimilation refers to the filtering or modification of input through one of the structures that the child has created. For example, a child pushes a ball and notices that it rolls. A child pushes a stroller. It moves too. The child is beginning to develop an action scheme or structure for pushing. Another child may be interested in dumping and filling. Wastebaskets are fun for this! Perhaps the child uses a shovel and pail and a pile of sand to fill and dump. The next day in the child's backyard baby pool, the same pail and shovel are used to try to fill the pail with water, using the same action that worked with sand. This child watches another child, who fills a cup with water and dumps it in a bucket. Abandoning the original scheme for filling and dumping, the first child imitates the other child and begins to pour the water into the pail using a cup. This child has modified the internal scheme for filling containers to fit what is at the time reality. A child who is not interested in an object or activity will not interact with it. But if the child does become engaged, assimilation and accommodation occur.

When a child encounters a new situation, if it is totally out of her realm of understanding, she will probably ignore it. For example, when a 3-year-old sees a copy of the *New York Times* on a table, she will probably ignore it. She may be more interested in the copy of *The Carrot Seed* that is partially covered by the newspaper. You may pass by both publications and be interested instead in finding your college catalogue of courses for next semester so that you can choose your classes. Both you and the child have an understanding of what a newspaper is. Your reality of a newspaper certainly differs from hers. Yet both of you ignore the paper as you see it. Each of you focuses instead on what interests you. We cannot possibly attend to everything we encounter, and of course, there is no need to do that.

When something unexpected happens, the individual realizes, "This is not what I thought it was." Von Glasersfeld (1995) points out, "The disappointed expectation generates a **perturbation** [emphasis added] (the condition of being perplexed) and this, in turn, may lead to a further examination, which then results in an accommodation (e.g., the person will create a new category)" (p. 374). Creating a new category involves mental activity. The child consciously coordinates what he believed to be the case with what surprised him. This mental activity is referred to as **reflective abstraction.** The child introduces relationships among the kinds of outcomes he expected in a situation and the outcome that actually occurred (Kamii & DeVries, 1993). However, "problems, which may have the power to trigger reflective abstraction, are problems raised by the subject, not problems that are merely presented by someone else" (von Glasersfeld, 1995, p. 378). This use of assimilation and accommodation is part of the formation of knowledge by an individual.

Knowledge is the result of interaction between a subject (the child) and an object (a toy, a trip to the park, a playmate). The child takes his notions of the experience into what he already knows; that is, he assimilates the object or experience. When he encounters an experience that doesn't fit with what he already knows, he is puzzled. This new object or experience becomes part of his mental structure through **accommodation**. He adjusts his structure to allow the new object to apply or perhaps creates a new substructure. The functions occur together. Here they are discussed separately to describe them for you, but in reality they occur together and should not be thought of as separate. Notice that as functions come into play, structures are modified. The functions remain the same throughout a lifetime. Organization and adaptation, including assimilation and accommodation, are always the functions, and their role does not change. However, as the child assimilates and accommodates, his mental structures change and are reorganized, perhaps by combining, being extended, or being replaced by another structure.

Structure

Piaget's work also focuses heavily on the description of cognitive **structure,** and it is this work, in particular, that helps us understand how knowledge is constructed. In studying knowing, much of constructivist theory focuses on the structures or mental components that each of us is constantly building or constructing. Perhaps as you read that sentence, you thought to yourself, "So that's why it's called 'constructivist theory.'" Notice that as that process occurred, you were constructing for yourself a new notion of the term *constructivism*. Perhaps you had not had a definition for it, or perhaps your previous structure was modified to accommodate the new information you received when you read this paragraph.

One of the Genevan researchers, Jean-Claude Bringuier, conducted and published a series of interviews with Piaget. During one of the interviews, Piaget explained a key point of constructivist theory: "Structures are not given in advance, neither in the human mind nor in the external world as we perceive and organize it. They are constructed by the interactions between the individual's activities and the object's reaction" (quoted in Bringuier, 1980, p. 37). When a child encounters a new situation, she relates it to something she already knows about. She was not born with the mental structure to understand the situation, and the situation or object itself does not give the child knowledge. However, she is constantly being intrigued by a range of experiences and objects. If the event is intriguing enough or if she can relate it in some way to something she has encountered earlier, she may attend to it. For example, when an infant who has a soft cloth ball encounters a rubber ball that looks similar, he will probably take in, or assimilate, the object as "ball" (a concept he has already created for himself). But as he acts on the new ball, dropping it and watching it bounce, he accommodates, or adjusts, his **scheme** for ball; that is, he extends and modifies the scheme. This adaptation, the bringing together of assimilation and accommodation, is referred to as **equilibration.**

We all frequently encounter situations, experiences, and objects to which we must adapt. We use those same functions, assimilation and accommodation, to construct our understanding of what we have encountered. Each of us constructs our own understanding, even when we all appear to be addressing the same object or situation. However, the functions, assimilation and accommodation, are stable and do not change with development. These functions continue to work in the same way whether the child is 3 years old and trying to make a car roll up a ramp or 12 years old and figuring out an algebra problem. The content that the child thinks about does change. It may become elaborated, or it may assume lesser importance. Sometimes totally new content is added. The result of cognitive activity is the creation of meaning by the child. Note that it is the child's cognitive activity that creates knowledge. The knowledge is not "out there" to be absorbed. Even when a child is able to repeat a teacher's words exactly as presented, his understanding of what he is saying is likely to differ from her understanding. For example, when a teacher says, "Put a period at the end of every sentence," it is certainly not difficult for many children to repeat that. But constructing the idea of sentence is not something that can be memorized. The following provides a classic example: Four-year-old Tina asked her teacher how to make an elemento. Her teacher was perplexed. After several tries to under-stand each other, Tina finally said, "You know, a,b,c,d,e,f,g,h,i,j,k,elemento, p."

CONSTRUCTIONS

1. Reflection

Let's say you are working on your computer and find that what you have done before doesn't work. For example, when you switch from one com-puter program to another, what you have always done to move a document to a folder doesn't work. Think about all the ways you could solve the prob-lem and list them in your journal. Compare your list with a classmate's list.

2. Analysis

Reread the opening dialogue among the study group teachers. Consider what each teacher said about learning and how it relates to the information about theory that you have just read. What might be each teacher's frame-work? (Of course, you don't have much information about the teachers at this point, but you can use what you have observed about them in Chapters 1 and 2.) Discuss your analysis in class.

Back in the library in Jennifer's school, the study group teachers are discussing the Fourth Conversation—Experiments with Children: The Discovery of Devel-opmental Stages (from Bringuier's *Conversations with Piaget* [1980], pp. 23–35). They had agreed to read this fourth conversation before today's meeting.

Kenisha: Let's each think of something a child in our own group learned this week and try to determine whether these stages of development fit real children. Be sure to remind us about how old your children are.

Jennifer: Okay, but I don't think the specific ages are that important. Isn't development supposed to be a progression for each individual?

Parul: Since I teach babies, it's pretty hard to know if they are learning anything. They can't even talk yet.

Sheila: In Head Start we have to teach them 10 letters. Today Sarita saw an *S* on the cards I'm using to check which letters they already know, if any. She said, "That's my name." So she has learned that, sort of, but I don't know when or how. According to the book, she should be in the preoperational stage, but the author didn't say anything about learning letters.

Ron: My students are definitely preoperational. In fact, I think a few of them are getting pretty close to concrete operations in some ways.

Matt: I need help. According to what I've read, my children should be developing a concept of logical necessity. But they are still always arguing over who has more of everything. Yesterday they were learning about money, and I gave them each 10 pennies. Martina spread hers out all the way across her desk and said, "Ha, ha, I got more than anybody." That started a big argument. Some of them agreed, and others said she was wrong. One second grader began to cry because she didn't think she had as many as Martina. She's the oldest in the class. You'd think she would know better. I tell you, I need help.

Jennifer: Maybe if we all look at this section of the reading together, we'll be able to understand what's happening in each of our classes. Would that work?

We'll leave the teachers now and consider what constructivist theory tells us about stages of cognitive development.

Stages of Development

Once Piaget had created a sense of the progression of development, he described a series of stages to depict how children's cognitive development moves forward. Certainly, there are exceptions—some children progress more slowly or more quickly than others—but all experience these stages of cognitive development. Piaget's interest was in "the common characteristics of structures of subjects (i.e., persons) who are at the same developmental level" (Vuyk, 1981, p. 11).

Piaget described four stages of development, providing general age ranges for each stage and general ideas of how a child responds to various questions or problems at each stage (Gallagher & Reid, 2002; Piaget & Inhelder, 2002). He used an interview approach to learn how children think. His method was not a form of test, and he did not intend that the approach be used to teach children to move to the next stage. Rather, he demonstrated that the significance of the stages is that as children interact with their environment and reflect, they construct new understandings for themselves and build new structures. He also demonstrated that children who are at the same stage of cognitive development behave in amazingly similar ways. Some people emphasize that children give wrong answers. Indeed, children do go through many wrong answers from an adult perspective, but knowledgeable adults accept children's thinking, work to understand that thinking, and support the child in moving forward based on knowledge of the child.

Sensorimotor Stage

Piaget described the first stage of cognitive development as the sensorimotor stage. Infants begin with preexisting biological structures and soon incorporate new elements. The infant readily grasps whatever is put into her hand (e.g., an adult's finger). As she encounters other objects, she must adjust that grasp. Soon the sucking reflex, which has been adapted from sucking a nipple to sucking a variety of other objects, is coordinated with the grasping behavior. When someone hands the infant a rattle and she grasps it, she will also try to suck it. As new elements are integrated and new behaviors are coordinated, we see the first signs of mental activity (Inhelder, Sinclair, & Bovet, 1974). These structures are action structures, based on the child's actions.

Preoperational Stage

As children enter the preschool years, "the semiotic function appears—language, symbolic play, mental images, and so forth, up until about the age of seven" (Bringuier, 1980, pp. 25–26). During this stage, the child can represent thought at a **preoperational** level; that is, she uses perception rather than **operations** to develop structures. These structures are more complex than sensorimotor structures because in all stages, transformations are constantly occurring, and within structures, the movement is from simple to more and more complex. As these transformations occur over time and through many experiences, the child rather suddenly "understands" a concept—it moves into consciousness—but the process has been ongoing for some time (Bringuier, 1980).

Concrete Operations Stage

At this point, at about age 7, the child has constructed or figured out for herself that problems can be solved based on logical necessity. The structure that the child previously held has been transformed from one that was prelogical. At about this time, the child is constructing operations and can use those operations to solve problems. Operations "are products of reflection and abstraction" (von Glasersfeld, 1995, p. 372). Gruber and Voneche (1995) define operations as "internalized actions that have become reversible" (p. 354). For example, the child constructs the meaning of addition and subtraction as being reversible processes—$7 + 3 = 10$ is the same as $10 - 3 = 7$.

Formal Operations

Once this stage is attained, at about age 11 and often much later, if at all, children and adults are able to think abstractly. The stage continues into adulthood, and thinkers no longer need to consider concrete objects in order to solve problems. Issues and values attract their attention, and their thinking can continue to develop in complexity. Piaget worked with his colleague, Barbel Inhelder, as she developed ideas for the formal operations stage of development (Tryphon & Voneche, 2001). Because this book deals with young children between birth and age 8, the authors have chosen not to focus on this stage. We strongly suggest that you study this stage as doing so will help you understand yourself and your choices when interacting with young children.

CONSTRUCTIONS

Research

Read a section of one of Piaget's books. Look for partial transcripts of interviews that demonstrate how children's thinking changes from stage to stage. Write in your journal ways in which you might use this information in your teaching.

Three Kinds of Knowledge

Constructivist theory delineates three kinds of knowledge: physical knowledge, logico-mathematical knowledge, and social knowledge (sometimes referred to as social arbitrary knowledge). Early childhood educators must construct an understanding of these kinds of knowledge because children (as well as adults) employ all of them in order to learn. The kinds of knowledge are closely interwoven, meaning that teachers should not try to focus on only one aspect of learning. Even when the child is very young, both physical knowledge and logico-mathematical knowledge always occur together.

Logico-Mathematical Knowledge

Logico-mathematical knowledge is the most difficult for us to understand because the idea is abstract and few theorists discuss it. It is a set of relationships that originate in the child's mind and are thus not observable. We can observe a child experimenting with ways to figure out how to zip his coat. From our observation, we decide that he is probably constructing physical knowledge about zippers. He begins constructing logico-mathematical knowledge if he begins to actively and consciously reason about the object (the zipper) and coordinate it with other objects in his environment (e.g., the coat's material, the need for a coat). This leads to the construction of relationship of a concept, which is logico-mathematical knowledge.

Previously, you read about the structures that one creates mentally through the process of assimilation and accommodation and equilibration. We saw that infants begin using reflexes and combine them to form sensory structures. As they use these structures to construct new knowledge, they begin to consider the ideas they are abstracting from their perceptions. When these lead to perturbations, they begin to consider different possibilities other than what they perceive. Although it takes several years, operations (an internally constructed system of actions) begin to develop somewhere around 7 years of age. Eventually, children construct for themselves the operation of reversibility, which leads to conservation and one-to-one correspondence and enables them to construct number. Because these ideas are quite complex, let's look at a few examples. One example of a structure that a child constructs is classification. This structure gives her a tool to use when she encounters a new experience. She decides how the new experience fits or relates to her previous knowledge. In the following example, Tina is probably too young to have constructed a true classification structure, but she has a good beginning:

At the snack table, four-year-old Tina was stuffing crackers into her mouth faster than she could chew. She gulped her cup of orange juice and belched loudly. Annabelle, who was sitting next to her and looking rather supercilious, said, "What do you say?" Tina replied, "Please." Her teacher, Ms. Farley, commented, "I think Annabelle was expecting something different." "Oh, yeah," Tina replied. "Thank you." Looking at Ms. Farley and Annabelle, Tina decided that wasn't the target either. With an embarrassed glance and then a smile of recognition, Tina said confidently, "Excuse me."

Tina had classified socially transmitted words into a subcategory of "words that I use to be polite." *Please, thank you,* and *excuse me* are such words, although politeness was surely a developing idea for her. Tina seems to be working on forming relationships between the uses of these words that her parents or teacher taught her and the times when saying each of these phrases would be appropriate. She realized that she was supposed to use one of these terms rather than "Gimme another cracker" or "This juice is good" or "You're mean." All she had to do was relate the situation (belching) with the expected socially transmitted nicety. In this example, we can observe logico-mathematical knowledge (Tina's classification system) being used with socially transmitted knowledge.

Let's look at another example involving classification and problem solving. A child who has had opportunities to draw with markers, pencils, and crayons may be introduced to drawing using a computer. He then classifies or groups the computer with other drawing tools. If he has already classified the computer as a tool for playing games, that classification may also remain. Over time, as the structure classification is repeatedly used, the child's structures become more complex. Eventually, he may create subcategories for the classification of tools for drawing. Perhaps two subcategories may be tools he uses on paper and tools he uses on a monitor. Another child who also has had experiences with computers may classify them as toys, tools to use at school, or as a vehicle for communicating with friends. In fact, both children may have created subcategories. Each child's use of the structure will be different. Each child uses the structures that he or she has created to solve problems. The following example provides a related scenario:

Marcus, a third grader, decides to illustrate his story. He considers using colored pencils, then printing his story and pasting the text on the illustrated pages. He also wonders if he could draw the illustrations using a computer and insert them directly into the text. Because he is not yet skilled at this approach but decides to try it, he asks his teacher for help.

One of the problem-solving strategies Marcus used in this situation was to consider the classification scheme he had already constructed. Another problem-solving skill he used was to find someone who was likely to have the information he needed. Probably as the result of a variety of experiences, he already had a classification for problem solving. A much younger child might whine or cry until someone helped him figure out what he seemed to need. The much younger child might also move on to another activity or throw his crayons on the floor or even hit a nearby child. You may have studied biology and can recall that plants and animals are assigned to groups distinguished by structure or other properties.

Another structure that children construct as they reflect on their interactions with the environment is conservation. When a person is able to conserve, he believes that if nothing is added or nothing is taken away, then the quantity, volume, or mass does not change. He also believes that the original condition can be produced again by reversing the transformation or change that produced the appearance of difference. Because this logico-mathematical concept is complex, let's look at an example. If you measure a quantity of juice, perhaps 4 ounces, into a short, fat glass, and then measure 4 ounces into a tall, thin glass, a young child usually believes that the tall glass has more. It looks that way to her. Her sensory structure is at work. If, to convince her that the quantities are equal, you empty the contents of the tall glass into a short glass identical to the other short glass, she will now believe that the amount of juice is the same in each glass. But if you pour the contents of one of the short glasses back into a tall glass, she will believe that now there is more in the tall glass. Over a fairly long period of time and with many experiences, the child will begin to reflect on situations such as these and decide that it just looks as if there is more in the tall glass, but the width of the short glass compensates for the height of the tall glass. She will also decide that since you didn't add anything or take anything away, the quantities couldn't possibly change. Furthermore, she may say that you could pour the juice from the tall glass to the short glass, reversing the situation, and demonstrate that the volume remains the same. We say that this child has constructed an understanding of conservation. If she has not yet constructed the necessary structure, merely telling her the answer we expect will not help her understand, although she may say our words back to us.

You may have observed a related situation when young children are working with clay. You carefully give two children identical balls of clay, and they agree that they each have the same amount. A 4-year-old may roll her clay into a long skinny snake and announce, "Now I have more." Her 8-year-old brother may believe that to be absurd. As a conserver, he knows that nothing was added or removed and that the mass of clay just appears to be larger because it has been elongated. He may demonstrate for her that rolling his out and then squeezing it back into a ball shows the reversal to the original state, and he may wonder how on earth the 4-year-old cannot see that. By now, you understand that the differences in the two children's thinking are based on the 4-year-old's use of a sensory structure, how the clay looks to her, while the 8-year-old has constructed the principle of logical necessity. Reflective abstraction led him to construct the notion of conservation, and for him, there is no question about the outcome.

Another major logico-mathematical construct that children begin to develop during the primary grades is seriation, which refers to the ability to organize objects or ideas according to magnitude. For example, a preschooler might organize manipulatives representing Mama Bear, Papa Bear, and Baby Bear into a series from small to large. By the end of the primary grades, children are often able to seriate a *greater* quantity of objects, and they can also use properties or identifiers other than size. As you teach, observe carefully how children address ordinary classroom situations. Depending on their age and the level to which their cognitive structures have been developed, children will solve problems in a variety of ways. As you saw in Chapter 2, your role is to provide support and opportunities for them to continue to construct more and more complex understandings.

CONSTRUCTIONS

Analysis

Reread the discussion the members of the teachers' study group had, focusing on Matt's comments about Martina, who spaced out her ten pennies and said, "Ha, ha. I have more than anybody." Based on your understanding of children's construction of knowledge, consider why Martina may have said this. Then decide how you would respond if you were Martina's teacher. Discuss your thinking in class.

Physical Knowledge

Peter, age 7 months, watches intently as the yellow and black foam ball slowly rolls toward him. With a swipe of his arm, he attempts to encounter the ball. He does, but the ball rolls away from him. Waving his chubby arms and looking intently at the ball, he scoots toward it and swipes at it again. He touches it, and it rolls farther away. He grunts in frustration. With his mother's prompting, his sister, Katie, puts the ball in both of his hands. Peter studies the ball and then puts it to his mouth, intent on investigating it by rolling his tongue over the indented surfaces of the ball.

What is going on in this seemingly mundane event? At this early age, Peter is beginning to demonstrate the roots of physical knowledge, one of the three types of knowledge that Piaget described (1967/1971). **Physical knowledge** is acquired as we touch, move, and physically investigate objects in our environment through our actions on them. A child explores the texture and weight of an object by handling, feeling, and even tasting it. To come to know properties of the ball, for example, Peter must touch and handle it, look at it closely, explore its surface, and maybe even smell it as he tastes it. Later, he will try other things, such as dropping, throwing, and rolling it. Try to imagine how Peter was feeling as he discovered those physical properties. Then think for a moment about gift shops or museums where signs say, "Do Not Touch!" If you have been in stores or homes where you had to restrain a child from reaching out to handle interesting items, you recognize the strong urge children—and adults—have for acquiring physical knowledge.

This type of knowledge stays with us our whole lives, though it is used more consistently by children and lessens somewhat with age, as we acquire more experience and develop the ability to picture objects in our minds. Still, people of all ages touch objects to know about them. This can easily be recognized in museums where touching is encouraged. You can see statues and objects of art that have had literally thousands of hands caress and explore them in order to know and appreciate them more fully. Why is this desire for contact with objects important? In the following sections, we discuss physical knowledge in more depth: how it is defined and why it is important for teachers of young children to understand as they consider creating curriculum with children.

According to Kamii (2000), "Physical knowledge is knowledge of objects in external reality." Having said that, she adds, "The ultimate source of physical knowledge is thus partly in objects, and physical knowledge can be acquired empirically through observation" (p. 5). That is, the object contains physical properties that can be observed. However, the inclusion of the word *partly* is important. The action of observation is part of the definition and helps to make a distinction between sensory experience and physical knowledge. Children do not need reinforcement from another person to acquire physical knowledge. The physical properties of the actual object reinforce the child's understanding (Wadsworth, 2003).

Action, for Piaget, meant mental as well as physical action, and although physical knowledge exists in an external sense, there is also an internal (or mental) part of noticing what happens as an object is pushed, squeezed, or dropped. It is this mental interpretation, or inference, that makes physical knowledge extend beyond sensory activity alone. As an example, you may pick up a melon in the market and press on the ends or thump it to determine its ripeness. You are not simply handling the melon, but rather taking mental action and paying attention to the feedback the fruit provides to come to a conclusion about its ripeness (Williams & Kamii, 1986). Thus, we know that physical knowledge is important in adults' daily lives.

Importance of Physical Knowledge

Observant teachers have often stated that children learn better when they handle objects, but why is that so? In *Physical Knowledge in Preschool Education*, Kamii and DeVries (1993) discuss why children's discovery of physical knowledge is important. One of the points they make is that children are curious and seek to make sense of their world. Investigating objects and materials in the immediate environment is part of their natural style of learning, one that they have experienced from the time they were infants. For that reason, a curriculum for young children that focuses on the discovery of properties of objects and materials will fit children's natural learning style and provide a basis for success. Children develop confidence in the knowledge they have learned through their actions on objects. The objects themselves give information and feedback to the learner; discovery of this information is not right or wrong and can be done individually. It is enhanced by interaction with another individual, who may model other interesting things to do with the materials or objects. This type of learning continues to be important for preschool and kindergarten-age children as they develop, though increasingly, young children will move from a reliance on real objects to representations of those objects. Even adults, especially when they are introduced to new information such as a new technology, benefit by working with objects and materials in a concrete form first.

A second and more theoretical reason for a focus on physical knowledge in an early childhood curriculum is its role in the child's acquisition of general knowledge of the world and the development of intelligence. As Piaget indicated over and over in his theory, the learner's action, both physical and mental, is critical for the development of intelligence. Humans do not just passively absorb knowledge; their actions and interactions with objects and other humans in their environment are the forces that provoke them to construct and reconstruct their theories and understanding about how the world works.

When teachers understand how children acquire physical knowledge, they can plan curricular events that enhance children's thinking and learning. They can also better gauge when and how to interact with children as they engage in physical knowledge activities. As mentioned earlier, physical knowledge is the information that exists in the world. It is "out there" in the real world, and it can be acquired by interaction on and with the object itself. When children interact with objects and focus on a certain property but ignore others, they are gaining information through a process Piaget called **empirical abstraction** (Kamii, 2000). "Empirical abstraction contributes to the child's development of physical knowledge" (Gruber & Voneche, 1995, p. 873).

In order to understand better what Piaget meant by this phrase, let's consider each word separately. *Empirical* means that something is found out or provable through experience or observation. *Abstraction* in this context means that something is taken out. Literally, the phrase means to take out or extract the knowledge through personal experience with the object. In a Piagetian sense, empirical abstraction is "directly drawn from observables (objects or material aspects of the subject's own actions)" (Gruber & Voneche, 1995, p. 873). As a young child acts on an object, he or she will focus on one property (perhaps color) and ignore the other properties (such as size and weight) (Kamii, 1982, 1989). An example would be that as a child examines a key that has a silver color and a jagged edge, the child will focus on either the property of color or the jagged edge but not both.

The Importance of Empirical Abstraction

Children engage in empirical abstraction when they construct physical knowledge (Gruber & Voneche, 1995). In addition, empirical abstraction is necessary for reflective abstraction. Reflective abstraction is the child's ability to make internal relationships between and among objects (Kamii, 2000) and be reflectively conscious of how he or she did it (Piaget, 2001). For example, when the child looked at the key, he focused on the color, which existed in the object. If another key, which was gold, had been next to the silver key, the child would have made an internal relationship of difference. The color of the keys is different. When the child noticed the color of the keys and focused on color, which was a property of the object, that was empirical abstraction. When the child used the two colors to construct a relationship of difference and was conscious of the coordination, that was reflective abstraction.

Learning about the properties that exist in different objects requires direct experience repeated over time. Children will not only repeat things they have done with objects, but also as they come to vary their actions with the object and try new things, they will elaborate the knowledge they have previously gleaned. In this manner, they learn new properties of the object and learn to expect certain reactions and responses as they interact with it. Over time, children will exhibit increased control of the object and may try similar actions on other objects. This exploration and the results of the exploration cause the child to trust his or her own ability to figure things out, which is of no small consequence for learning in the future.

Let's return to our teachers as they discuss physical knowledge activities in their classrooms:

Parul: After reading about Dr. Kamii's work on physical knowledge, I can really see lots of examples of my babies learning physical knowledge. It's very exciting to me to watch them discover their world and to explain what they're doing to their parents. These babies are all going to be so smart!

Jennifer: I'm not convinced that that's enough to make them smart, Parul. They really don't know what they're doing, so how does that lead them to be smart on tests by the time I get them? Everyone seems to think discovery learning is so wonderful! Maybe it is for infants, and the professor in my master's class at the university is encouraging us to teach science as discovery learning, but I don't have time for the children to discover everything. They have to know content.

Matt: Whoa, wait a minute. You're comparing apples and oranges here. Babies are very different from third graders. Do you really think you can generalize about the role of discovery across age groups like that? I think discovery is still important at age 9, but maybe balancing discovery with other types of knowledge is appropriate for your third graders too.

Kenisha: I think I agree with Matt, Jennifer. I'll give you an example. My kindergartners have been working in the float-and-sink section of the science center. I have a whole bunch of items in a container for the kids to experiment with, but first they have to make a prediction. Then they can try it to see if it floats or sinks and whether it does what they thought it would do. After they've done that a lot, we've talked about the things that make the items that sink different from the ones that float.

Sheila: Do you use big words like *prediction* with them? I bet they don't even know what that means.

Kenisha: Well, at first we use the word *guess;* then I pair it with the word *prediction.* They love big words. Anyway, it seemed that the kids started making predictions by just paying attention to the size of the object. Now they don't seem to be using only that one idea as to what makes it float or sink. I hear them beginning to vary their predications, and I think they understand more about properties of items that float versus sink. The best part to me is they're learning this physical knowledge from the objects and not from me.

Sheila: Kenisha, would you videotape that activity and bring it to our next meeting? I'd like for us to really look at it and discuss it. If your kindergartners are learning as much as you seem to think, I could certainly use that video in my room.

Kenisha: Sure, Sheila. But how would you use the videotape in your classroom?

Sheila: I can show it to my students, and they can learn which objects float and sink by watching. Then we'll do a worksheet on water displacement so they'll have the right answers about floating and sinking.

Ron: I just want all of us to avoid thinking that physical knowledge is science or science education or the discovery method for teaching science. Physical knowledge deals with the child's intellectual development. Don't you remember? Kamii and DeVries [1993] pointed out that science or science education or the discovery method deals with teacher-organized content that the teacher teaches or transmits to the child.

Matt: That's right, Ron. I just love the example Piaget used to distinguish between "discovery" and "invention." I think I read about it in one of Kamii's books: something like Columbus discovered America— but it was already there; but man invented the automobile—it wasn't there before [Kamii & DeVries, 1993].

Kenisha: So what you are saying is that physical knowledge deals with the child's construction of knowledge, not the instruction or discovery of scientific knowledge.

What do you think about Sheila's idea of showing a video of a float-and-sink activity? In addition to constructing physical knowledge, the children were also acquiring logico-mathematical knowledge. Physical knowledge and logico-mathematical knowledge are not totally separate from one another. Remember the definition of physical knowledge: Because it includes mental action, physical knowledge isn't just sensory input. Remember when we defined empirical abstraction, we pointed out that reflective abstraction (necessary for logico-mathematical knowledge) was necessary for the child to recognize the properties of difference. Watching a video of other children may provide them with ideas to try out, but it denies children the opportunity to develop their own physical knowledge of the objects.

We will conclude this section on physical knowledge by taking a brief look at the use of objects in classrooms with young children, as well as the role of the teacher in encouraging physical knowledge activities.

The Role of Objects

Objects and materials hold an important place in children's development and education. Think about this for a minute. Whether children have access to expensive toys, Montessori materials, people, or everyday objects in homes and classrooms, they interact with them with fascination as they repeat activities and invent new ones. How do they use objects?

According to Kamii and DeVries (1993), children use objects to act on and observe the properties related to movement (such as push, pull, roll), the properties related to change (mixing, melting, cooking), and the properties that don't fit into either category (shadow play, playing with mirrors). For example, when a 6-year-old child pushes a doll's carriage along a sidewalk, watches it roll down into the driveway, and then runs to catch it, the child is both observing and acting on the object (the carriage). When a 5-year-old boy helps his mother stir and then bake cupcakes for his birthday, he is mixing and cooking. In this example, he is primarily observing the blending of the ingredients and the cooking of the batter, but he also acts on those ingredients by stirring. And when the 3-year-old child peers into a corner mirror in his child-care room, smiles, sticks out his tongue, and then walks away, he is observing his own actions. In each of these examples, the children act on the objects and observe their actions.

Sinclair (1994) describes how children might use the objects and their properties to interact with others. Because children view humans, as well as materials, as objects to act on, Sinclair's work documents the simultaneity of the child's acting on and interacting with two kinds of objects (materials and humans) at the same time. First, children use objects as a means of collaborating with a partner. At different ages, the focus may be different. For example, you may see toddlers giving to and taking objects from one another. The focus is not on the object itself but on the action between peers. In this case, the object provides the means for social interaction. In fact, watch toddlers for a while, and you will notice that an object being used by another child is attractive simply because someone else has it (Verba & Musatti, 1989). Second, children use objects for shared activities with other children. In this situation, the object and peers appear to have equal focus. The children do pay attention to the objects and may transform their use in play. For example, in housekeeping play, a block may become a telephone. Here it appears that children imitate, share, and extend the use of objects as they play, and there is reciprocal interaction. In block play, you may see a group of children planning together as they build and use shared materials (although they may still want objects that other children have). The materials help sustain the interaction with both peers and objects.

Finally, children use objects in ways that focus on the objects, their properties, and reactions to the child's actions on them. This is most closely related to the way most teachers think of the child's acquisition of physical knowledge. In this context, children use objects to experiment, elaborate, combine, and perhaps even create new objects or activities. Teachers may also use objects to provoke curiosity and initiate activities about particular content they want to introduce or to extend.

Children Constructing Knowledge

As you can see, objects may serve a number of different functions that are all valuable in different contexts. Clearly, the provision of real objects and primary or raw materials is an important component of learning environments for children of all ages. Thoughtful teachers will know how to use objects in these different situations to enhance children's learning and the teaching goals chosen for focus at the time. Let's examine this statement further.

Suppose that the teacher has decided from observing two toddlers sitting together and handing toys back and forth that the goal for this interaction is the acquisition of physical knowledge. At this early age, children have much to learn about the giving, taking, and sharing of objects and how their actions affect other children. The children are not focusing on the object as much as on one another and the process of give and take. They are acting on both the other child and the object as they construct physical knowledge. The way the teacher responds is based on the goal of the activity and the children's focus at that point. Thus, the teacher might encourage the children's interactions of exchanging the toys or might focus on the properties of the toys.

Earlier in this section, we discussed Sinclair's research (1994) on children's purposes for objects. One of her points documented how children focus on objects, their properties, and the child's action on them as their goal. First, think about yourself and your use of objects. Have you ever had the experience of doing something with an object and then being unable to recall what you did? Sometimes we seem to do things automatically, or without consciousness of what we are doing. This can happen with children too, so the idea that children learn simply by handling manipulatives or objects is not necessarily true. They must use the objects in a mindful manner.

As you have probably determined, physical knowledge activities are found primarily in the science curriculum. Interestingly, some teachers believe that they are fostering the child's development of physical knowledge by simply putting different objects on a table labeled "The Science Corner." In such a site, children observe and handle objects, but there are no planned activities to help children make further connections between objects and their world. Granted, the children will gain some knowledge about the properties of the objects, but unless they are encouraged by questions and have activities and problem-solving opportunities that are of interest to them, they are manipulating materials in a mindless or minds-off manner.

Physical Knowledge and Curriculum

Although physical knowledge is most closely aligned with the area of science in the curriculum, it is not just the science curriculum. We have said this before but want you to understand this important distinction between the curricular area of science and the role of physical knowledge in the child's intellectual development. Children may use objects from biology, chemistry, and physics to act on objects and observe the results of their actions. For example, children may feed and care for a class pet or plant a garden (biology), mix paint for a mural (chemistry), or use a pendulum to knock down blocks (physics). Chaille and Britain's (1996, 2002) book, *The Young Child as Scientist: A Constructivist Approach to Early Childhood Science Education,* is an excellent source for a constructivist approach to the science curriculum.

Children may use physical knowledge in other curricular areas. Many teachers encourage children to use objects in math activities. For example, if the children are planning a party for the class, the teacher might have them decide how many cups of punch would be needed for each child to have two cups. (When we say that teachers may use objects for math activities, we are not talking about commercially prepared materials and objects that attempt to use the actual object to teach place value or number.) Content in social studies relies on items used by cultures and individuals over time to enhance the understanding of people living here before us. In art, children act on objects to create and design. For example, they might use brushes, canvas, clay, and paint in their work. See Table 3.1 for examples of physical knowledge activities in the classroom.

Table 3.1 **Examples of Physical Knowledge Activities in the Curriculum**

Target ball	Water play	Woodworking
Pendulums	Shadow play	Marbles
Pulleys	Cooking	Mixing solids and liquids
Rollers	Mirror play	Ramps
Balls	Block play	String

CONSTRUCTIONS

1. Observation

Visit a local child-care center and kindergarten classroom. Identify the children engaged in opportunities to construct physical knowledge. Write observations that document the children's use of movement to act on objects, the children's observation of change to act on objects, and other actions that seem to be physical knowledge but don't fall into either category. Bring your thoughts to class to discuss with a peer.

2. Observation

Videotape a group of children engaged in a physical knowledge activity and share the tape with a classmate. Ask your classmate to analyze the tape based on what he or she knows about physical knowledge. Then analyze your classmate's tape.

3. Reflection

Drawing from information about the three types of knowledge, jot down your ideas about a more appropriate way to have third-grade children learn about sinking and floating activities. Label the types of knowledge your suggestions would exemplify.

Social Knowledge

Mary Jane, the mother of 10-month-old Darbi, was overjoyed when she held her daughter one morning and Darbi said, "Ma Ma." Mary Jane couldn't wait to tell her best friend that Darbi had finally called her Mama. How did Darbi come to call her mother Mama? Darbi was at a place in her language development when she was verbalizing consonant-vowel combinations such as *ma, da,* and *ba.* In interactions with her mother, Darbi heard her mother use *Mama* in reference to herself. Mary Jane had called herself *Mama* while interacting with Darbi. Mary Jane had named herself for Darbi. Through interactions over the course of Darbi's young life, she had heard her mother call herself *Mama.* The word *Mama* stands for mother and is the name that Mary Jane wants Darbi to call her. When Darbi verbalized the consonant-vowel combination *mama,* Mary Jane assumed Darbi was referring to her, became excited, and showed Darbi that she was very pleased by what Darbi had uttered. Mary Jane could just as well have called herself *Bubba,* and Darbi would have associated the name *Bubba* with her mother. In Mary Jane's culture, the word *mama* is arbitrarily used by some people to name one's mother. The use of the term *mama* to represent a female nurturer is a social convention agreed on by those who choose to use it.

Three-year-old Clint couldn't wait for his mother to pick him up from preschool because he had something important to tell her. When she asked what he wanted to tell her, he said he had learned to count to 100 at school. She was somewhat skeptical because she had heard him count only to 5. But she could tell he was very proud of this achievement, so she showed her excitement by asking him to count for her. Clint said, "One, two, skip a few, a hundred!" He had memorized this chant from one of his friends at school. His accomplishment did not indicate that he understood what the numbers meant, only that he had been able to recall words from memory.

Some parents mistake word recall for understanding of concepts. Parents may think that children have greater understanding than they really do when they recite the alphabet or count to ten. Children can learn to do these things without understanding what they mean. It is not uncommon for some parents to become embarrassed when their child utters profanities in public that she has heard at home. But parents usually know that the child does not understand what she has said. She is only repeating something she has heard and memorized.

In his study of the human body, second-grader Donito has learned the names for various body systems such as the circulatory, nervous, and digestive systems. He found these words in a book he checked out from the school library. Now he has a name, the circulatory system, for the idea of movement of blood through the body.

The preceding are three specific examples of how children acquire social knowledge. Social knowledge or conventional (arbitrary) knowledge (DeVries & Zan, 2012) is arbitrary truth agreed on by groups of people. It is knowledge passed or transmitted from one person to another, usually through language. Examples include the alphabet, names for things, social customs, and social rules for doing certain things such as shaking hands when you meet someone. Social knowledge comes from culturally agreed-on customs and traditions. Piaget studied children's social interactions and conventional knowledge, including knowledge of games and rules. In describing social knowledge, Piaget (1970) wrote, "Social life . . . provides the totality of practical rules and bodies of knowledge arrived at collectively and passed on from one generation to the next" (p. 67). Piaget differentiated between social and conventional knowledge and moral judgment. Moral judgment is arrived at through the coordination of different perspectives on what is right or good behavior. It reflects moral reasoning about situations, taking into consideration multiple perspectives; therefore, it is not arbitrary. Social knowledge is not reasoned through but given ready-made. Examples include social knowledge of your telephone number, address, and Social Security number.

Constructivist researchers have used the term *social knowledge* to refer to knowledge that is transmitted from person to person (Chaille & Britain, 2002; Kamii, 2000; Kamii & DeVries, 1993). Names, labels, rules, customs, and conventions are then passed from person to person and generation to generation. Social knowledge is not arrived at logically. For example, it is not likely that someone would be able to deduce a telephone number logically. People do not usually use logico-mathematical reasoning to come up with their telephone numbers. Those numbers are usually assigned by the telephone company. We do not construct dates for holidays that are also arbitrary, such as celebrating St. Patrick's Day on March 17; names for things such as the name *dog* for furry animals; or rules such as wiping your feet before entering a house. These are all examples of social knowledge.

Source of Social Knowledge

The source of social knowledge is other people. Through interactions with others, children learn the names for things. For example, teachers tell children the names for alphabet letters, numerals, seasons of the year, and dinosaurs. Names for things are arbitrarily agreed-on conventions that cultures use to communicate among people. Names for things can be changed by groups of people; for example, Washington's Ronald Reagan Airport used to be called National Airport. Although the reasons given for such changes are derived logico-mathematically, the names are not. Although the source for physical knowledge is in objects, the source for social knowledge is in people. Cultural names, traditions, holidays, and rituals are transmitted from person to person. They cannot be derived through logico-mathematical reasoning or observed in objects.

All knowledge, whether physical or social, is constructed within a logico-mathematical framework. Even knowledge that is transmitted, such as telephone numbers, is classified in ways that make sense. For example, a telephone number can be classified according to location by its area code. The number 405–744–7125 is located in Oklahoma because it has an Oklahoma area code. Teachers tell children the names for various dinosaurs. But children use logico-mathematical reasoning to differentiate the category of dinosaurs from the category of farm animals by making relationships of size, function, era, and other characteristics. Memorizing the state capitals is another example of socially transmitted knowledge. State capital names can be found in a book or on a Web site, or can be given by the teacher. See Box 3.2 for examples of social knowledge.

BOX 3.2 EXAMPLES OF SOCIAL KNOWLEDGE IN CURRICULUM CONTENT AREAS

Literacy: Names of alphabet letters, punctuation marks, standard spelling, reading from left to right and top to bottom, manuscript and cursive handwriting, conventions for written forms such as letters, grammar rules

Mathematics: Names of numerals, rote counting, algorithms

Science: Names of natural objects, animals, plants, and seasons; teacher demonstrations of experiments

Social studies: Names of countries, cultural customs, rituals, conventions, rules and traditions, flag salute, calendar

Expressive arts: Names of colors, songs, poems, stories, folktales, finger plays, rhymes, chants, plays

---

The Importance of Social Knowledge

Social knowledge is important because it helps children know the names of things. Children who know and use names and labels for things can communicate with others by using this information to express their thoughts and feelings. It would be difficult to communicate without naming things. Social knowledge is also important because it helps people understand why certain things are done in certain cultures. Social conventions, such as stopping at red lights, help the culture run more smoothly (in this case, there should be fewer accidents). Social knowledge is a type of code that facilitates the way we interact with others.

Difficulties can arise when we do not know the social conventions of a culture we are visiting. For example, some hand gestures in American culture are considered obscene in other cultures. The only way to acquire this information is for someone to tell us. In some countries it is an accepted social convention and even the law to drive on the left side of the road, whereas in the United States the appropriate side is the right side. Knowledge of such social conventions is constructed through interactions with others who know and communicate the social conventions. Social knowledge helps children know what to call things, how to act within a certain social context, and why rituals are used.

Social Knowledge and Cultural Transmission of Information

It is important for teachers to understand all three types of knowledge. Understanding the three types enables teachers to respond to children based on the type of knowledge that the child is constructing. Understanding physical knowledge helps teachers plan environments with appropriate physical objects that children can use to learn about how objects work. Understanding social knowledge helps teachers know when to respond to children by telling them names for things and when to encourage children to construct relationships through experimentation and reasoning. Many names for things must be told to children. Children do not construct names for alphabet letters, for example; they must be told. But they do construct spelling words based on patterns that make sense to them.

It is important, however, to recognize that curriculum is more than social knowledge. Children cannot learn everything through social transmission. They must actively construct knowledge through a logico-mathematical framework.

Difficulties arise when teachers attempt to teach everything as if it is social knowledge. This problem has resulted in teacher-directed instruction for rote memorization of information. Some knowledge can be told to children, but other knowledge is best learned through active construction and making relationships of how one thing is related to another, such as the idea that 5 is related to 3 and 2. The predominant mode of instruction in schools continues to be teaching through telling. This robs children of the opportunity to construct knowledge and ultimately robs them of their ability to think for themselves. They become dependent on the teacher to tell them the correct answer.

Kamii and Joseph (2004) have described the harmful effects of teaching algorithms in mathematics instruction. Children who are taught mathematics as if it were social knowledge or algorithms to be memorized do not learn to think on their own. They mechanically apply the algorithm or formula for solving a problem. Teaching mathematics as social knowledge instead of as logico-mathematical knowledge hinders children's thinking so that they no longer use their ability to reason through a problem. They just memorize and apply the formulas without thinking whether they make sense. Kamii and Joseph's research has shown that this type of teaching is harmful to children. Logico-mathematical knowledge, such as mathematics, should not be taught as social knowledge.

Science is another content area that is often taught as social knowledge to the detriment of children's thinking. For example, teaching the solar system in kindergarten by having children memorize planet names does not help children understand complex concepts such as the characteristics of planets, the relationships of planets to one another, or orbital regularities. In fact, undue emphasis on memorizing planet names can extinguish children's interests in science. Science then becomes just another subject for which they memorize meaningless information. Chaille and Britain (2002) have shown that children construct theories and conduct experiments to test their theories in similar ways as scientists.

By understanding the differences among physical, social, and logico-mathematical knowledge, teachers can better facilitate children's knowledge construction. They will know when to respond to children with a name for something and when to encourage children to figure out relationships. It is also important for teachers to understand the interrelationship of the three types of knowledge. All three types are usually involved in most learning situations. For example, in block play, children learn about the physical properties of blocks through building with them. They learn that some blocks are shaped differently from others, some roll, some are curved, some work better on the bottoms of buildings, and others work best stacked on top. Children construct logico-mathematical relationships in block play, such as angle, force, and stability. They also learn social knowledge, such as the words for bridge, skyscraper, and tower. Just about every learning activity involves all three types of knowledge. Children do not differentiate among the types. But teachers can use the types to understand children's learning and how to respond in ways that will promote rather than hinder children's thinking. Think of how the three types of knowledge are involved in each of the following activities: easel painting, water play, reading a story, writing a story, and riding a tricycle.

Social Knowledge and Its Relationship to Curriculum Content

Curriculum in schools has been traditionally viewed as content areas. Reading and language arts, mathematics, science, social studies, and expressive arts are typical content areas. Social knowledge is embedded in all these curriculum content areas, although it is more pronounced in some and less in others (see Box 3.3 for examples of social knowledge in curriculum content areas).

BOX 3.3 EXAMPLES OF SOCIAL KNOWLEDGE IN CURRICULUM CONTENT AREAS

Examples of Social Knowledge in Curriculum Content Areas

Literacy: Names of alphabet letters, punctuation marks, standard spelling, reading from left to right and top to bottom, manuscript and cursive handwriting, conventions for written forms such as letters, grammatical rules

Mathematics: Names of numerals, rote counting, algorithms

Science: Names for natural objects, animals, plants, seasons, teacher demonstrations of experiments

Social studies: Names for countries, cultural customs, rituals, conventions, rules and traditions, flag salute, calendar

Expressive arts: Names for colors, songs, poems, stories, folktales, finger plays, rhymes, chants, plays

---

As previously mentioned, to teach mathematics as social knowledge is to undermine children's invention of mathematics. Just because children can give the names of numerals in sequential order does not mean that they understand numerical relationships. Adults tell children the names for numerals, but children must construct number relationships for themselves.

In the teaching of reading, social knowledge again plays a minor role. Teachers must tell children the names for alphabet letters and how to spell irregular words, but children should be encouraged to construct knowledge of print, word patterns, and the use of words in communication in active ways based on children's purposes and needs to communicate with others. Phonics drill and practice is another example of teaching reading as social knowledge instead of focusing on the logico-mathematical relationships involved in understanding words and word patterns. The issue should not be whether to teach phonics, but rather should focus on how children come to understand print and how teachers can encourage that understanding. Many children do actively use phonetic strategies for deciphering words. Teachers can encourage children to use their own invented strategies for making sense of print (Taylor, Branscombe, Burcham, and Land, 2011).

Science is a content area in which all three types of knowledge are evident for understanding nature, scientific processes, and names and labels for scientific information. Teachers who rely on objects alone, such as nature objects, rocks, birds' nests, and fossils, do children a disservice. Although studying nature objects are important, what is more meaningful to children is to be able to ask their own questions and have opportunities to explore their questions using observation, experimentation, discussion of hypotheses with others, and analysis. Science teaching should help children become inquirers. In combination with an inquiry approach, teachers can tell children the names for objects and scientific phenomena without forcing them to memorize meaningless lists of information.

Social knowledge is most evident in the area of social studies in which children learn about their own and other cultures, social traditions, and cultural customs. For example, a project on Japan might involve learning Japanese words for numbers and colors, traditions such as origami, folk tales, and foods. All of these topics rely on social knowledge that is transmitted through telling children about these various aspects of Japanese culture. In addition, children will learn about Japanese cultural objects and artifacts, resulting in physical knowledge of these objects. They will also use logico-mathematical reasoning to compare and draw conclusions about differences and similarities between Japanese culture and American culture.

Expressive arts, such as music, drama, and art, rely on physical knowledge coupled with social and logico-mathematical knowledge. Songs, finger plays, rhymes, and chants involve social knowledge, as do plays and reenactments of stories. Art projects, such as painting, collage, woodwork, and drawing, involve physical knowledge to a large degree. Logico-mathematical knowledge is constructed when children create their own songs and plays and experiment with art media to express their thoughts and feelings. It is important for teachers to consider teaching in ways that promote active knowledge construction of all three types of knowledge and not just focus on teaching for social transmission of information. See the following Curriculum Strategies that foster the three kinds of knowledge in your teaching.

CURRICULUM STRATEGIES: FOSTERING THREE KINDS OF KNOWLEDGE

- Respond to children based on the type of knowledge. For physical knowledge, structure activities and experimentation with objects. For logico-mathematical knowledge, encourage children to make relationships and formulate and test theories. For social knowledge, tell children content that they cannot construct for themselves, such as names of the days of the week.
- Teach for knowledge construction and not for memorization.
- Ask children questions that provoke reasoning, perspective taking, and problem solving.
- Model inquiry for children. Let them hear you puzzle over your own questions.
- Engage children in activity that has interest, purpose, and challenge for them.
- Assess children's real work through documentation of artifacts and portfolio entries. Encourage children to evaluate their own work.

Social Knowledge and Assessment

The majority of standardized tests used today to assess achievement do not measure understanding. They focus on measuring the most trivial information that is primarily taught through social transmission or teaching as telling. Children can and do memorize information to use on tests, but this memory work should not be mistaken for understanding. Curriculum is more than social knowledge. Appropriate assessments of children's understanding include observations; anecdotal records; and artifacts, such as drawings and stories, that reflect children's thinking and demonstrate what they are able to do in terms of tasks that have meaning and interest for them. Portfolio assessment of children's work would be a more appropriate replacement for standardized tests and would reflect the view that curriculum involves all three types of knowledge.

CONSTRUCTIONS

1. Observation

Observe an activity in a kindergarten classroom. Identify the types of knowledge involved in the activity. Discuss with others how to plan activities that promote active knowledge construction.

2. Reflection

Recall how you learned to read. Describe your learning in terms of the three types of knowledge.

3. Analysis

Write a letter to parents in which you explain the difference between teaching mathematics as social knowledge and teaching mathematics as logico-mathematical knowledge. Include examples that make your points clear.

Representational Thought

Eighteen-month-old Quantavious loved his pretend golf clubs. He carried the putter with him everywhere he went. When his grandmother flipped the light switch with her hand to turn on the lights, Quantavious watched very carefully. He spent the next few days attempting to reach the light panel to move the switch. Finally, he looked at his putter, held it up to the light switch, and pushed. Much to his amazement and glee, the light switch moved, and the lights came on.

Three-year-old Anna maneuvered her wheelchair to the art easel, anchored herself so that she could reach the paint brush and paints, and then reached for the brush to begin experimenting with blue paint. Because she wanted to make long brush strokes, she moved her head closer to the paper. After 15 minutes, she looked up and exclaimed, "I'm ready to hang my painting so that it can dry."

Three 4-year-olds hurried to the Choice Board to select the dramatic play center; they wanted to play "county fair." They had decided to dress up like clowns and march around the center. Once they began their play, they decided to pretend they were clowns who were driving a clown bus to pick up people in the parking lots and take them to the fair.

Five-year-old D.J. crawled on the floor with the fingers on each of his hands grasping two unit blocks. As he zoomed by, the teacher asked what he was doing. "I'm skating," D.J. replied. His teacher had brought in in-line skates since they were studying the theme of wheels.

A group of 5-year-olds took a cardboard box and transformed it into their representation of a pickup truck as one of their projects for their theme of wheels. Brandy, one of the group's members, spent hours painting and designing the doors of the truck. As she put the final touches on her door by painting lettering on it, she exclaimed, "It'll have the restaurant's name on it just like my father's van."

Henry, a first grader, did not really like to write, but his first-grade teacher wanted him to write and publish a book for the class library. As he rode the bus home, he puzzled over a story to write. When he arrived home, everyone was in a tizzy. His older brother shouted for him to pick up the burlap bag and get into the car. On the way to the hospital, his mom explained that his father had been bitten by a rattlesnake and needed to get to the hospital. When they arrived at the emergency room, Henry's mom told him to take the bag to the nurse. When he handed it to the nurse, she asked, "What's inside?" Henry's mom replied, "It's the rattlesnake that bit my husband. I thought you needed to see it." The nurse dropped the bag, screamed, and ran from the room. Henry thought, "I've got my story for my book! I can even draw pictures for this one!"

Kaying was excited when her third-grade teacher explained that they were doing a research report for their theme on the oceans. She wanted to study whales and use the Internet to learn more about them. When she went to the library for her research time, Kaying found not only pictures of whales but also a video of whales swimming and making their noises. She even found an address to e-mail an oceanographer who studies whales. Kaying was so excited as she wrote her report, downloaded the pictures, and drew her representations.

These children are all representing their ideas about their worlds through play, drawing, problem solving, and oral and written language. Piaget and his colleagues view these as manifestations or forms of **representational thought.** Representational thought is different from logico-mathematical thought because it is influenced by the quantity, quality, and nature of the sign systems a learner experiences. Furthermore, representational thought is the "thought of social relationships or coordination of individual minds" (Piaget, 1955, p. 9).

At first, representational thought is a personal system of presenting known actions. As the child becomes interested in letting others know what he or she knows, that child's message becomes social and is influenced by culture, socioeconomic status, language, religion, parents' education, and even the political climate of the times. It will also be influenced by his or her reflection on the way those components shape meaning. For example, when children at a summer enrichment program became interested in making greeting cards, they wanted to make ones that fit their needs as well as the needs of the entire summer program. One 5-year-old said, "I'm going to make my daddy a Father's Day card because he's so special. It has to have writing in it like a store-bought card." When the teacher asked her when her family celebrated Father's Day, the child said, "I don't remember, but this will let my daddy know how much I love him." This child was representing her understandings of holidays to her father and others in her group. She was representing her world of known actions to others, as well as coordinating what she knew with what she had learned from others.

"Pre-verbal, sensory-motor intelligence progresses to where the child needs some kind of representation for further cognitive progress and where his cognitive structures make such representation possible. Observational research shows that early symbolic behavior occurs only after objects have been endowed with certain physical and conventional properties and after certain kinds of creative organizational behavior have appeared" (Sinclair, 1970, p. 36). Although language is the most noticeable kind of symbolic functioning, it is only one of many. Children use mental imagery, deferred imitation, symbolic play, drawing, computerized graphic representations, work with clay, and dance and movement, as well as language, to represent what they know. Furthermore, they use such representations to image objects that are no longer present. The better able they are to present what they know, the better they can control the relationships necessary to understand their worlds (Forman & Kuschner, 1983). In other words, the act of representing requires the child to use what Furth (1969) calls "double knowledge" (p. 96). "When a child uses a box as a bed in his play, he knows what a bed is and what a box is; precisely because of this double knowledge he can use one as a symbol for the other" (Sinclair, 1970, p. 42).

Representation consists of coordinating signs or symbols so that people can understand each other. The fact that the child has moved beyond motoric thought dominated by direct perception to thinking about more than the appearance of things allows him or her to begin to understand that one thing could represent another (e.g., a block could represent a car). In order to understand representational thought, one must first understand the semiotic function. Because the focus of this book is curriculum and ways that theory guides and informs curriculum, this chapter will provide a very brief discussion of semiotics. **Semiotics** is the sign-symbol system that humans use to make and provide meaning to self and others. The signs consist of signifiers, such as words, numbers, notes, and graphic icons (found on computers), that represent the signified, or meaning, quantity, or sound. These signifiers are behaviors that have been used to represent something else. Because written and spoken language can be used to describe most other sign systems, it is the most complex system. Other systems, such as gestures, written musical scripts, money, written words, and street signs, also represent meaning but not with the generative property that language has.

Let's see what the teachers are saying about their understanding of representation and its importance:

Parul: One of the parents designed and made a huge train from cardboard boxes for the infants and toddlers. The 1-year-olds just wanted to run into the engine, peep out the window, and then run outside to the train. It was as if they were playing peek-a-boo and thinking, "When I'm in the train, you can't see me, but when I am outside, you can." The 2-year-olds' play was different. They would fill the engine with a pretend gas pump, pull an imaginary cord for the whistle, and wave to their friends in the room. What do you think this play means to a constructivist? I'm trying to use it in my parent conferences, but I don't really understand what I'm seeing.

Jennifer: You are talking about the way children represent their understanding of the world through deferred imitation.

Sheila: I think they're just playing! Parents are not going to want you to tell them about their children playing in a make-believe train. They want to know whether the children can recognize their colors and count to five.

Ron: I disagree with you, Sheila. These children are engaged in deferred imitation; that is, they're trying to copy or imitate an earlier behavior they saw. Parul, you said that one of the children pulled an imaginary cord for the whistle. That child was mentally representing or remembering what had happened earlier. This is an example of the double knowledge we read about last week.

Sheila: What do you mean?

Parul: The children had to know about boxes and about trains in order to use the box to represent a train.

Jennifer: You've got it!

Sheila: Yeah! But the 1-year-olds didn't do anything but run in and out of the box. Running in a classroom should be a health and safety issue.

Parul: Come on, Sheila! The children were well supervised and weren't "running" but were moving quickly. I think I'll just continue to observe and read more about this representational stuff.

The Child's Ability to Represent

Infants use representations as early as a few months of age. When they smile or frown after looking at their mother or caregiver, they are using the earliest sign system to meet their needs. For example, when infants look up and see their mother, they search for a signal before responding. If the mother signals approval, the infants will continue with their planned action: a big smile. By the third month, most infants attempt to imitate others. For example, when the mother sticks out her tongue at the infant, the infant will imitate that action. Within the first year of life, infants can produce gestures, such as nodding or shaking their heads, to convey a message to an adult or child. Furthermore, toddlers between 1 and 2 years of age often use movement or dance to convey a message. This is the beginning of deferred imitation, or imitation of an action that happened at an earlier time. However, we must remember that although the infant is using early forms of representing, the purpose of that representation is a desire for success or practical adaptation. If it is a desire for success, then the infant wants to be fed or noticed. If it is practical adaptation, then we must remember that the infant adapts to things or the body of another person (a mother or caregiver, for example) but without socializing the intellect. The infant does not have the ability to reflect, elaborate, or organize his or her thoughts through reflection and reasoning (Piaget, 1955).

Toddlers between the ages of 18 and 24 months are progressing from sensorimotor intelligence to some kind of representational intelligence. They do this through the internalized process of "spontaneous and internal regroupings which are equivalent to mental deduction and construction" (Piaget, 1955, p. 3). They are able to solve some kinds of problems and evoke images mentally rather than by relying primarily on sensory and motoric experimentation. For example, Zack and Megan were playing with the stuffed snake in the 2-year-old's room. Zack made a hissing sound and then ran up to Megan and put the snake on her shoulder. Megan took the snake and hissed back. These two children used deferred imitation and were able to assimilate the snake (an object or thing) to its actions (their imitation of the snake's actions).

Because 2-year-olds are just beginning to use representational intelligence, their thinking is more practical than representational (Forman & Kuschner, 1983). For example, they may know the difference between a motorcycle and a tricycle, but they cannot represent the relationship between the motorcycle's motor and its movement. The child zooming through the play yard after sitting on a motorcycle is representing the function of the object (the cycle), not the relationship. As they construct more knowledge through their play and interactions with objects, children begin to construct relationships between the structure and function of those objects within their environments.

Symbolic play is a second manifestation of representation. Like deferred imitation, it is an external representation of a mental image. The child takes an object and uses it to represent something else. For instance, in the earlier example, D.J. used blocks to represent in-line skates. Although he was using imitation in that he was imitating the ways he had seen in-line skaters skate, he was formulating a way to represent the in-line skates (the blocks). When D.J. created the symbol for the skates, he was engaging in symbolic play. Thus, in symbolic play, a child uses a systemic approach to create symbols at will in order to express everything in that child's life experience that he or she cannot formulate or assimilate by means of language alone (Wadsworth, 2003). Symbolic play is essential as children attempt to describe, elaborate, and explain their play scenarios to playmates so that they will join in the play (the social experience).

Mental imagery is an internal representation (symbol) of objects and past experiences. The mental images are not exact or accurate copies of the objects or experiences but rather static imitations of sensory perceptions much like a photograph (Branscombe, Castle, Dorsey, Surbeck, & Taylor, 2000; Wadsworth, 2003). The child uses mental imagery to coordinate the appearance of an object with reasoning about that object or the action of the event with reasoning about the event. As the child begins this process, he or she forms relationships between differing points of view (the real and the reasoned).

At about 2 years of age, children begin to use spoken language. This manifestation of representation shows that the child is able to represent the object with symbols in the form of spoken words. At first children use one-word sentences, but by age 4 they have mastered or constructed the use of spoken language. Spoken language allows them to interact socially with others, to elaborate concepts and relationships, and create rules.

Children construct notions about the production and interpretation of the written word. Drawing, writing, and computerized graphic representations are all forms of representation that older children use. Whereas the 2-year-old holds the crayon, brush, or pencil and scribbles, the 5-year-old's representations are more realistic. Children's intent is to make drawing, writing, and computerized graphic representations realistic. Box 3.4 provides examples of children's representations in classrooms. One characteristic of young children is that they draw what they think, not what they actually see (Wadsworth, 2003). By ages 8 or 9, children are able to draw what they see.

As children develop, they continue to construct knowledge about ways to represent what they know. Older children use the written word as a form of representation (Taylor, Branscombe, Burcham, Land, 2011). Just as with other kinds of representation, children move through developmentally ordered levels as they construct their notions about making meaning through writing. Ferreiro's (1990) research with young children's writing serves as the seminal work in this area. She found that children move through several levels as they construct notions about the production and interpretation of the written word. According to Ferreiro, children must first distinguish between two modes of graphic representation: drawing and writing. Through their experimentation with written symbols, they realize that any written system is a set of forms that is arbitrary and ordered in a linear fashion. Next, they discover ways that drawing and writing relate to each other. As they do this, they follow the organizational principle that "letters are used to represent a property of the objects of the word (including humans, animals, etc.) that drawing is unable to represent" (e.g., their names) (p. 16). Their next step is to recognize ways that letters are organized to represent the names of objects so that those letters are readable, interpretable, and meaningful. Once children have done this, they must solve the problems of how many letters are necessary for something to be able to be read (according to Ferreiro's research, children maintain that three letters are necessary for the formation of a word). For example, they would not view *of* as readable or a word because it has two letters. Ferreiro calls this the *principle of minimum quantity* (p. 17). The other problem children solve is that of variations of letters within a word, which is more of a qualitative than a quantitative problem.

In the second developmental level of children's understanding and representing the written word, they grapple with differentiation between pieces of writing. They want their letter strings to have interpretations other than their own intentions. Furthermore, they want those graphic differences within a string to support different intentions for the readers. These decisions must be worked out before the children address the relationship between the sound pattern of the word and the written representations of the word.

The third level is the "phonetization" of the written representation (Vernon & Ferreiro, 1999). Within this level, children create hypotheses about different principles of written language. Once they understand the last principle, alphabetic hypothesis (using letters of the alphabet to make words), they understand the "intrinsic nature of the alphabetic system" (Ferreiro, 1990, p. 22). The next problem that they must address is the orthographic features of the language, such as punctuation marks, uppercase and lowercase letters, and blank spaces.

Children who have experienced a print-rich preschool and kindergarten environment have moved through the three levels that Ferreiro describes. In fact, many experiment with using punctuation marks, making capital and lowercase letters, and writing meaningful stories and poems. During the early primary school years, children continue to work on writing construction and interpretation. Production, fluency, and communication become major goals for them. They read their own writings, question whether others can read their writing, and develop strategies to make their written messages readable by others. They also experiment with the text composition (a letter, poem, story) and features of those compositions as they convey the intended meaning. Children use social interaction and play as they refine their compositions. For example, they may reenact their written stories or join peer editing groups (Taylor, Branscombe, Burcham, & Land, 2011; Britton, 1982; Caulkins, 1994).

In addition to writing, children in the primary grades use theater, music, dance and movement, puppetry, and computerized graphic representations (Norton, 1997; Resnick, 1998, 2012). When children write their plays and then engage in play production, they are building from their preschool use of dramatic play and symbolic play. Dance and movement also build from earlier constructions. As more teachers are using computers in their pre-school and primary school classrooms, computerized graphic representations are becoming a viable form of communication for children. The computer, graphic representations made with the computer, and digital manipulatives are physical manipulatives that children can use to represent their under-standings. For example, with digital manipulatives, children can create their own simulations and new forms of media, such as animated cartoons (Res-nick, 1998, 2012). See Box 3.4 for examples of representational thought in the curriculum.

BOX 3.4 EXAMPLES OF REPRESENTATIONAL THOUGHT IN THE CURRICULUM

Child-made books
Children's art work
Children's structures that they build
Children's designs on the computer
Children's writings
Children's plays and puppet shows
Children's movement, dance, and music
Children's interactions with other children

Representation is necessary for children to understand their worlds. Al-though influenced by outside experiences, representation is an internal pro-cess that develops as part of intellectual development. The child's main purpose for representation is to bring discontinuities of action and events together to make them more continuous. For example, what happened yesterday can be represented and related to what is happening today. When children construct such relationships and reflect on them, they become aware of the relationship between what they know about a subject, what their audience knows as a result of their representation, and what is generally known about that subject.

CONSTRUCTIONS

1. Observation

In teams, observe and photograph or videotape toddlers, preschoolers, kindergarten children, and primary children. Study those photos or video clips and write down examples of their use of representation.

2. Journal Entry

Write a journal entry in which you explore ways you will encourage children to represent what they know.

3. Research

Write a summary and reaction to two articles about the role of representation in children's thinking. Discuss those articles with a classmate. Have the classmate read and write a reaction to your articles.

SUMMARY

- Learning takes place through active knowledge construction in which children act on objects, interact with others, and make sense of their experiences by relating one idea or attribute to another.
- Constructivist theory and research explain how children construct knowledge.
- Constructivist theory and research inform teaching and curriculum planning.
- Jean Piaget was a genetic epistemologist whose theory of constructivism advanced what we know about how children develop cognitively.
- Piaget defined intelligence as the ability to adapt to new situations.
- Adaptation occurs through the functions of assimilation (taking in information) and accommodation (modifying knowledge based on discrepant information), resulting in equilibration (process of cognitive balance).
- Using the process of assimilation and accommodation, children create cognitive structures to help them make sense of how one thing relates to another.
- Piaget formulated four stages of cognitive development: sensorimotor, preoperational, concrete operational, and formal operational.

- Piaget named the mental activity of thinking about how one thing relates to another as constructive abstraction.
- Empirical abstraction, that is, getting knowledge through observation of an object's attributes, is different from constructive abstraction because it does not require the active construction of relationships.
- Representational thought is the use of signs and symbols to stand for ideas.
- Children use representational thought in mental imagery, deferred imitation, symbolic play, drawing, language, and movement.
- Piaget described the three types of knowledge: physical, logico-mathematical, and social.
- Physical knowledge is the knowledge of objects in external reality constructed through interacting with objects.
- Logico-mathematical knowledge is the knowledge of how one thing or event relates to another.
- Social knowledge is conventional or arbitrary knowledge, such as names and dates for important events, that comes from other people.
- All three types of knowledge are interrelated and constructed through a logico-mathematical framework.
- Children's actions, both physical and mental, are critical for the development of intelligence, as are interactions with others.
- Constructivism is an important theory for appreciating children's understanding.

Resources

Books

Piaget, J. (1962). *Play, dreams and imitation in childhood.* New York, NY: Norton.

Piaget, J. (1965). *The child's conception of number.* New York, NY: Norton. (Original work published 1941)

Piaget, J. (1941/1965). *The child's conception of time.* (A. J. Pomerans, Trans.). New York, NY: Ballantine. (Original work published 1946)

Piaget, J. (1976). *The grasp, of consciousness: Action and concept in the young child.* (S. Wedgewood, Trans.). Cambridge, MA: Harvard University Press. (Original work published 1974)

Piaget, J., & Inhelder, B. (1967). *The child's conception of space.* (F. J. Langdon & J. L. Lunzer, Trans.). New York, NY: Norton. (Original work published 1948)

Piaget, J., & Inhelder, B. (1969). *The early growth of logic in the child.* (E. A. Lunzer & D. Papert, Trans.). New York, NY: Norton. (Original work published 1964)

All six books are essential to understanding Piaget's work. Each book addresses an area of a child's thinking. The books contain the research findings from Piaget's work.

Web Sites

Jean Piaget Society http://www.piaget.org/index.html

This Web site is an overview of the Jean Piaget Society and its work. The Web site contains a students' page, recent publications, conference information, and news. It's an excellent resource.

PART 2

WHAT ARE KEY COMPONENTS OF CONSTRUCTIVIST CURRICULUM?

Constructivist curriculum is created when teachers base their curriculum decisions on constructivist principles about how young children learn. The four chapters in Part 2 of this book offer perspectives on key components of a constructivist curriculum. Chapter 4 presents a perspective on authentic tasks, choice, and decision making, and explains how their inclusion in the curriculum is of importance for children, families, and teaching. Chapter 5 presents a perspective on social interaction, play, and project work. Chapter 6, on problem posing, problem solving, and the role of reflection, explains how these elements help children, families, and teachers become life-long learners. Chapter 7 presents a perspective on community, distinguishing this constructivist perspective from others. All four chapters challenge you to think about how constructivist aims and explanations about how young children learn influence your curriculum decisions. In addition, Part 2 provides insight into how early childhood professionals include children and families as partners in curriculum decision making.

4

AUTHENTIC TASKS, CHOICE, AND DECISION MAKING

Chapter 4 is designed to help you construct a deeper understanding of three of nine key components of constructivist curriculum. It expands the information presented in Part 1 by helping you better understand the role of authentic tasks, choice, and decision making in the construction of knowledge. This chapter provides a rationale for the value of an active classroom that fosters children's interest, experimentation, and cooperation with teachers and peers. In addition, this chapter shows how authentic tasks, choice, and decision making can promote reasoning and autonomy, as well as help you meet the content-area standards and the developmental levels for which you are preparing to teach. After reading this chapter, you should have a deeper understanding of

- why authentic tasks, choice, and decision making are necessary to learning;
- what kinds of tasks, choices, and decision-making problems are appropriate for young children, their families, and their teachers;
- how authentic tasks, choice, and decision making can be integrated into any required curriculum; and
- how the diverse needs of all can be met through the use of authentic tasks, choice, and decision making.

Introduction

The six teachers Kenisha invited to her school in September to form a study and support group are meeting in the church that houses Sheila's Head Start class. They have recognized that they differ significantly in their understanding of constructivist principles, as well as in their appreciation of the need for that understanding. However, they have agreed to continue to meet to discuss their questions about how these constructivist assumptions can work in real classrooms. They are interested in sharing points of view about how they can become better constructivist teachers and still meet all of the requirements put forth by their administrators, state standards, national content-area standards, and licensing and accreditation requirements.

Sheila: I'm so glad you all agreed to come visit my school. As you can see, it's not very fancy, but I'm really happy here.

Kenisha: I can see that you love your work with the kids as much as I do, and I can tell that you're as concerned as I am about how we can get others to understand that what we do is important.

Sheila: Thanks, Kenisha, that's a great compliment coming from you.

Parul: This place is very relaxed and quiet, Sheila, and I thank you for inviting us here. Maybe we'll be able to talk some more about those constructivist assumptions we learned about earlier and try to figure out how we can use them in all our different settings.

Jennifer: I already know the one that applies to my setting! I agree that kids learn from other people in their culture and society, and I know that I'm the one who's responsible for what my kids learn. The assumption I've got some trouble with is related to making choices. I just don't see how giving kids a choice is going to help them learn.

Ron: I know what you mean, Jennifer, because I'm having trouble involving children in decision making when no one else in my school is doing it. I think I know why I should do it, but I just can't figure out how to do it.

Matt: Well, the assumption that I want to discuss is the one related to the use of authentic tasks. I think that the things I'm doing are authentic, but how can I be sure?

Kenisha: Well, let's get started and see if we can relate our concerns about these ideas to what we've just learned about the three kinds of knowledge.

The Role of Theory

Piaget (1970) was an advocate of what he referred to as **active methods** for educating children. He held that children develop the ability to think more readily when teaching methods allow them to be physically active, involved in manipulating objects, and experimenting with things. He held that children also learn through interacting with others and by being mentally involved through reflecting on the results of their actions. Central to his active methods is his reference to authentic work on the part of the learner. Piaget (1970) states,

> When the active school requires that the student's effort should come from the student himself instead of being imposed, and that his intelligence should undertake authentic work instead of accepting pre-digested

knowledge from outside, it is therefore simply asking that the laws of all intelligence should be respected (p. 159).

However, he also held that "the most authentic research activity may take place in the spheres of reflection, of the most advanced abstraction and of verbal manipulations (provided they are spontaneous and not imposed on the child at the risk of remaining partially uncomprehended)" (Piaget, 1995, p. 712). In other words, the mental activity involved in the learning task is itself an authentic task.

According to Piaget (1995), the active methods he proposed are much more difficult to practice than are the more traditional approaches of lectures, drills, and demonstrations. He suggested that these methods "require a much more varied and much more concentrated kind of work from the teacher" (p. 712). For a variety of reasons, traditional educators do not seem to appreciate or value the active approach. Active approaches allow children more freedom to move about the room and to talk with one another. Often, this creates a problem for traditional educators, who believe that classrooms must be quiet in order for children to learn. Another concern that traditional educators have expressed is that active methods are not sufficiently structured. Consequently, these traditional educators believe that teachers cannot be sure that all of the children are mastering the content sufficiently. Finally, traditional educators hold that active approaches take too much time, and they are not willing to provide the time sufficient for including these approaches. They reason that they have too much to accomplish with all of the objectives and content they are required to teach.

Authentic Tasks

The teachers are discussing the use of authentic tasks.

Ron: I'm really glad to be here today. I needed to talk to someone. Remember the constructivist assumptions that we talked about last time we met? Well, I know that they're necessary to my curriculum, but I just can't seem to get a handle on how to use authentic tasks in this first-grade class, especially when most of the teachers at my school think that I need to be teaching decoding skills and subtraction. Can anyone help me?

Sheila: I don't know if I can help, but I do know what you mean. I'm always hearing criticisms about how I haven't prepared my kids for kindergarten, but I question how meaningful it is to these kids to learn to

	say the letter names. They're far more interested in talking about the animals that they've seen on those long bus rides they have to take every day.
Kenisha:	And I'll bet that they know a lot about those animals too! Too bad that kind of knowledge isn't considered necessary to be "ready to learn," but I don't think they get tested on that.
Matt:	Yes, Kenisha, I agree that the children's knowledge about animals is important, but the more interesting question to me is how we can get children involved in authentic tasks related to school content areas like reading and math. So is that our challenge for today?
Ron:	Yes, I would love to explore ways that could make learning to read and doing math more interesting for the kids. And I would love to be able to show how this approach is more successful than what the others in my school are doing.
Sheila:	Be careful here, Ron. What we really want to explore is how kids can be motivated to want to learn to read, write, and do math. I wonder if that is possible.
Jennifer:	Of course, it is possible! My kids get so many points for every book they read and for every problem they get right on their worksheets. When they have free time, they can use these points to shop at the school store. Most of the kids work really hard for these points so they can get something that they wouldn't be able to have otherwise. That seems pretty authentic to me!
Matt:	Yes, I can see where you think it is authentic, Jennifer, but do you ever wonder if they would continue to read and compute if there was no reward for doing it? Doesn't your approach motivate them to get the reward rather than to want to read and do math?
Jennifer:	Well, I don't know. I guess I've never thought about it that way.
Matt:	Parul, we haven't heard from you. What do you think about our question for today?
Parul:	Well, I have to confess that how we can get children involved in authentic tasks is not of particular interest to me as an infant teacher. However, I'm fascinated thinking about what these youngsters might consider an authentic task. And I'd love to explore how I could use authentic tasks to foster an infant's ability to learn to walk.

Authentic tasks are those that the learner considers necessary, significant, or engaging. They are tasks that learners engage in either because they are intrigued by a topic or by an action on an object and its result, or because they have some kind of adaptive value for the learner—in other words, they satisfy a genuine need to know. Authentic tasks provide the motivation for learning or create the need to know in the learner, as you will see in the following example taken from a kindergarten classroom.

Why We Need to Learn to Write: A Scenario From Barbara Thompson's
Kindergarten Classroom

A small group of children had played in the block center for the entire center time, making a structure that they wanted to use the next day for dramatic play. Ordinarily, the children were expected to take down whatever they had built during cleanup time. However, today this group of children wanted to leave the structure assembled; they were not yet through with it, and they still had not had the opportunity to play in it. As a group, they decided to approach Mrs. Thompson regarding this idea.

John: Mrs. Thompson, we haven't finished yet, and we want to leave our blocks like they are until tomorrow.
Lee: Yeah, cuz we haven't even had a chance to play in it.
Latisha: And we worked really hard making it.

Mrs. Thompson took the idea to the class for a discussion, and the class decided that it would be fair for the structure to remain in place for the next day. John, Lee, and Latisha went home happy.

The next morning the children rushed to their classroom only to find that their block structure had been taken down and all of the blocks had been returned to the shelves. They were quite upset and wanted to find out why this had happened, so they went to Mrs. Thompson to see if she knew. Mrs. Thompson told them that she didn't know what had happened; their block structure was still standing when she went home. However, she promised the children that she would try to find out what had happened. In the meantime, Lee, John, and Latisha began their building all over again. When center time was finished, Mrs. Thompson called the group together.

Mrs. Thompson: I found out what happened to your building.
Latisha: What?
Lee: Yeah, what?
Mrs. Thompson: The custodian put the blocks away because he had to sweep the carpet, and he didn't know that you wanted it saved.
John: Well, let's go tell him that we want it saved today.
Mrs. Thompson: But he isn't here now. He doesn't come to work until long after we have gone home.
Lee: Then how are we going to let him know that we don't want him to take it down?

John:	I know! We could write a sign to put on it.
Mrs. Thompson:	That might work, John. What would your sign say?
Latisha:	I know what it should say: "No touch!"
John:	Yeah, I like that!
Lee:	Let's get busy.

Together, the children found a large piece of paper and figured out how to write the sign. It read "NO TCH" (translated No Touch) and was placed on the block structure that day. The next day when they returned to their classroom, the structure was still standing.

Writing the "No Touch" sign was an authentic task for this group of children because it let them communicate with someone who was not in the same place at the same time as they were. After this incident, Mrs. Thompson reported a flourish of "No Touch" signs by classmates who wanted something of theirs left undisturbed.

Why Authentic Tasks Are Essential for Children, Teachers, and Families

In the *Science of Education and the Psychology of the Child,* Piaget (1970) states that education consists of helping learners adapt to their physical and social environments. This process of adaptation refers to the means by which the learner adjusts to the physical and social world. According to Wadsworth (1978), learning to talk is an example of an adaptation that infants make, in that using speech makes it easier for them to communicate to others. These adaptations occur spontaneously as children make sense out of incoming information by either incorporating this information into what they *already* know (assimilation) or modifying what they already know to account for the new information (accommodation). These two processes are complementary and together achieve the balance necessary for successful adaptation.

Gruber and Voneche (1995) suggest that play and imitation are two avenues for cognitive growth that educators should use. They note that play is primarily assimilation; it is an activity in which "established schemes are exercised rather than changed" (p. 694). They assert that this is why play is fun. Imitation, on the other hand, is primarily accommodation; it is the process by which children change what they already know to adjust to the new information. DeVries (1987) cautions that play and imitation should be thought of not as opposites but rather as complementary processes by which children transform earlier symbolic play schemes into deeper and more accurate reflections of reality. She states, "For Piaget, the capacity to work is not something opposed to play and imposed on the child by adult instruction, but is something that develops out of the play interest" (p. 28).

While you will learn more about the role of play in Chapter 5, it is important in this chapter to understand the complementary role of imitation and how it helps the learner perceive a task as authentic. For example, most youngsters in our society imitate driving a car. The very young child might use a block and vocalizations that imitate the sound of a motor to symbolize driving a car, a 4-year-old might sit on someone's lap and pretend to drive by turning the steering wheel, and a teenager may practice going back and forth in the driveway in preparation for a driving test. All are ways of adapting to the learner's social world through play and imitation since most young Americans perceive being able to drive a car to be an authentic task.

Authentic Tasks Foster the Motivation for Learning

Authentic tasks are essential for children, teachers, and families because they build on the learner's need to know and provide the motivation for learning. When teachers use authentic tasks to approach content that might be thought of as mundane or boring, they find that the children value and become excited about what they are doing, and their parents appreciate and marvel at what the child is learning. An e-mail from a first-year teacher in New Jersey who was bravely using authentic tasks documents this idea.

Multiple Perspectives: From the Classroom

Anna Hall, a second-grade teacher who spent her first year in a suburban district in New Jersey, shared the following.

Good old parent conferences. Over the past two days I have met with the parents of all of my students except one. While preparing for these conferences, I felt apprehensive and worried that the parents would not be satisfied with the evidence of learning that I was providing with my small assessment folders. I was pleasantly surprised and energized to find out how supportive and excited all of the parents were about the classroom environment that I have created. When you take off down a long and unknown road, it is easy to keep your focus on the fog in the distance instead of noticing how far you've come. I think the feedback from these parents has allowed me to sit back for a minute and realize that even though this is my first year and I am constantly learning better ways of doing things, I am still a good teacher and a good person. The compliments about the little things remind me that I take much of my enthusiasm and energy for my job for granted. For example, so many parents commented on how meaningful spelling words have become to their child this year because I take them out of their child's own writing and ask them if there are other words they would like to learn. I also was comforted when a number of parents mentioned that their children now write at home for fun and love sharing their writing with their family. One child who was never interested in reading has recently asked to spend his birthday money at the local bookstore. All of these comments have flooded me with joy, and for the first time, I actually miss those little kids.

It is clear from the example that, for this teacher, an authentic task is to be a good teacher. The comments she received from the parents of her students supported her decisions about how to approach the content areas related to literacy. An authentic task for the parents was to oversee their children's education. This example documents the parents' satisfaction with the progress their children were making and with the fact that their children were now not only reading and writing but also valuing those processes. This example verifies that the use of authentic tasks in literacy learning provides the intrinsic motivation for children. Consequently, this example demonstrates how teachers, parents, and children are motivated through the use of authentic tasks.

Motivation is a complex subject. It includes the motives one has to pursue a particular learning task or endeavor or to take a particular action. Earlier, you heard one of the teachers in the study group tell about how she used a point system to motivate children to read and write. This teacher was using a form of extrinsic motivation, a positive reinforcement. Constructivist teachers prefer building on more intrinsic forms of motivation such as curiosity and interest. Table 4.1 describes the major kinds of motivation.

According to DeVries (1987), Piaget's active methods assume the child's spontaneous interest in the topic at hand or a motivation based on a genuine need to know about the topic. Constructivist educators recognize that the use of authentic tasks takes advantage of children's spontaneous interest so as to foster the kind of physical and mental activity necessary for intellectual growth and development.

Constructivist teachers recognize that when children are engaged in authentic tasks in which they are spontaneously interested, they will construct the knowledge necessary to meet the teacher's objectives. Additionally, they understand how these tasks will help the children better think about complex problems and become wiser decision makers. They also appreciate a busy classroom and quickly learn to differentiate between chaos and constructive activity. The biggest difficulty constructivist teachers face is to determine how to appeal to the child's spontaneous interest with authentic tasks that will result in

Table 4.1 **Kinds of Motivation**

Kinds	Sources	Examples
Extrinsic	External to the learner	Praise, rewards, grades
Intrinsic	Internal to the learner	Intention, purpose, need
Interest	Internal to the learner	Curiosity, adaptive value, fascination

Table 4.2 **Authentic Purposes for Content-Area Learning**

Oral language	We tell stories to entertain, inform, and share.
Listening	We listen to enjoy, to receive information, and to share.
Reading	We read for information and enjoyment.
Writing	We write to remember and communicate.
Counting	We count to determine how many.
Measurement	We measure to find out how long, high, tall, or wide something is.
Operations	We add, subtract, multiply, and divide to solve problems.
Geometry	We use spatial boundaries to determine what we have, where we can go, what we can do, and how we can make things fit.
Science	We use objects and actions to test out ideas.
	We use reflection to raise questions about things we don't understand.

the child's ability to learn what the schools expect children to learn. Thinking about the **authentic purposes** for each of the content-area topics that they are expected to teach can provide teachers with a way to begin thinking about how to appeal to the child's spontaneous interest. Authentic purposes build on the usefulness of the learning from the child's perspective and provide the intrinsic motivation to learn the content. Authentic purposes for many of the content areas taught in early childhood are presented in Table 4.2.

Authentic Tasks Foster Intellectual Development

Authentic tasks are essential for children, teachers, and families because they build on the learner's need to know and foster their intellectual development. According to Labinowicz (1980), Piaget identified four factors that in combination account for the intellectual development of children: maturation, experience, social interaction, and equilibration. Teachers must understand how all four of these factors support the use of authentic tasks to foster children's learning in the subject matter teachers are required to teach.

Maturation refers to the fact that as children grow older, their mental structures become more highly organized and operational. This development is natural and seems to be related to the maturation of the nervous system, which is not complete until around the fifteenth or sixteenth year (Piaget, 1970). While this maturation is a necessary condition for intellectual development and allows for more advanced ways of conceptualizing experience, it is not solely sufficient for intellectual development.

Experience in the same content area over time provides children multiple opportunities to think about that content in different ways. As you read in Chapter 3, both physical and logico-mathematical knowledge are constructed as children act on objects in experimental ways and as they think about the results of those actions. In other words, the construction of these types of knowledge requires active physical and mental experience. Consequently, children must have many opportunities to actively explore their physical and social worlds in order to develop intellectually. Authentic tasks in which children are actively involved allow the physical and logico-mathematical experiences necessary for intellectual development.

Social interaction, presented more fully in Chapter 5, is an important factor in the intellectual development of the child. According to Piaget (1970), "the social development of the child proceeds from egocentrism toward reciprocity, [and] from assimilation into a self still not conscious of itself to mutual comprehension leading to the constitution of personality" (p. 175). Authentic tasks provide significant opportunities for children to interact socially with groups of children, teachers, and parents to exchange points of view and to develop intellectually.

Equilibration, the most important of the four factors (Labinowicz, 1980), refers to the process of interaction between the child's mind and his or her physical reality—the process of adaptation discussed earlier. According to Labinowicz (1980), equilibration is the factor that coordinates the three other factors. It is the active process by which the children act on objects, are puzzled when the outcomes of their actions do not conform to what they anticipated, continue to experiment using different actions and objects, and refine their original thinking to accommodate to the new information learned through their own actions. Engaging in authentic tasks allows many opportunities for the child to experiment, to be puzzled, to transform his reasoning, and to be "the mainspring of his own development" (p. 46).

Authentic Tasks Allow for the Construction of All Three Kinds of Knowledge

Authentic tasks are essential for children, teachers, and families because they build on the learner's need to know and allow for the construction and use of all three kinds of knowledge. Think about what you might consider an authentic task for yourself. Perhaps you have invited friends over for dinner, and you have to go to the grocery store to buy the food for that dinner. From this perspective, going to the grocery store would be considered an authentic task necessary to your goal of preparing dinner for your friends. In doing this shopping, you would have to think about the food preferences of your friends (social knowledge), the kinds of foods that you can afford (logico-mathematical knowledge), and the foods that are healthy for you to eat (physical knowledge). Most authentic tasks are naturally integrated, so they hold the potential for the construction of all three kinds of knowledge. The following is an example.

Becoming a Rattlesnake: Young Children at Play

During a theme on camping, Kayla and Austin were playing in a small tent in their classroom. Four-year-old Austin and 5-year-old Kayla were pretending that they were out in the woods camping in the tent. As their play progressed, Kayla decided that she wanted them to become rattlesnakes that would make noise outside the tent and scare the campers. Becoming a rattlesnake became an authentic task for Kayla and Austin. First, they went on the Internet and found a picture of a rattlesnake. As they studied the picture, they planned how they would make the rattles and how they would use them. Next, they went to the drinking fountain and got two small paper cups. They filled one of the cups with sand from the sand table and taped the other cup on the top of the first cup. Using masking tape, they sealed the edges of the cups so the sand could not escape. Next, they taped string to the small cups and tied them to their ankles. Then they played rattlesnakes by crawling on their stomachs and shaking their rattles to scare the campers. They crawled all around the tent in which they had previously been the campers.

Making themselves into rattlesnakes was an authentic task for Kayla and Austin. It arose out of their curiosity about rattlesnakes, which arose from the camping theme. In the process of carrying out the symbolic play, the children constructed a relationship between the sound of the sand in the cup and the sound of the snake's rattles. They played out the relationship between campers and snakes, represented snakes through their handmade rattles and their body movements, and learned the name of one particular kind of snake. This example documents how engagement in authentic tasks allows for the construction of all three kinds of knowledge.

The Kinds of Authentic Tasks That Should Be Considered

Using authentic tasks to engage the spontaneous interest of children requires planning. Teachers and parents have to recognize that it is not always possible to predict which tasks will appeal to their children. According to Piaget (1970), teachers should analyze all curriculum decisions to ensure that they have given consideration to "the significance of childhood, the structure of the child's thought, the laws of development, and the mechanism of infantile social life" (p. 151). Authentic experiences in all content areas should be developed around the teacher's knowledge of children and the subject matter to be taught. For example, authentic art experiences should take into consideration "a teacher's knowledge of patterns of artistic and aesthetic development, consideration of the intentions of children as they make art, and the recognition of significant content in the subject of art and art's relationship to other disciplines" (Taunton & Colbert, 2000, p. 68). After giving consideration to their children's learning needs and the subject matter to be learned, teachers and parents can begin to brainstorm a number of authentic tasks, which can be classified into three rather distinct categories.

Exploratory Tasks

The catalyst for exploratory tasks is the child's curiosity. Children explore all the physical characteristics of objects and many of the possibilities of their actions on objects. Authentic tasks in this category invite children to explore objects and events in their physical and social realities. Exploratory tasks offer children opportunities to test out their hypotheses about their actions on these materials. Exploration may be as simple as exploring a new object, like the yellow and black foam ball described at the beginning of the physical knowledge section of Chapter 3. This scenario offers a good picture of a simple exploratory task. What Peter learns from this kind of exploration is knowledge about the texture, movability, and holdability of the ball. He will construct this knowledge through his actions on the ball and his awareness of the result of his actions on the ball.

A more complex type of exploratory task could be conducted by a small group of children who face a complex problem. For example, in one second-grade classroom, a small group of children were curious about what kind of things would and would not dissolve in water. They tried a variety of different materials and watched them over time, recording their findings. They found that soft, pillow-like mints dissolved in less time than hard peppermint candies of the same size and that sand would never dissolve. The children worked on this task for many days and grouped the materials they used into those that would never dissolve, those that dissolved slowly, and those that dissolved almost immediately. Then they began to hypothesize about how all the materials in each group were alike.

When planning for exploratory tasks, teachers must appeal to the children's curiosity, their ability to touch and manipulate things in their environment, and their ability to test out their ideas in resourceful ways. Teachers should consider how to build on children's interest when they introduce materials in the classroom. For example, some materials work well at the beginning of the year, and others should be introduced throughout the year so that children can continue to be curious about new things. Additionally, teachers should consider ways to help children think about new ways to explore familiar objects in the classroom.

Problem-Solving Tasks

The catalyst for problem-solving tasks is the children's state of **disequilibrium,** or recognition that a problem exists. Children solve problems in order to resolve their puzzlement and reach a higher level of equilibration. You will learn much more about the problem-solving process in Chapter 6, but for now, you need to understand how these kinds of tasks differ from exploratory and purposeful tasks. Disequilibrium exists in the mind of a child when she becomes aware of a contradiction in her thinking and recognizes the problem. According to

Labinowicz (1980), "learning begins with the recognition of a problem (disequilibrium)" (p. 53). Once they recognize a problem, children go through a problem-solving process that sometimes produces unpredictable behaviors, errors in thinking, or vacillation, until they reach a higher level of equilibration. One simple example of problem solving is a vote held in a classroom of young children. For example, in a class of 21, 18 voted yes. One child then said, "We don't have to see how many 'no' votes there are, because the 'yes' votes have won!" This put one of the "no" voters in disequilibrium because her vote was not counted. She said, "That isn't fair because I didn't get to vote." This child's problem relates to fairness; she thinks that every vote should be counted. This is a problem from her point of view. She will be able to work through the problem with peers and the teacher as she counts the "no" votes to solve her dilemma of fairness. Through repeated interaction of this kind of problem solving, the child will construct the understanding of why it is not necessary to count the "no" votes.

Forman (1996) presents a more complex type of problem-solving task in a video titled *Jed Draws His Bicycle: A Case of Drawing-to-Learn*. By having a child draw a picture of his bicycle to show how it works, Forman sets up a task that creates a state of disequilibrium in Jed's mind as he becomes aware that his thinking about how the parts work is not clear. He goes through a process of looking at the bicycle, altering the errors in his drawing, returning to the bicycle, and again changing his drawing. Through careful observation and correction of earlier errors in his drawing, Jed learns to think more specifically about how the bicycle works and how to represent that in his drawing.

When planning for problem-solving tasks, teachers must set up situations that have the potential to create disequilibrium in children's thinking. Also, they "should select materials that make the child become conscious of a problem and look for the solution himself. And, if he generalizes too broadly, then provide additional materials where counter examples will guide him to see where he must refine his solution" (Piaget & Duckworth, 1973, p. 23). For example, when working with objects that sink and float at the water table, a child might generalize that big things sink and little things float. The teacher might then present objects that are small yet sink and objects that are big that float. Another example would be to ask the child how to make an object that sinks float.

Purposeful Tasks

The catalyst for purposeful tasks is the child's need to know, which is often related to a need to accomplish some intrinsically motivated goal. According to Piaget and Garcia (1974), a task is purposeful when children have their reactions to material problems reinforced by "the necessity of finding a solution to them" (p. 27). Purposeful tasks satisfy some internally constructed aim or goal. An example of a purposeful task, described earlier in this chapter, is the child's need to learn how to drive a car; it is purposeful because the child needs to know how to do this to become an adult. In the same manner, learning to read becomes a purposeful task to the child when she sees that reading is an important thing adults in her society do or that learning to read will lead to the intrinsic pleasure of enjoying a good book or gaining information. Children are motivated to learn what they see adults doing as a "genuine part of living" within their culture group (Holdaway 1986, p. 58). Through observation, participation, and practice of the purposeful task, the learner reaches the point where she no longer needs assistance and announces, "I can do it by myself" (Taylor, 1991, p. 10).

When planning for purposeful tasks, the teacher has to "change the adult-child interactions so that they become children-classroom-adult interactions" (Taylor, 1991, p. 11). Teachers need to plan projects that allow children many opportunities to talk together, question together, and complete purposeful tasks together. The teacher's role shifts from being a dispenser of knowledge to that of an adult learner who asks questions with the children about the tasks or projects that should be undertaken. In this role, the teacher is able to use the children's information and questions as the basis for the curriculum. One of the most important teacher roles is to determine what the children deem to be purposeful tasks and to build the curriculum around those tasks.

How We Use Authentic Tasks in the Integrated Curriculum at School and at Home

As you learned in Chapter 1, there are many ways to define curriculum. However, the way teachers organize the content to be taught and the teaching methods they choose help determine whether the curriculum is constructivist. It is possible to offer opportunities for children to engage in authentic tasks in a separate-subjects curriculum, but an integrated curriculum offers better possibilities for children to engage in meaningful authentic tasks. The National Association for the Education of Young Children suggests that an integrated curriculum is more appropriate for young children (see Box 4.1).

BOX 4.1 INTEGRATED CURRICULUM

For 3- through 5-year-olds: Curriculum content from various disciplines, such as math, science, and social studies, is integrated through themes, projects, play, and other learning experiences, so children develop an understanding of concepts and make connections across disciplines.

For 6- through 8-year-olds: The curriculum is organized and integrated so that children acquire a deeper understanding of key concepts, skills, and tools of inquiry of each subject area, are able to apply their knowledge in different areas, and also understand the connections between and across disciplines.

Source: S. Bredekamp & C. Copple (1997). *Developmentally appropriate practice in early childhood programs* (rev. ed.). Washington, DC: National Association for the Education of Young Children. Reprinted with permission from the National Association for the Education of Young Children.

The following three scenarios illustrate the use of authentic tasks in three different contexts.

Authentic Tasks to Foster Letter Writing in the Second-Grade Classroom

In a multiage first- and second-grade classroom, the children were working through a number of projects related to their theme on the African savanna. The animals of the savanna fascinated many of the children, and they were making three-dimensional life-sized replicas of many of these animals. One 8-year-old named Eddie became interested in the African elephant. This elephant's large, fan-shaped ears first attracted Eddie, but as he began learning more about the beast, he became more intrigued by the fact that the elephant carried a significant amount of weight on his four small feet. During a teacher conference, Eddie asked how much weight the elephant carried on each foot and how that would compare with the amount of weight he carried on each of his two feet.

Working together, the children devised a task for Eddie. Using paper divided into 1-inch squares, Eddie would be able to estimate how many square inches there were in each of his feet as compared to each of the elephant's feet. Then, using the weight of the elephant and his own weight, he could compare how much weight each carried on 1 square inch of their feet. Eddie agreed that this was a good plan and started. He traced around both of his feet on the squared paper and went to the scales in the nurse's room to determine his weight. However, he was not sure how he could find out how many square inches there were in each of the elephant's feet or what the average elephant weighed. He talked about his dilemma with his classmates, and one of them knew of a zoo in a nearby city where Eddie might be able to get his information.

At that point, Eddie had a brilliant idea: He asked the teacher if he would help him learn to write a letter. He wanted to ask the people at the zoo to tell him what the elephant weighed and to trace all four of the elephant's feet on the four sheets of squared paper he was sending along with his letter.

Learning to write the letter became an authentic task to help Eddie get the information he needed about the elephant so that he could complete his project. From the teacher's perspective, this was the time to teach Eddie how to write a letter, a language arts standard for second grade. The letter was sent, the zoo responded, and Eddie learned how to write a letter. More important, he completed the task and learned that the elephant carried much more weight per square inch than he did, and he loved sharing that fact.

Authentic Tasks Foster a Deeper Understanding of Propulsion in a Kindergarten Classroom

In a kindergarten classroom, the children were engaged in a number of projects related to Australian animals. As they were gathering information about some of these animals, they learned that the red kangaroo can jump as far as 29 feet in distance. Because the children couldn't estimate how far that was, the teacher took them outside, put down a piece of masking tape, had the children use their foot rulers to count out 29 feet, and put down another piece of masking tape.

The youngsters were amazed that anything could jump that far and began to ask questions such as "I wonder how far I can jump?" and "Can I jump that far?" In order to answer their questions, they made a plan to have everyone take a turn starting at the first piece of tape and jump as far as they could. Then, others would put down a piece of tape where each child landed and write the name of the jumper on the tape. When that activity was complete, the children wanted to talk about who had the longest and shortest jumps, so they got some paper and graphed their jumps from shortest to longest. Then, Joni wondered how many of her jumps it would take to jump as far as the red kangaroo could. With this question in mind, the children cut pieces of string as long as their jumps and replicated them until they reached the 29-foot mark. They counted and graphed the number of replications it took to jump as far as the red kangaroo. They agreed to count the replication that crossed the tape as their last jump and didn't worry how far the string stuck over the 29-foot mark.

When they graphed the number of replications, they were surprised to find that the people whose jumps were longer on the first graph had lower numbers on the replications graph, and they couldn't figure out why that was so. It took a lot of discussion before some of them began to understand.

Then another thing happened that really surprised the teacher. Danny found some information that suggested that the red kangaroo uses its tail to help it jump so far. The children wanted to figure out if there was something they could do to make their jumps longer. One group looked at some of the pictures of Olympic jumpers and decided to try a jump with a running start and compare it to their other jumps. Another group looked at how the tail was used to push or propel the kangaroo forward. This group set up an apparatus with a flexible board, a fulcrum, and a cabinet to hold one side of the board down. Then they tested their jumps using the board in a manner similar to a diving board. Both groups found that propulsion jumps were greater in distance than were jumps from the starting line.

Authentic Tasks Foster Balance in the Infant and Toddler Classroom

A teacher at an infant center was interested in exploring how she could use authentic tasks to foster infants' ability to learn to stand, balance on their feet, and begin to walk. She found that it was fun and challenging! She tried to place some favorite toys in spots where they were visible to the infants but not reachable without standing up, reaching out, or climbing up the steps. It was amazing to see what happened. Those babies worked long and hard to get the toys. One boy used the railing to stand up and get his balance, then let go of the railing to reach up and grab the teddy bear, lose his balance, and sit down again. Then he would start all over. A small girl picked up one of the cloth balls, crawled a little bit, dropped that ball, and crawled to the next one. She used the clear plastic steps to try to stand and reach it. Then she threw that ball down and tried for the next. The teacher thought that it was really interesting to observe how the infants' interest in the toys motivated them to move, and

---

CONSTRUCTIONS

1. Research

Observe in classrooms of children at different ages to see if you can find children who are or are not engaged in some kind of sustained activity that seems to be self-motivated. Take field notes on the kind of behaviors you observe that seem to suggest whether the activity is authentic from the children's point of view. If possible, talk with the children to see if you can determine what motivated their activity.

2. Analysis

Compare and contrast the behaviors of the children related to their goals.

through this process, how they refined their abilities to stand, balance, and walk. She learned a lot about how to use authentic tasks to foster the development of motor skills.

Choice

The teachers have now come together to talk about why choice is considered a key component of a constructivist curriculum.

Jennifer: I can now see the usefulness of authentic tasks because they help kids meet the state and national standards, but I'm afraid that choice is a different matter. I think kids have to learn that they don't always have a choice in things and that they have to do some things whether they like it or not.

Matt: I understand how you feel, Jennifer. Remember that Piaget said that it was the teacher's job to figure out how to use the information he offered. So maybe during this session, we can talk about the role of choice in the classroom, and then you can think about whether you can use it.

Kenisha: You know that choice is an emotional topic in our society, and we may disagree about the role of choice in general. I mean, look at the heated debates about antiabortion and the right to choose, the right to choose about prayer in school, and even the right to choose your children's school.

Ron: Wow, Kenisha, I hadn't even thought about choice in that way. I was thinking more about letting the kids choose which color to make their flowers.

Sheila: I'm like you, Ron. I really didn't think about children having to make serious choices like adults do. I was thinking about the same kinds of choices you were, like choosing the story for the day or choosing a center to work in.

Parul: Well, even those choices are too complex for infants and toddlers, but I am interested in learning about choice.

Why Choice Is an Essential Component for Children, Teachers, and Families

Two major theories have shaped early childhood educators' views about the role of choice in the classroom. Erik Erikson's theory of psychosocial development suggests that during the early childhood years, children have to resolve three or four conflicts positively. If they resolve these conflicts successfully, then children will develop ego strength through their sense of trust, autonomy, initiative, and industry. If they do not resolve these conflicts successfully, they will develop an ego characterized by a sense of mistrust, self-doubt, guilt, and inferiority (Tribe, 1982). Abraham Maslow's motivational theory suggests that there are two basic kinds of needs: deficit needs and self-actualizing needs. Deficit needs are those that when not met cause illness. They include physiological, safety, and belongingness needs. Self-actualizing needs are those that are motivated by creative impulses. They include self-reliance, esteem, self-fulfillment, and competence (Tribe, 1982). This theory suggests that it is necessary to help children meet all of the deficit needs so that they can become self-actualizing.

Influenced by these theories, most early childhood educators hold that children should have many opportunities to make meaningful choices in the learning process. They maintain that providing choice fosters the child's interest and engagement. Their belief in choice is grounded in the notion that individuals have power over their lives and that by making choices, they become more self-reliant and independent.

These values are not commonly shared by cultures that hold that children should learn from the adults in the culture and not through contrived situations (Gonzalez-Mena, 2001). Parents teach children in ways that are more compatible with their cultural and ethnic values. However, in all cultures, the deficit needs must be met in order for the more self-actualizing needs to appear.

Choice Fosters Thinking About Alternatives

From a constructivist perspective, choice is an individual activity that is essential to cognitive as well as social development. Choice requires the child to think about how the alternatives are similar and different. This kind of mental activity allows for the construction of the logico-mathematical relationships of sameness and difference. These relationships work in concert with other previously constructed relations and have the potential to transform earlier kinds of thinking. Let's say a child is given a choice of which of two shirts to wear to school. He has to think about the alternatives and the criteria he will use to choose. He knows that his red shirt and his blue shirt are both comfortable ("both" being a relationship of sameness and "comfortable" being a necessity), but the red one is dirty (a relationship of difference with "cleanliness" being a necessity). Thus, he chooses the blue one to wear. These kinds of choices increase his ability to choose from a number of possibilities the ones that, by necessity, meet his criteria for selection. This continuous kind of activity holds the potential for later combinatorial reasoning, a formal operational ability.

Choice fosters the child's ability to think about the many possibilities available to choose from and the necessity to limit those possibilities to those that are the most essential to the solution of a problem. For example, Piaget (1987) asked 5-, 6-, and 7-year-olds to arrange two houses and a tree "so people can go and eat the apples" (p. 108). He then looked for their ability to produce multiple combinations by adding three, four, and five houses and asking them to place them in any way possible that all might be able to go and eat the apples. Oli, a 5-year-old boy, constructed 19 combinations with two houses, 13 with three houses, 19 with four houses, and 13 with five and six houses. Piaget explains that when Oli made his first combination, he might not have thought of any other pattern; thus, it might not have been a choice. "If he had not thought of anything else, there would be no choice; but if, before acting, he hesitated between 'above' and 'on both sides etc.' [related to the placement of the tree and the houses], then the action he carried out is the result of a choice, so that the alternative that was not chosen remains a possibility to be materialized in the next construction" (p. 111). From this perspective, "what produces possibilities is the gradual process of becoming conscious that there are choices—in other words, the emergence of the notion of choice in the subject's mind" (p. 111). Thus, choice initiates the child's ability to think about possibilities.

Choice Fosters Wise Decision Making

Because choice is individual, it helps children consider many possibilities related to a particular situation and allows both children and adults to base their decisions on what they hold to be true and just rather than on what someone else tells them to think. Moral autonomy is the ability to make decisions about what is just and fair by yourself, without being influenced by rewards or punishment and after considering all points of view. Intellectual autonomy is the similar ability to make intellectual decisions about what is true by yourself. Consequently, allowing children opportunities to make choices fosters both moral and intellectual autonomy and helps children become capable decision makers.

Another way in which choice fosters wise decision making is when children don't always get their first choice. For example, a child might want to play in the block area, but the block center is full. This problem helps the child learn how to rethink a choice when the first choice is not available. It also allows the teacher to be empathic in responding to help the child think about other areas in the room where space is available and to leave the choice to the child.

Choice Fosters Acceptance of Responsibility

Piaget (1997) suggests that there are two different moralities and that they are in opposition to each other. The **ethic of authority** is the ethic of duty and obedience that leads to the acceptance of **retributive justice,** a sense of justice based on the dispensing or receiving of punishment. This is opposed to the **ethic of mutual respect,** that is, the ethic of goodness and autonomy that leads to the acceptance of **distributive justice,** a sense of justice based on equality and fairness to all involved in the break of the social bond. Those who subscribe to the ethic of authority advocate the use of expiatory punishment—punishment that is arbitrary, vindictive, and not necessarily related to the misdeed for which the child is being punished. An example of an expiatory punishment would be missing recess play time for talking back to the teacher. Those who subscribe to the ethic of mutual respect advocate the use of **reciprocal consequences.** Such consequences are still retributive but are not arbitrary or vindictive, are always related to the misdeed that necessitated them, and are employed because the misdeed breaks the social bond of mutual respect between the transgressor and those who were transgressed against. An example of a reciprocal consequence is rebuilding the block tower if you knock it down. Choice helps children construct a relationship between the choices they make and the consequences that follow as a result of making those choices.

Multiple Perspectives: From the Classroom

Anna Hall taught second-grade and spent her first year in a suburban district in New Jersey. This perspective was one of many e-mails she sent to one of the authors during her first year of teaching.

So many of my children do not know how to handle choices and responsibilities because adults in their lives often make decisions for them. Because of this assumed helplessness, they are unable to make good decisions when faced with life circumstances. Adults think they are doing so much for their children when they do everything for them, but in reality they are hindering their children's ability to think and make choices on their own. Sure it takes more effort on our part to constantly offer choices and consistent consequences for poor choices, but it is in this effort that our children learn values and internalize the importance of trying to make good decisions. I can't wait to get to school tomorrow and ask my children what they think their responsibilities are in my classroom and at home. I will also ask them about five things they would like to have control over that they don't have control over right now. It will be interesting to hear them think. That is my most favorite sound in the world, noisy thinking.

Piaget (1997) discussed six classes of consequences of reciprocity that he ordered from the most to the least severe. These consequences offer teachers a way to deal with misbehaviors in the classroom that is consistent with constructivist tenets.

Exclusion From the Social Group

Children issue exclusion when one child is not willing to behave in ways required by the social group. The child has broken the social bond. For example, a group of children may refuse to play games with a cheater. If he cheats only once, the cheater may be given a second chance. However, if the child continually cheats, the exclusion might become permanent. Another example could be that the children or the teacher excludes a child from working in the block center because she regularly takes the blocks from other children's constructions. The exclusion might be temporary until the child agrees to behave appropriately or permanent if the child is not willing to change her behavior.

Natural Consequences

Natural consequences are those that are immediate and material. Piaget (1997) gives many examples, such as a child having a cold room because he broke the window, a child being put to bed because he pretended to be sick, or a child not being believed because he was not truthful. In the classroom, this could be as simple as the children having to go without having a black marker to use because the cap was left off, and as a result, the marker tip dried and no longer makes a mark. It is reciprocal in that the members of the social group approve of the consequence and do not set things right, such as replacing the broken window, letting the child get out of bed when it is discovered that he is not sick, or replacing the dried-out marker.

Depriving the Transgressor of the Thing Misused

This kind of consequence helps the child come to understand her relationship to the social group. If the child does not take care of community property, others will not be able to use those things. An example of this kind of consequence would be depriving a child of the use of the classroom crayons because she broke the ones she used into little pieces or not allowing a child to take books home because he tore pages out of one of them.

Doing to the Child What He or She Has Done

This kind of consequence is what Piaget refers to as simple reciprocity. For example, other children may refuse to help the child who wouldn't help them, or they tell on the child who told on them. These are simple forms of reciprocity that can help the child understand the result of her actions. However, Piaget suggests that forms of reciprocity can become absurd when they result in the swapping of one bad thing for another. DeVries and Zan (2012) suggest that this consequence is often not suitable for teachers to use with children and that sometimes children use this consequence in punitive ways.

Restitution

This consequence allows for justice in a way that is not punitive by simply making things right again. For example, if a child knocks another child's block structure down, the child could simply take the time to rebuild the structure. At the art center, the child spills a jar of paint on the floor, so she gets the materials and cleans it up. DeVries and Zan (2012) suggest that apologies freely given can be considered restitution.

Censure Only

The purpose of censure is to help the child who has misbehaved understand that he has broken the bond of mutual respect. The censure is not imposed by authority, and is without any other form of punishment. It is based on a breakdown in the relationship, and that breakdown causes the child to feel the pain associated with that breakdown. Examples are when one child will no longer play with another because he hits and kicks or when a teacher responds to a child who has done something wrong by saying, "I am so disappointed in you."

The Kinds of Choices That Should Be Considered

When considering how you might use choice in your classroom, you will want to consider the children's maturation, experience in making choices, and ability to make choices, as well as the kinds of choices that you are comfortable offering.

Limited Choice

Limited choice is a good way to begin with children who have had little choice-making experience. Limited choice refers to the number of alternatives from which the child is to choose. A good rule of thumb is the younger the child, the fewer the number of alternatives. For example, with toddlers, you might offer a choice of a saltine or an animal cracker for snack. With a kindergarten child, you could offer putting the blocks away by himself or inviting a friend to help. Some choices are limited by necessity. Notice that in the example, the child was not given the choice of leaving the blocks on the floor. Nor could we allow the child unlimited choices in what to do and where to do it. Limited choice allows you to provide for those things that you consider necessary to the care and education of the child, while at the same time offering the benefits of choice.

Authentic Choice

In authentic choice, the child understands that the alternatives are equal and that his peers, parents, or teachers will not judge the selection of either one as wrong. For example, suppose a child is told that she will have to either straighten up or leave the room. The child chooses to leave the room, and then the teacher gets angry with the child because she made the wrong choice. This would not be considered an authentic choice because the teacher did not really intend for the child to make the choice she made. According to Piaget, a choice is not a choice unless the child can think of another alternative. In other words, the child needs to have had experience with both alternatives in order for the choice to be authentic. If you asked the child whether he would rather have a peanut butter and jelly or a tuna fish sandwich for lunch, and the child has never had a peanut butter and jelly sandwich, then the choice is not authentic. Only after having tasted both kinds of sandwiches would the child be able to make an authentic choice.

Purposeful Choice

A purposeful choice is a choice that appeals to the child's spontaneous interest in a topic, a real need to know, or a means to accomplish a goal. For example, in a study of Australia, a child might become fascinated with marsupials and choose to do a project related to the red kangaroo. Teachers can use instructional strategies that allow for considerable purposeful choice in what and how the children study the content. The accompanying Curriculum Strategies includes some suggestions for ways to include purposeful choice in your curriculum.

CURRICULUM STRATEGIES:

Using Choice

1. **Organize your classroom as a workshop for children.** Think of your classroom as you do your home. At home, you have a place where you cook, a place where you sleep, and a place where you read. Organize and furnish your classroom in the same fashion so that the children have a place to read, a place to write, a place to use the computer, a place to build, a place to draw, a place to experiment, and so forth. Then children can choose to go to the part of the room they need to use to complete some part of the task they are working on.

2. **Use a choice board.** A choice board is a freestanding board with a representation of every work area in your room. These representations can be pictures of the area drawn by the children, photos of children

in the areas, written names of the areas (for older children), or any combination of these. Under the representation of each area should be hooks for children to hang their name tags on to indicate they are choosing that area. The number of hooks available under each area should correspond to the number of children who can be in that area at the same time. The number of choices on the choice board should always exceed the number of children in the room, so that even the last child who comes to the board has a choice.

3. **Have planning sessions with individual students.** Talk with each student about how his or her work is progressing. Discuss what he or she would like to see included in the next week's work. Use a chart to record what was learned this week and what he or she would like to learn during the next week.

4. **Use a helping hands chart.** Put up a chart that has important jobs that children could complete weekly in the classroom, such as feeding the gerbil, peer teaching, running errands, and making the lunch count. Ask children to volunteer for these responsibilities by hanging the hand with their name on it under the job they choose.

How We Use Choice in the Integrated Curriculum at School and at Home

Helping children learn to make choices and accept the consequences of those choices is easy in an integrated curriculum that has children working on many different kinds of projects related to the topic under study. Usually, the curriculum is organized around a theme. The following scenarios illustrate the use of choice in three different contexts.

Choice to Foster Reading in Literature
Discussion Groups in the Third Grade

A third-grade teacher was interested in using choice in her classroom but was worried about how that might affect how well she would be able to meet all the required standards for third grade. She appreciated how teachers in the lower grades were implementing choice, but knew that her third-grade children would be tested on the standards. She thought about how she could use choice in the reading program and came up with an idea that really worked for her. She was already reading to the children daily, but she always selected the books to be read. So one of the things she did was to put up a chart that asked for the titles of books that the children or students would like her to read. They really liked that, and she was surprised at the quality of books requested. She also implemented literature discussion groups. She decided that rather than assigning children to the groups or to certain texts, she would offer them limited but authentic choices for getting into a literature discussion group. She chose three books of which she had multiple copies that were appropriate to the reading levels in her classroom. Then she read just a little out of each of the three to the children to let them know a bit about the story and the writing style, and then told them a bit about each of the authors. She put a copy of each of the three books by the interactive white board with titles written on the board. She told the children to put their names on the board beside the book they would like to read. As it turned out, she had two rather large groups—one of nine and one of seven—and one rather small group of four. Then she allowed thirty minutes of silent reading a day to be used reading the book chosen. They were given time to write about what they had read in their response journals and then 15 minutes to talk to each other about the book. The teacher was excited to see how eager the children were to read and talk about the books and began to realize how powerful choice could be.

Choice to Foster Physical Knowledge in Preschool

A Head Start teacher had been hesitant to do too much with physical knowledge activities, activities that invite children to move and change objects, and to observe growing plants and animals. Every time she tried it in her classroom, the children just seemed to go wild and she couldn't manage them. She had attended an inservice session about organizing the classroom like a workshop. She thought about what she had learned and then started to work. She set up a place for dramatic play, for construction, and for painting and drawing. Then she decided that she would create a place for physical knowledge activities that would accommodate only four children. She set up a choice board so that once four children selected that center, it was closed. She put out only enough materials to engage four children at a time, and she kept a record of all the children who chose to go to that center. Once she knew that every child had had an opportunity in the center, she would change the materials. The kids loved it and took no time to adjust to the fact that they couldn't all be there at one time. The choice board helped this Head Start teacher have a physical knowledge area in her room and still maintain an orderly classroom.

Choice to Foster Addition in a First-Grade Classroom

A first-grade teacher started thinking about choice and how to use it in his classroom. One of the important standards for first grade is related to number operations. The National Council of Teachers of Mathematics standard (2000) says that children in K–2 should be able to "compute fluently and make reasonable estimates, develop and use strategies for whole-number computations with a focus on addition and subtraction, and use a variety of methods and tools to compute, including objects, mental computation, estimation, paper and pencil, and calculators" (p. 78). The teacher made a number of math games for first grade recommended by Kamii and Housman (2000) and then invited the children to play the games when they came in the room at the beginning of the day. He let the play continue for 30 minutes every day while he completed the attendance and lunch reports. Children started to arrive at school early just to play the games. He let the children choose the games they wanted to play and the friends with whom they wanted to play. It really worked for him, and the children said that it is their favorite time of the day.

CONSTRUCTIONS

1. Journal Entry

Write about an experience that you have had as a learner when you were allowed to make a choice related to your school tasks. Try to think about how you felt about the choice you made and remember as many of the details as you can. If you cannot recall ever being allowed to make a choice, then write about a choice that was made for you that you did not think was a good one. Remember how you felt about it at the time.

2. Reflection

Reflect on your experience with choice making. Try to identify how you felt during the process and after the choice was made. Do you think that those choices had an impact on your learning?

Decision Making

The teachers begin to discuss the next topic on their agenda, decision making.

Matt: I know that we're going to talk about decision making in the classroom, and quite honestly, I can't find any reference to decision making in the Bringuier [1980] book.

Kenisha: I couldn't find it either, and I must say that I'm having a hard time differentiating between choice and decision making. After all, isn't making a choice making a decision?

Ron: I wondered about that too, Kenisha, but I'm also interested in finding something that I can read related to how to use decision making in the classroom.

Sheila: Every day we make decisions about our teaching and about how kids are doing, but I never thought about involving children in the decision-making process. I wonder what kinds of decisions are appropriate for preschoolers.

Parul: Yes, and is it possible to do decision making with infants and toddlers? I know a woman who teaches parents about how to do infant massages, and she has the parents ask the infant if he or she wants a massage. Then if the infant does something like smile, they go ahead and do the massage. On the other hand, if the infant turns his head away, they don't give the child the massage. I guess that could be considered decision making, couldn't it?

Jennifer: Wow! That's wild. Whoever heard of asking an infant a question! I don't think that the kid really knows whether he's saying yes or no, do you?

Parul: Maybe it's just my culture, but, yes, I do think that they do.

Why Decision Making Is Essential for Children, Teachers, and Families

Decision making differs from choice in that it can be a group process as well as an individual process. Choice is always individual. Additionally, sometimes we make choices that we may never make again. For example, you may choose to do an activity that you have never done before just for that reason: You want to try it. After trying it, you know that you will never do that again. On the other hand, decision making seems to be more long term, and you have to live with your decisions for a while before amending them. For example, if you decide that you are going to meet someone for dinner every Wednesday night, then you expect to do that for a while.

One of the primary reasons for engaging teachers, parents, and children in decision-making activities is to foster intellectual and moral autonomy. Children and adults who engage in decision making together develop a sense of mutual respect and are better able to make informed decisions about what is true (in the intellectual realm) or what is fair or just (in the moral realm). DeVries (1987) suggests that in order for teachers to become constructivist teachers, they must learn to make decisions about curriculum based on what they know about how young children learn. This holds for parents, as well, because parents serve as their children's first teachers. If teachers, parents, and children all engage in decision making together, they will all benefit from the sense of cooperation and self-regulation that results from this process.

Multiple Perspectives: From the Classroom

Here is another e-mail from Anna Hall, a second-grade teacher who spent her first year in a suburban district in New Jersey.

I find myself counting down these last days of school, not because I am tired of my kids but just because I'm tired. This year has been the longest transition period of my life. For the first time I had to accept that I wasn't going to be one of the best at what I was doing, at least not for a few more years. There were so many things I wanted to do but physically and mentally couldn't fit in. I am so ready to spend the summer thinking and reflecting on what worked this year and what I would like to change for next year. Some days I'm proud of the progress I see in my kids and some days I feel guilty wondering if I didn't teach enough of this or enough of that. In the end, I'm beginning to realize that kids are kids. They are constantly soaking up knowledge and it was more important for them to be in an exciting classroom with a clueless teacher than in a boring classroom with a teacher who knew it all. I'm proud and happy with my first year. I think I have been extremely lucky and blessed with a supportive staff and an excellent fun-loving principal and with students who have loved me and kept me on my toes. I know I have learned more this year than I ever have before, and I am excited about all there is still to learn. Here's to teaching, the job that allows for life-long learning.

Decision Making Fosters Concepts of Fairness

DeVries and Zan (2012) suggest that one of the purposes for using decision making in the classroom is to promote feelings of necessity about rules and fairness. Unlike choice, which initiates the child's ability to think about possibilities, necessity requires the child to think about how possibilities must be limited or constrained. According to Piaget (1987), "necessity is the result of a top-down procedure that at each step diminishes the number of possibilities and correlatively increases the number of impossible choices" (p. 115). Thus, as children engage in decision making, they think of as many possibilities or solutions as they can. Then they have to think about which of these possibilities need to be eliminated because they may not be just or fair in the moral realm or true in the intellectual realm.

Decision Making Fosters Self-Regulation

Piaget (1970) suggests that "life is essentially autoregulation" (p. 26). By this, he means that, as both biological beings and intellectual beings, children grow through the continual development of their own self-correcting systems. DeVries and Zan (2012) suggest that when children make decisions, they construct a sense of ownership for the decisions made. This ownership helps children move from obedience to decisions made by adults to an awareness that decisions are agreements among peers, that these agreements govern their actions, and that the group can change these agreements when they think it necessary. Thus, children move from obedience to autonomy and begin to recognize the social participation required to be self-governed.

Decision Making Fosters Responsibility

One of the most difficult things to learn is to accept the responsibility for your decisions. It is much easier to blame someone else when things do not turn out the way we want them too. When young children make decisions, they do not always make wise ones. If the teacher is unwilling to let children experience the consequences of their decisions, the children will not advance in their ability to make wise decisions. Therefore, teachers must be willing to let young children experience the consequences of their decisions whenever possible. DeVries and Zan (2012) suggest that when children make decisions and live by those decisions, they construct a sense of a shared responsibility for the things that happen in the classroom and for how the group members work together.

Decision Making Fosters Mutual Respect Among Teachers, Parents, and Children

DeVries and Zan (2012) hold that fostering an atmosphere of mutual respect is one of the major objectives of involving children in decision making. This atmosphere is one in which adults and children are self-governed and cooperate with each other. Piaget (1997) differentiated between obligation due to unilateral respect and mutual respect. *Unilateral respect* refers to the kind of respect a child has for the parent. If the parent delivers a rule, the child will follow the rule out of obligation and respect for the parent. Through group discussion, children begin to hear differing points of view and begin to develop a respect of cooperation, or mutual respect. Piaget (1997) suggests that children advance from a feeling of unilateral respect and obligation to the parent to a feeling of mutual respect for others, and through this process they construct an understanding of obligation to the social group.

The Kinds of Decision-Making Opportunities We Should Consider

Decision making can be both individual and social. Many different classroom occasions provide opportunities for both individual and group decision making.

Peer-Group Decisions

There are many occasions when teachers can bring children together for discussions and decision making in the classroom. Peer-group discussions can relate classroom rules and their infractions, classroom arrangements, topics for group study, or moral issues about specific problems that arise in the classroom. Making peer-group decisions provides opportunities for children to think about the feelings and characteristics of others.

Peer-group decisions can be made in a variety of ways. In some cases, children will discuss and negotiate the topic so that the decision is made through consensus. Voting provides another way for decisions to be made. Voting often promotes disequilibrium when young children realize that their vote was not the majority vote. Resolution of this kind of disequilibrium can help children move to a more coordinated perspective of the problem solution.

As children learn to agree to the decisions of the majority, they move from unilateral respect to a mutual respect based on cooperation and self-regulation. According to Fuqua (1999), children in constructivist classrooms who have been encouraged to discuss and decide on rules think of the rules as mutually determined agreements rather than as laws passed down from an authority. She found that kindergarten children in constructivist settings reasoned at a higher level of moral reasoning than did children in nonconstructivist settings. DeVries (1987) developed a questionnaire, provided in Box 4.2, that teachers can use to compare the way their children think about rules when they enter school to their thinking at the end of the year.

One of the most effective ways to involve children, teachers, and parents in the decision-making process is to hold parent-teacher conferences, with the child present at the conference and carrying a major role in it. In order for this

---

BOX 4.2   QUESTIONNAIRE TO DETERMINE CHILDREN'S PERCEPTIONS OF RULES

1. What is a rule?
2. Why do we have rules?
3. Who should make the rules in a classroom? Why?
4. Should teachers have to follow the same rules as children? Why?
5. What rules do we need in our classroom? Why?
6. What should happen if a person breaks a rule?
7. Can rules be changed once you make them? How do you decide whether a rule should be changed?

Source: R. DeVries & L. Kohlberg (1987a). *Programs of early education: The constructivist view* (pp. 158–159). New York, NY: Longman.

to be effective, children need to be involved in self-evaluation through regular conferences with the teacher. Teachers help the child prepare a portfolio that documents her best work and the areas where she is having the most difficulty. The child should be involved in the selection of items to be put in the portfolio, and the teacher should have an equal voice. For example, the child will be able to show the parents what she considers her best piece of writing and explain her reasoning to her parents. The teacher may select another piece that he thinks is the best and will be able to give the reasons for his selection. During the conference, the teacher and the parents listen while the child explains what she is doing well and what she needs or wants to work on. When the child has finished, both the parents and the teacher ask her questions. Then, together they make decisions about what needs to come next and how they can help bring that about. Through this process, the teacher, parents, and child are working cooperatively to guide the child's continued growth.

Individual Decisions

While most of the time we think about decision making as a group process, we also need to understand that we make decisions individually. These decisions may be at the conscious level, or they may be decisions that the child is not consciously aware he is making. Some of those decisions will be *intellectual decisions,* or those children make related to what is true. Piaget states that intelligent thought is conscious, "which means that it is adapted to reality and tries to influence it; it admits of being true or false (empirically or logically true) and it can be communicated by language" (quoted in Gruber & Voneche, 1995, p. 85). For example, when playing the game of double War, two children may disagree about who has the higher quantity on the two overturned cards. When a conflict like this occurs, each child has to verify what is true. One child may base his decision on counting, while the other may base her decision on the logic that they both have one card with 5 and her 6 is more than his 4. Regardless of the methods they use, they should both find that their answer is the same and is true.

Moral decisions are those that are related to what is fair and just, and they occur frequently in the active classroom. Some of these can be resolved through group discussions, but many are made on an individual basis. For example, a child may decide that it was not fair that another child got to work in the block center during all of center time. The next day, this same child may reason that it is fair for her to stay in the block area all day because someone else did it the day before. Moral decisions are made regularly in situations where children have to share materials, space, and responsibilities.

Other decisions, *pragmatic decisions,* are those that children make regarding what they want to do for their project work, with whom they want to work, when they want to have their snack, and with whom they want to sit. These kinds of decisions take up a lot of the children's time and relate to the organization of time, space, materials, and people.

All three kinds of individual decision making are important to the child, and all three help the child become more self-regulated.

How We Use Decision Making in the Integrated Curriculum at School and at Home

Facilitating individual and group decision making is easier in an integrated curriculum because the need to make decisions arises naturally out of the project and theme work. However, the teacher may also find that, in this kind of setting, she needs to bring the group together to establish rules of conduct or discuss problems. Some teachers have learned more about the role of decision making in the classroom by using it in their classrooms. The following scenarios illustrate how teachers have used decision making in three different contexts.

Rule Making in the Kindergarten Classroom

In a kindergarten classroom, a boy brought in a praying mantis, and the other children wanted to know if they could name it and keep it in the room as a pet. They had a class discussion and talked about how they could provide an appropriate environment for it in the classroom. The next day, one of the parents donated a glass terrarium large enough to provide sufficient space for Mary Ann (the class voted on this name). Some of the children went to the library to find out what Mary Ann might like to eat and drink. Others tried to find out what they needed to put in the terrarium so that Mary Ann would feel at home. At last, the terrarium became a real home for Mary Ann. The children found a space in the classroom to put the terrarium. Now the question for decision making was, How many people can go visit and watch Mary Ann at one time? The children offered a number of suggestions that ranged from two to eight. Reasons supporting their answers were "If there were only two, you could walk around and see Mary Ann from different sides," and "I think it should be six, because lots of people will want to choose this center." The teacher recorded each suggestion on the whiteboard with a bit of the reason beside it. Then one of the children said, "Why don't we try out these ideas?" They all decided that was what they wanted to do. They split into a group for each suggestion and then started a discussion. The teacher was amazed that the children all agreed that the number should be two, because it wasn't too crowded like four or eight, and they could move around to another side if they wanted. The teacher remarked that this was the first time she had consensus in a discussion, and no one tried to break this rule.

Moral Dilemma Discussion in the Third-Grade Classroom

A third-grade teacher tried something a little more structured. She used one of the books written by Lorraine Goolsby and Rheta DeVries (1994c) that set up moral dilemmas with no clear right or wrong outcomes to help children think about more than one perspective. She thought using these books would be a good way to start decision-making discussions. Since these books don't have an ending, the children can offer suggestions about what should happen next. She read them the story titled *When a Friend Steals*, about a boy who doesn't like to get up in the morning so he never has time for breakfast. When he gets to school, he is hungry, so he sneaks food out of others' lunches and eats it. Finally, the parents and the children figure out what is happening, and they have a discussion about the fairness of taking others' food and about how they could help solve the problem. This teacher was very surprised that her students liked talking about the problem. Somehow it seemed highly significant to them. And she was amazed at the good solutions the children developed.

Using the Scooter in the Preschool Classroom Sharing

A teacher of a Head Start class for 3-year-olds thought that perhaps her children were too young to work on decision making, Then she found she had a problem because three of the youngsters fought over who was going to get to use the scooter at playtime. She had tried everything she could think of, but nothing seemed to work, so she decided to have a discussion with the three who were having the problem. She started out by saying that there was a problem with the scooter every day and that she was not going to put it back in the playground until they worked out a way to play with it. She was using one of Piaget's sanctions, but she said that she would sit and talk with them until they worked out a solution. Charles said, "We could take turns." Lavaris responded, "That don't do no good, cuz you ain't never give up your turn." The teacher asked, "Is there a way we could make turn taking work?" It was very quiet for a while and the teacher thought that she had lost them. Then Liam said, "You could get more scooters." She agreed that while that was a good idea, she didn't have any money to buy any more scooters. Finally Charles said, "What if we count the times we go around the circle and each take five turns. Then we have to get off 'til you two take your five turns." The teacher smiled and asked, "Do you think that you could do this?" and they agreed that they could. They did it for that day. The teacher was surprised, yet doubtful that she had seen the last of the problem.

SUMMARY

- Authentic tasks, choice, and decision making are important to children's construction of knowledge and self-regulation.

- Authentic tasks provide three kinds of motivation for learning and intellectual development.
- Authentic tasks are important in the construction of all three kinds of knowledge.
- There are three basic kinds of authentic tasks: exploratory, problem solving, and purposeful.
- Choice requires thinking between alternatives.
- Choice helps children become wise decision makers.
- Choice and the consequences that result are important in helping children understand and accept responsibility for their actions.
- Group decision making fosters the child's conception of fairness.
- Individual and group decision making are important in the development of self-regulation and mutual respect.
- Teachers can promote authentic tasks by providing the materials for exploration, the time for children to engage in problem-solving activities, and the discussion and implementation of purposeful projects. Teachers can use individual conferences and group discussions to help children learn to make good choices and wise decisions.

CONSTRUCTIONS

1. RESEARCH

Observe children of different ages playing the same game, such as Candyland, Hi-Ho Cherry-O, or Chutes and Ladders. What is the teacher's role as they play? Does this role vary according to the ages of the children? How?

2. RESEARCH

Try using limited choice with a group of 3-year-olds. How did they respond when making these choices? What did you learn from this?

3. RESEARCH

Observe in at least three different classrooms. Then interview children in these classrooms using the DeVries questionnaire to determine what they perceive to be the rules.

4. ANALYSIS

Compare and contrast the children's perception of the rules in their classroom with the teacher's perception of the rules.

5. RESEARCH

In one classroom, have a group of children vote about a real issue they are facing—for example, what they should buy for the classroom with the $25.00 they earned by collecting aluminum cans or which book they want to hear this morning. Observe how the children handle the task of voting. How do their behaviors relate to their cognitive development?

Resources

Books and Articles

Goolsby, L., & DeVries, R (1994a). *When a friend refuses to share.* Cedar Falls, IA: Regent's Center for Early Developmental Education.

Illustrated story for teachers to use in conducting moral dilemma discussions. Tips for using the book are included.

Goolsby, L., & DeVries, R. (1994b). *When a friend eats more than her share.* Cedar Falls, IA: Regent's Center for Early Developmental Education.

Illustrated story for teachers to use in conducting moral dilemma discussions. Tips for using the book are included.

Goolsby, L., & DeVries, R. (1994c). *When a friend steals.* Cedar Falls, IA: Regent's Center for Early Developmental Education.

Illustrated story for teachers to use in conducting moral dilemma discussions. Tips for using the book are included.

Readdick, C., & Douglas, K. (2000). More than line leader and door holder: Engaging young children in real work. *Young Children, 55*(6), 63–70.

Yelland, N. (2000). *Promoting meaningful learning: Innovations in educating early childhood professionals.* Washington, DC: National Association for the Education of Young Children.

Videos

DeVries, R., & Zan, B. (2001). *Friendly hands and friendly words: Four-year-olds make classroom rules.* (Available from Regent's Center for Early Developmental Education, Cedar Falls, IA)

Authors Rheta DeVries and Betty Zan use Piaget's research on moral development to show why inviting children into the classroom rule-making process can contribute to young children's moral development.

Forman, G. (1996). *Jed draws his bicycle: A case of drawing-to-learn.* Amherst, MA: Videatives.

Retrieved from https://www.videatives.com/store/node/1859

5

SOCIAL INTERACTION, PLAY, AND PROJECTS

This chapter presents a constructivist perspective on the importance of social interaction, play, and projects to children's learning. Chapter 2 gave many examples of how children learn when they are interested and are given choices among authentic activities. Chapter 3 described the three interrelated types of knowledge that children construct: social, physical, and logico-mathematical. This chapter expands on the role of social interaction in the construction of social knowledge and provides examples of how children construct all three types of knowledge within the sociomoral atmosphere of classroom communities. This chapter presents a strong rationale for the value of play in general and in classroom settings in particular. This chapter also discusses project work from a constructivist perspective. In today's schools with much emphasis on accountability and testing, time for social interaction, play, and projects has been curtailed to children's detriment. This chapter provides a rationale for the necessity of social interaction, play, and projects in the curriculum. These activities are not only important for children's development and knowledge construction but are also vital to their health and well being. After reading this chapter, you will have a better understanding of

- how learning occurs through social interaction, play, and projects;
- the role of social interaction in the development of interpersonal understanding, friendships, and perspective taking;
- the value of play in curriculum;
- project work from a constructivist perspective; and
- how teachers can support social interaction, play, and projects.

Introduction

The teachers' group is discussing the common attitude of parents, other teachers, and administrators that play is a waste of time and work does not get done when children are playing.

Kenisha: We have a problem at my school with people who don't understand why play is important to young children. Some of the teachers think play is just a waste of time and that we don't have enough time to cover the curriculum, much less let kids play. How do you deal with that attitude?

Matt: We have the same problem at my school, and it's getting worse. Two weeks ago, a parent who lives across the street from the school called the principal and complained. She said the kids were spending too much time outside for recess and weren't learning anything! Now our principal is thinking about doing away with recess!

Jennifer: Well, maybe we should get rid of recess. The kids just get rowdy and come in all hyper from playing outside. Sometimes it's very hard to get them settled down to work again.

Parul: Well, I don't know about older children, but my infants and toddlers learn so much when they play. Just the other day one of them used the toy cell phone to call her mommy. She pretended to talk to her mommy and sang her a song.

Kenisha: But that's just it …! All children learn through play. They learn about social roles when they act out being firefighters, they learn geometry and spatial relationships when they build with blocks, and they learn how to create and solve problems when they work on projects like making a kite. Everybody gets something from play, even adults. I bet you all play at something. I like to play in local theater productions. So how can we get parents and others to value play?

Sheila: We have play days for all our families. We organize a play day about once a year at a time when most families can attend. Then we set up play activities that are part of our curriculum. The kids get to show off the activities to their parents, so the parents can see what their children are learning. It's fun too!

Jennifer: I don't think my parents would go for that. They want to see test results to know that their kids are learning.

Ron: I tried something a few years ago that helped my parents understand the importance of play for their children. Instead of sending worksheets home that kids had done like some teachers do, I wrote objectives for each classroom activity based on our Common Core curriculum. When children completed each activity, they took home the description of the objectives they had fulfilled. That way, the parents knew their kids were learning from play. It really helped to communicate my program goals to parents.

Sheila: What about the parents who don't read English?

Ron: I had it translated for them.

Matt: I saw a TV special the other day that said children today have much less play time than they did 15 years ago. If schools outlaw play, this will make the problem worse. One of the teachers at my school who values play is working on a committee of the state early childhood organization to write a position paper on the value of play. The organization plans to send it to legislators and school administrators.

Kenisha: I hope they get it written soon! I'd love to send a few copies to people at my school.

The Role of Social Interaction, Play, and Projects in Children's Learning

The three topics in this chapter—social interaction, play, and projects—refer to the planned and spontaneous activity of children in group settings. In addition, all three serve as mediums through which children experience curriculum and construct knowledge. Piaget's ([1932] 1965) research on how knowledge is constructed showed that social interaction and play are important in children's learning. Children develop the ability to take another's perspective through interactions with peers. Vygotsky ([1930–1935] 1978) also studied how social experiences influence children's development. Just as Piaget's work did, Vygotsky's work showed how social interactions are a necessary and important factor in child development. Vygotsky also said that children with disabilities particularly need social interactions with peers because they tend to become socially isolated due to their disabilities. Constructivist educators and advocates of the Reggio Emilia approach (Helm & Beneke, 2003) have described children's project work as a medium for social interactions and play based on children's inquiry.

Peer interactions lead to perspective taking. **Perspective taking,** the ability to understand another's viewpoint, is a necessary condition for the functioning of classroom communities. More will be said about classroom communities in Chapter 7. Piaget studied perspective taking and children's moral reasoning through their play activities and described how children construct their ideas about rules and fairness through their interactions during play. Similarly, constructivists have long maintained that children develop perspective taking through interactions in inquiry and project work. Projects provide authentic learning opportunities in which children can choose activities based on their interests and a need to know. They can explore their own questions through inquiry that leads to more meaningful and long-lasting learning. Perspective taking and inquiry help children to develop autonomy, the ability to make decisions for themselves considering the correct and right things to do. Schools are not always receptive to child autonomy.

When you consider your own learning, how important is social interaction to your learning? What types of social interactions have you experienced recently that confirmed your thinking, challenged your thinking, or provided a meaningful shared experience for you and those involved in the interaction? Social interaction, play, and projects have posed difficulties for some educators because of their perceived need to control choices in learning objectives, materials, and activities. Social interaction, play, and projects run counter to the old-school approach of telling children what they need to know and how they need to know it. Schools and educators are not always receptive to the complexity of classroom life when children express their autonomy in choosing based on their interests. Traditional education has long perpetuated heteronomy and conformity, not autonomy, the aim of constructivist education. When children have opportunities for social interaction, play, and projects, they are more likely to develop the ability to self-regulate, or autonomy. Therefore, constructivist educators value social interaction, play, and projects as central to curriculum, not as frills that can occur only when real work has been completed. Social interaction, play, and projects are real work in constructivist classrooms.

Social Interaction

When children interact with each other, they share their needs, desires, thoughts, and feelings with others who also share theirs. Through interactions, children learn they are both different from and similar to others. Although they come to understand and appreciate others' views, it is not without difficulty, as you will see in this preschool example.

When Perspectives Clash

Alisha and Robert were constructing vehicles with lock-blocks in their preschool block building center. Alisha reached for a set of wheels to add to her vehicle at the same time that Robert grabbed the wheels for his vehicle. The children played tug-of-war with the set of wheels, neither willing to give in.

Alisha:	Let go of the wheels. I want them for my car!
Robert:	No! I saw them first.
Alisha:	But I want them bad!
Robert:	You let go. I want them badder!
Teacher:	Alisha and Robert, you seem to have a problem. You both want the wheels. There is only one set of wheels left and two of you. How will you solve this problem?
Alisha:	Give them to me. I saw them first!
Robert:	No, I did. Give them to me!

Teacher: Okay. Both of you can't have the wheels at the same time. Have you thought about taking turns using the wheels? Or building something with the blocks that doesn't have wheels?

Robert: But I need this car!

Alisha: My car won't go without wheels!

Teacher: Since the two of you want the one set of wheels, but you both can't have them, I will put the wheels away. When the two of you decide on a solution that both of you agree on, let me know, and I will get the wheels. Let me know if you want me to give you some suggestions.

Conflict in social interactions prompts a need for perspective taking. In this example, the teacher has turned the problem back to the children for them to solve. In order to solve it, each must take the other's perspective into account and decide on a solution that will accommodate the desires of both. For example, they may decide to take turns with the one set of wheels. Or they might work together to create a vehicle with the one set of wheels and take timed turns playing with it. Or Robert may offer Alisha a toy in exchange for getting to use the one set of wheels. While more will be said about problem solving in Chapter 6, it is important to understand that children learn to take another's view through interactions that may involve conflict.

Piaget's theory emphasizes the importance of social interaction.

Piaget's Social Theory and Children's Development

Piaget (1973) identified social interaction as one of the four major influences on development. He wrote about the role of social interaction in various publications, including *The Moral Judgment of the Child* (1932/1965). In *Sociological Studies* 1965/1995), he wrote that social interaction is necessary but not sufficient for intellectual development and that social adaptation is just as important as any other form of adaptation, including physical adaptation. In social adaptation, children learn the culture of their environment through interactions with adults and other children. In pointing out the importance of social interaction, Piaget (1965/1995) wrote,

> everywhere where subject-to-object relations are present, and this is so in sociology as elsewhere, even and especially if the subject is a "we" and the object is several subjects at the same time, knowledge arises neither from the subject nor the object but from the inter-dependent interaction between them, so as to advance from there in the dual direction of an objectified exteriorization and a reflexive interiorization. (p. 27)

Thus, Piaget viewed social interactions as important in knowledge construction due to the potential for **reciprocity**, the two-way exchange that occurs when one person interacts with another. As a result of reciprocity, a common or shared understanding emerges when people interact. Piaget (1965/1995) wrote that cognitive and social development are interrelated and go hand-in-hand; they do not occur separately. Children develop cognitively within a social context and socially within an intellectual context. Their emotions play an important role in cognitive and social development by energizing their actions in directions reflecting their values and interests. For example, just as children choose play materials they find interesting and pleasurable, children develop friendships with other children they like and with whom they have experienced positive shared experiences. Without emotions and interest, cognitive development cannot occur. For Piaget, affectivity (emotion and interest) is the fuel that makes intellectual development run. Children become engaged intellectually when they are pursuing their own purposes.

The Interrelationship of Social, Cognitive, and Moral Development

DeVries (1997) has elaborated on Piaget's social theory and the interrelationship of social, cognitive, and moral development. In outlining the progression of development, Piaget described movement away from a state of egocentrism in early childhood toward a sense of reciprocity and autonomy in later childhood and adulthood. **Egocentrism,** for Piaget, is the inability to take another's point of view. The child is able to understand the world and daily situations only from his or her own perspective. Egocentrism is not the same thing as selfishness or self-centeredness, which imply an understanding and disregard for another's perspective. In the previous example, Alisha and Robert couldn't understand each other's desire for the wheels because they couldn't **decenter** from their own desires. They were focused on their own needs to the exclusion of understanding that others have similar needs as well.

Another example of egocentrism may occur when a toddler stands between his mother and the TV screen she is watching, obscuring her view. The child does not understand why his mother is upset: Since he can see the TV, he does not understand why she can't see it too. The child's intention is not selfish or malicious but reflects his inability to understand the situation from anyone's perspective except his own. In Piaget's terms, he can't decenter from his own perspective to consider the perspective of someone else. To decenter would mean he could consider multiple perspectives simultaneously. Children gradually develop the ability to decenter and perspective take.

Furthermore, egocentrism means that the only point of view that exists for the child is his own. He does not understand that there are other viewpoints or what those other viewpoints might be. As a child interacts with others, and especially as the child's perspective comes into conflict with another child's perspective, the child recognizes first that the other does not view the situation in the same way. Later, he develops an understanding of what the other child's perspective is and how it is different from his own. At this point in the child's development, he can coordinate his perspective with the others and engage in cooperative behavior. To **cooperate** means to act in coordination with another's perspective for the mutual benefit of those concerned. For example, when two children are fighting over one ball, they may come to conclude, due to the conflict and their own desires, that they both can't have the same ball at the same time. In order to make sense of or resolve this conflict or disequilibrium, they may decide to take timed turns with the ball or play catch with it together. Through this reciprocal interaction, they have come to appreciate the other's perspective and to cooperate for mutual benefit.

Peer interactions help the child break away from egocentrism and become more autonomous in her relations to others. Autonomy, or self-regulation, is the ability to act based on considering the relevant variables including the differing perspectives of others. Autonomous decisions are based on what is the right or correct thing to do, regardless of external reward or punishment. Peer interactions in which children are equals provide a means for autonomy to develop. While adult-child interactions are also important in children's social and cognitive development, it is unlikely that equality can be achieved in these interactions since the child typically views the adult as an authority figure. The adult-child relationship is not equal, resulting in the child's deference or conformity to the more powerful adult's wishes.

Piaget claimed and others have substantiated (Castle & Richards, 1979; Rubin & Ross, 1982; Selman, 1980) that movement from egocentrism toward reciprocity is accomplished through social interaction. Social interaction provides the context in which children begin to consider that others have viewpoints different from their own and begin to figure out what those differences are and how to coordinate their perspectives with the differing perspectives of others. Piaget said that interactions with peers provide an opportunity for children to experience equality in relations with other children. This equality occurs among children when there is equal power in the relationship, providing an opportunity for reciprocity. There is an equal give and take among children who can choose to attend to or ignore the ideas of peers. When points of view differ, the child may experience disequilibrium. As a result, he may recognize the difference in perspectives, decenter from his own perspective, and consider the other child's perspective as well as his own.

Game play is a means for understanding moral reasoning. Piaget studied children's social interaction in games, specifically in the game of marbles, to understand their moral reasoning. He found that children progress in their ability to think about such issues as fairness through interactions. Gradually, children become increasingly willing to submit to mutually agreed-on game rules. Very young children believe that rules are externally imposed by authority figures such as adults. Older children believe that rules can be agreed on and changed through the consensus of those involved in the game. This movement reflects the progression from heteronomy, or external regulation, toward autonomy, or self-regulation. As children learn that they can self-regulate their behaviors without having to depend on adults to tell them what is right or correct, they become more autonomous in their relationships and actions.

Piaget also studied children's moral reasoning through their responses to interview questions about moral dilemmas. His ideas about moral development were subsequently presented as stages of moral reasoning (Kohlberg, 1984). The stages progress from egocentrism, in which children view what is right as obedience to higher authorities, to the highest stages (attained by few adults), where right is viewed as treating others the way one wishes to be treated and acting autonomously on universal principles such as justice and equality.

Children learn moral reasoning through social interactions in which they are exposed to differing viewpoints that reflect various stages of cognitive development. Children tend to be open to a stage of reasoning that is one stage above where they are. They tend to tune out reasoning at lower stages. When children have opportunities to engage in moral discussions, they have a chance to explain their ideas to others and to think about others' ideas in relation to their own. Such discussions promote their development of moral reasoning (DeVries & Zan, 2012).

Levels of Interpersonal Understanding

Selman and Schultz (1990) based their levels of children's interpersonal understanding on Piaget's theory and stages of perspective taking. DeVries and Zan (2012) applied these stages to children's behaviors, resulting in an understanding of how children enact their moral reasoning when interacting with others. Selman and Schultz describe two types of social interactions. One type, termed **negotiation,** occurs when there is tension or disequilibrium in the interaction, such as a dispute over a toy. The second type, called **shared experiences,** occurs when there is no tension, disequilibrium, or conflict, and the interaction is friendly. Each type of experience can be analyzed in terms of four levels of enacted interpersonal understanding, ranging from level 0, egocentrism, to level 3, mutuality (see Table 5.1). Teachers can use these levels to understand children's moral reasoning in relation to others.

Table 5.1 **Selman's Four Levels of Interpersonal Understanding**

Level 0	Egocentric: impulsive level
Level 1	Unilateral: one-way level
Level 2	Reciprocal: reflective level
Level 3	Mutual: third-person level

Source: R. L. Selman & L. H. Schultz (1990). *Making a friend in youth* (p. 29). Chicago, IL: University of Chicago Press.

Children progress from an egocentric state, level 0, in which they are unable to consider other perspectives, to level 1, in which they are aware that other perspectives exist but act in ways to maintain their own perspective. In level 2, they recognize different perspectives and act on this knowledge in a reciprocal or give-and-take manner, and in level 3 they collaborate with others based on a mutual view of the situation. Movement through the levels is a function of experiences children have in their interactions with each other.

DeVries, Reese-Learned, and Morgan (1991) analyzed children's enacted interpersonal understanding in three classrooms using Selman's levels. The classrooms they studied reflected three different approaches to teaching children: the behaviorist, eclectic, and constructivist views. All three classrooms had children from similar backgrounds and experiences. The researchers found that children in the constructivist classroom were more advanced in their interpersonal understanding and were able to resolve more conflicts constructively than were children in the other two groups. They attributed this difference to the sociomoral classroom community that existed in the constructivist classroom in which children were engaged in moral discussions and rule making and were encouraged to be autonomous. Such classroom communities offer opportunities for children to make choices and consider others' viewpoints in relation to their own. Constructivist classroom communities are also places where children have daily opportunities to interact and develop friendships. Friendships become increasingly important as children move through school. The following interaction between two friends took place in the multiage classroom of one of the authors of this book.

Multiple Perspectives: From the Classroom

Sammy, a 5-year-old who had been physically abused by his parents, began the program by withdrawing from all the children. He would not speak, make eye contact, or play with anyone, including me, the teacher. He kept his head down most of the time and didn't do much, despite my efforts to engage him in conversation and in play.

For several weeks, the children and I tried our best to interest Sammy in our activities. While most children eventually stopped trying to communicate with Sammy, one child kept trying. Three-year-old Garrett never gave up on Sammy. In his energetic way, Garrett would try to take Sammy's arm and get him interested in block building or in a variety of other activities Garrett liked, such as trying on all the hats in the dramatic play area. He would put them on Sammy, who would passively let him. The day things changed was when Garrett sang a song to Sammy while playing our class guitar. Sammy, in the cowboy hat Garrett had put on his head, lifted his face to Garrett, and for the first time I saw Sammy's eyes shine and his face come alive with a smile I will never forget. It was a joyous moment and a breakthrough for Sammy.

Garrett would play for Sammy every day, and it wasn't long before Sammy joined in the singing and playing. I never quite understood why Garrett persisted when other children didn't, but I feel Garrett's persistence and his music brought Sammy into our classroom community. I wish I could say that Sammy continued to make great strides in his interactions with others and in engaging in activities, but that was not the case. However, he made one good friend in Garrett and learned that there was at least one person who would not give up on him and who could always make him smile. Garrett learned that persistence pays off. I learned a lesson too about the power of social interaction and friendship.

Friendships and Social Interactions

Friendships play a major role in creating classroom community. Friendships represent bonds of attachment among individuals, which keep group members united and willing to cooperate. But friendships don't come into being automatically. A teacher cannot will children to be friends with each other. Friendships take time and social interaction to develop. Friendship means that between two people, there is a level of trust, attraction or interest, and cooperation. In order to maintain a friendship, cooperation is necessary. In peer relations, friendships tend to be somewhat equal, in that each person has equal power to give and take when necessary to preserve the relationship. Through friendships, young children learn how to reciprocate to keep friends and learn that constant discord or acting on only their own self-interests without considering the other will lead to loss of friendships.

Selman and Schultz's (1990) levels of interpersonal understanding can be applied to friendship (see Table 5.1). These levels reflect the progression of understanding from lower levels in which young children's friendships are characterized by interests in similar toys and activities, with an egocentric view having little or no regard for the other's perspective, to higher levels of reciprocal behaviors based on an understanding of the other's perspective and a desire to reciprocate or accommodate to the other perspective in order to maintain the relationship.

Friendships are important to children's well-being. You may have heard a young child say, "If you give me a cookie, I will be your friend," or "You're not my friend. You can't come to my birthday party." Young children often associate friendship with concrete objects or events, whereas older children are more likely to associate friendship with psychological factors, such as similar values or interests. Regardless of age, children experience emotional attachments and responses to their friends. When friendships dissipate, children experience feelings of sadness and loss.

In describing how being friends influences social interaction, Burk (1996) compares maintaining friendship to Piaget's idea of equilibration. When disequilibrium or discord is felt in the relationship, there is an attempt to bring the relationship back to a state of harmony (**equilibrium**) by accommodating or renegotiating the relationship. Burk says this is a form of cooperation, or coregulation, in which individuals work together to resolve the conflict. Shared experience occurs when there is a lack of tension in relationships.

Gilligan (1982) describes two ways of relating. The first is a morality of responsibility and care, indicating connections with others. The second is a morality of rights and justice focused on separation. Selman and Schultz (1990) have written similarly in defining two types of social interactions: negotiation and shared experiences. They describe the need for negotiation when there is tension or conflict in an interaction, such as when children have a difference of opinion or a conflict of interest in play materials or activities. Children develop and use negotiation strategies. These range from use of force, such as hitting or yelling; to one-way demands, threats, or bribes; to persuasion or deferring to the will of the other; and finally to suggesting a mutually satisfactory compromise (DeVries & Zan, 2012). Social interactions help children develop negotiation strategies and lead to an understanding of more effective strategies to prevent future conflict (Zan, 1996).

Shared experiences occur when there is equilibrium in a relationship with no need to resolve conflict (Selman & Schultz, 1990). Shared experiences are pleasant, calm, and friendly, and they help build connections and happy memories among friends (DeVries & Zan, 2012). Developmental levels can also be identified in shared experiences. At lower levels, there may be unreflective contagious imitation, such as children making funny faces together. At the next level, there is expressive enthusiasm, such as expressing excitement at being together, and at higher levels children reflect on the good times they experience in activities that involve shared common goals or commitments (DeVries & Zan, 2012).

Most teachers prefer shared experiences to conflict interactions calling for conflict negotiations. However, children benefit from both types of experiences.

It is important for teachers to recognize the potential for conflict to lead to meaningful learning. Through conflicts, children learn how to negotiate and generate satisfactory compromises. Teachers should view conflicts as an important part of the curriculum for young children and look for opportunities to support children in these situations (Zan, 1996). The following example shows how two children, with their teacher's help, negotiate a conflict. The children are working together on the same drawing of a nature walk they recently took with their kindergarten class.

Julie:	Let's put flowers all around the tree.
Mei:	Yeah! Some tulips and those yellow ones.
Julie:	Don't forget the leaves. Mine are going to have thorns.
Mei:	Remember the bee? I want to put a big ole bumble bee right here!
Julie:	No, Mei, you can't do that. You'll make it too big.
Mei:	That's how I make them.
Julie:	You will ruin our picture if you do that!
Mei:	It will look good.
Julie:	Teacher! Teacher! Mei's ruining our picture!
Teacher:	What a colorful picture! I can tell you remembered the colors of the flowers we saw on our walk. What's the problem?
Julie:	Mei wants to draw a big bee, and it won't look right.
Mei:	It will too!
Teacher:	So Mei wants a bee in your picture, but you don't?
Julie:	It won't look right. She draws them too big.
Teacher:	I've seen Mei's bees. Sometimes they are big. But she wants to put one in your picture. So the two of you need to decide what to do about the bee. Can you think of a way to do your picture so that both of you are happy with it?
Mei:	I could draw just one bee.
Julie:	I don't want a bee! You can go make your own picture with bees!
Mei:	I could make it little! Would that be okay?
Julie:	Okay. Why don't you put it up high?
Mei:	Yeah! I'll put it in the sky!
Teacher:	Way to go! The two of you cooperated! I can't wait to see your special picture!

Not all children's conflicts can be easily negotiated. Sometimes children are not able or ready to take the other child's perspective. Sometimes children refuse to budge from their positions to accept compromises, even when the teacher offers reasonable alternatives. When children become destructive of materials or each other, teachers must intervene. Using punishment produces negative effects such as blind obedience or rebelliousness and is not advocated by early childhood professionals. Instead of punishment, Piaget described using **sanctions by reciprocity.** "Sanctions by reciprocity are directly related to the act we want to sanction and to the adult's point of view. They have the effect of motivating the child to construct rules of conduct from within, through the coordination of viewpoints" (Kamii & Livingston, 1994, p. 61). Sanctions are described in more detail in Chapter 4. Can you recall the last time you and a friend experienced a situation calling for negotiation and compromise? What strategies did you use to overcome the conflict? Were they effective?

Teaching to Promote Social Interaction

DeVries and Zan (2012) describe the constructivist sociomoral classroom atmosphere as a community in which children are respected and learn to respect others. Children learn respect through interactions with teachers who show them respect and guide them to consider the consequences of their actions on others. In a constructivist community, teachers provide blocks of time in which children can interact with each other and with adults. Teachers do not squelch conflicts among children, but rather use them as opportunities to help children see the other child's perspective. When conflicts occur, teachers encourage children to think about the situation from all viewpoints and generate possible solutions.

Group meetings provide opportunities to discuss conflicts. Another way to promote social interaction is to hold group meetings in which the teacher helps children discuss how the class as a whole can solve a problem. Children may even vote on a preferred solution to the problem and then act on the solution. Group meetings allow children to express their emotions and ideas and to listen carefully to the ideas of others. Teachers encourage children to listen carefully to what the other person is saying and to determine whether they agree with the other's ideas or have a different idea. Group meetings can also become opportunities to discuss moral dilemmas as they arise and consider what would be the right thing to do in a difficult situation. Such interactions during group discussions lead to advances in children's thinking, their moral reasoning, and their enacted interpersonal understanding.

Perspective taking is encouraged by asking children to consider situations from the viewpoints of others. For example, suppose one child has hit another. The teacher might ask the aggressor how the other child might feel and how he would feel if someone hit him. Then the teacher may ask the child to come up with some alternatives to hitting, such as using words to express his desire to have a turn. Teachers can model appropriate ways to gain entry into play groups. For example, a teacher may take an excluded child by the hand and model speaking to a group of children in play: "It looks as if you need a horse on your farm. Robert makes good horse noises. How about including him?" Or the teacher may suggest that Robert offer to gather needed play materials for the group. Robert will learn strategies that will enable him to become an accepted play participant.

Teachers can engage children in creating classroom rules or guidelines as daily situations arise that call for agreed-on rules to regulate activity. Children who work collaboratively with teachers to create rules are more likely to understand why rules are necessary and are more likely to follow the rules they create (Castle & Rogers, 1993–1994). Piaget said that autonomy is the ability to create rules. Mutually agreed-on rules indicate group self-regulation. Teachers can reduce their adult authority as much as possible by playing games as an equal game partner with children and by encouraging children to do their own thinking, resolve peer conflicts, and express autonomy in their actions. Teachers can encourage social interaction by providing time in the schedule for play and collaborative projects. For examples of how to promote social interaction see the following Curriculum Strategies. More will be said about this in the following sections of this chapter.

CURRICULUM STRATEGIES: PROMOTING SOCIAL INTERACTION

- Blocks of time for interactions, group meetings, play, and collaborative projects that emphasize respect for others
- Emphasis on sharing and listening to the diversity of viewpoints in the group
- Group discussions of conflicts and moral dilemmas as they arise
- Group shared experiences of memorable and pleasant events
- Creation of classroom rules jointly with children
- Reduction of teacher's adult authority whenever possible, such as in game playing

---

CONSTRUCTIONS

1. Research

Observe children's interactions in a preschool classroom. Look for examples of interactions involving tension and subsequent negotiations of the tensions. Look for examples of interactions not involving tension (shared experiences). Compare the two types of examples in terms of classroom context. What was happening in the classroom when the interactions occurred?

2. Interview

Interview children who are 4, 6, and 8 years old. Ask, "What makes a good friend? What do you like best about your friends?" Compare their responses.

Play Is an Important Part of the Curriculum

The Role of Play in Learning

All early childhood educators agree that play is important to learning, although they may define play in different ways (Bodrova & Leong, 2007; Brown & Patte, 2012; DeVries & Zan, 2012; Fromberg, 2012; Taylor, Branscombe, Burcham, & Land, 2011). Yet a crisis in early childhood education exists today as many schools and programs relegate play to recess time and do not include it in the curriculum. Some schools have eliminated recess altogether and provide no time during the school day for play. In this section, you will learn about these different viewpoints, with an emphasis on a constructivist view of play and ways to promote play among children.

Play Is Important for Children and Adults

When was the last time you played? How would you describe what you did? Was it a solitary activity or fun among friends? Did you learn something new or look at the activity in a new way? Why did you play?

Everyone plays, even adults. People play at hobbies, sports, video games, and with new ideas. Some corporations, such as Microsoft, encourage employees to play by providing time during the workday and facilities for play at the work site. Some corporate executives believe that play rejuvenates the brain and leads to a more focused and creative work environment. This idea is based on research showing that play frees the mind to explore different associations, leading to new connections among ideas (Bruner, 1985; Isenberg & Jalongo, 2006). It has also been shown that play rejuvenates the body, leading to a healthier mind-body connection (American Academy of Pediatrics [AAP], 2011). The architect Frank Lloyd Wright attributed his interest in architecture and his innovative designs to playing with Froebelian materials as a child. Froebel designed many play materials and activities including paper folding, paper pricking, and block play. Wright was given a set of Froebelian blocks as a child, which influenced his designs.

> The smooth shapely maple blocks with which to build, the sense of which never afterward leaves the fingers; so form became feeling. These primary forms were the secret of all effects . . . which were ever got into the architecture of the world. (1943, p. 34)

Play has numerous interpretations. Play has been defined in various ways through history. Maria Montessori (1965), the noted physician, humanitarian, and educator, defined play as children's work. She respected children's play because she felt that through play, children learn about the world and the reality of how things work. Froebel, founder of the kindergarten, viewed play as important not only for what children learn about the world, but also for the spiritual significance of play. Froebel felt that through play, children learn about the unity of God, nature, and humankind. He designed special play materials including small blocks, influenced by his knowledge of the structures of crystals in nature (Brosterman, 1997). Freud felt that play was a means of expressing and releasing emotions and tensions (Monighan-Nourot, 1992). Vygotsky (1976) claimed that play was important for the child's adaptation to the social world. Bruner (1985) showed that children who first interact with materials in free play were better problem solvers in later tasks with the same materials than were children who had not played with the materials. Many child development and early childhood researchers have explored the various aspects of play: stages of play, types of play, and the relationship of play to various areas of the curriculum such as literacy (Bergen, 1987; Garvey, 1977; Kamii & DeVries, 1980; Taylor, Branscombe, Burcham, & Land, 2011; Wasserman, 1992; Wohlwend, 2011). For example, several research studies show the benefits of pretend play, including the strengthening of cognitive capacities, sustained attention, memory, logical reasoning, language and literacy skills, imagination, creativity, and understanding of emotions; and the ability to reflect on one's thinking, inhibit impulses, control one's behavior, and take another person's perspective (Copple & Bredekamp, 2009).

In a study of preservice early childhood education teachers and the meaning of play, Sherwood and Reifel (2010) found that the seven participants did not define play in the same ways. For each participant, play seemed to have an individualized meaning consisting of multiple parts, such as child determined, creative and imaginative, fun, not focused on a specific outcome, physically active, socially interactive, less academic, relaxing, positive, games, swinging, toys, and playground. How does your definition compare to theirs?

A commonly accepted definition of **play** among early childhood educators is activity that is engaged in for sheer enjoyment or pleasure, not aimed at a particular goal and with elements of active engagement, interest, and spontaneity (Fromberg, 2002). Chaille (2008) contends that the elements of interest, experimentation, and cooperation must be present in order for active learning to occur through play. Piaget (1962) defined play as assimilation in which reality is assimilated to the child's schemes or view of the world, as opposed to accommodation or change in schemes to fit the external environment. In other words, children at play explore a variety of relationships without feeling the need to accommodate to any external demands for changing their ideas or behaviors. For example, in play, a log can become a horse on which a child rides to round up imaginary cattle, a block becomes a fire truck used to save a burning house, or children assume roles to act out a family dinner. Play as assimilation means that children can try on a variety of roles, use play materials to represent real-life objects and events, and create outcomes that would not happen in real life, such as building a tower to the moon.

Play has been described developmentally as social participation by Parten (1932), who identified a progression from play that is uninvolved to onlooker play and then to solitary, parallel, associative, and cooperative play. Social interaction plays a major factor in a child's progression through the levels to cooperative play. Vygotskians Leong and Bodrova (2012) described five stages in a child's make-believe play: first scripts; roles in action; roles with rules and beginning scenarios; mature roles, planned scenarios, and symbolic props; and dramatization, multiple themes, multiple roles, and director's play (p. 30).

Piaget (1962) studied children's play and identified four kinds of play based on stages of cognitive development: practice play (functional, exploratory, or sense-pleasure play), symbolic play, games with rules, and construction play. **Practice play,** which begins in infancy and continues throughout life, involves repetition of structures or behaviors the child can do for the pleasure of doing them, such as batting at a toy hanging across a crib. For an adult, it might mean repeatedly throwing a basketball into a hoop. It typically does not involve much learning of anything new, although it may result in improving an existing skill.

Symbolic play begins about the end of the first year or the beginning of the second year of life and is characterized by make-believe and representation of an absent object. Examples of symbolic play would be imitating the actions of an elephant's trunk by swinging one's arm, using a candle to represent a symphony conductor's baton, or assuming the role of an airplane pilot and acting out flying a plane. Piaget thought that pretend play helps children take control of experiences in which they have little control in real life. Symbolic play is evident in groups of preschool children who spontaneously form loose play groups to enact certain themes, rituals, or stories. It is a rich medium for the development of the ability to take another child's perspective because it involves many communications in which children negotiate who will play what role and who will do what. For adults, symbolic play may take the form of simulations, such as race car driving in video games or playing a role in a local theater group.

In **games with rules,** children who play agree that the play will be governed by rules. They also agree on what the consequences of rule infractions will be. This type of play begins when children create rules to govern their play enactments and when they engage in formal games, such as board games. Games with rules involve interest in playing the game, self-initiated competition, and cooperation in order to keep the game going. Interest in games with rules continues into adulthood. A variation on games with rules is child-invented games in which children create their own games and rules for them. Inventing games allows children to express their autonomy in the type of game and rules they create and in their ability to interest and sustain play of their games with others (Castle, 1998, 2012). More will be said about invented games in Chapter 6.

Constructions play begins to emerge with school-age children who desire to make products that represent objects in the real world, such as through constructing a board game, a model airplane, or a model farm. Some view constructions as a midway point between play and work (Chaille & Silvern, 1996). Constructions include elements of playing with materials for the pleasure of the play plus producing a product, which involves goal-directed activity. Constructions are common in adult play and hobbies, for example, in model building, gardening, and crafts.

Play and the Three Types of Knowledge

Children construct knowledge through play. In a single play activity, such as sand play, children may construct three types of knowledge:

1. Physical knowledge is constructed as the child sifts sand through her fingers and notes the graininess of it, a physical property of the sand.
2. Logico-mathematical knowledge is constructed as the child constructs the relationship between dry sand and the sand she mixes with water to make sand pies.
3. Social knowledge is constructed when the child plays with another child to make a structure out of the sand and learns a new term from the other child who talks about "our sandcastle."

All three types of knowledge of sand are constructed through the child's logico-mathematical framework, which connects sand to other concepts, such as that sand is different from water but both can be poured into containers. Play is a complex activity that cannot be easily categorized into one type of knowledge, as the preceding example shows. However, for the sake of describing how play relates to the three types of knowledge, they will be separated in the following descriptions.

Play and Physical Knowledge

Physical knowledge is constructed in play with materials, toys, and other play objects. As children handle, push, pull, throw, aim, and roll objects, they learn about the objects' physical properties, such as a ball is round, will bounce, and will roll when put on a hard surface. Infants and toddlers spend much play time exploring objects and observing their physical properties. They will repeat the same actions numerous times, such as banging a toy on the floor for pleasure while sustaining an interesting event within their control. Constructivists distinguish between object play in which the child is thinking about the objects and her actions on them and play in which the child is manipulating objects without making conceptual relationships. Object play without mental action does not result in knowledge construction.

Play and Logico-Mathematical Knowledge

Play is a rich medium for developing logico-mathematical relationships. For example, through water play, children learn which objects float and sink, which containers hold more than others, and which objects are better than others at transporting water from one place to another. Children engage in experimentation in play by using objects and actions to test their ideas. For example, a child constructing with lock-blocks may wonder whether she can construct a row of blocks that will reach all the way to the art easel. A small group of children may try to figure out how to build a block structure that will hold and provide a frame for a blanket to serve as a circus tent.

Play and Social Knowledge

Social knowledge, or conventional knowledge, including the names for things, is constructed in play with others. When preschool children play store, they learn about the social roles of customer, cashier, and shelf stocker. They may learn the names of store products, such as cornflakes; how prices are scanned from a bar code; or new terms such as *dime, quarter,* and *dollar.* They also learn about the social interactions and rituals involved in shopping.

Kindergarten Play: A Discussion

During center time in Dana Richmond's kindergarten class, 18 children choose from a variety of centers and play materials, including easel painting, games, construction materials, musical instruments, nature study, water table, and dramatic hospital play. During large-group discussion after center time, the children discuss what they did in their play.

Mrs. Richmond:	I saw many interesting things happening at centers today. Is there someone who learned something new you didn't know before?
Jasmine:	Me and Rosa poured water, and I learned that the water goes out faster from the sieve than out of the bucket. It makes lots of streams out the holes.
Sara:	I learned the hermit crab will stick its head out if you blow on it! I blew on it, and Carissa got scared! She wouldn't do it.
Carissa:	I didn't want it to bite me!
Jason:	Molly, Jeff, and me built a landing place for the hospital helicopter to land on. We wanted to make it round. We used blocks, and it took a long time to make it round. We're going to build it better next time.
Mrs. Richmond:	Why was it important that it was round?
Jason:	Because the big blades that spin around make a circle. We had to have a place big enough for the circle it makes.
Amy:	I listened to Caitlin's heart beating through the stethoscope. It went bump *bump*, bump *bump*, bump *bump*.
Caitlin:	Amy's heart sounds like a drum!
Carlos:	I made a collage just like the pictures in our book *Frederick*. Teacher, we need some gray paper. I had to use brown. But it looks okay.
Brandon:	Zac and I took apart the telephone and found where the bell is that rings when someone calls. Teacher, what's the black part called that has the little holes in it?
Mrs. Richmond:	Brandon, that's called a receiver. You hold one end of it to your ear and listen to the person talking to you. Megan, you and Heather and Blane looked as if you were having fun with the drums and tambourines. Were you creating a song?
Megan:	We were playing band. We had to march in a Fourth of July parade.
Heather:	I got to play the drum this time.
Mrs. Richmond:	What did the rest of you do?

Grant: We played Don't Tip the Waiter. The bigger pieces really
                    make the tray spill more than the smaller ones.
Desmond: Me and Aidan played on the white board. We made up a
                    story about three pigs.
Mrs. Richmond: It's amazing how much I learn just by listening to all the
                    things that you have learned at our centers!

Play Issues

There are several issues related to play that affect early childhood education.
We will focus on some of these, such as the difference between work and play,
the inclusion of play in the curriculum, and the decrease in play time available
to children today due to a cultural devaluing of play. All the issues described
here pivot around the perceived value of play to young children's learning.
What's important to keep in mind is that constructivist educators view play as
an important medium for the child's knowledge construction. Through play
children learn self-regulation, oral language, symbolic generalization, school
adjustment, social skills, the ability to delay gratification, cognitive decentering,
metacognition, the development of mental representations, and the ability to
use symbols and engage in abstract thinking (Leong & Bodrova, 2012).

When Does Play Become Work?

Montessori viewed children's play as their work. **Work** is usually thought of as
goal-directed activity that may or may not be pleasant to do. Many teachers
today, concerned about test scores, view work as important and play as a waste
of time, because they perceive that children are not accomplishing set goals in
play. Some teachers allow play only during short recess periods during which
children are allowed to release pent-up energy so that they will be able to con-
centrate on their work better. In general, play is not valued in today's schooling,
where the focus is on prescribed goals and accountability through testing.

Whether an activity is counted as a play activity or as work is really up to
how the child perceives it. Piaget said that the child, not the adult, determines
whether an activity is play or work. Some activities begin as play and develop
into work when a child determines a specific goal, objective, or product to be
accomplished in the activity. Cooney, Gupton, and O'Laughlin (2000) found
that kindergarten and first-grade children perceived some activities as a blending of play and work. Such activities also included elements of shared control
of classroom activities among teachers and children, as well as spontaneity.
They found that a playful disposition helped children imagine alternative possibilities and could be necessary for success in an increasingly unpredictable

world. Ranz-Smith (2012) describes the transition from play to work based on Gardner's (2007) "5 minds" framework that considers play to be undefined and based on child-generated activity and work as defined, primarily by the teacher. When children's activity moves from play to work, it is goal oriented and focused on accomplishing a task. Such a framework that replaces the false dichotomy between play and work can be used to help teachers, administrators, and parents understand that play is important and should be included in the school curriculum. Teachers who strive for a developmentally appropriate program "recognize the importance of both child-guided and adult-guided learning experiences. In supporting children's deep engagement in creative experiences and child-guided activities, teachers find opportunities to enhance children's thinking and learning" (Copple & Bredekamp, 2009, p. 296). Adults in general and especially teachers play an important role in expanding play and facilitating the play interactions of children with their peers (Stanton-Chapman & Hadden, 2011).

Play in the Curriculum

Play serves to integrate curriculum. Early childhood educators have long valued play as an important part of the curriculum. Children themselves do not think of learning as being in separate content areas such as mathematics and science (Fromberg, 2012). In play, children show how content is integrated in their thinking. Play then becomes a natural way to achieve **curriculum integration,** in which areas of the curriculum are connected within a unifying theme or project. For example, children may play at building a city with blocks. This involves figuring out how many blocks are needed for each building (number concepts), which shapes will make the most stable bridge across the river (physics), how to create street signs and billboards (literacy and art), what types of buildings to include, such as a school or office building (social studies), and where the streets will run (mapping/geography).

Block play is one form of play that can be studied for the integration of all curriculum areas into the play, especially spatial relationships and mathematics. Block play contributes to all areas of the curriculum: language arts/literacy, social studies, science, art and expression, mathematics, and physical education (Hirsch, 1996). Unfortunately blocks are not generally seen in programs beyond preschool or kindergarten. Yet blocks have powerful potential to influence children's critical thinking, problem solving, and creativity. For example, in a study of 6- and 7-year-old boys from low socioeconomic status (SES) families, Park, Chae, and Boyd (2008) showed that block play is a way for children to learn mathematical concepts in place of more traditional math lessons, especially because children from low socioeconomic backgrounds have limited access to such materials at home. They said, "Those children's block play at school will not only compensate for the academic disadvantage, but also provide them less stressful learning experiences and more emotional support from adults than would traditional mathematics lessons" (p. 162). Block play benefits all children's learning by providing opportunities for them to construct relationships and patterns that will help them throughout their schooling.

In a study of children age 1 to 3, Miyakawa, Kamii, and Nagahiro (2005) focused on children's logico-mathematical thinking constructed through play with blocks and an incline. They concluded that the development of logico-mathematical knowledge as a network of interrelated mental relationships is a better goal for preschool mathematics education than isolated objectives, such as ability to sort, recognize shapes, and understand words such as "first" and "second" (p. 292). Kamii, Miyakawa, and Kato (2007) studied children from 1 to 4 years old and found the new spatial relationships that children made as they grew older also changed the classificatory, seriational, numerical, and temporal relationships they made.

Saracho (2012) identifies stages of block building and offers suggestions for the block play of children with special needs, including assisting them to the block center, supporting their physical block play, helping them move blocks from one area to another, and modeling block building for them. Block building can provide opportunities for all children to collaborate in constructing block structures and developing social skills.

Block play can also be an opportunity for teachers to encourage cross-gender play groups. While boys tend to spend more time in the block area than girls who spend more time in dramatic play, teachers can incorporate dramatic play props into the block center and can encourage boys and girls to build with blocks together. By age 6 children play with same-sex peers much more than with other-sex peers (Maccoby & Jacklin, 1987; Martin & Fabes, 2001). Children learn gender stereotypes from adults and peers that contribute to gender segregation. Teacher intervention may be necessary to help children break away from gender stereotypes.

Developmentally appropriate classrooms set aside large blocks of time (30–45 minutes) for child-initiated play, including block play, through the primary school level. Children can choose to play at various interest centers, from woodworking, to dramatic play, to art. Through play, children learn to express themselves verbally and symbolically, understand how objects work, and regulate their behavior in relation to the behavior of others. They learn how to express their feelings through art, drama, and storytelling. They learn how to take risks and create something new. In addition, play is one of the most effective means of reducing children's stress and anxiety (Jessee, Wilson, & Morgan, 2000). Schools that value play recognize that academic and socioemotional objectives can be achieved through play.

Research on literacy learning shows that children who are encouraged to play in literacy-rich classroom environments learn to write and read within the meaningful context of play episodes (Ferguson, 1999; Owocki, 1999; Patton & Mercer, 1996; Taylor, Branscombe, Burcham, & Land, 2011; Wohlwend, 2011). Play is important to children's knowledge of narrative, make-believe, and pretend play. Teachers can facilitate children's make-believe play and understanding of story through providing props; encouraging children to make their own props and describe how they are using an object in a pretend way; planning field trips, literature, and videos to expand children's play themes; and helping children plan their play and discuss the roles and themes of their play (Leong & Bodrova, 2012).

Play and literacy activity are similar in that both involve the ability to transform the meanings of objects or actions. Symbolic play helps children learn that symbols can represent events just as black marks on paper represent names, objects, or stories (Owocki, 1999). Print is visible everywhere in literacy-rich classrooms (see Box 5.1). Labels identify centers, areas of the classroom, and objects, such as the classroom clock. Paper and markers are not just located in the art or writing centers but can be found in other areas, such as in the housekeeping and sociodramatic play center. Electronic white boards are accessible for children's literacy activities. Good children's literature is in abundance. Stories dictated or written by children are visibly posted. The teacher encourages children to write their ideas, make lists, produce class newsletters, and communicate with others through written messages. For example, a play center with a restaurant theme may contain menus, posted specials of the day, and pads and pencils for writing orders. Children can make signs naming the restaurant, locating the rest rooms and telephone, and numbering the tables. An airport play center would allow children to write arrival and departure lists, destination names at gates, and tickets. A nature center could include a chart for recording growth of plants and watering times. Children can write the rules for their invented games plus instructions on how to play the game. Teachers can help children extend their ideas in print in meaningful ways reflected in their play themes.

BOX 5.1 CREATING LITERACY-RICH CLASSROOMS

- Label objects such as clock, light switch, bookshelves, blocks, pets, plants, and computers.
- Label centers such as writing, library, art, manipulatives, sociodramatic play, and nature centers.
- Display children's writing, stories, lists, and group stories or dictations.

- Provide a variety of good children's books in all centers where appropriate.
- Provide a variety of writing materials, paper, pads, journals, markers, and pencils in as many centers as appropriate.
- Encourage children to write their ideas in journals, stories, lists, plans, letters, and games; on the classroom electronic white board; and in class newsletters.

Play and Children With Special Needs

All children have a right to play. It is important for early childhood teachers to help overcome an adult attitude that children with disabilities are incapable of play. When adults do not allow or facilitate the play of children with disabilities, their development suffers. Play helps children with disabilities construct knowledge, master motor skills, and develop social skills important to interacting with others. Teachers can consider not only the type of disability a child has but also the child's interests in making modifications to facilitate play.

Kangas, Maatta, and Uusiautti (2012) studied the play of autistic children. Group play tends to be difficult for many autistic children due to lack of social skills. Autistic children tend to engage in more sensory motor play but not much symbolic play. They need adult help and tend to benefit from more structured play activity, such as having play scripted for them. Other suggestions include using stories to initiate play, using electronic games, and encouraging the imitation of the play behaviors of others. Autistic children may need extra help in establishing and maintaining relationships and interactions with peers.

Children with physical difficulties benefit from inclusive playgrounds that have been modified to facilitate their movement and use of play equipment. For example, wide pathways and ramps for wheeled vehicles, accessible routes, and decks and stationary bridges that give access to elevated play equipment help provide the same types of play experiences as for children with no disabilities (Frost, Wortham, & Reifel, 2012). Children with emotional difficulties benefit from having opportunities to act out emotional experiences through play with caring adults. Play therapy has greatly benefited children suffering from abuse and trauma.

Play, a Four-Letter Word

DeVries, Zan, Hildebrandt, Edmiaston, and Sales (2002) describe a political issue involving play-oriented curriculum. Many traditional educators view play as aimless activity and do not include it in the curriculum. Some educators view play as a time of unstructured activity in which teachers do not intervene. Other educators may give lip service to the value of play in curriculum, while disguising didactic activities as "play." DeVries et al. call for a constructivist approach in which play is integrated with social, emotional, moral, and intellectual goals and not relegated to the periphery of the curriculum. They say that teachers can support play by interacting with children in ways that expand their thinking. A well-placed question at just the right time may engage children in constructing relationships that they hadn't thought of before.

Play has become a four-letter word to some educators who view it as a waste of time. Unfortunately, some educators are too quick to ban play and move into drill on isolated literacy skills such as phonics. The work ethic has always played an important role in American society and in American schools. Children in classrooms are often admonished to stop playing around and get back to work. Traditional educators may associate play with worthless activity that interferes with children getting their work done. This attitude toward play results in the reduction of play at school and even at home. Wohlwend (2011) says it is time for play to be redefined as a new twenty-first century literacy that can help improve new technologies, invent new uses for materials, and imagine new possibilities.

In a study of parents' perceptions of their children's learning through play, Bongiorno (2012) found parents' perceptions of children's learning through play fell into the categories of cognitive, social and emotional, language and literacy, and physical learning. She calls for parent-education programs to increase engagement of parents in their children's play, more time for play at home, and advocacy for play becoming an integral part of the curriculum at school.

Play is disappearing from some schools. Work in schools is activity that teachers perceive to be under their control, while play is activity initiated by children who don't have enough work to do (Fromberg, 1990). In most public schools, children are grudgingly given small amounts of recess time (10–20 minutes) if any at all during which they can play with minimal adult supervision. The word *recess* implies a break from the important activity of the day: work. Teachers give children control over free play at recess because they do not value it. In order to improve test scores and increase time spent on academic content instruction, many schools have decreased recess time, and some have banished it entirely. Children today have less play time than they did 20 years ago, and children in the United States have significantly less than those in many other countries, including Japan (Alexander, 1999). Lack of play time and increasing engagement in sedentary media activities such as video games contribute to the current health problem of childhood obesity.

Play Advocates and Guidelines

All early childhood professional associations, including the National Association for the Education of Young Children (NAEYC), and other professional associations, such as the International Play Association (IPA) and the American Academy of Pediatrics (AAP) advocate for play in early childhood programs and for at least one hour each day of physical activity. The United Nations Convention of the Rights of the Child includes the right to play (Stroud, 1993). The NAEYC declared that play is an important vehicle for children's development and must be incorporated into all accredited early childhood programs (Copple & Bredekamp, 2009).

The IPA and the Association for Childhood Education International (ACEI) have produced position papers on the importance of play. ACEI believes that play will become increasingly more important to children as they experience increased pressure to succeed in all areas of life. ACEI guidelines for play in early childhood programs include providing appropriate, safe, and inviting environments, including planned outdoor play environments, and carefully planned curricula, including play activities (Isenberg & Quisenberry, 1988). Almy (1984) says that play is as essential to the child's development as adequate food and rest. She says that play is valuable because through play, children's interests are self-directed and free from external rules, except for the ones they impose on themselves, and are concerned with experimenting with possibilities.

Teachers and parents have an important role in supporting children's play activities. Adults can support play by playing with children, providing large blocks of uninterrupted time for play, providing a variety of play materials, planning play with other children, and respecting children's play for the important role it has in learning. The following curriculum strategies provide more guidelines for supporting play.

CURRICULUM STRATEGIES: SUPPORTING PLAY

- Provide large blocks of time for child-initiated play.
- Encourage children to play with ideas and to develop a playful disposition.
- Plan activities that call for creativity and inventiveness.
- Provide a large variety of play materials and spaces for play to occur.
- Play with children and model how to enter an existing play group.
- Encourage children to plan what they will play.
- Provide follow-up discussions after play focusing on what children did and why.

CONSTRUCTIONS

1. Research

Observe kindergarten-age children at play. Look for examples of practice play, symbolic play, games with rules, and constructions in play.

2. Interview

Interview three first-grade teachers at different schools, asking them about the amount of play (recess) time, indoors and outdoors, children have during each day at school. Compare their responses.

Projects

Projects are sustained, in-depth activities initiated by children or children and teachers together for the purpose of studying a topic in depth to increase understanding and appreciation. Children may express an interest in bubbles; with their teacher's help, they may engage in a project to learn about bubbles—how they form and why they don't last very long. A bubble project can lead to experimenting to determine which substances make the longest-lasting bubbles, how to form bubbles around objects, and how to make bubble art. One child may learn about the role of bubbles in carbonated drinks, while another child tries to build bubble structures on a table top. All the children may help in making a giant bubble in the middle of their classroom. The project ends when children lose interest and stop generating questions to explore.

The use of projects in curriculum can be traced back to John Dewey and his idea of learning through experiences. Early childhood educators have always advocated the use of projects as a meaningful part of curriculum (Copple & Bredekamp, 2009). Project work has been acclaimed in the Reggio Emilia schools in Italy, where children may be actively involved in the same project for several months. Reggio teachers encourage children to use a variety of media, paint, constructions, and drama to express their project work. Edwards, Gandini, and Forman (1993/1998) describe project work as children's use of a hundred languages to represent their perceptions in words, drawings, sculpture, sound, drama, and movement. One example they give of how curriculum is integrated in project work is the construction of an amusement park for birds that took several months and was shared with parents and the community.

Project work may be similar to what some refer to as themes or units, although themes and units are often more teacher directed, while projects are more child directed (Katz & Chard, 2000). Projects are opportunities for children to raise their own questions to learn more about a topic. Project work provides opportunities for children to explore their own interests, take initiative, make choices, and assume responsibility for their learning with their teacher as a facilitator of their work. The teacher may plan activities, field trips, speakers, and special events, and gather appropriate materials for project work.

Project Work From a Constructivist Perspective

Project work in a constructivist classroom may not look much different from project work in a traditional classroom. What distinguishes constructivist project work are the goals that constructivist teachers hold for education and the attention given to constructivist principles. For example, constructivist project work would emphasize child interest, experimentation, and cooperation (DeVries & Zan, 2012). Interest can free up or stop a child's engagement in project work. For example, one child may spend much time drawing maps of the slaves' escape routes through the Underground Railroad, while another child, who has little interest in mapping, writes stories from a slave's perspective. Teachers who understand what interests children will be able to facilitate their projects. Teachers can also share their own interests with children, who may then become interested in a topic they hadn't before thought about. For example, a teacher may encourage interest in mapping by sharing how the American slaves sewed symbols in quilts to show the way to freedom.

Children experiment by acting on objects and observing what happens. Experimentation involves errors. Constructivist teachers encourage children's experimentation and appreciate the value of learning from errors. Constructivist teachers cooperate with children by engaging them in making choices, sharing their interests, and experimenting with them. Through cooperation with others, children develop reciprocity—how to give and take with others in ways that maintain the relationship and facilitate the activity. Chapter 6 will revisit experimentation and learning from errors.

In choosing projects, child interest plays an important role. However, not all project themes may be appropriate. Projects should have intellectual integrity and educational worth (see the following curriculum strategies related to projects).

CURRICULUM STRATEGIES: PROJECTS

- Encourage child-initiated interests, topics, and questions. Brainstorm possible topics, and guide the selection.

- Provide a variety of ways a child can choose to express understanding, for example, through writing, drawing, storytelling, and drama.
- Encourage experimentation and problem solving, including making errors and learning from them—for example, predicting, estimating, hypothesizing, and reflecting.
- Facilitate cooperation with others in shared experiences as well as engagement in individual activity: small group, large group, paired, and individual project work.
- Help children make relationships and connections to how things work. Point out how results from one child's work connect to the work of others (e.g., maps show the route similar to the ways that stories describe the route).

Teachers must decide whether certain topics, such as "bears," will sustain learning that is significant and has value. Some topics, such as "carnivals," may be fun but may not provoke thought or much learning. The teacher's role is to guide the choice of project topics into areas rich for learning that will sustain children's in-depth inquiry, such as a project on the human body.

Examples of Projects

Infant-toddler programs should focus on simple themes, such as movement, transporting objects, stacking objects, causing an effect on an object, and creating sounds. One example focused on movement would be a project about balls since balls move in interesting ways when touched or thrown, and balls come in a variety of shapes and sizes, leading to surprise in how they respond when dropped and to problem solving. A project on balls might engage infants and toddlers in play with a variety of balls. Young children would learn that balls come in different sizes, weights, and colors; some have designs, some have solid colors, some are transparent, and some have inner lights and sounds that make interesting effects when thrown, bounced, or manipulated. Teachers could provide a variety of balls: inflated, plastic, cloth, wooden, and paper. Some balls bounce; others do unexpected things when dropped, such as bounce sideways or make interesting sounds (chimes, squeaks, rings). Children experiment to learn how their actions affect the balls (cause-effect relationships).

Teachers could use giant balls to help children explore body movements such as rolling around on the top of a giant ball. Teachers and children could play games of rolling, throwing, and catching balls. Older toddlers may experiment with aiming balls at blocks or rolling them down roller boards and ramps.

Teachers can read books about balls and sing simple ball songs with children, such as "Roll the Ball." Teachers can use descriptive words such as *round, large, small, soft, hard, striped, red, blue,* and *bouncy.* A project on balls would encourage the construction of physical knowledge.

A preschool project might focus on trash as a result of children's interest in watching the garbage truck empty a dumpster. Children may decide to recycle reusable trash into projects, such as building with cardboard containers that are empty of paper, food, or appliances. Children may recycle paper to use in writing or drawing. Some children may want to know what happens to trash after it is picked up. This curiosity may lead to a field trip to a recycling center or dump. Some children may wonder how much trash each child or the center produces in a day. Others may become interested in decomposition. These interests can lead children to experiment, interview, ask more questions, and share what they learn about trash. This project would focus on construction of logico-mathematical, physical, and social knowledge.

The beginning of kindergarten may prompt a project on the school. Children may take a tour of the school, visiting the library, cafeteria, gym, office, and playground. Some children may want to learn more about the cafeteria. They may interview cafeteria workers, take inventory of the kitchen, or create their own cafeteria in the sociodramatic play center. Some may want to learn more about the people who work at the school. They may visit the principal, janitor, and resource teachers to find out what they do. Others may be interested in the school building. They may make drawings or maps of the building. Children's interests may take them in a variety of directions. The teacher may suggest that they pool their results in a book about the school that they can share with their families. This project would help familiarize children with the new setting and increase their knowledge of and comfort with this new place.

A first-grade project might be on inventing games (see Box 5.2). The teacher could provide a variety of games, such as board games, dice, cards, and group games, plus time for playing games. Children could brainstorm various types of games, including games from other cultures. The teacher, the children, and their families could save clean discarded materials to be used in making games, such as cardboard containers, egg cartons, meat trays, bottle lids, plastic toys or pieces from discarded games, balls, paper, and tape.

The teacher could encourage children to plan a game by drawing it on a large piece of paper and creating written rules for the game. Children could then construct their games and present them to the class during author's chair time. They could play each others' games and give feedback. Game inventors could then modify their games based on feedback from others. The teacher could invite a younger or older class in to play the games or have a game night for families. An invented games project would encourage construction of logico-mathematical, physical, and social knowledge (see Box 5.2).

BOX 5.2 INVENTED GAMES PROJECT

Reasons to Encourage Children to Invent Games

- Encourages child choice, decision making, problem solving, and self-regulation
- Supports inventiveness, creativity, imagination, design, and implementation of child's own plan for a game that others would find interesting
- Integrates all areas of curriculum: literacy, mathematics, science, social studies, expressive arts
- Helps children learn to make good rules for themselves and others in regulating behavior
- Helps children learn to take the point of view of others, to compromise and negotiate conflict in constructive ways
- Helps children learn why rules are meaningful within the social context of game playing
- Promotes physical object activity, such as throwing, aiming, pushing, pulling, and rolling

Invented Games Project Activities

- Playing games in indoor and outdoor group games
- Discussing rules and why they help us
- Inventing games in small groups, pairs, or individually
- Constructing games and teaching them to others
- Modifying games to make them better (similar to editing a story)

Invented Games Project Investigations

- Comparing games from different cultures and eras
- Categorizing games by type: board, card, dice, physical skill, chance, strategy
- Predicting results of using various strategies in playing games
- Trying out different ways of keeping score
- Investigating class members' preferences for different games

---

Culminating Activity: Game Fair/Family Night

- Invent games in small groups. Invite another class in to play the games. Invite families to game night.

Children's Reflections on Invented Games Project

- Discuss what children have learned from this project.

Children's Comments on Inventing Games

"I learned how to make them. When I get bored, I play with them."

"It's fun to make them, and you get to talk a lot."

"I like them because you can help your friends, and they're fun when you're finished."

"I learned how to make them. It's a way to improve yourself by making the game. It's like your first masterpiece."

Second-Grade Project: The Human Body

Nancy Simpson's second-grade class in Stillwater, Oklahoma, became interested in the human body when one of the children had to spend time in the hospital for corrective foot surgery. During a group discussion, the children showed a strong interest in the surgery and in what happens to the human body to make surgery necessary. As a group, they decided to do a project on the human body. They had many questions to pursue—for example, What are the parts of the body? How do the parts work together? How can we keep the body healthy?

Mrs. Simpson brought a variety of materials to the classroom for the children to explore, including books; diagrams; three-dimensional models; microscopes; plastic body parts; a human skeleton; X-rays; and actual animal organs, such as eyeballs, a liver, and a heart from a cow. A medical doctor, the father of one of the children, was a guest speaker. He planned on a 15-minute presentation but found the children had so many questions that he stayed for an hour and promised to return at a later date to see the children's project work.

The children took a field trip to the hospital, where they toured the building and participated in the orientation given to child patients. They went to the hospital cafeteria and learned about nutrition in planning patients' meals. An orthopedic intern talked to them about preventing bone injuries.

Within a week of beginning the project, the classroom was decorated with a body drawing of each child with organ systems drawn and labeled. The children researched the circulatory system on the Internet. They made models of organs out of clay. They made body-part trading cards with pictures of the parts drawn on one side and descriptions of their functions on the reverse side. The cards were popular and were traded frequently. The cards helped the children learn the individual functions of the body parts. The body drawings helped them learn how the parts worked together.

The children wrote stories about their bodies and drew detailed diagrams of various body systems. When the doctor returned to the class, he couldn't believe how much the children had learned. The project continued for 2 months until the children's interest began to decline. Before they were done, they had mapped all body systems; had created books on nutrition, body building, and protective clothing; and had written a fictional book about an invisible body. They shared their knowledge with the kindergarten class and helped those children draw and cut out their own body shapes. They also presented a skit on Mr. Bones and how to keep bones strong. They invented games, including a body trivia game. They also grew bacteria cultures from their own mouth and nose swabs. They observed the growth of the cultures and discussed the importance of mouth and nose care.

The children expressed their learning through discussing the topic, asking questions, observing, writing, drawing, researching, analyzing, and reflecting on what they had learned. At the end of the project, Nancy Simpson (1994) commented,

> We were having a great time, but were the kids really learning? I wondered. (Why do we doubt ourselves? I knew they were learning, but what if someone didn't believe me?) So I made a fourteen page booklet for each child.
>
> On each page was an incomplete sentence and plenty of room for words and an illustration: My Body, My Heart . . . I gave the children large blocks of time to work on their My Body books. The results surpassed my expectations. When I looked at the final chapters in our second grade science textbook, they paled by comparison. I could not find a single worksheet or idea that seemed appropriate to use. Thank goodness I did not limit this group of learners to information in the textbook. (p. 26)

CONSTRUCTIONS

Analysis

Analyze the project work in the second-grade example just described. Look for examples of the three types of knowledge (physical, social, and logico-mathematical) in the children's activities. Draw some conclusions about their construction of knowledge about the human body.

SUMMARY

- Social interaction, play, and projects are important to children's learning.
- Social interaction is important to the development of perspective taking, reciprocity, and friendship.
- Children construct all three types of knowledge (physical, logico-mathematical, and social) through play.
- Play issues center around the perceived value of play to learning.
- Projects give children opportunities to learn within the context of a topic about which children have questions they want to explore.
- Teachers can promote social interaction, play, and projects by giving choices, encouraging interests, providing a wide range of materials and experiences, and asking questions that prompt children to think about what they want to know more about.

CONSTRUCTIONS

1. ANALYSIS

Observe social interaction in a group of kindergarten children. Use Selman and Schultz's levels of interpersonal understanding to analyze children's interactions. What do you conclude about the group you have observed?

2. RESEARCH

Observe a preschool group of children at play. Follow three children and record the frequency of their interactions with peers. Include the gender of those peers with whom they interact. Code each interaction in terms of negotiated interaction or shared experience. What do you conclude from this research?

3. RESEARCH

Plan a play day for a group of young children and their families. Include these topics in your written plan:

- Purpose of the play day
- Setting, equipment, and facilities
- Types of play activities
- Schedule of activities
- Assessment of the play day

4. ADVOCACY

Develop a position paper on the importance of play to share with parents, teachers, and administrators.

5. RESEARCH

Surf the Internet looking for sites that would help primary teachers find resource materials for classroom projects.

Resources

Books

DeVries, R., & Zan, B. (2012). *Moral classrooms, moral children: Creating a constructivist atmosphere in early education* (2nd ed.) New York, NY: Teachers College Press.

DeVries and Zan provide a rationale, based on Piaget's work and their own research, for creating a sociomoral classroom atmosphere. They offer practical ideas for creating classroom community with children that enhances their sociomoral development.

Edwards, C., Gandini, L., & Forman, G. (Eds.). (1993/1998). *The hundred languages of children: The Reggio Emilia approach to early childhood education in Reggio Emilia, Italy.* Norwood, NJ: Ablex.

This book describes the Reggio Emilia approach, which could be considered a model for students and teachers who want to use close observation and documentation of young children.

Gallas, K. (1994). *The language of learning: How children talk, write, dance, draw, and sing their understanding of the world.* New York, NY: Teachers College Press.

This book provides many practical ideas on how teachers can enable children to communicate their knowledge of the world, not just through writing, but through all the arts. The author addresses the importance of creating classroom community.

Guddemi, M., & Jambor, T. (1993). A right to play. In *Proceedings of the American Affiliate of the International Association for the Child's Right to Play,* September 17–20, 1992, Denton, TX. Little Rock, AR: Southern Early Childhood Association.

This book includes chapters by multiple authors documenting the importance of play to children's health and development. The book gives suggestions for how teachers can support children's play.

Helm, J. H., & Beneke, S. (2003). *The power of projects.* New York, NY: Teachers College Press and Washington, DC: National Association for the Education of Young Children.

This book provides a rationale for using projects in the curriculum with many examples of projects.

Helm, J. H., & Katz, L. (2010). *Young investigators, the project approach in the early years* (2nd ed.). New York, NY: Teachers College Press and Washington, DC: National Association for the Education of Young Children.

The authors in this book provide a rationale for using the Project Approach with young children. They offer suggestions for implementing a project approach and provide many examples of projects, including projects on nature, using cameras, and the fire hydrant.

Johnson, J. E., Christie, J. F., & Yawkey, T. D. (1999). *Play and early childhood development* (2nd ed.). New York, NY: Longman.

The authors emphasize the importance of play to child development and draw from research literature on play to support their rationale.

Kamii, C., & DeVries, R. (1980). *Group games in early childhood education: Implications of Piaget's theory.* Washington, DC: National Association for the Education of Young Children.

This book defines physical knowledge and gives suggestions for facilitating the construction of physical knowledge through group games. It is full of examples of games teachers can do in classrooms.

Katz, L. G., & Chard, S. C. (2000). *Engaging children's minds: The project approach* (2nd ed.). Norwood, NJ: Ablex.

Katz and Chard define the project approach and give many suggestions and guidelines for engaging children in in-depth project work. The book provides numerous examples of real projects.

Owocki, G. (1999). *Literacy through play.* Portsmouth, NH: Heinemann.

The author describes what is meant by a literacy-rich environment and gives suggestions for creating such a classroom environment in which children come to literacy through play. She discusses a rationale for literacy through play, as well as ideas for assessing children's literacy as they play.

Piaget, J. (1932/1965). *The moral judgment of the child.* New York, NY: Free Press.

In this book, Piaget reports on his research on children's moral reasoning. He describes two types of morality and the stages through which children progress from heteronomy to autonomy.

Roskos, K., & Christie, J. (2000). *Play and literacy in early childhood: Research from multiple perspectives.* Mahwah, NJ: Erlbaum.

The book offers research on play and literacy supporting the importance of play in the literacy curriculum.

Shores, E. (1992). *Explorer's classrooms: Good practice for kindergarten and primary grades*. Little Rock, AR: Southern Early Childhood Association.

This book offers numerous practical examples of developmentally appropriate practices. The author addresses the necessity of play in early childhood education.

Vygotsky, L. S. (1930–1935; 1978). *Mind in society: The development of* higher *mental processes*. V. John-Steiner, S. Scribner, & E. Souberman (Eds. & Trans.). Cambridge, MA: Harvard University Press.

This book describes Vygotsky's ideas about child development, including the importance of play.

Wasserman, S. (2000). *Serious players in the primary classroom* (2nd ed.). New York, NY: Teachers College Press.

This book provides a theoretical rationale for play in the curriculum. The author describes an approach to promoting children's active learning through play.

Wien, C. A. (Ed.). (2008). *Emergent curriculum in the primary classroom: Iinterpreting the Reggio Emilia approach in schools*. New York, NY: Teachers College Press and Washington, DC: National Association for the Education of Young Children.

This book gives many examples of an emergent curriculum incorporating children's projects and what they learn from them.

Web Sites

Alliance for Childhood http://www.allianceforchildhood.org
American Association for Childhood Education International (ACEI) http://www.ACEI.org Position paper on the essentials of play
Association for the Study of Play http://www.tasplay.org
Clearinghouse on Elementary and Early Childhood Education (ERIC/EECE) www.ericeece.org and ceep.crc.uiuc.edu/eecearchive/index.html (archives)

This site offers a vast amount of professional literature on early childhood education, including research reports on social interaction, play, and projects.

Convention on the Rights of the Child http://www.unicef.org/rightsite
Eleanor Duckworth's Critical Explorers http://www.criticalexplorers.org
International Play Association (IPA) http://www.ipaworld.org
Kaboom! Nonprofit for creating play spaces http://www.kaboom.org

National Association for the Education of Young Children (NAEYC) www.naeyc.org/naeyc

This site is full of information, resources, and professional literature on early childhood education. Various position papers on topics such as play are available at this site.

USA Affiliate of the International Play Association http://www.ipausa.org
The Playful Brain http://www.theplayfulbrain.com

Important Documents on Play

Almon, J., & Miller, E. (2011). *The crisis in early education: A research-based case for more play and less pressure.* Alliance for Childhood, www.allianceforchildhood.org
Hirsh-Pasek, K., Golinkoff, R. M., Berk, L. & Singer, D. (2009). *A mandate for playful learning in preschool: Presenting the evidence.* New York: Oxford University Press.

Research on how play meets curriculum goals.

American Academy of Pediatrics [AAP]. (2001). *The importance of play to promoting healthy child development and maintaining strong parent-child bonds* [Clinical Report]. www.pediatrics.org
Isenberg, J. P., & Quisenberry, N. (2003). *Play, essential for all children: A position paper of the Association for Childhood Education International.* http://www.acei.org

Project Approach

The Project Approach http://www.projectapproach.org/project_approach.php

This site provides many examples of real project work in early childhood classrooms.

6

PROBLEM POSING, PROBLEM SOLVING, AND REFLECTION

This chapter is designed to expand on problem posing, problem solving, and reflection as aspects of inquiry and experimentation related to children's interests and ideas. In addition, it is intended to guide you as you learn more about your role as a developer of constructivist curriculum.

After reading this chapter, you will have a beginning understanding of

- the roles of interest, awareness, and disequilibration in learning and teaching;
- the importance of children's problem posing and solving;
- the recognition and use of child-generated problems;
- the role of the teacher in problem posing and solving;
- the role of reflection for both children and teachers; and
- the importance of respecting the thinking of children.

Introduction

Let's rejoin our teachers as they begin to grapple with these important aspects of the implementation of curriculum.

Jennifer: I want to be the discussion leader today because finally we're getting to something in curriculum that makes sense for my third graders. At least problem solving is part of the state content standards in math and science. I mean, play is fine for younger children, but this is more like real school—you know, *academics*.

Matt: Okay, Jennifer. I'd like to start out by saying that I still don't agree with the way you are thinking about play. Older children benefit by play too. But here's another issue to untangle: I think that in constructivist classrooms, problem solving is more than just part of the math and science content, if that's what you mean by academics. I believe it's much broader in its importance for curriculum and learning. What do some of the rest of you think?

Parul: I think problem solving is important for my babies too, but it's on a different level, so I'm not sure it applies in the way you mean, Jennifer. They certainly aren't solving math problems yet.

Sheila: Oh, gosh. Do you mean my Head Start kids need to be solving math problems to be ready for kindergarten? They're really smart, but they don't all recognize the numbers or how many each number really means yet.

Kenisha: Here's how I'm thinking about it. I think Matt is right—when constructivists focus on problem solving with children, it's more than content based, and it is not related to any algorithm in math! So Parul and Sheila, hold on, and see if this makes sense. From our reading, we know that constructivists believe we should use authentic problems and the interests of children to lead in to projects and investigations. Questions the kids have, whether they ask them or not, can be viewed as problems. You start where they are.

Jennifer: Well, it's a "problem" in my class if the kids get low scores on math questions, but I'm curious about where you are going with this. Do you mean that the *kids* set the entire curriculum? How can we keep our jobs and have kids score well on tests if we don't set the problems and teach them the right answers? Ron, you must feel the pressure: Your children are in first grade, where they have to start understanding all the content on tests. Where are you on this?

Ron: Boy, I'm confused. I do know I have to teach the children certain core content this year. How can I be sure they get it if I just follow their interests to set the curriculum in my room? But I remember that last year when I was student teaching, we used a lot of Kamii's ideas for everyday problems for math—you know, things that made a difference to the kids, like dividing lock-blocks fairly, so they were really interested in finding out the answer. I hate to be wishy-washy, but I need to know—now—how I ought to be approaching curriculum. How can I get all of this constructivist stuff to fit with the school requirements for content, which seem to increase every year? The core curriculum we've been mandated to include doesn't seem like it can be taught in any way but directly!

Like Ron, you may have questions about how constructivists can match the way children learn with school- and state-mandated content knowledge. We will explore this topic together in this chapter as it relates to science and in other chapters as well. Let's start with some other information about important aspects of children's learning, which shows why constructivists work with children as they do.

Awareness, Disequilibration, and Learning

As we mentioned in earlier chapters, Piaget felt that interest is the fuel that drives learning. He said, "A person won't ever solve a problem if the problem doesn't interest him. The impetus for everything lies in interest, affective motivation" (quoted in Bringuier, 1980, p. 50). So the question we must answer is, how can interest enhance classroom learning? To answer this question, let's look more closely at some of the cognitive processes involved in developing an interest.

The first step in the development of knowledge is that the activity or topic is something the child is aware of and motivated to understand better. Children are increasingly characterized as natural scientists because of their curiosity (Gopnik, 2012), but they are sometimes unaware of problems that are beyond their levels of understanding or outside of their experiences. When children have no experience with a particular topic or question, they do not yet have a conscious awareness of the possibilities for interesting involvement. This can be the case with curriculum that is preset by educators or curriculum developers, who focus on content without considering how children construct knowledge or the knowledge of the individual children involved. An example of this occurred in a public school kindergarten located on an O'odham Tash-Salt River reservation in central Arizona.

A school committee mandated the use of a social studies workbook in all the kindergarten classrooms. In part, the workbook was chosen because of a unit on Native Americans. Strangely, pictures in the workbook depicted Native Americans as people who dressed in feathered headdresses and lived in teepees. The native children in this area did not identify with the people in those pictures because they do not wear that kind of headdress in their tribal celebrations, and their tribes' traditional homes are not teepees. In fact, most of the children live in mobile homes separated from one another by large tracts of desert.

This section of the workbook was taught right before an event called "Indian Day." The children were initially excited to have "Indians" come to the schoolwide celebration. However, when the day arrived, the "Indians" were local performers, dressed in their own tribal costumes, and were the children's own families and neighbors. The "Indians" they expected were not in attendance, and they did not understand themselves to be "Indians."

This example points out a lack of awareness on at least two levels: adults, who are unaware of how young children think, and children, who are unaware of meanings and content that adults assumed they had integrated into their understanding. If curriculum developers and other adults decide that content is of interest or important to children but it is not, children cannot think about the information in the way adults assume they will.

This example underscores the importance of teachers knowing how a child thinks about events, information, and activities in his or her everyday world, what is of importance for the child to know, and what problems are interesting to a child at a particular time. It is this focus on the thinking of learners rather than on content that differentiates a constructivist approach from traditional teaching. In fact, curriculum cannot be considered to follow a constructivist approach when the focus is on content rather than on the child's thinking.

Recent research points to striking similarities between how children and scientists learn. Children have been found to use data to formulate and test theories and hypotheses, and they learn from the data and ideas of one another (Gopnik & Tenenbaum, 2007; Gopnik, 2012). Constructivist teachers endeavor to follow the motivational lead of children's interests and to capitalize on these natural learning activities. Once a child expresses an interest, that often brings into play a strong internal desire to investigate, find solutions to the problem, or understand better. In this process, children encounter many more questions that engage their curiosity and drive to explore in order to understand.

This process takes time, but must be respected and encouraged. As was discussed in Chapter 3, children enjoy doing things over and over again. Although adults frequently want to hurry them and direct their attention to "content," there are solid reasons for encouraging children to repeat and elaborate activities until they are ready to shift activities. Why is this so? Piaget says that the individual's cognitive growth often remains unconscious until after problem solving or resolution of a perturbation occurs (Bringuier, 1980). Think back to the example of Jaime and the different kinds of juice in Chapter 1. As she developed a broader category for juice, she enhanced her understanding of the concept "juice." It didn't happen with the first encounter but instead emerged with repeated exposure to juices of other types. At points of disequilibration, new understandings began to be integrated into her earlier concept of juice. When there was a transformation—a shift toward better understanding—cognitive progression occurred.

It is important to understand that no one can give this understanding to the child, nor can anyone demand that the child think. Teachers can provide opportunities for children to encounter experiences that may help them develop awareness of interesting questions, but the process of disequilibration occurs only when the child recognizes an inherent contradiction and begins to make a shift in thinking as a result. In summary, the first step in the development of knowledge is to provoke the child's attention. Children's curiosity makes them natural scientists, but only if the topic to be studied is something that interests them.

Constructivist teachers have an important role to play: They must provide children with questions, activities, and different points of view that, in one teacher's words, "complicate the children's thinking," or encourage disequilibration. This teacher-generated problem posing is a critical feature of child-teacher interaction. This strategy has been termed **critical exploration** and is intended to encourage disequilibrium:

> Such a method is adapted to educational purposes by questioning children about how they would approach a problem and how they arrived at their answers. The teacher presents children with further problems, based on those the children have already solved (or not solved), to see what rules or generalizations the children have formed. Often the children are given a second problem, especially in mathematics that, if solved by the procedure used to solve the first problem, would lead to an incorrect answer. Thus by setting up a conflict situation, the teacher notes whether the disturbance causes an adjustment and consequent avoidance of future errors (Gallagher & Reid, 1981, p. 150).

Some examples of questions that can promote critical exploration are provided in Chapter 2. Another example of this kind of question occurred as part of research on identity constancy of young children. This study extended the work done by DeVries on animal identity (1969) that involved changing the identity of Maynard the cat by using a mask of a dog. This study investigated young children's beliefs about the identity constancy of humans. In this later study, Santa Claus was the subject of identity constancy research (Lieberman, 1977).

With parental permission, preschool-aged children were asked to view a videotape of a familiar adult as she dressed up in a Santa costume. Before the costume was donned, the children had to recognize and name the adult. (If they could not, they were not included in the study.) Once the child could identify the woman as Miss Pat (one of the teachers in their classroom), the child watched the video, which showed the teacher putting on various items of the Santa Claus costume. Periodically, the video was paused, and the child was asked, "Who is this person now? Is it Miss Pat or is it Santa Claus?" Typically, after the beard, hat, and boots were in place, children responded that she had become Santa. The complicating question was then posed to the child: "What happened to Miss Pat?" There were three types of responses. For some children (response 1), the visual transformation overcame the logic; Miss Pat "disappeared like magic," and the identity discrepancy went unnoticed. She simply no longer existed. For others (response 2), the complicating question created apparent disequilibration, and children struggled to reconcile the conflicting information. Others (response 3) clearly knew that Miss Pat was only dressed up and remained the same person they had recognized earlier.

It is important to note the different responses. Children whose logic was derailed by a visual change of appearance (response 1) were certain but illogical in comparison to adult logic. Children who were uncertain (response 2) were beginning to be aware of conflicting information. For example, a child might reason that "Miss Pat 'became' Santa, yet she looks like my teacher. Who is this really?" In the case of the third response, the child has resolved the conflict, and, despite the perceptual change, the child knows "Santa" is still Miss Pat. Constancy of identity has been achieved. The key is to understand the importance of posing the right question to the right child to encourage disequilibration.

It is this type of question that constructivist teachers pose to children in order to provoke their thinking. As a result of the teacher's question or another child's opinion or idea, the child may be provoked to reconsider his thinking. Children may also realize inadequacies in their own thinking unprompted. However it occurs, the process of disequilibration is of critical importance in constructing knowledge.

As the examples illustrate, awareness and disequilibration are important to both children and teachers: They are crucial elements of internal meaning making. Basing curriculum plans and interaction with learners on awareness and disequilibration is difficult because these processes are not visible. Doing so demands that teachers listen carefully to the conversation and the thinking of children and comprehend how children understand a topic at that time. Taking these and other dynamic processes into account sets constructivist teachers apart from others because their interactions in classrooms are based on the science of how children learn rather than on content or the traditional culture of teaching as telling. Let's return now to the question of the distinction between problem posing and problem solving.

CONSTRUCTIONS

1. Journal Entry

Visit a group of children and ask them to explain something to you. If possible, tape-record the conversation. Listen carefully for the logic that individual children use in their explanations. See if you can detect how each one has come to the understanding that is shared. In your journal, jot down your ideas to share with a peer.

2. Analysis

Play the recording for your peer, and together discuss the hypotheses you made in your journal. See if you can further understand the thinking of the children.

Problem Posing and Problem Solving

DeVries (personal communication, 1993) described the kinds of experiences that are beneficial to learners of all ages as they transform knowledge:

> A constructivist takes the position that the learner must have experiences with hypothesizing and predicting, manipulating objects, posing questions, researching answers, imagining, investigating and inventing, in order for new constructions to be developed.

As you notice, the focus is on the activity of the learner. Piaget advocated for what he termed *active methods*, which are captured in the description by DeVries. Piaget (1972) stated, "The aim of education is to form the intelligence rather than to stock the memory, and to produce intellectual explorers rather than mere erudition" (p. 51). It is through the active use of the mind that structures are built, as we saw in Chapter 2. These activities are all part of the broad umbrella of **inquiry,** which is an active search an individual (or group) undertakes to resolve a cognitive conflict or to satisfy a curiosity. According to Lindfors (1999) and Novack (1964), inquiry is seeking for truth, information, and knowledge. It is the set of behaviors involved as people struggle for reasonable explanations of phenomena about which they are curious. Inquiry is "the action of asking." Broadly speaking, inquiry involves these behaviors:

- Questioning and wondering
- Investigating and exploring
- Problem solving
- Confronting errors and misconceptions
- Interpreting information
- Seeking to make meaning out of information and experiences

Problem posing and solving are key components of inquiry and constructivist classrooms, and thus we discuss them in more detail in the section that follows.

Problem Posing

Traditionally, children have solved the problems teachers and parents posed to them—problems thought to be relevant to what they must know. In the quest for better test scores, recent school reform efforts have given credence to the belief that child-generated **problem posing** is an important component in developing math and science content understanding (Gopnik, 2012; Moses, Bjork, & Goldenberg, 1993; National Council of Teachers of Mathematics [NCTM], 1991/1995; Silver, 1994). Yet because they engage children in investigating, formulating, representing, and reasoning, problem posing and problem solving are at the heart of how children learn (English, 1997; Wasserman & Ivany, 1988).

Problem posing involves generating new problems and questions to explore a given situation, as well as reformulating a problem while solving it (Silver, 1994). Problem posing may occur anytime during problem solving: before, during, or after. Thus, it is more inclusive than the process of problem solving, although the two terms are closely related and often intertwined. Brown and Walter (1993) contend that students who pose their own problems are better motivated to solve them. Duckworth (1973) elaborates on this idea by suggesting that when children raise questions for themselves and figure out how to try to answer them, they have an opportunity to progress in their thinking. She wrote about this in an essay titled "The Having of Wonderful Ideas":

> The right question at the right time can move children to peaks in their thinking that result in significant steps forward and real intellectual excitement; and . . . although it is almost impossible for an adult to know exactly the right time to ask a specific question of a specific child . . . children can raise the right question for themselves if the setting is right. Once the right question is raised, they are moved to tax themselves to the fullest to find an answer (p. 264).

The right setting includes the sense of community and social interaction, as discussed in Chapter 5, and a climate that encourages children to explore their own ideas and celebrate the important ideas they encounter. Wonderful ideas do not emerge from nowhere; they build on the foundation of other ideas. This is the heart of the active method. Children benefit in many ways when their engagement in problem posing is recognized and used in curriculum development, including the following:

- Empowering children to explore problem situations and to pursue information that is personally relevant and satisfying
- Promoting inquisitiveness

- Providing teachers and parents with clues about the way the child is thinking
- Engendering flexible thinking
- Encouraging children to view themselves as competent thinkers and learners, whose problems are of interest and value to others (English, 1997).

In addition to the intellectual benefits of child-generated problem posing, there is a second reason that problem posing is of particular interest to constructivist teachers. Because teachers need to consider the interests and needs of children when developing curriculum, they need ways to discover what those interests are. But when children are not yet verbal or unable to express their ideas clearly, how does the teacher know their interests and needs? We believe there are ways to understand this, as you will see in the section on creating curriculum around child-generated problems.

Problem Solving

In contrast to problem posing, problem solving consists of structured activities, such as recognizing that a problem exists, representing the problem, choosing and developing a plan for solving the problem, carrying out the plan, and evaluating the results (Beyer, 1987; Mayer, 1992). Problem solving with very young children does not require such rigid steps and should be done informally. As children move into the later primary grades and beyond, more structured steps can be appropriate, especially when knowledge of a structured sequence of steps is required in grade-level standards.

In a constructivist classroom, problem solving should incorporate the broad aspects of inquiry and include investigative activities. Stated in scientific terms, problem solving engages children in the intellectual processes of observing, describing, comparing, classifying, measuring, questioning, predicting and hypothesizing, gathering data, verifying, interpreting and inferring, generalizing, synthesizing, and evaluating. Notice that these activities comprise the work of all scientists. In fact, when you compare the activity of scientists and children, you see that both scientists and children are adept at wondering and exploring; both struggle to make meaning out of experiences in the natural world and find unique ways to explain their reasoning (Gopnik, 2012). They value and benefit from dialogue with their peers, and hypothesize, conduct research, and seek to verify their answers (Chaille, 2008; Chaille & Britain, 1996). How are these activities carried out in a classroom?

Invented Games

One of the most enjoyable problem-solving activities of primary-school-age children is invented games. As mentioned in Chapter 5, invented games are rich sources of social development and peer interaction. The opportunity for problem solving is just as rich. In fact, both problem posing and problem resolution are present as children determine what game to invent, how to play it, and what strategies to include. Following the suggestions of Kamii and DeVries (1980) and Castle (1990), such a project was undertaken by two teacher-researchers (Surbeck & Glover, 1992).

The teacher and children in a second- and third-grade multiage classroom had decided to launch a study of the environment. As a way of engaging the children, the teacher presented the idea of creating games focused on ecology. Because the children had played many games, they were familiar with the format and curious about how they could be game makers themselves. One of the first steps was to plan how to proceed. Together the class came up with the procedure shown in Box 6.1.

BOX 6.1 CHILDREN'S STRATEGIES FOR GAME MAKING

1. Choose a topic for the game.
2. Research to get information and facts.
3. Decide how to play the game.
4. Make a rough draft.
5. Make the game board and cards.
6. Write the rules of the game.
7. Name your game.
8. Test your game with other people.

The research took several weeks while the children read and gathered information. They did whole-group reading, individual reading with an adult, and some additional research at home. Once they reached the stage of designing their game boards and cards, they considered and tried out organizational strategies. As the rough drafts of the games emerged, problem solving was in full swing. Not only did they have to coordinate the mechanics of the design of the game, but they also had to develop strategies of how to play, win, and evaluate the correctness of the content and suggested strategies for winning. The games literally took on their own lives. The room was alive with children learning and using information about ecology that cut across many topics, and there was lively dialogue, which challenged children to coordinate points of view with others. This occurred not only as they played the games they created, but also as a result of feedback when they played their games at home with parents and siblings.

While the content that children learned was impressive, the richest opportunities came from the process of inventing. As Chaille and Britain (1996) wrote, "Real science incorporates many things to which young children are most particularly open: creative thinking and problem solving, experimentation and invention" (p. 18). Table 6.1 lists the concepts and skills used in constructing a board game.

In reflecting on their experience of game making, the children assessed the strengths and challenges of the game project. Most informative to the teachers was the sense of power the children gained as a result of their experience. For example, Deanna said, "The game I made up about the rain forest was the best thing about being in Mary's class so far." Libby echoed the same sentiment: "When I was done, I felt like the best kid in the world." These emotional reactions are important, as Duckworth has stated: "That's the absolute key to it—owning the ideas—but not only in the sense of the emotional side of it. It's not only that you feel good that you came up with this idea; it's also that you don't have the idea unless you've created it" (quoted in Meek, 1991, p. 30). As elaborated in chapter 5, autonomy is a critical goal to develop in the early years.

Finally, there is one more point to be made about the importance of problem posing and solving with children. Although constructivist teachers recognize the power of child-generated problem posing and solving as it relates to content knowledge, their perspective has the larger goal of developing autonomous thinking and self-efficacy in children. This learning-to-learn process is far broader than particular content knowledge. As the invented game project

Table 6.1 **Concepts and Skills Used in Constructing a Board Game**

Likenesses and differences	Probability (e.g., the chance of landing on a card space)
Writing and reading directions	Sorting and classifying
Odd and even numbers	Conservation of resources
Sequencing	Quantitative comparisons
Number ordering	Money notation
Taking turns	Money concepts (credit, cash)
Matching numbers	Moral and ecological responsibilities
Problem setting and solving	Multiplication
Place value	Mental arithmetic
Revision	Adding
Counting	Identifying coins
Making predictions	Memory
Spatial relationships	One-to-one correspondence
Light and dark shades of color	Relative length

Source: E. Surbeck & M. Glover (1992). Seal revenge: Ecology games invented by children. *Childhood Education,* 68(5), 281.

illustrates, children can go far beyond content information when they are allowed to think, create, and solve problems. Children progress toward the goal of autonomous thinking with repeated opportunities to exercise their innate capacities. Problem posing and solving begins in infancy and continues for a lifetime if it is encouraged and nurtured.

CONSTRUCTIONS

Reflection

Using your journal, discuss a recent problem that you posed and solved. What were your feelings during the process? Elaborate on Duckworth's quotation on owning the idea and specify how the process was beneficial to your own thinking.

Problem Posing, Problem Solving, and Curriculum

Younger and older children pose problems using different means. Using child-generated problems as a source of curriculum in classrooms keeps the learner in the center of what occurs in the classroom. This section examines how problems that are posed by children and by teachers can give direction to content.

Across the early childhood age span (birth to age 8), children exhibit curiosity, and they engage wholeheartedly in experimentation and problem solving if they are given the opportunity. Very young children do pose problems to investigate, but they don't state them the way adults do. In fact, the youngest children may say nothing at all! Children pose problems through the actions they take on objects and materials, as well as through interactions with others. Older children can verbalize problems that they are curious about, and they become quite good at this when teachers encourage it. Children's questions and interests can determine curriculum, but there is more to it than that.

Curriculum Sources

Like Jennifer, some teachers believe that children are the only ones who determine curriculum in constructivist classrooms. This is a misconception. Teachers are critical decision makers in the determination of curriculum, and their judgment about what is worth pursuit, in the whole group or individually, is part of their professional responsibility. Remember what we said earlier about awareness? Sometimes children don't know what they don't know. Teachers who understand how children work to determine meaning, what interests children, and what they will need to know can introduce them to interesting questions and important content. Increasingly, content knowledge for young children is being proscribed by local, state, and even common curriculum demands across states. Thus, these requirements, as well as the interests of the teacher, are also sources of content. As discussed in Chapter 1, curriculum should have many sources, but they should be thoughtfully balanced so that they include play and children's interests, needs, and abilities, as well as the questions they pose (Almon & Miller, 2011; National Board for Professional Teaching Standards [NBPTS], 2012).

Because children are progressing in all developmental domains during early childhood, developmental tasks are also vital sources of curriculum. Curriculum also should emanate from unique or spontaneous events that affect the children in a particular class or group, as we saw in the example in Chapter 2 of the birds flying into the window. Let's look more closely at both children and teachers as curriculum sources and how teachers use that information with a constructivist perspective.

Interests, Needs, and Abilities of Children

First, think about the youngest children. If they do not ask a question directly, how can you tell what they are working on or are interested in investigating? What kinds of problems do children pose through their behavior that can be useful for curriculum development? First, let's consider the example of Peter in Chapter 3. Remember Peter and his encounter with the ball? What question or problem is he focusing on? Because we can't get inside his thought processes, you must **infer** by rereading the observation of what he was doing. (An *observation* is an experience that is obtained through one or more of the senses. An *inference* is an explanation of an observation.) Asking a series of questions of yourself as you observe a child can guide you in making reasonable inferences.

Infants focus intently on people, events, and objects that interest and challenge them. If you wrote or thought of questions related to the focus of Peter's visual attention and his quest for physical knowledge about the ball, you are on the right track. In addition, questions that take into account the child's perseverance and the number or type of actions he used in pursuit of the ball would also yield interesting clues to the problem Peter was engaged in. The key for understanding his questions comes from close attention to his focus and his actions and sounds. It is probable that his questions or problem would be like these:

"What is a ball?"
"How does it feel?"
"What happens when I touch it?"
"What does it take to move or hold the ball?"

Here's a second example, demonstrated by Peter's 2-and-a-half-year-old sister, Katie. Katie, an energetic, outdoor- and water-loving child, has been given a sandbox built by her grandfather. Although the arrival of the sandbox has been a topic of discussion for a week, this is her introduction to both sand and the sandbox. The square box, settled neatly into the side of the lawn, has been filled with new sand and covered with a top that fits snugly. Katie jumps up and down in excitement as her mother and Grandpa take the lid off the box. Inside the box, in addition to the sand, are a bucket, a shovel, a sieve, spoons, a funnel, and a miniature cake pan, as well as small plastic containers. With sparkling eyes and little encouragement, Katie gets in the sandbox, first sitting down in the seat built into the corner. Moving quickly, she squats and picks up the shovel, plunging it into the sand. Using too much force, she lifts the shovel up quickly, and sand goes flying in the air. It lands in her hair and on her clothes. Surprised, then laughing, she picks some up in her hand and throws it up in the air. "Keep the sand in the sandbox, Katie," cautions her mother. Looking at her mother with a mischievous expression, she picks up another handful. She lets it trickle between her fingers. She looks at it intently, then pats her hands together. With her mom's encouragement, she begins to fill the bucket, using the shovel. When the bucket is about half full, she drops the shovel and grabs the funnel. After looking at the narrow end, she pours sand into it and watches as all the sand runs through it onto her shoe. She repeats this activity several times.

Katie's mother begins filling a small container with sand and pats it down hard as Katie watches. Her mother turns one of the containers over and says, "Look Katie. I made a birthday cake." "Oh, yeah, birfday cake," she responds. Singing her own rendition of "Happy Birthday," Katie repeats her mother's actions, making two more cakes. Then Katie spies the hose, a favorite and familiar object. She runs to get it and brings it back to the sandbox. She looks at her Grandpa and says, "You turn it on, Cawpa?"

Like Peter, Katie was posing a series of questions as she experimented with the sand and objects in the sandbox. Some of them may be these:

"What is the texture and nature of this material called sand?"
"How does sand move when it is thrown, poured, dropped, or patted?"
"Are there rules for playing with sand?"
"What different shapes can I make with sand?"

"What can I do with the different items that are in the sandbox?"
"What happens to sand if I add water?"

These inferred, behaviorally posed questions provide avenues for curriculum development with very young children (Chaille & Britain, 1996, 2002). Especially with children under the age of 3, a need for exploration and the developmental tasks they are experiencing provide the foundation for curriculum (see the following Curriculum Strategies for examples)

CURRICULUM STRATEGIES: CURRICULUM FOR YOUNGER CHILDREN

- Follow the child's emergent interest.
- Consider the developmental milestones that a child is displaying and plan activities that encourage the next step.
- Expose the child to experiences that provoke curiosity and surprising reactions of objects.
- Plan physical knowledge activities as suggested by Kamii and DeVries.
- Play simple, culturally appropriate games with children that also link to cognitive capabilities (for example, peek-a-boo with an infant).
- Respond to vocalizations with language and eye-to-eye interaction with the child.

Creating Curriculum

What could be done to build on Peter's interest? It is appropriate to meet his developmental abilities and needs by encouraging his interest in objects and allowing his natural curiosity to lead his playtime. Of course, safety must also be considered. It is also recommended that Peter be encouraged to strive to obtain the object of his interest, though not past the point of frustration. This helps him learn to coordinate his actions of eye and hand and also his ability to grasp and hold objects. Physical development and coordination of actions provide very young children with many challenges, and they all require practice, as any mother of a newly crawling or walking child will readily tell you.

After Peter investigates the ball, the teacher should model other things to do with it, such as rolling it or giving it to a playmate. The adult's language about the object and attention to the child's activity all add to his discovery of knowledge.

In many respects, the same is true for Katie, although her ability to represent knowledge and her enhanced language skills and mobility will also guide the teacher's actions. With very young children, the role of the adult is twofold: (1) provide safe and varied contexts within which experimentation can occur; and(2) facilitate developmental progression by providing language, materials, and experiences to expand on the child's current understanding and level of functioning.

As we suggested in Chapter 3, physical knowledge activities are paramount during the period of birth through age 3, and these activities comprise appropriate content. In recognition of this, Kamii and DeVries (1993) established criteria for good physical knowledge activities with young preschool-age children. These criteria are shown in Box 6.2.

BOX 6.2 PHYSICAL KNOWLEDGE CRITERIA FOR MOVEMENT OF OBJECT ACTIVITIES

The child must be able to produce the movement of an object by his own action. (Peter makes the ball roll by hitting it with his hands or feet.)

The child must be able to vary his action. (Peter can kick or bounce the ball as well as hit it.)

The reaction of the object must be observable. (When the ball moves, Peter tracks the trajectory.)

The reaction of the object must be immediate. (Once touched, the ball moves.)

Source: C. Kamii & R. DeVries (1993). *Physical Knowledge in Preschool Education* (p. 8).

CONSTRUCTIONS

1. Analysis

Think back to the discussion of the three types of knowledge in Chapter 3. What type of knowledge is Peter learning? What about Katie? Which type of knowledge is predominant in each example? What developmental needs and abilities does each child express?

2. Practice

Using the criteria for physical knowledge activities, design the next developmentally appropriate activities for each child, based on the problems each child posed in his or her behavior.

3. Reflection

Using the questions posed by the behavior of each child, describe how you would explain your curricular activities to parents in each situation.

You might be thinking that the questions or challenges posed through a child's interest and development may appropriately serve as curriculum for young children but not for older children in kindergarten or primary grades, where testing and standards make teachers accountable for content. Let's consider two examples of how curriculum could emerge from the interests and talk of older children. The first is the story of how one teacher used the interest of a child with special needs to lead him to skills he needed to learn. The second example presents questions posed by first-grade children during science.

Building Curriculum From Children's Thinking

Close observation of individual children and topics about which they express interest can lead the teacher to insights for curriculum development and direction. Such topics may become evident in drawings children choose to create as well as in daily conversations they have with their peers and yourself. While this example focuses on the interests of a child with special needs, curriculum can be built around the interests of any learner.

Multiple Perspectives: From the Classroom

In a book titled *Charlie's Ticket to Literacy*, multiage teacher Mary Glover (1999) describes her experience with Charlie this way:

Charlie, a premature infant, suffered a hemorrhage in one part of his brain at birth. This affected his integration of visual information, which delayed both his motor development and his reading development. Charlie was fortunate. Thoughtful and caring family members and friends surrounded him, but life still was not easy for Charlie. In his pre-school and school environment, his attainment of physical and perceptual tasks was considerably behind that of his peers. He was highly sensitive, timid, and spoke in a very soft voice.

In the midst of those challenges, Charlie also displayed exceptional strengths and abilities in other areas. For example, although he still had difficulty with one to one correspondence in math in second grade, he could remember scoring details of professional football games that happened a year before. Charlie posed a challenge for me when I became his second grade teacher. Each teaching year seems to bring at least one child who challenges you to go beyond what you already know. Your usual bag of tricks, your familiar teaching practices seem useless for this particular child. The questions are many, the answers elusive. That year, Charlie was that child for me. I was fascinated by his complex mind and at the same time I wondered if I was really qualified to be his teacher.

To know where to begin, I carefully observed Charlie. I recorded the experiences he wrote about, the pictures he drew, the thoughts he shared, and the ways he interacted with the other children. As he showed me himself, as a person and a learner, I began to trust myself as a teacher, believing that Charlie would lead me in the right direction. And he did just that. My research into Charlie's interests led me to recognize the potential of Charlie's obsession with the National Basketball Association (NBA), which emerged during first grade. Through his drawings, I uncovered his expert knowledge of the players, teams, scores and games. This was the basis for our work together for the next two years. Through the books he was motivated to read and write, the math problems he was intrigued to solve, and his unique place in the classroom community as the NBA expert, Charlie learned basic skills and, perhaps more important, confidence in his abilities as a learner. The techniques I used to assist Charlie in mastering literacy and math skills included the following, which were required in our second grade classroom of all children:

Writing individual pieces, which often became books
Teacher-child dialogue journals
Articles for the school newspaper
Information logs
Word problems in math that came from his interest (in basketball).

The result of the two years of work was a child who became self-assured as he read, wrote and worked math problems related to his obsession. Although he still had a great deal to learn, the skills he needed were in place, because we used his passionate interest in sports to engage him in becoming literate and numerate and to find authentic tasks to feed his success and confidence. In fact, he was very successful after this foundation: last year, Charlie graduated as valedictorian of his high school class (Awakening Seed School, 2000).

Building Curriculum From Children's Questions

The second example begins with a group of children engaged in discussion, called a Science Talk, about the weight of water and ice. The question that they started with was, Why does ice float? (Gallas, 1995). In this transcription of an audiotaped scenario, you will notice that children are constructing ideas about this question. In the process of thinking out loud, they are generating theories. A **theory,** similar to a **hypothesis,** is an explanation of a specific phenomenon or a guess that guides an investigation. A theory is more inclusive than a hypothesis, consisting of several hypotheses linked together.

This is how the children addressed the question, Why does ice float?

Vera: Yeah, but my question is . . . why should ice float, if, if water sinks, because ice, ice, you see if we put some water on a scale, and then ice, what would the water weigh? It would hardly weigh anything, and if we put ice on the scale, it would weigh something, but then why would it not, why does water sink and if it doesn't it won't weigh anything? And why would . . .

Danny: Uh, Vera?

Vera: . . . ice float if it does weigh something?

Danny: Um. How would we, um . . .

Chloe If you put it in something, then it will make it heavier.

Vera: You could try a scale. Oh, I know, I think I know! Maybe it's the amount of water, maybe it's the amount of water that made it heavier, and, the . . .

Danny: Vera?

Vera: . . . the ice, the, um and there was a little bit of ice and there was more water than the ice.

Ollie: Vera?

Roberto: There is a way. There is a way to weigh water, like Mr. P. said. He took a piece of tape and he writed it. He make numbers on it so there is a way to weigh water. Vera is right.

Ari: Or you could put it on a scale.

Teacher: Or you could put it on a scale.

Vera: Or you could *pour it* on a scale? Or you could pour, um a bucket of water onto a scale, but I doubt my mom and dad would let me do that (Gallas, 1995, p. 17).

As this example shows, children will generate their own theories when allowed and prompted to do so.

Gallas (1995) has suggested that such theory building during Science Talks encourages children to conceptually try out new ideas and see if they make sense. In Science Talks, children closely follow what research scientists do—that is, talk with colleagues. Gallas has proposed that curriculum most appropriately emerges from the discussions among children and that the silencing of the teacher in these exchanges is critical to the development of thought. The role of the teacher during this strategy is to be silent, so the power of the teacher does not override the thinking of children. In children's exchanges, ideas are revealed, challenged, abandoned, refined, and transformed. In the process, misconceptions emerge. Rather than being viewed as mistakes to be corrected, these so-called wrong ideas offer reflective teachers further information about the way that children think. In fact, misconceptions are also theories; many scientific discoveries have resulted from mistakes and the imaginative thinking that characterizes them.

The work of Forman and her colleagues (Forman & Kraker, 1985) has suggested that older children employ two phases of problem solving: the invention phase and the verification phase. During the **invention phase,** children seek to come to reasonable hypotheses. Often, this work is collaborative, as children discuss the merits of one another's ideas. The **verification phase,** the search for evidence of truth, may cause conflict among children as they try to "prove" their position to one another. While teachers intuitively act to squelch conflict, a constructivist teacher will encourage the different points of view and coach children to disagree in ways that allow for many interpretations and viewpoints. It takes courage for individuals to state what they believe to be true or right, and stating one's beliefs is an absolute necessity in the development of autonomous thinking. That is one of the reasons that Piaget's goals of education, found in Chapter 1, included sociomoral objectives. Children can consider multiple perspectives and develop courage to state their own ideas. For more curriculum strategies for problem posing and problem solving with K–3 children, see the following Curriculum Strategies.

CURRICULUM STRATEGIES: PROBLEM POSING AND PROBLEM SOLVING WITH K–3 CHILDREN

- Observe children to determine the problems they find interesting, and record them for individual children as well as groups of children. Plan activities to follow up on those interests.
- Interview children about their interests, listing their suggestions. Engage children in a discussion about choices for the next project to undertake. Keep the interview documentation for reflection.
- Use a K-W-L (what we know, what we want to find out, what we learned) chart to record the thoughts and questions at the beginning of a topic or project.
- Provide a chart for new questions that arise, encouraging children to write them down for later discussion.
- Employ the play-debrief-replay technique as described in "Children and Reflection" later in this chapter.

- Engage children in inventing games of their own; children can guide the selection of a topic, choosing from a wide variety of interests.
- Encourage each child to be an expert in an area of personal interest. Refer children to one another for information on that topic.
- Document the progress of projects and children with photographs for later reflection and discussion with children and their parents.

CONSTRUCTIONS

1. Analysis

What theories did children propose in response to the question, Why does ice float? What can you determine about the children's knowledge based on what they said in their discussion?

2. Research

What informal investigations or project could this discussion prompt? Web or outline the possibilities for exploration.

Building Curriculum From Teachers' Interests

Because teachers are a vital part of the classroom community, their interests and knowledge should also provide direction for the content of projects and studies carried out in the classroom. Like Charlie, Anita Ramsey, a third-grade teacher at Red Mountain Elementary School in Mesa, Arizona, is an avid professional sports fan, though her interest is in football. Three years ago, she realized that the fathers of many of her third-grade children were National Football League (NFL) fans also. With the goal of involving fathers more actively in their children's education, Anita set out to create a football tracking program, and she has been expanding on it as curriculum in her classroom ever since. This is a description of how she used her interest to engage that of her students.

Each child is assigned an NFL team, and they use information about the team to incorporate math, reading, and writing into lessons centered on the sport. For example, students chart which teams win, and they calculate the different scoring combinations the team could have made to get their score. (For instance, with a score of 20, the team might have scored 2 touchdowns with points after [7 + 7] and 2 field goals [3 + 3], or, they may have scored 2 touchdowns with points after [7 + 7] and a touchdown [6], missing the point after.) Children use a map and mile scale to calculate how far their team had to travel for the away game that week. They also use statistics and probabilities for the Super Bowl at the end of the season. Literacy is not ignored; children write letters to their team as well as to pen pals, located over the Internet, in their teams' home cities. As the children get more interested and involved with the project, they use the information they compile to create and read charts, graphs, and tables, all of which is content on the third-grade state-mandated test.

Ramsey admits that the project initially draws moans from the third-grade girls. She states that "those disappear after the first few weeks." As one of her students, Breana, commented, "The more I understand it, the more it gets interesting to me" (Romero, 2000, p. B1).

This example presents just one way that the interest of a teacher can be used to lead children to expand their understanding of a new topic. The fact that children learn to apply knowledge required by the school and state is no accident. To ensure this, Mrs. Ramsey initially poses the problems for investigation, keeping the required state standards in mind. In the process of responding to her questions, however, the children pose and solve many other problems of their own creation.

Building and Balancing Curriculum: Standards, Core Content, and Accessing Information With Young Children

While there is a strong demand for early childhood teachers to provide direct instruction of content based on standards and Common Core information, constructivist teachers resist this approach for both theoretical and practical reasons. Often, such content is based on adult ways of thinking. Teachers who understand the way that young children think find ways to make important content accessible through active learning and build upon familiar information to help children make connections to the content. They know that some of the abstract information is beyond the comprehension of their learners, since it occurred in the distant past or is of a highly abstract nature. Constructivist teachers know that telling children information of this sort is not likely to result in retention; thus, they act autonomously and professionally to advocate for their students, providing foundational skills and concepts in more meaningful ways (Almon & Miller, 2011; NBPTS, 2012). This issue is more fully discussed in Chapter 10 on assessment.

CONSTRUCTIONS

1. Analysis

Using the "Curriculum Strategies: Projects" in Chapter 5, review the NFL project just discussed and determine how to ensure a constructivist perspective.

2. Reflection

Look back at the standard and project described in "Curriculum Strategies: Using Standards" from Chapter 1; list additional ideas about problems or questions you think children might pose as part of this project that could also meet school curriculum standards.

Reflection

The teachers have met again, this time to talk about the role of reflection in a constructivist classroom.

Sheila: Before we start our discussion tonight, I just want to tell you all something. I've *really* learned a lot about the way kids think from all of you and from the reading and dialoguing we've done. I think Piaget's theory really does work.

Matt: Thanks, Sheila, I knew you would see how brilliant I am with a little time. I could lead you to greatness.

Ron: Oh, yeah, Matt. Sheila's growth is all due to you! That sounds contrary to constructivist theory to me.

Parul: Sheila, what have you learned that you didn't understand before? In fact, maybe this is a good time for all of us to reflect on the progress in our understanding of Piaget's theory and constructivist classrooms. Would the group like to spend a few minutes on that?

Matt: Hey! I thought we were going to talk about reflection, not engage in it.

Kenisha: The rest of you seem to agree with Parul. Let's do take a few minutes, but before we get into that, can we define what we mean by reflection? How do you think it fits with a constructivist approach?

Jennifer: Yeah, I'm up for that. My principal keeps saying I would benefit by being a reflective practitioner. I'm not sure what she means. I don't have time to sit around and just daydream about the kids in my class, though I'd really like to.

The processes learners use to reexamine and extend their understanding are of critical importance in a constructivist classroom. **Reflection** is the practice or act of analyzing our actions, decisions, or products by focusing on the process of achieving them (Killion & Todnem, 1991; NBPTS, 2012). It involves analyzing and making judgments about what has happened, and it is integral to every aspect of learning. It precedes, is a part of, and occurs after learning. Some of the activities that encourage reflection are writing, especially journal writing, and all forms of self-questioning, assessing both yourself and the situation. A second aspect of this activity is linking those thoughts to previous and predicted experiences. Schön (1983, 1987) has written extensively about the importance of reflective practice in education. He describes two types of reflection: reflection on action, or thinking back about something, and reflection in action, or thinking about something in the midst of actions. Both types are important for teachers and children, since, according to Wilson and Jan (1993), reflection touches most of the processes of the mind.

In constructivist theory, reflection is most clearly related to logico-mathematical knowledge because it demands reconsidering an idea or event and linking it to something else. Like reflection, logico-mathematical knowledge is not observable, occurring as an internal event. Reflection is a process inherent in the construction of logico-mathematical knowledge. Unfortunately, teachers often ignore this activity in their plans for classroom interactions. Reflection with children can occur during the course of a day, for example, at the end of an activity or during and after a group project. Although the systematic process of reflecting is most often discussed in regard to the decision-making responsibilities of teachers, it is a critical part of a constructivist perspective on curriculum with young children. Let's examine the importance and role of reflective thinking with children and then turn to its importance for the teacher.

Children and Reflection

Just as Jennifer did, you may wonder what it means to be a reflective practitioner and to engage in reflection in the classroom. The process of reflection as defined here is integral to terms you have encountered earlier in this book. In Chapter 3, you encountered the words *empirical abstraction* and *reflective abstraction*. Both of these mental operations embody the same characteristics as reflection—mental activity, or sense making—that encourages us to develop connections and relationships and to link prior experiences to our current thinking. As we pointed out in Chapter 3, many teachers mistake learning through the senses as a constructivist approach. They have translated Piaget's notions of the active method only literally. For those teachers, hands-on manipulation of materials may be considered sufficient for children to understand content. This is inaccurate and denies children the core of constructivist learning, the opportunity to build solidly on the knowledge they already have by linking it to other content, and to reexamine the things they understand at that time.

If reflection is so important, how can you as a prospective teacher be sure you incorporate it into your classroom practice? Although each of you will create your own ways of building time for reflection into your classroom, here are some suggestions that others have developed.

Some programs include reflection as part of their curricular approach. For example, the teachers trained in the High Scope curriculum (Weikart & Schweinhart, 2013) incorporate an element of planning and review in their daily schedule for each of the preschool-age children in their classes. As you will read in Chapter 9, in the High Scope program, children are first asked to decide on a plan for their imminent activity and then to implement the plan. After the period of time is over, they are asked to review and discuss what they did. In this way, review and **evaluation** are systematically included.

At the primary level, Wasserman and Ivany (1988) have developed an approach to science called *play-debrief-replay*. Wasserman and Ivany believe that play is most like science inquiry. They advocate giving primary (and older children) time to play, or mess about with ideas and materials. Then they bring children together in groups to discuss, analyze, and critique what they did and learned. Finally, the children are invited to play again, or replay, using their extended knowledge.

Rather than focusing on a particular content area, Australians Wilson and Jan (1993) suggest many strategies to engage children in reflection and metacognition, or thinking about their own thinking. Their book *Thinking for Themselves* (1993) provides concrete guidelines for planning strategies for the reflective learning of young children. Some of their strategies include negotiating learning with children, using questions to develop questioning and thinking skills in children, learning logs, concept mapping, and self-assessment. An example of the use of learning logs to encourage reflection is the use of double-entry logs. The children divide the page into two sections. One side is used to record information and procedures related to topics of study. The other side is used for personal connections and responses to the content discussed.

However reflection is integrated into the curriculum, it is intended to extract meaning from the experiences of the learner. Effectively done, it enables students to use their observations and experiences to heighten conceptual awareness, discover meanings, and lay the foundation for further learning. Earlier in this chapter, we discussed critical exploration, or questions that complicate the child's thinking. As Duckworth noted (quoted in Meek, 1991), it takes a lot of on-the-spot reflection to pose questions to the right child at the right time. We now turn to focus on the importance of reflection for teachers.

Teachers and Reflection

A substantial body of literature exists about the importance of reflection in teaching and its role in the professional development of teachers (Carter, Cividanes, Curtis, & Lebo, 2010; Henderson, 1992; Jalongo & Isenberg, 2000; NBPTS 2012; Schön, 1983, 1987; Surbeck, Han, & Moyer, 1991; Tom, 1985). As we discussed previously, reflection is a key to active learning and sense making for all learners, teachers included. Specifically, one cannot be a constructivist teacher without being reflective. According to Henderson (1992), all teachers are concerned with subject matter or content. Constructivist teachers ask questions of themselves that emphasize at least two additional considerations:

1. What is the relationship between what I am trying to teach and children's past experiences?
2. What is the relationship between what I am trying to teach and children's personal purposes?

As you have learned, the constructivist approach to learning places the focus on the learner. The constructivist teacher believes that learning is a complex interaction among the learner's past experiences, individual needs and interests, interactions with others, and the content requirements. Reflecting on these questions and answering them leads constructivist teachers to examine their own teaching practices. Reflecting on your teaching is a way to make you aware of how you teach. It is a method of self-assessment. How each of you implements your unique approach to classroom practice will be determined by the sense you make of your past experiences and your personal purposes in being a teacher.

Reflective practice engages the teacher in a cycle of thought and action. Like the constructive process itself, the cycle can be activated only when you are engaged in both action and reflection. Smyth (1989) poses questions that demand answers if one is to be both a constructivist and a reflective practitioner. The questions include these:

As a teacher, what do I do?
What does this mean?
How did I come to be this way?
How might I do things differently?

CONSTRUCTIONS

1. Reflection

In your journal, using both your past experience in teaching and projected teaching roles, answer Smyth's questions for yourself.

2. Research

Read back through this chapter and list the roles of the teacher that have been discussed. Then look back at what you wrote in your journal.

3. Reflection

Compare the two pieces of information. How do you see yourself in the role of the teacher? How did you come to that determination? Write about the differences and why the differences exist between roles suggested in the chapter and your own ideas of the teacher you'll become.

Teacher Advocacy and Autonomy

As teachers or teachers-to-be, your engagement with these questions now not only will prepare you to become a reflective practitioner, but also will give you an opportunity to engage in constructing your own ideas about teaching and learning. It will be part of your role as a constructivist teacher to be articulate in advocating inquiry-based learning and a constructivist approach with parents, your peers, and administrators. Why is this so important? We have repeatedly said that children should be encouraged to follow their own interests and to trust their own thinking. When children are taught this way, they learn that their ideas are valuable and important, and they learn to trust their intellectual tools and capability to find and create information on their own. It is important to recognize that a constructivist approach requires courage on your part. To many adults, childlike thoughts seem silly and inconsequential. In the rush to accelerate cognitive growth and test scores, the way children think is held up to ridicule, and content deemed important on tests is literally force-fed to children, to the exclusion of their own curiosity and knowledge base of experience (Miller & Almon, 2009; Almon & Miller, 2011). Gruber (1973) captures the challenge for teachers:

How can we create a world in which a childlike thought will be treated with the respect it deserves? In which the child will know he has that respect? Perhaps this is the right way to read Piaget's work for its educational significance—not as a fixed chronicle of stages in the emergence of a specific inventory of concepts, but as the model of a [person] who respects children's thinking. Their thinking, like Darwin's, is "childlike"—questioning, searching, following unexpected leads, inventing, discovering. Their thinking is creative, especially when it is permitted to function freely and is respected as all such thought ought to be (p. 103).

Being an advocate for constructivist approaches requires that teachers use their own developing theories about teaching and learning in order to develop autonomy as a professional. As Schwebel and Raph (1973) state, "One opportunity a teacher must have is free use of her intelligence. Lacking that, she is no boon to any classroom of children no matter what other qualities she has" (p. 278). What are steps you can begin to take at this point in your career to develop the courage to be autonomous? Following are suggestions, though only you can determine which will fit for you at this time. Keep in mind that like children, your thinking is valuable, and your insights into your own teaching and learning theory will be unique to you.

Developing Autonomous Teaching

- Observe children closely and keep notes on the thinking of children.
- Listen for the logic that children employ. While it may not yet follow adult logic, it will reveal a great deal about how they are making sense of their world.
- Practice respect for the knowledge that children have by using techniques that you have read about in this book; use children's responses to verify your thinking rather than depending on administrative mandates or advice from other teachers.
- Practice sharing your emerging teaching and learning theory with a like-minded peer. Supporting one another in understanding children's thinking helps further your knowledge, intuition, and insight.
- Be active in professional organizations and read articles and books that will further your implementation of constructivist practice.

It is unfortunately a well-known fact that teachers in America are held in low esteem. Part of the reason is that most people have gone through public education that has embedded within us old educational conceptions. The teacher is historically viewed as a mere transmitter of the knowledge that others have deemed important for children to know and be able to do. Teaching from a constructivist approach invites you to use your own intelligence and rely instead on the science of how children learn. It is an exciting and interesting challenge that will benefit the next generation of children. As you develop in your career, we anticipate that you will find many rewards for the courage you take now in becoming a teacher.

SUMMARY

- Interest, awareness, and disequilibration play crucial roles in the learning of children and teachers.
- Inquiry is an integral part of problem posing and problem solving.
- Children benefit cognitively and affectively when they pose and solve their own problems.
- Children provide interesting and valuable contributions in setting curricular direction.
- Teachers' interests and professional responsibilities also determine curricular content.
- Reflection is the process by which humans make sense of experience and is a crucial aspect of a constructivist approach to teaching and learning.
- Taking a constructivist approach to teaching and learning relies on active methods and a respect for the thinking of children.

CONSTRUCTIONS

1. RESEARCH

Observe children in a setting such as a child-oriented museum or in a classroom that encourages active investigation of materials. How do children investigate materials? What problems do children appear to pose for themselves? What role do materials play in provoking and sustaining child interest?

2. RESEARCH

Visit three classrooms where projects are used as a curricular strategy. Interview a small number of children in that room about the project. How did they start this project? What are their thoughts about the project? What do they find most interesting, and why? What else would they like to study?

3. ANALYSIS

Reflecting on your research observations and interviews, write in your journal about the problem-posing and problem-solving aspects of project work. Address the following questions: (1) How will children be encouraged to pose problems for themselves? (2) What role will you play as the teacher in promoting both inquiry and reflection? (3) How will children be prompted to think deeply and to go further with their topic?

4. ADVOCACY

Write a one-page newsletter to share with parents about the benefits of children's inquiry and reflection.

Resources

Books and Articles

Brown, C. P., & Lee, J. (2012). How to teach to the child when the stakes are high: Examples of implementing developmentally appropriate and culturally relevant practices in prekindergarten. *Journal of Early Childhood Teacher Education, 33,* 332–348.

This article addresses what early educators can do to focus on children's needs in high-stakes contexts.

Christenbury, L., & Kelly, P. P. (1993). *Questioning: A path to critical thinking.* Urbana, IL: National Council of Teachers of English.

This book provides helpful examples and direction in developing and posing questions.

Copenhaver, J. (1993). Instances of inquiry. *Primary Voices, K–6* (Premier Issue), 6–14.

This article shares many classroom-based suggestions and examples of inquiry with young learners.

Glover, M. K., & Giacalone, B. (2001). *Surprising destinations: A guide to essential learning in early childhood.* Portsmouth, NH: Heinemann.

The story of how multiage learning evolved when two classes worked together on a regular basis.

Graue, E. (2011). Are we paving paradise? *Educational Leadership, 68,* 7.

Reminds teachers of the knowledge base of child development and the benefits of a play-based, child-centered kindergarten.

Hazen, R. L., & Trefil, J. (1991). *Science matters: Achieving scientific literacy.* New York, NY: Doubleday.

Provides content background in science appropriate for primary-aged learners.

Harlan, J. D., & Rivkin, M. S. (2008). *Science experiences for the early childhood years: An integrated affective approach.* Upper Saddle River, NJ: Pearson/Merrill Prentice Hall.
  Provides concrete guidance in developing integrated topics of study with young children.

Heard, G., & McDonough, J. (2009). *A place for wonder: Reading and writing nonfiction in the primary grades.* Portland, ME: Stenhouse.
  Shares a framework for integrating literacy into centers, projects, and clubs with children.

Hunkins, F. P. (1995). *Teaching thinking through effective questioning* (2nd ed.). Norwood, MA: Christopher-Gordon.
  Provides guidelines for questioning and interacting with learners.

Miller, E., & Almon, J. (2009). *Crisis in the kindergarten: Why children need to play in school.* College Park, MD: Alliance for Childhood.
  This document provides a rationale for active teaching and learning based on research.

National Association for the Education of Young Children [NAEYC]. 2011. *The Common Core State Standards: Caution and opportunity for early childhood education.* Washington, DC: National Association for the Education of Young Children.
  NAEYC's position paper raises thoughtful assessment and critique of these standards.

Paley, V. G. (1981). *Wally's stories.* Cambridge, MA: Harvard University Press.
  This is an instructive glimpse into a preschool class and the thinking of the children within it.

Seifert, P. (2000). Inquiry in the kindergarten. In J. W. Lindfors & J. S. Townsend (Eds.), *Teaching language arts: Learning through dialogue* (pp. 103–118). Urbana, IL: National Council of Teachers of English.
  Provides examples of investigations appropriate for young learners.

Steele, C. F. (2009). *The inspired teacher: How to know one, grow one or be one.* Alexandria, VA: Association for Supervision and Curriculum Development.
  Details a continuum of teacher growth to describe how inspired teachers respond to separate teaching skills.

Whitin, P., & Whitin, D. J. (1997). *Inquiry at the window: Pursuing the wonders of learners.* Portsmouth, NH: Heinemann.

This book gives helpful guidelines for developing the processes of inquiry, including rich examples of studies that evolved out of the curiosity of children.

Web Sites

Accomplished Teacher by Smartbrief www.nbpts@smartbrief.com
   Offers daily news, current educational resources, and curricular ideas related to practices of accomplished teachers across all certification areas, including early childhood. Teachers can subscribe without being board certified by registering for the news brief at www.nbpts.org

Alliance for Childhood www.allianceforchildhood.org
   A research and advocacy group of leading early childhood educators who promote policies and practices that support children's healthy development, and love of learning. Policy briefs available on the Web site address many current issues such as play, technology, and child health.

Classroom Connect www.wentworth.com
   Provides resources for teachers, with links to schools.

Co-Vis Project www.nwu.edu/mentors/welcome.html
   This site can match mentors with students to work on long-term projects in science.

Defending the Early Years www.deyproject.org
   This organization is a nonprofit project of the Survival Education Fund, which seeks to rally educators to take action on policies that affect the education of young children.

Edutopia www.edutopia.com
   This site features curricular approaches based on research designed to share workable ideas and to provoke thinking about how technology can personalize education for students.

Eisenhower National Clearinghouse www.enc.org
   The Eisenhower National Clearinghouse for Mathematics and Science Education provides resources, activity guides, and links to schools.

Globe Program www.globe.gov
   An international environmental science and education partnership is shown on this site.

NAEYC's Technology and Young Children Interest Forum www.techandyoungchildren.org.

This forum seeks to lead discussions and demonstrate best practices using technology to benefit young children.

National Institute for Play. www.nifplay.org

This agency brings together diverse play scientists and practitioners to inform others about the transformative power of play. Resources provided include videos from *The Promise of Play*, a three-episode award-winning PBS series about play.

7

THE ROLE OF COMMUNITY

In this chapter, you will learn what community means from a constructivist perspective. Chapter 1 described how the teachers' group became a community to support one another. Chapter 5 explored the role of social interaction in children's learning. This chapter will expand the discussion to include what children learn when they come together in a community as they do in early childhood classrooms. The idea of a community of learners in programs designed from a constructivist perspective is similar in some respects yet different in others from the commonly held notion of community as a gathering of individuals. In this chapter, you will read about examples that make this distinction clear. Constructivist classroom communities are special places in which children learn the importance of mutual respect in a caring environment where they feel a sense of belonging in unity with others. This chapter gives suggestions for creating classroom community based on constructivist principles. Planning a classroom environment from a constructivist perspective will be discussed, with numerous examples from real classrooms. In addition, this chapter will describe expanding community beyond the classroom in connecting with others in other classrooms, programs, and settings.

After reading this chapter you will have a better understanding of

- how to create classroom community and develop a sociomoral classroom atmosphere;
- the importance of providing for physical, emotional, and intellectual safety;
- how to promote children's autonomy;
- the role of shared experiences in creating community;
- how to expand community to include families and others; and
- how to include children in planning the classroom environment.

Introduction

According to one second grader, "*Community is where you and me come together to make we.*" Community can be created anywhere individuals come together with

Piaget's (1965/1995) work also defined two types of morality: heteronomy, or morality through external regulation, and autonomy, or morality through self-regulation. It is through cooperative social interactions with other children that a child develops autonomy. It is also through reciprocity in social interactions that a child develops a sense of justice. When constructivist teachers create classroom community, they plan experiences that will help children develop as individuals as well as together as a group committed to helping each other and to resolving issues of social justice. In such settings, children develop a sense of justice, fairness, and responsibility for themselves and each other. In addition, through shared experiences, children develop emotional ties to each other and to the group. Working through problems in fair ways and having pleasant shared experiences form the foundation for classroom community.

DeVries and Zan's (2012) book titled *Moral Classrooms, Moral Children: Creating a Constructivist Atmosphere in Early Education* is based on what they call the first principle of constructivist education: to establish a sociomoral atmosphere of mutual respect. Respect is important for community to exist. The sociomoral atmosphere refers to all interpersonal relations in a classroom. Their book details how to promote a constructivist sociomoral atmosphere. They begin the book with descriptions of three types of classrooms, which they refer to as the Boot Camp, the Community, and the Factory. They refer to research (DeVries, Haney, & Zan, 1991; DeVries, Reese-Learned, & Morgan, 1991) showing that children in the community classroom were better able to self-regulate, were more advanced in sociomoral development, used more strategies for solving conflicts, negotiated more successfully with each other, and had friendlier shared experiences than children from the Boot Camp or the Factory. The sociomoral atmosphere they describe includes a teacher who respects children, gives choices, encourages and guides children through solving conflicts, and creates opportunities for children to engage in shared experiences. Children are able to share feelings, make choices, and cooperate with others.

Kohlberg and Lickona (1987) describe classroom community as intellectual and emotional bonds of connectedness to a larger whole. They suggest creating a just community by involving children in making rules and setting consequences, having group discussions about moral dilemmas, and engaging children in group decision making about life in the classroom. They stress that bonds of caring among children are necessary to create and maintain a just community. It is not enough to focus on fairness. Children who care for one another become more vested in maintaining fair social interactions. To participate in such discussions and decision making engages children in democratic processes that help them become contributing members of their communities.

CONSTRUCTIONS

Research

Read a chapter from *Moral Classrooms, Moral Children* or one of the research articles by DeVries and her colleagues. Identify the essential characteristics of a sociomoral classroom atmosphere. How do these characteristics compare to classrooms where you have observed or participated?

Multiple Perspectives: From the Classroom

Kristi Dickey's Second-Grade Classroom Community

I teach a second-grade class in Stillwater, Oklahoma, of 10 boys and 9 girls. My students are ages 7 and 8. I am involved in a looping program at my elementary school; I teach first grade and then move on to second grade with the same group of children.

My classroom space is organized so children feel ownership of the classroom. Areas are well defined, and materials are easily accessible to children. This feeling of ownership encourages students to be responsible for their learning. They get the necessary learning materials independently rather than depending on me to get things for them. Marsha gets Unifix cubes to help her with story problems in math, Herb and Cori use magnifying glasses when observing their terrariums, and Carol prefers to read silently in the bathtub in the reading area. Because students are allowed this independence in space and material selection, our respect for each other's differences grows. The children are able to appreciate each other as individuals when they are allowed to choose an area and materials that will help them all be successful on their own levels.

Creating Classroom Community

Classroom communities should be caring places (Copple & Bredekamp, 2009; Hyson & Taylor, 2011). Creating classroom community is not a one-person enterprise. It takes a teacher who sets creating community as a curriculum goal and children who learn to recognize the need to value working together. Kohn (1998) describes the caring classroom community as a safe place where children do not fear being humiliated or punished and in which they feel comfortable to disclose their thoughts and feelings to others. Noddings (2005) has similarly written about the importance of a curriculum of care in schools. She says that schools need to move away from competition toward creating communities that are supportive of children. She advocates a curriculum in which children learn to care for themselves, others, animals, plants, and the earth. As children's communities expand to a global level, caring for the world becomes increasingly important. Creating classroom community does not occur overnight. It takes time, patience, energy, and sensitivity on the part of the teacher. It also takes children who see the sense in working together.

Where to Begin?

As they say, begin at the beginning. Focus on your thoughts about classroom community. Reflect on your own experiences as a learner in a caring classroom. Think about ways you might incorporate some of your own positive experiences into classrooms where you work with young children.

CONSTRUCTIONS

1. Journal Entry

Write a journal entry about an experience you had as a learner in a caring classroom community. Recall the experience in as much vivid detail as you can. Write about your feelings about being in that place, about the teacher, and about your classmates. If you have never been fortunate enough to have an experience in a caring classroom, then write about your worst classroom experience.

2. Reflection

Reflect on your journal entry. Pick out those characteristics of your classroom that made it a caring or uncaring place.

3. Analysis

Analyze what role you, your teacher, and your classmates played in contributing to the caring or uncaring classroom atmosphere. What elements can you draw from your reflections to assist you in creating your own classroom community?

Caring Communities

Caring classroom communities will extend to others outside the classroom when they enter and become part of the classroom. Those outside the classroom community entering it for the first time may lack appreciation for what they encounter in a caring community. If they do not see children sitting quietly doing the same teacher-directed task, they may wonder if real learning is taking place. Caring classroom communities may be busy places with children engaged in a variety of tasks, excitedly discussing what they are doing. In order to help classroom visitors appreciate what they encounter in her classroom community in Stillwater, Oklahoma, second-grade teacher Nancy Simpson gives each visitor a guide as they enter the door. Her Visitor's Guide, shown in Box 7.1, describes what happens in a caring second-grade classroom. The last line in the guide says it all: a group of people with a shared history and a shared vision.

BOX 7.1 VISITORS' GUIDE

Welcome to Second Grade
IN OUR CLASS YOU WILL SEE:

LEARNERS ENGAGED IN THEIR WORK. Children make many choices about what to learn and how to learn it. With these choices comes commitment to the chosen task. For instance, when Space is the topic, one child may do research about Mars and another about astronauts. Both the resources and the end product of that study will be different.

INVITATIONS TO CHILDREN. Children are offered inspiration, possibilities, suggestions, from which they decide for themselves exactly how to pursue their own learning. For instance, writing topics are discussed at length, but the actual choice of what to write about lies with each child.

QUALITY IN CHILDREN'S WORK WHICH COMES FROM OWNERSHIP. Children are eager to share the results of their work. They eagerly participate in Author's Chair, display their handmade books, hang their work in a hallway for others to see. Pride of ownership comes from honest investment in their work.

CHILDREN MAKING AUTHENTIC CHOICES. Only when children can freely choose and live with the results of those choices do they grow in their decision-making ability. During Author's Chair, for instance, other children offer comments and questions for the author, but final decision about revisions rests with the original author. During silent reading time, children choose which books they read.

TEACHER AS LEARNER AND LEARNERS AS TEACHER. Areas of expertise are readily shared by all members of the class. No individual is presented as "the expert." Rather "resident experts" are those who are informed about a particular topic.

DIVERSITY. The unique characteristics of each individual are celebrated as we grow. We recognize that each person starts at a different point and learns at a different speed, but the important thing is that each is learning.

LISTENING AND TALKING. Discussion is an important avenue for learning. The views and understandings of each are valued.

CURRICULUM EXTENDING BEYOND THESE FOUR WALLS. Learning is enhanced with print materials brought into the classroom, photographs, guests who visit, field trips to other locations.

ROUTINES, NOT RUTS. Children know what to expect, but we expect to change if a more appropriate learning opportunity presents itself.

A GROUP OF PEOPLE WITH A SHARED HISTORY AND A SHARED VISION.

Source: From Nancy Simpson, second-grade teacher, Stillwater, Oklahoma.

There are many benefits of caring communities:

- Children and teachers want to be there and like coming together.
- Children are more motivated to learn.
- Children are more collaborative and eager to work together to solve problems.
- Children develop better problem-solving strategies.
- Children develop more appreciation for the usefulness of group rules.
- Children and teachers are more relaxed and more likely to be creative.
- Children and teachers are more likely to express emotions in constructive ways.

The Absence and Presence of Community

One way to consider the importance of community is to focus on its absence. Classrooms devoid of community are places in which teachers make most decisions about content, learning experiences, rules, and how things will be done. Teacher-centered classrooms can stifle children's creativity and thinking. Teacher-centered classrooms may give the appearance of communities because children in such classrooms look as if they are in control. They are engaged in accomplishing tasks given by the teacher. Some administrators, principals, and program directors like these classroom environments because they remind them of their own schooling experiences. However, teacher-centered class-rooms are not true communities in the way community has been defined in this book because children are not cooperating in a constructivist sense. They are obeying the adult authority, sometimes without thought of what they are doing or why they are doing it. Such classrooms are often controlled by teach-ers through intimidating children, either with fear of punishment or focus on getting rewards. Individual children are encouraged to do their own work, and the focus is on individual accomplishment.

In contrast, caring classroom communities are individual and group focused at the same time. Teachers work with children to decide what will be studied and how, to create classroom rules and procedures, and to celebrate individual and group accomplishments. Children have choices and learn to consider how their actions affect the group. In caring classroom communities, children can't do whatever they want. Children's choices must take into account their impact on others in the community. The freedom to choose is offset by feelings of ob-ligation to the group. Children are not free to harm others or to interfere with the functioning of the community as a whole. This integration of choice with community is the foundation of democracy (Kohn, 1998). In communities, the freedom to choose is offset by feelings of obligation to the group.

In creating a classroom community it is important to keep in mind that help-ing children learn to cooperate with others takes time. It also includes mo-ments of difficulty when perspectives clash and conflict, accompanied by strong emotions, and demand immediate attention. Children do not learn to resolve conflict in a vacuum. They learn to do this with the assistance of a teacher who guides them in negotiating solutions that are agreeable and fair to all con-cerned. Teachers can learn to guide children by observing them closely, listen-ing to them carefully, and withholding their adult authority whenever possible to allow children to suggest and to reach their own solutions to problems. See the following Curriculum Strategies for information related to creating com-munity in an infant-toddler classroom.

CURRICULUM STRATEGIES: CREATING COMMUNITY IN AN INFANT-TODDLER CLASSROOM

- Create a welcoming classroom entry by decorating the door with the children's photos and art work.
- Design an inviting parent space complete with informational bulletin board.

- Label children's cubbies or lockers with their names and photos.
- Have three-way conversations among teacher, parents, and their child.
- Plan socials for families, such as potluck dinners or picnics, to promote home-classroom connections.
- Invite families to observe and participate in the program.
- Be sensitive to families' differences and special requests.
- Plan daily shared experiences such as children's arrival and departure songs and fingerplays.
- Play with children and encourage their play with each other.
- Point out to children the helpful things they do for others.
- Use appropriate touch and voice tones to convey caring feelings to children.
- Use the words *we* and *our* to refer to the whole group.
- Provide multiples of favorite toys to prevent conflicts over the same toy. When multiples are not possible, discuss the need to share and model how to share a toy with someone.

Creating a Safe Community

Classroom communities should be physically, emotionally, and intellectually safe. Classroom communities should be safe places for children and teachers. A sense of safety means freedom from fear of harm physically, emotionally, or intellectually. Unfortunately, in today's world there can be no guarantee of classroom safety. Teachers must do the best they can in providing safety within the limits of their school context and become acquainted with emergency procedures.

Physical Safety

In planning a safe environment, consider a child's point of view. Classroom communities should be places where children can move freely without getting hurt. It is impossible to prepare for all possible ways in which children can get hurt, but every teacher should try to do this. Anticipating and preventing physical harm is critically important to children's safety. Begin by surveying the physical environment both inside and outdoors for potential physical threats to safety. You can do this first with children absent and then again with children present, observing where they go and how they handle equipment and materials. It's also advisable to get down on the child's level to look for things you might not see from your adult perspective.

The physical environment should be free of electrical hazards, such as electrical cords that can trip children or invite them to pull on the cord, appliances that are plugged into outlets and may cause electrical shock, or uncovered electrical outlets. It should also be a safe place to explore for children who may fall. Look for hard, sharp table edges or wobbly furniture that won't support a child's weight. Remove these and any other obstacles to safe exploration. This is especially critical for infant and toddler classrooms.

Make sure surfaces are safe for walking, crawling, or sitting on the floor. While water sources such as sinks are important to have in classrooms, make sure that floor surfaces don't get slippery with spilled water. Water-absorbent floor coverings with grip backings may be needed in these areas. All materials should be clean before and after use. Involving children in the cleaning will help them learn responsibility for classroom materials. Cleaning table tops and the water table daily will cut down on the spread of infectious diseases. Encouraging children to use tissues and to wash their hands frequently will also help prevent illness. Classroom communities should be safe, comfortable, and supportive of children's activities.

It is important for children to learn that the classroom community is a place where they will not be physically harmed by others. Teachers can send this message by preventing physical attacks and encouraging children to talk about their problems instead of using physical force. Teachers can model the use of words to express one's feelings. They can also encourage children to think of ways to get their needs met that don't hurt others. Teachers can send the message, "I will not let others hurt you, and I will not let you hurt others." This shows the teacher's responsibility in maintaining a physically safe community. Class discussions of the importance of working together to prevent physical harm can give children a chance to share perspectives and learn more effective ways to be together.

Professional Guidelines for Classroom Safety

Major early childhood organizations, such as the National Association for the Education of Young Children (NAEYC), provide guidelines for classroom safety. In addition, other professional organizations, such as the American Academy of Pediatrics, provide guidelines that are useful to teachers in planning for classroom safety. Safety guidelines can be found in the publications and on the Web sites of these groups. Some resources include the following:

National Association for the Education of Young Children, *Developmentally Appropriate Practice in Early Childhood Programs, Revised Edition*: www.naeyc.org/naeyc

American Academy of Pediatrics: www.aap.org

Consumer Product Safety Commission: www.cps.org

Physical Comfort

Classroom communities should be not only physically safe but also physically comfortable. Physical comfort can take the form of objects brought from home; home furnishings, such as curtains, pillows, and comfortable chairs; and items that relieve stress, such as fish aquariums, pets, water play, soothing music, and comfortable noise levels. If children are hungry, tired, or worried, teachers should help them meet these needs in appropriate ways. Extra snacks can be provided, and private spaces can be arranged for children who need a break from the group. Older children can take responsibility for getting their own drinks and going to the bathroom. Systems for regulating these activities can be kept by children themselves, as illustrated in Box 7.1, a classroom sign-out sheet used in Nancy Simpson's second-grade classroom. Children can be encouraged to self-regulate leaving from and returning to the classroom with a sign-out sheet for which they take responsibility.

BOX 7.2 CLASSROOM SIGN-OUT SHEET

NAME: WHERE: TIME: TIME:

A simple sign-out sheet simplifies classroom routine. I began using the sign-out sheet to keep from being interrupted so many times by students going to the bathroom, to the library, or to the office for Vaseline. I've discovered many benefits to this system.

If I need a child, I can look at the sign-out sheet and see where he or she is. I don't have to try to remember who told me they were going where.

If there is trouble in the bathroom, I just look at the sign-out sheet. It provides either an alibi or incriminating evidence.

If I suspect a child is avoiding, say, math, I look at the sign-out sheet for several days and see if there is a pattern of signing out every time we begin hard math. If it is just a "bodily function routine," I can usually make a suggestion about handling it another way so it doesn't interfere with class work. (I noticed one was signing out every time I began to read aloud after lunch. I suggested she stop by the bathroom on the way in the building from recess so she wouldn't miss the beginning of the story every day. She was appreciative.)

If a parent asks about trips to the bathroom, I have a record to check easily. I also mention to the children that if I notice they are going an excessive amount, I need to let their parents know. Sometimes that might mean they are getting sick and don't even realize it yet.

To indicate where a student is going, abbreviations are easily understood: r.r. for restroom, lib. for library, off. for office.

I use an inexpensive digital clock until I am sure children can tell time quickly and easily on a regular clock. Although it is good practice for telling time, I don't want this to be a test.

In a nutshell, a sign-out sheet documents the goings and comings of each child and frees me from many unnecessary interruptions.

RESTROOM, ETC... SIGN-OUT SHEET

Who where time time
rr 9:41 9:41
rr 9:52-9:53
rr 9:53-9:59
L! 9:55-9:57
10:06
R.R 10:20 - 10:21
Teacher Workroom 10:24
Office 10:29 - 10:32
rr 10:38_
rr. 10:39 10:41
rr 10:39 - 10:40
rr 12:43 12:44
12:43
L. 2:41 - 2:44
3:03
rr 3:20 - 3:21
3:21 -3:21
rr. 3:22 . 3:23

Nancy Simpson

Classroom sign-out sheet.

Source: From Nancy Simpson, second-grade teacher, Stillwater, Oklahoma.

Emotional Safety

Just as children need to be free from physical harm, they also need to be free from psychological harm. It is important for teachers to take the emotional pulse of the classroom to ensure that the environment is emotionally healthy. This can be done by observing whether children are stressed out by undue classroom tension. Classroom environments should be relaxed yet productive. There should be a relaxed and productive atmosphere that is apparent to anyone entering the classroom.

Children should feel free to take risks without fear of punishment or intimidation. They should be able to share their ideas and feelings with others without feeling they may be humiliated or insulted. If children do not feel free to express their emotions, they will not view the classroom as a community, in the sense of being able to understand others' needs in relation to their own. Because children have such different thresholds for emotional distress, teachers should help them discuss and process their emotions both privately and in group discussions.

It is important for all children's emotions, both positive and negative, to be recognized and accepted. For example, the mother of a daughter who was beginning kindergarten became perplexed when her child expressed strong negative emotions about going to school. Her daughter would cry and say she didn't want to go back to kindergarten. The mother soon learned that the kindergarten teacher had recently scolded another child in a loud voice. The teacher's view of discipline was to yell at the children. The daughter was not accustomed to adults who yelled. She was fearful that her teacher might yell at her too. She became very upset and did not feel comfortable in this classroom.

Children should feel a legitimate ownership of their emotions at the same time they are learning to express them in constructive ways. It is only in having their emotions accepted by others that they can learn to accept the emotions of others. Teachers can reassure children that it is okay to have strong emotions and to talk about them, but it is not okay to act on them in ways that harm others.

Emotional Comfort

Children should feel emotionally comfortable in that they look forward to being in their classroom with each other. In the overall balance of classroom life, children should experience more positive emotions, such as happiness, joy, and interested engagement, than negative feelings of sadness, anger, or hopelessness. The classroom community should be primarily an emotionally joyful place. Teachers can help children develop an emotional balance by helping them learn to process their feelings and cope in constructive ways with their

negative feelings. In one program for 3-year-olds, the teacher and children referred to themselves as "friends." In some of their group times, they shared stories about what friends do for each other, listened to books about friends, and
discussed what it means to be a friend.

Regular classroom meeting times can provide an opportunity for children to
discuss feelings in authentic ways. One such program at the elementary education level, the Responsive Classroom approach, uses Morning Meeting (Kriete,
2002) time as a daily practice for children to discuss topics important to them,
including emotional events in their lives. Such Responsive Classroom activities
have been shown to improve student achievement as well as teacher-student
interactions and provide emotional support for children (see the Responsive
Classroom Efficacy Study, www.responsiveclassroom.org).

Intellectual Safety and Comfort

The teacher's motto, like the physician's, should be to do no harm. This applies
to physical, emotional, and intellectual harm. Physical and emotional harm are
easily seen. Intellectual harm is less easily recognized and may not become evident until years later, when teachers become aware of older students' lack of
motivation or interest in curriculum content. Kamii has addressed this problem of traditional teaching that shuts off children's thinking. When teachers
focus on getting the correct answers and correcting incorrect answers, children
learn to try to give the teacher what she or he wants instead of trying to figure
out their own solutions. Kamii (2000) says, "In traditional teaching, when the
teacher says that an answer is correct, all thinking stops because there is no need
to think any more" (p. 202). To encourage and sustain children's intellectual
curiosity, it is important to give them opportunities to study those things they
are most interested in. It is also important not to correct their errors. Children
will learn to correct their own errors and in doing so will develop autonomy as
learners.

Children need to feel intellectually safe and comfortable. In order to do this,
they need opportunities to be actively engaged in activities, projects, and experiences that are of interest to them. Mindless teacher-directed activities that
children find pointless but feel compelled to do will destroy interest. Teachers can kill intellectual interest by dominating children with their own teacher
objectives and activity plans. Teachers should strive to find out what interests
children, what they want to know more about, and what they are passionate
about and provide opportunities for children to pursue their own questions.
This book provides numerous examples of how to do this by giving choices
and engaging children in problem posing, problem solving, projects, play, and
authentic tasks.

Sharing Experiences and Forming Bonds

Classroom communities form only when there is affection among members of the community. Chapter 5 discussed the importance of social interactions and the development of friendships. Communities emerge when individuals get to know each other, begin to like each other, develop attachments to one another, and become better friends. Teachers can facilitate friendships by discussing with children what it means to them to be a friend and to have a friend. Teachers can point out the importance of cooperation and helping in friendships and how these acts improve community life for everyone. Friendship can become a curriculum topic for study. Teachers can demonstrate what it means to be a friend through their actions and through pointing out the actions of children who are helpful to others.

One characteristic of friendships is having enjoyable experiences together. Over time, friends develop a history of shared experiences, which they can recall to remind them of the bonds that have formed among them. Teachers can encourage this type of enjoyable shared experience among children and provide opportunities for children to remember and relive these experiences as they appreciate their history together as a community. One simple example of this is the kindergarten teacher who created a wall-sized classroom calendar containing a large square for each day of the month. At the end of each day, the children would decide which object to attach to that day's square that would represent what they did together that day. At the end of the month, the teacher would engage the children in a discussion of all the shared experiences they had during that month. The wall calendar was concrete documentation of the experiences that helped the children develop an appreciation for their shared experiences as well as a sense of the passage of time during a month.

Spontaneous and Planned Shared Experiences

As mentioned in Chapter 5, Selman (1980) and DeVries and Zan (2012) have described the importance of shared experiences in forming friendships and in creating a sociomoral classroom atmosphere. They describe shared experiences as interactions among children when there is no tension, such as friendly interactions when children are playing together. Shared experiences can occur spontaneously as children interact. For example, two children playing in the dramatic play area may imitate a third child who is making dog noises. The threesome then enjoy making dog noises and laughing as they do. They are enjoying each other's company and engaging in a mutual activity that helps them come together as friends. Among older children, for example, a child who is writing a story about her cat may be joined by a friend who also begins a story about a cat. The two share cat stories while enjoying each other's company. A third example of a spontaneous shared experience would be a small group of first-grade children who are interested in researching "The Star Spangled Banner." One of them draws a large American flag; another finds out who wrote the music and when it was written; and the third finds out the significance of fireworks on the Fourth of July. When they regroup, they spontaneously sing the song while they act out raising the flag and exploding fireworks, to the delight of those around them. It then becomes a ritual that they can do on request. It also becomes an enjoyable memory that bonds them.

Shared experiences can also be planned (recall the kindergarten example of a monthly calendar). A preschool teacher engaged children in the construction of a swamp in the water table. They saved the vegetable peels from a class soup-making project to become swamp weeds in the water table. They also decided what props, such as boats and plastic animals, should be placed in the swamp. Then they enjoyed playing in the swamp water table for one day. This became an activity that was frequently recalled at other times and became an enjoyable common memory. Sharing experiences helps children develop community. Reflecting on shared experiences strengthens community.

Reflecting on Shared Experiences

Having shared experiences helps children develop affective bonds with one another. Reflecting on those experiences helps them remember and appreciate those experiences and maintain the bonds they have created. Teachers can engage children in discussions of the experiences and in keeping a class history through various documentations of events, such as the monthly calendar. Teachers can suggest that older children write and draw about their shared experiences in their writing journals and share them during Author's Chair, when written work is read to each other and constructive feedback is given to the author. Teachers and children can keep a class scrapbook of experiences that can be posted on the class Web site and/or taken home and shared with children's families. There can be a place in the scrapbook for parents to write comments to be shared during group time. Children's work can be displayed in the classroom as a reminder of what they have done together.

Creating Community Through Story

Teachers can help create classroom community through children's literature that embodies themes of community, such as Heine's book *Friends*. They can also use literature to discuss difficulties that disrupt community, such as Fox's book *Feathers and Fools* and Dr. Seuss's *The Butter Battle Book*. Paley, a former kindergarten teacher, has written about the use of story enactment in the experiences of her kindergarten children. Her books, such as *Wally's Stories* and *The Kindness of Children,* are filled with stories created by her children as they struggled to learn to live with each other in their classroom community. Paley encouraged children to create and act out stories that had importance in their everyday lives. Through stories, the children became connected to each other and developed into a caring community.

Gallas (1994) is another primary teacher who has written about the importance of story to children's understanding. She has described classroom life and how children talk, write, dance, draw, and sing their understanding of their world. Classroom community is created through these shared experiences.

There are many children's books that promote community:

The Day the Earth Was Silent by Michael McGuffee, 1996, Bloomington, IN: Inquiring Voices Press

Fish Is Fish by Leo Lionni, 1970, New York, NY: Pantheon Books

Friends by Helme Heine, 1982, New York, NY: Margaret K. McElderry Books

The Busy Beaver by Nicholas Oldland, 2011, Tonawanda, NY: Kids Can Press

Koala Lou by Mem Fox, 1989, New York, NY: Voyager Books

Sam by Ann Herbert Scott, 1967, New York, NY: McGraw-Hill

Sea Monster's First Day by Kate Messner, 2011, San Francisco, CA: Chronicle Books

Swimmy by Leo Lionni, 1968, New York, NY: Pantheon Books

The Table Where Rich People Sit by Byrd Baylor, 1994, New York, NY: Charles Scribner's Sons

Will I Have a Friend? by Miriam Cohen, 1967, New York, NY: Collier Books

Creating Community Through Shared Decision Making

To be a member of a community means that you have some control over what happens there. Chapter 4 addressed the importance of decision making. Engaging children in making important decisions about classroom life helps them develop responsibility for their community. Of course, there are some decisions that teachers need to make without involving children. These decisions often have to do with institutional requirements and child safety. For example, a teacher may decide that the back door to the classroom will not be used because of the possibility that children will get hurt by the heavy door, which gets blown shut by strong wind. In that case, the teacher tells the children that they will not be opening that door and explains why. Teachers who teach with intentionality know that it is important to plan the classroom in order to be supportive and encouraging as well as to scaffold children's learning, but also to involve children in making decisions as well (Gronlund & Stewart, 2011). Teachers who observe children's comfort levels can plan challenging activities that give children a sense of security and support (Epstein, 2007).

Children can actively participate in classroom decision making. But there are also many aspects of classroom life that children can help decide. For example, they can decide on topics of study that have interest for them. They can make choices about how they will represent their learning: through drawing, writing, storytelling, or in other ways. They can decide what is their best work and present that work and their rationale to each other and to their families. Teachers can give children choices about a great number of things—for example, whether to spend more or less time in self-initiated activity time, where to go on field trips, and what guest speakers will be asked to visit the classroom. Children can vote on their choices during group discussions. DeVries and Zan (2012) say that voting encourages self-regulation, exchanging points of view, the ideas of equality and cooperation, and the usefulness of written symbols in recording votes. The more children help choose classroom experiences, the more ownership they feel with the class and the more unified the community becomes.

Some suggestions for child choice include these:

Infant-toddler program: Simple choices such as between toys, activities, and books
Preschool: Choices among classroom centers and activities at centers
Kindergarten: Choices in project topics and activities
First grade: Choices in topics to write about
Second grade: Choices of times at which to complete work
Third grade: Choices in selecting best work and providing a rationale for choices

Multiple Perspectives: From a Teacher

Second-grade teacher Nancy Simpson decided with her children to study World War II. The children read, wrote, interviewed relatives, and invited war veterans to visit their classroom. Some educators and parents had concerns about this topic being studied in second grade. In response to these concerns, Nancy wrote this description of her experience:

World War II in Second Grade?

Different is not necessarily bad, but parents are asking why you are studying World War II in second grade. A question always causes me to pause and reflect. Don't we always wonder, "Am I doing the right thing?" But student responses left little doubt in my mind of the value of this extended unit of study.

I returned to my classroom and posed the question to the real experts on teaching and learning, the students. "Some people wonder why we are studying World War II in second grade. What would you tell them?" Here are some of the children's answers:

"We hear from our families that a lot happened in World War II. Sometimes stories are on the news and in the newspaper. We weren't alive then, and if we hadn't learned about World War II in school, we wouldn't know what everyone was talking about."

"When we grow up, we can help the world be a place for peace. We want to make choices that don't start another war. Wars are scary and dangerous. I didn't know that before."

"And besides that, now we can talk to our grandparents about something they are really interested in. When I ask questions, they have something to tell me that we both care about. They are pleased to see how much I know about World War II."

I couldn't have said it better myself!

Rule Creating

Engaging children in making classroom rules is another way to create community through shared decision making. Teachers can lead rule discussions when problems occur that make it necessary to set rules. As situations occur, such as children getting upset when others destroy their block constructions or art projects, teachers can call the group together to discuss the problem and brainstorm solutions. Unless children perceive a need for rules to regulate behavior, they are not likely to see the sense in teacher-imposed rules. That is why it is more meaningful to discuss rules as they become necessary rather than in the abstract. Rule discussions can expand into discussions of appropriate consequences when rules are violated. Although younger children tend to create consequences that are much more punitive than adults would, they can be guided by teachers to consider the appropriateness of consequences and to commit to those consequences that would be just and fair.

Second-grade teacher Nancy Simpson has one classroom rule: Do what you're supposed to do all the time! She feels this one rule covers all situations. She also thinks that by the time children arrive in second grade, they have had many experiences with classroom rules. By second grade, most children have developed ideas about what is considered appropriate school behavior. For preschool-age children, discussions of rules as they become necessary and posting of the rules help children understand that rules protect everyone in the class.

Rule creating promotes children's autonomy. In classrooms where children have had experiences playing games with rules and creating their own games and rules, children are more likely to understand the usefulness of classroom rules. Young children do create rules for games they invent that are similar to classroom rules, in the sense that they regulate fair behavior (Castle, 1998).

Multiple Perspectives: From a Teacher

Kristi Dickey, a second-grade teacher in Stillwater, Oklahoma, describes how she sets rules with her students.

The children and I establish the classroom rules early in the year during class meetings. After the children have had experiences in our classroom, we brainstorm a list of guidelines that can help our classroom be a safe and happy place. I purposely wait until we have been in school for several days, so that children will be able to give input that is meaningful and also realize the necessity of having some sort of boundaries and guidelines for behavior. These shared and lived experiences create a feeling of community and are the basis for the rules that evolve. These rules may change as children add to, delete, or create a new set of rules for certain situations.

Young children tend to look at rules as a set of arbitrary demands imposed on them by adults. When asked to come up with their own set of rules, they often come up with a list of don'ts. This year was no exception. Our first rule list was No punching. No kicking. No pushing. No chair fights. No running. Help people when they are hurt. Talk nice. Respect the work of others. No jerking. No yelling . . . always listen. No picking up others. No pulling hair. As we went on, the rule list was quickly becoming a "don't" list of all the terrible things that the children could think of. When I saw the direction in which we were headed, I asked the students if any of these bad things on the list ever happened in our room. "Of course not! No!" were the replies. I suggested that maybe instead of writing down all of the things that we do NOT want to happen, that maybe we should list the good things that DO happen in our classroom, so that anybody entering might feel safe right away. I asked what the things are that we already do that make our classroom a good place to be. This is how our current list of rules came to be. After voting to accept the rules, all members of our class, including me, signed the list. A word describing our class was voted on (Welcome to our "AWESOME" class!) No student has suggested any changes to the rules, but several students have referred to them during times of conflict with another student. The rules hang on the inside of our classroom door, where they are easily read and seen regularly. They say,

Welcome to our AWESOME class!
We try our best at everything.
We use our best manners.
We always work hard.
We are nice to everyone.
We help other people.
We respect others.
We have fun in class!

CONSTRUCTIONS

1. Research

Generate a list of what you consider to be appropriate rules for a preschool classroom.

2. Interview

Observe a preschool classroom for any signs of posted rules. Interview the teacher about how her classroom rules are created and enforced. Interview three preschool children in the classroom you observed about what they think their classroom rules are. Compare their ideas to those of their teacher and to your own list of rules.

Class Discussions

Teachers can engage children in making decisions by leading class discussions on both positive and negative issues that need deciding. A classroom agenda book (Nelsen, Lott, & Glenn, 2000) can serve as a place where children can record an issue to become an agenda item for a class discussion. The teacher and children together select from the agenda book issues that affect the entire class and discuss them. All perspectives on the issue are shared, without drawing negative attention to individual children. The class discusses helpful ways in which they can resolve the issue and then makes a commitment to act on what has been decided. This process helps children learn that individual desires must sometimes be forfeited for the good of the group. The choice that is made is a group choice, not an individual choice. And the group then takes responsibility to act on the choice.

Planning the Classroom Environment

The teachers' group is having a discussion on involving children in making decisions about classroom space.

Parul: Classroom rule discussions might work well for older children, but with infants and toddlers, you're wasting your time. I've found that when there is a conflict between children, redirecting their attention to more appropriate activities works best. I may offer a simple choice between two activities. For example, I might say, "Hitting hurts people. I can't let you hit Sara. And I won't let Sara hit you. So let's find something else to do. Do you want to play with this ball or this fire truck?" Redirection usually works with infants and toddlers.

Matt:	I think children of all ages like to have choices. Remember the problem I was having with children being rude to each other? The other day we had another fight break out. So I thought this would be a good opportunity to have a class problem-solving discussion. The children identified the problem as some children upsetting the block constructions of others. Through their discussion, they figured out that some children leaving the art table run through the block area on their way to the housekeeping center. Although not intentionally, they knock down other children's block constructions. And this leads to fights. We discussed what we could do about this. They decided it would work better to move the blocks to another part of the room where there would be less traffic. I can't believe I hadn't thought of doing that myself!
Kenisha:	What a great example of class decision making!
Sheila:	Matt, did you try it out?
Matt:	Yes. The children helped move the blocks across the room. Although it did cut down on fights, they are still pretty rude to each other.
Jennifer:	I would take their recess away if they were rude.
Ron:	If changing the blocks helped a little, why not have more class discussions? You could ask them to come up with alternatives to saying rude things. If they could solve one problem, I bet they could work on this one too.
Matt:	I guess you've given me another homework assignment!

Planning Involves Making Many Decisions

What would your ideal classroom look like? How would you organize classroom space to prevent traffic problems? How would you arrange materials accessible to children to promote their independence? In an ideal world, teachers would know in advance what their assignments will be and which classrooms they will have. They then would have ample time and materials to create their ideal classroom arrangement. In the real world, most teachers work within the classroom constraints they find themselves in, such as rooms without windows, sinks, or outdoor access; furniture made for larger children with desks instead of tables; and material resources that are almost nonexistent, such as 100 sheets of construction paper and one box of markers to last the whole year.

Creativity comes in handy in planning a classroom environment. It also helps to know where to find free and inexpensive materials. Regardless of the situation, classroom environments should be planned with children in mind and should be appropriate to their age and individual needs, including necessary adaptations. There is no one recipe for planning a constructivist classroom environment. Every classroom will have its own look and ambiance, based on the teacher, the age and characteristics of the children, and the resources available. Constructivist classroom environments don't require expensive material, and they can be created in just about any location. The energy in the classroom comes from a teacher who is thinking about curriculum from a constructivist point of view and from children who are actively engaged in a program that encourages their thinking, social interaction, and autonomy through accessible materials and an environment responsive to their actions.

On the first day of class, an elementary school special education teacher moved all the desks into the hallway before the children arrived. As they arrived, she told each one to move a desk into the classroom to a place he or she wanted to be. She also told them that if later they decided they wanted to move to a different location, they would have to give her a reason for their request. The children took responsibility for their choices of location. This teacher gave them many opportunities to make decisions about classroom life.

Who Plans?

Initially, the teacher plans the classroom environment to meet children's physical, emotional, intellectual, social, and moral needs. To the extent possible, the teacher engages children in planning the environment. Children can take responsibility for caring for materials, class pets, and plants; for cleaning up; and for other tasks that need doing. They can also take responsibility for displaying their work on walls, tables, and bulletin boards. A constructivist classroom environment is responsive to children's activity. Space, furniture, equipment, and materials will move and change in response to what children are doing at the time (Chaille & Britain, 2002). Flexibility is the key to organizing a constructivist classroom. The teacher should remain open to the many possibilities that will emerge from children's ideas and purposes.

A constructivist classroom environment is responsive to children's activity. In one preschool classroom, the teacher planned a concept center based on children's current interests or inquiries. For example, she created a center about boxes that displayed a great variety of boxes of all shapes, sizes, colors, designs, and functions. Activities at the center included stacking and nesting boxes, building box constructions, creating things from boxes, such as swimming pools or homes for pets, and making boxes from a variety of materials. Children's interests focused on things made from boxes, such as homes, schools, mailboxes, hatboxes, jail cells, and jewelry boxes. She knew when to change the center based on children's waning interest.

Multiple Perspectives: From a Teacher

Kristi Dickey, a second-grade teacher, comments on classroom space:

In our classroom, lessons, centers and activities change as units of study change. Changes also occur as children's interests evolve. Some activities require more space than others. When we have class meetings, children push the tables away from each other to create a large space in the middle so we can place our chairs in a circle. When an in-depth study of the rain forests of the world led us to create our own version of a rain forest inside a giant bubble, furniture was arranged to accommodate the construction.

Children are able to select or create their own working space much of the time. Use of space and materials changes as I make daily observations regarding student use and as students themselves decide that changes are necessary.

Making Adaptations for Children With Special Needs

Children with special needs must be considered in planning any classroom environment. Teachers adapting to special needs must work closely with parents and special education services to make sure that children are comfortable, challenged in appropriate ways, and have the resources they need to benefit from their classroom experiences. Technology has been used to help children with special needs to better function, see, hear, move, communicate, write, and express their ideas and feelings in classroom settings. To the greatest extent possible, children with special needs should be engaged as members of the classroom community.

Teachers can adapt environments to special needs. In one preschool, for example, a partially paralyzed child with limited bodily movement learned to paint with her teacher's help. She first started with a brush held between her teeth. Later, the brush was attached to a special helmet she could wear. She would use the brush to apply paint to paper attached to a slant board designed to be at her level as she sat in her wheelchair.

There are many ways in which children with special needs are educated. Some attend classes with other children with special needs. Others spend some part of the day in regular classroom settings and the remainder of the day in a special class. And still others spend the entire day in a regular classroom. Placement decisions are a function of extent of special needs, parent preference, and ability of the school to adapt the environment and materials to meet individual needs.

In one Midwestern school, educators work together to provide opportunities for children with special needs to spend time in regular classrooms. In one second-grade classroom, the teacher and children have created a caring classroom community. Joel, a child with mental disabilities, spends part of his day in this community. The children view his time with them as precious and hate to see him leave. They would like for him to stay with them all the time. They care for Joel and view him as a contributing member to their classroom community. They make space for him, invite him into their activities, assist him as needed, laugh with him, share their work with him, and ask him for help. Joel enjoys being with them and enjoys being challenged in his thinking as he challenges the thinking of the other children. He loves to participate in their activities and looks forward to being with them each day.

The Project Approach helps connect children with special needs with their peers. Using the Project Approach with children with special needs helps teachers focus on each child's strengths and interests, not just their deficits (Lickey & Powers, 2011). Project work is conducted at children's various abilities and encourages collaboration across all ability levels, helping all children benefit from working together in project activities.

Community Beyond the Classroom

Classrooms are not isolated entities existing on their own. They are part of larger communities. A classroom may be part of a larger school, center, or program. In turn, schools, centers, and programs are also located within communities, represented by outlying neighborhoods, towns, or cities. Children's ideas about classroom community broaden to include the communities beyond the classroom. There are times when it is appropriate to go beyond classroom walls to learn more about the community at large.

Forming Bonds With Families

A constructivist classroom community includes the families of the children in the classroom. Family participation in classroom life is ongoing, spontaneous, and planned. One effective means of communication from classroom to home and from family to family is the family journal. The family journal goes home to each family on a rotating basis and communicates what is happening in the classroom as well as families' comments about classroom life and home life. A family can use the journal to find out what their child does at school and also to communicate their ideas and responses back to the teacher and to other families. One example of a family journal is a classroom scrapbook of everyday events. The scrapbook goes home to families and includes blank pages for families to write comments. It serves to connect classroom life with family life.

Teacher-parent communications should be reciprocal and continuous. The younger the child, the more involved are the families in the child's program. In infant and toddler programs, parents visit every day as they drop off and pick up children. Teachers have more opportunities to discuss the child's daily activities because they see the parents every day. It's also easier to give parents written communications about the program when they are there in person. Parents who visit the program every day can observe the program and learn what their child has available to do each day. When children reach third grade, they may arrive and leave on the school bus or with a carpool. The teacher may have limited or no contact with parents. Written communications may get lost from school to home and the reverse. Family-school communication becomes an ongoing challenge.

If you were a parent, in what ways would you like to be involved in your child's classroom? What would it take for you to feel welcome as a parent? How can you use your own parent perspective, if you are a parent, to create a welcoming environment for parents to your classroom? In one third-grade classroom, parents are the first source of the larger community. There is a classroom open-door policy for parents. The third-grade teacher encourages parent participation in all aspects of the classroom. She arranges programs and the monthly Authors' Fair to accommodate parents' schedules, and drop-ins are greeted with enthusiasm.

Invitations for family involvement are issued on a continuing basis, and the teacher makes a concerted effort to know the families personally. One thing that has come from this is the mother-daughter book club. The teacher noticed that six or seven of the girls were ordering the same books from the monthly book club. She suggested that perhaps the girls would like to form a reading circle. From there the idea took shape and grew into the mother-daughter book club. The mothers and daughters get together in one of the homes each month. They vote on which book to read and decide on the hostess for the next month. Mothers and daughters read the book. Some read it together; other pairs read separately and engage in book talk as they read. The host family provides a treat for the meeting, usually one that fits with the story in some way, and they prepare an activity that furthers comprehension. When they read *The Twenty-One Balloons*, they actually did a balloon launch (Rogers, 1999).

Including families in the program is one way to appreciate the cultural diversity that exists among families in the program and to provide ways for families to participate with others from a variety of multicultural backgrounds and diverse values and traditions (Ponciano & Shabazian, 2012). Teachers can help children discuss cultural differences within the comfort of a caring classroom atmosphere as well as welcome families into the conversation by encouraging them to participate in classroom activities and to communicate directly and indirectly through media such as the family journal that rotates among families, the classroom newsletter, and the classroom Web site that may contain a space for parents to share their ideas. Engaging families in these ways helps families become acquainted and connected to the classroom community. Another way to engage families is through family literacy projects for both children and families whose first language is English and for those learning English. Children and families can be affected in positive ways, including increased knowledge of print and understanding of the meaning of print through having opportunities to participate in family literacy programs (Harper, Platt, & Pelletier, 2011).

Forming Bonds With Other Classrooms

Sometimes teachers and children perceive a need to connect with other classroom communities. One regular first-grade classroom adopted an early childhood special education classroom. The adoption was proposed after a group discussion in which the first-grade teacher mentioned the special education class because she and the special education teacher were friends. A child then revealed that she had a good friend in the other class. One thing led to another, and the first-grade class invited the special education class to their school to play games. The game day was very successful. It was followed by an invitation from the special education class to the first-grade class to join their swim activity at the local YMCA. The two classes sent messages and invitations to each other throughout the school year. At the end of the year, the first-grade class became cheerleaders for the special education students at the Special Olympics. Both classes felt they were a part of a much broader community that went beyond their own classrooms. See the following Curriculum Strategies for more ideas for involving families.

CURRICULUM STRATEGIES: SUGGESTIONS FOR INVOLVING FAMILIES

Inside the Classroom

- Create a place just for parents in the classroom or school with refreshments, reading materials, and comfortable chairs.
- Design a parent bulletin board filled with program information.
- Set up a parent station where parents can read and write notes from and to the teacher.
- Provide a sign-up sheet for parents to volunteer to read, work with children, or share something of interest.
- Provide resources, books, and toys for parent checkout.

From the Classroom to the Home

- Send notes, letters, newsletters, family journals, and the class scrapbook home to parents.
- Phone, e-mail, or visit families.
- Design a class Web site accessible to parents.

Connecting Families

- Plan family events where families can meet, get acquainted, and share information.
- Have socials, potluck dinners, afternoon teas, open houses, and book, art, and author fairs for families.

Buddy Programs

Sometimes older children buddy up with younger children for tutoring, reading books, or participating in other special events. For example, fifth graders may spend part of their day in kindergarten sharing books with younger children. An older and younger child will buddy up, get to know each other, and share their perspectives on books with each other. The kindergarten children look forward to visits from their buddies. In one such program, the fifth graders acted out the story of "The Three Little Pigs" for the kindergarten children. This created an interest in the kindergarten children to act out stories. They videotaped their plays to share with the older children and with their families at the school open house.

Another example is inviting children from other classrooms to share something special. In one kindergarten class that was doing a project on musical instruments, a fourth grader they invited to the class brought his trumpet. He explained how the trumpet worked and played it for them. They wrote him a thank-you note afterward.

Collaborative Projects

Classrooms often collaborate on projects together. In one elementary school, a first-, second-, and third-grade primary wing spent two hours each day in Team Time. During Team Time, the three grades formed multiage groupings. A sense of community spread among the three classrooms. The children all knew each other better. The older children would look out for the younger children at recess, in the cafeteria, and during other parts of the day.

Another example of collaborative projects occurred when a second-grade class became involved in an invented games project over a period of several weeks. They planned, constructed, and played their invented games. They decided to invite the first-grade children in to play their games. This activity was so successful that they then invited the third-grade class to play their games. During a class discussion following the two events, they analyzed playing with the two different age groups. They talked about what the first graders did with the games and how difficult it was to get the first graders to play the games by the rules they had invented. They decided that playing the games with the third graders was much more interesting because the third graders asked them questions about their games that challenged their thinking and led to refinements in their games.

Community Beyond the School

Field trips are the typical way that classes venture out into the community. Going to such places as art galleries, children's museums, a dairy, factories, farms, and public services such as the post office is a great way to expand and enrich curriculum. Community members can also visit the classroom and share their own stories with children. Russell Dougherty Elementary School in Edmond, Oklahoma, invited families and citizens to a celebration of community. At the celebration, the school displayed the work of students who had researched the history of their community. The children produced a manuscript summarizing their historical study, with stories, drawings, songs, poems, and other graphic documentation.

Students in Linda Skinner's second-grade classroom shared their work that resulted from field trips into the community and interviews with community figures who visited their classroom. One child wrote a summary of what she learned when two community leaders came to visit. She learned from talking to them that her school was named in honor of Russell Dougherty, the first person in their community who had been killed in World War II. This child's idea of community was deepened to include the notion that sometimes people die in wars in order to preserve their communities and their country. What the students learned from this project, in which there was interaction between the school and the community, was greater and more personally meaningful than what they would have learned from a textbook.

Service-Learning Projects

Service-learning projects provide opportunities for children and teachers to give service in some form to the community. Examples of projects include collecting food for the needy; clearing trash; making items, such as colorful placemats, for local nursing homes; and sponsoring events, such as a health fair for the community. These projects help children learn why service is meaningful.

Kristi Dickey's second graders decided to participate in their own service-learning project when a parent came to their classroom to tell them about a needy family in the community with four children. The children brainstormed a list of perishable and nonperishable food items to make a well-balanced meal and volunteered to bring at least one nonperishable item from each home. They were also concerned about providing clothing for the four children since winter was approaching. Mrs. Dickey asked the fourth-grade teacher if her class would like to cosponsor the family. The other class also wanted to participate. Children from both classes brought food and money from home.

When food, clothing, and money had been collected, both classes met to sort items. They brainstormed ideas for how to spend the money. They generated a list of items, including coats, socks, shoes, winter clothes, underwear, and gloves. The fourth graders estimated costs for each item. Children and parents volunteered to visit a local store to shop for items on the list. There were four shopping groups, one for each child in the family. Each group was led by a fourth-grade student with a specific list and a budget. They shopped for the items, compared prices, and found the best bargains. Of the $220.00 they had collected, the shoppers received $0.14 in change, showing their ability to estimate costs accurately.

In reflecting on the project, Kristi said,

> The significance of the service-learning project was big for the family we helped. It was also significant for the second- and fourth-grade children and their teachers and parents. The evidence of learning was great. While all my children approached this idea with a helpful attitude, I sensed that many of them could not relate to being truly needy in terms of food and clothing needed to survive. When we were given a specific family with ages of children that my students could identify with, they immediately responded, "What if that were me?" This opened the door for many discussions on needs and wants. Our community awareness grew as the project took life.
>
> They began to realize what it might be like not to have the necessities of life. Marsha said, "What will happen when they run out of food?" Her comment brought home the fact that doing our good deed with one family one time wasn't going to solve the problem of hunger forever. My students now view themselves as instrumental in helping the community. I asked them to reflect on the project. Jarred, a second grader, wrote, "Helping the adopted family was the best thing I did in my life. It made me feel

good. I don't know why it made me feel good. I want to do it again one day. Because I want that feeling again. I think it changed me as a person."

Service-learning projects help children develop an ethic of care. In a constructivist classroom community, children care for each other. When they are encouraged to go beyond their classroom walls, they extend their care to the broader community. In a study on care in the classroom, Rogers (1999) wrote, "Does the spirit of community help create a place of caring? I would have to conclude from my study that the formation of community establishes the opportunities to practice caring in authentic ways and leads to encounters with caring practices. The competence of children to interact is heightened by the experiences associated with community. Experiences of donating, helping, benevolence, and consideration for other people contribute to community and the essence of a caring classroom" (pp. 187–188). When children experience a caring classroom community, they bond with each other and their teacher. They learn respect through being respected and showing respect to others.

CONSTRUCTIONS

Research

Interview five to seven first-grade children of both genders. Ask them what examples they can give of care in their classroom. Analyze their responses for what care means to them.

SUMMARY

- Creating classroom community so that children are physically, emotionally, and intellectually safe is important to children's well-being.
- Teachers can *create* rules with children, plan the classroom environment together, and provide opportunities to reflect on shared experiences of the group.
- When children learn to cooperate in community with others, they develop autonomy.
- Expanding classroom community to include others outside the classroom, other classes, older children, families, and community members enriches children's experiences of community.
- Classroom communities are caring places.

CONSTRUCTIONS

1. Research

a. Observe in an infant and toddler, Head Start, and public school first-grade classroom. Compare the three classrooms on characteristics of classroom community.

b. Find a professional journal article that describes service-learning projects in early childhood education.

c. Visit a local early childhood program where a variety of services are offered for children and families.

2. Analysis

a. Interview an early childhood teacher about how she or he creates classroom community with children.

b. Design a classroom floor plan that promotes physical, emotional, and intellectual safety. Make a list of materials for your ideal classroom that would help create a caring classroom community.

3. Advocacy

a. Participate in a community group activity designed to promote family involvement.

b. Create a buddy system, such as reading buddies, for younger and older children. Share your idea with local teachers and administrators.

Resources

Books and Articles

Casto, K. L., & Audley, J. R. (2008). *In our school: Building community in elementary schools.* Turner Falls, MA: Northeast Foundation for Children.

The authors, influenced by the Responsive Classroom approach, write about a framework for building a school-wide community focused on common knowledge, routines, gatherings such as school meetings, yearly events such as festivals, and involved families.

Chaille, C., & Britain, L. (2002). *The young child as scientist: A constructivist approach to early childhood science education* (3rd ed.). New York, NY: Longman.

This book gives many examples of children raising and exploring their own questions in an attempt to better understand the world and how it works.

Connolly, P., Hayden, J., & Levin, D. (2007). *From conflict to peace building: The power of early childhood initiatives.* Redmond, WA: World Forum Foundation and NIPPA-The Early Years Organisation.

The authors share stories of early childhood practitioners and children around the world about their struggles and successes in dealing with the consequences of conflict and war on young children. The stories show how early childhood programs can be a vehicle for peace and help injured children overcome the trauma of violence.

DeVries, R., & Zan, B. (2012). *Moral classrooms, moral children: Creating a constructivist atmosphere in early education* (2nd ed.). New York, NY: Teachers College Press.

The authors provide a rationale, based on Piaget's work and their own research, for creating a sociomoral classroom atmosphere. They offer practical ideas for creating classroom community with children that enhances their sociomoral development.

Gallagher, K. C., & Sylvester, P. R. (2009). Supporting peer relationships in early education. In O. A. Barbarin & B. H. Wasik (Eds.), *Handbook of child development and early education: Research to practice* (pp. 223–246). New York, NY: Guildford Press.

This article presents ways for adults to support children's peer interactions with benefits to children's ability to take another's perspective.

Gallas, K. (1994). *The language of learning: How children talk, write, dance, draw, and sing their understanding of the world.* New York, NY: Teachers College Press.

This book provides many practical ideas on how teachers can enable children to communicate their knowledge of the world, not just through writing but through all the arts. The author addresses the importance of creating classroom community.

Guddemi, M., & Jambor, T. (Eds.). (1993). A right to play. *Proceedings of the American Affiliate of the International Association for the Child's Right to Play.* Little Rock, AR: Southern Early Childhood Association.

This book includes chapters by multiple authors documenting the importance of play to children's health and development. The book gives suggestions for how teachers can support children's play.

Helm, J. H., & Beneke, S. (Eds.). (2003). *The power of projects.* New York, NY: Teachers College Press and Washington, DC: National Association for the Education of Young Children.

This resource helps teachers use projects in working with children of poverty, children with special needs, and English language learners.

Helm, J. H., & Katz, L. (2011). *Young investigators: The Project Approach in the early years* (2nded.). New York, NY: Teachers College Press and Washington, DC: National Association for the Education of Young Children.

This book describes how to use the Project Approach with young children including dealing with various issues such as incorporating standards into project work, involving parents, and using technology.

Kamii, C., with Houseman, L. (2000). *Young children reinvent arithmetic: Implications of Piaget's Theory* (2nd ed.). New York, NY: Teachers College Press.

The authors provide research evidence and classroom examples of how children actively construct their knowledge of arithmetic.

Kohn, A. (1999). *The schools our children deserve.* Boston, MA: Houghton Mifflin.

Kohn blasts traditional education with its emphasis on competition and testing and advocates for a constructivist approach to education. He offers numerous examples of how to create classroom community.

Lickey, D. C., & Powers, D. J. (2011). *Starting with their strengths: Using the Project Approach in special education.* New York, NY: Teachers College Press.

This book helps teachers learn about the benefits of project work to children with special needs. Project work helps children build on their strengths, not focusing on their deficits.

Lindfors, J. (1999). *Children's inquiry: Using language to make sense of the world.* New York, NY: Teachers College Press.

The author describes child inquiry and its importance to learning. She gives many examples of how teachers can support children's inquiry.

Nemeth, K. N. (2012). *Basics of supporting dual language learners.* Washington, DC: National Association for the Education of Young Children.

This book offers important suggestions for early childhood teachers in working with children and families who are dual language learners. The author offers many suggestions to both teachers who speak the language of the child and to those teachers who don't.

Noddings, N. (2005). *The challenge to care in schools* (2nd Ed.). New York, NY: Teachers College Press.

The author advocates for an ethic of care in schools, which should be an important part of curriculum at all levels.

Owocki, G. (1999). *Literacy through play.* Portsmouth, NH: Heinemann.

The author describes what is meant by a literacy-rich environment and gives suggestions for creating such a classroom environment in which children come to literacy through play.

Paley, V. G. (1981). *Wally's stories*. Cambridge, MA: Harvard University Press.

Paley, a former kindergarten teacher, shares vignettes of children's stories that reflect their understanding of themselves and each other as they work together as a classroom community.

Paley, V. G. (1999). *The kindness of children*. Cambridge, MA: Harvard University Press.

The author presents stories of children's kindness drawn from her teaching experiences.

Smith, C. A. (1993). *The peaceful classroom*. Beltsville, MD: Gryphon House.

This book should be helpful to teachers who want to create a peaceful classroom community. The author gives numerous examples for how to promote peace in children.

Stone, J. G. (2001). *Building classroom community: The early childhood teacher's role.* Washington, DC: National Association for the Education of Young Children.

The author discusses the importance of respect and creating a caring classroom environment.

Vance, E., & Weaver, P. J. (2002). *Class meetings: Young children solving problems together.* Washington, DC: National Association for the Education of Young Children.

This is a how-to book about using class meetings to help solve classroom problems and disputes.

Wien, C. A. (Ed.). (2008). *Emergent curriculum in the primary classroom: Interpreting the Reggio Emilia approach in schools.* New York, NY: Teachers College Press and Washington, DC: National Association for the Education of Young Children.

This book includes examples of how various primary teachers have interpreted the Reggio Emilia approach into an emergent curriculum that comes from the interests and questions of children.

Web Sites

American Academy of Pediatrics www.aap.org

This site gives current information and guidelines on young children's health and medical issues including research on the importance of play to children's development.

Consumer Product Safety Commission www.cps.org

This site gives guidelines for child safety.

Center on the Social and Emotional Foundations for Early Learning http://csefel.vanderbilt.edu

This is a national resource site sponsored by the Office of Head Start and the Child Care Bureau that offers materials, videos, and resources to help teachers support young children's social emotional competence.

Critical Explorers http://www.criticalexplorers.org

This constructivist site provides many examples and resources for teachers wanting to do an inquiry based curriculum.

National Association for the Education of Young Children www.naeyc.org

National Association for the Education of Young Children (NAEYC) *Developmentally Appropriate Practice in Early Childhood Programs (Rev. Ed.)*

This site has abundant professional information about the field of early childhood education. It also has various position papers that can be downloaded.

Responsive Classroom www.responsiveclassroom.org

Various activities associated with the Responsive Classroom approach, such as Morning Meeting, have been shown through research to result in higher levels of achievement as well as in improved teacher-student relationships.

Teaching Tolerance www.tolerance.org

This site is a project of the Southern Poverty Law Center and provides articles and resources for teaching regarding diversity and respect for differences in schools.

PART 3

WHAT ARE CONSTRUCTIVIST PRACTICES?

In Parts 1 and 2 of this book, you read about how children learn and about how that learning is supported by teachers who understand and implement constructivist theory. In this part, you will learn about how the theory can be implemented in designing curriculum. Chapter 8 addresses what is expected of teachers and what teachers expect of children. We also consider ways in which teachers can gradually implement a constructivist approach. Because there are specific established constructivist strategies available for your use, you have many possible starting places. This chapter also provides information about meeting standards and working with other adults.

In Chapter 9, you will examine some constructivist models of instruction, with particular attention to the thinking behind the models. After reading the chapter, you will have clear information to help you consider existing models and those that may be developed in the future. This chapter helps you examine curriculum models in light of the components of a constructivist model. Many specific examples show you how you can apply constructivist theory in early childhood settings and how various practices and activities relate to particular models.

Chapter 10 demonstrates that a constructivist approach provides a variety of opportunities and expectations for assessment and evaluation. You will find clear examples of ways in which you can continue to implement a constructivist approach while providing meaningful and appropriate records of progress made by your class and by individual children.

All three chapters in this part challenge you to think about how you might implement and evaluate a constructivist curriculum. We hope you will enjoy the many details provided to help you implement all the parts of a constructivist curriculum, using a well-integrated, authentic approach.

8

BUILDING A CONSTRUCTIVIST CURRICULUM

Learning about theory and related practice is essential for you as a future teacher. In addition, you will need to be prepared to address a range of personal and interpersonal expectations. In this chapter, you will learn about ways to implement a constructivist curriculum. After reading this chapter, you will have a better understanding of

- what to expect of yourself as a constructivist teacher;
- how to help children understand expectations;
- how to introduce a constructivist approach gradually;
- how to address standards within your plan;
- how to work with a broad range of students;
- how to gain the support of administrators and parents; and
- how to work with other adults assigned to the same classroom.

Introduction

The teachers' constructivist study group has gathered at Parul's infant-toddler center late in the afternoon for their discussion. At this center, some of the babies and toddlers stay until 6:00 p.m., so quite a few children are still present.

Jennifer: I don't know how you stand it, Parul: What do you do when all those babies start crying at once?

Parul: Actually, in many ways, they aren't that different from your primary children. When they're tired or hungry or don't know what to expect, their behavior changes. Our very young children can't say, "I need a nap."

Matt: Oh, come on, Parul. No one in my class is going to say, "I need a nap."

Ron: Yes, but you can sure tell when they're getting tired of what's going on in class.

Sheila: Yeah, and with preschoolers, I know right away that if they have been sitting at circle time too long, I'd better get them up and moving.

Kenisha: Exactly, and even if I've told them the routine a million times, I still have to let them know what to expect.

Ron: Hey, I've been teaching for several months now, and I'm still trying to figure out what *I'm* supposed to be doing!

Matt: That sounds like a great place to start today: What's expected of teachers and children in classrooms when we use constructivist principles? I'm going to grab one of those brownies Parul made, and then let's get started.

All teachers want to know what is expected of them. Even long-time teachers recognize that community standards change, new programs are put forward, or a new principal or director is assigned to the school. Children also need to know what their teachers expect. This is quite apparent at the beginning of each school year or when a teacher begins to use a new approach such as a constructivist approach. Let's look first at teachers.

Expectations of Teachers

As you proceed through your teacher preparation program, you are learning about what being a professional teacher means. When you begin to implement these ideas, you begin to take stock of which ones fit your teaching personality and style. You also identify which areas you need to reflect on and study more. In this section, we will consider teacher expectations that, when addressed, will make using constructivist principles realistic for the beginning teacher.

Ethical Behavior

Teachers are expected to behave ethically. Studying the NAEYC *Code of Ethical Conduct and Statement of Commitment* (1998/2011). provides an excellent starting point and will be a tool to which you will turn throughout your career. Another NAEYC publication, *Ethics and the Early Childhood Educator: Using the NAEYC Code* (Feeney & Freeman, 2011), provides additional support. The National Education Association (NEA) has published a code, as has the Division for Early Childhood of the Council for Exceptional Children (2007).

One of the chief challenges to ethical behavior is the principle of confidentiality. Teachers are expected to respect the confidential nature of their interactions with children, families, and colleagues. It is sometimes difficult to adhere to this principle when teachers get together in the lounge. Although a conversation about some delightful comment a child made may be acceptable, criticizing a child or family is certainly inappropriate. Child or family issues that the teachers deem as serious should be discussed with appropriate personnel only. As you familiarize yourself with policies and procedures provided by your state and district, you will develop a better sense of who can provide help to a child. Although these requirements may seem overly specific, they are designed to protect the child, the family, and the teacher.

Ethical dilemmas wouldn't be dilemmas if they weren't challenging. A wise practice to establish early in your teaching career is to find and collect resources that you can use when an ethical dilemma occurs. Perhaps your resources will include colleagues or faculty members and contact information for them. Perhaps the local chapter of your professional organization may be included as a resource. These will help you as you learn to make the best decisions rather than using an ambivalent approach and continuing to be distracted by the problem. Recognition of the importance of ethical behavior is one of the marks of professional teaching.

In terms of curriculum, the principle that takes precedence over all the others in the NAEYC *Code of Ethical Conduct* (2012) is this: "Above all, we shall not harm children. We shall not participate in practices that are disrespectful, degrading, dangerous, exploitative, intimidating, emotionally damaging, or physically harmful to children" (p. 3).

Knowledge Related to Content

Every school, child-care center, or district has particular content that is often prescribed by age or grade level. Whether these are detailed or general, your responsibility will be to become familiar with the standards and to have a working knowledge of the content. For example, in the area of physical science for grades K–4, children are expected to learn about the properties of objects and materials (National Research Council, 2008).

Knowledge related to content for young children requires a number of resources. First is your own wealth of knowledge. Accurate knowledge about a wide range of topics is essential for teachers, not because they will be trying to transmit this knowledge to children but because it is impossible to encourage children to express their thinking and to guide them without knowledge. For example, in one preschool classroom, children constructed a tree trunk from cardboard, attached branches, and painted their creation.

Over the year, they observed a tree growing in their playground and modified their own tree to resemble the playground tree. Their teacher needed to be able to answer their questions about changes in leaves, about why the tree doesn't just fall over as their cardboard tree had done initially, and what makes the tree grow. While they observed the tree in the yard, children noticed insects, birds, and squirrels on it. They wondered why the creatures were there. Resources such as books, the Internet, and a local botanist were helpful. Although most of the children were not yet readers, their work consisted of hypothesizing, observing, and gathering and analyzing data. A teacher who knew nothing about trees could not be effective in guiding their discussion. Furthermore, the teacher's expressed interest helped sustain the children's interest.

CONSTRUCTIONS

Analysis

Obtain a copy of the *Next Generation Science Standards* (National Research Council, 2013). Read the account of a teacher encouraging her class to engage in an investigation. Make a list of what the teacher did or said that helped the children to extend their thinking. What knowledge do you think the teacher had in order to respond to the children's conjectures as she did? What materials did she have or obtain in order to support children's work? Compare your analysis with what your classmates determined.

Knowledge About Policies and Procedures

An essential preparation for teaching is to obtain the policies and procedures manual that your district and school use. Study this manual carefully. For example, what do you do when a child who is ill comes to school or when a child burns himself or herself in a classroom cooking experience? If there is a school nurse, the answer is easy, but today many schools have no nurse or perhaps have only a part-time health aide. Another example involves an increasingly occurring situation relating to a child's noncustodial parent. What can you tell the parent? What if he or she comes to take the child to an appointment? You'll also need to know the procedures that you must teach the children, such as those for tornado drills, "stranger danger" situations, and what to do if they arrive at school late.

Organizing Furniture and Materials

As a constructivist teacher, you'll want to be sure that your classroom is organized so that you can implement curriculum using a constructivist approach. Is there reasonable time and space for children to work together? Are there places to which children can retreat for thinking, reading, and just having a little extra space? Because few classrooms are as spacious as teachers would like, they have to find ways to organize materials, arrange tables, and eliminate unneeded furnishings.

You must ensure that materials and furnishing are aesthetically pleasing and that they represent a range of cultures and characters of both genders. Check the materials. Are they durable enough for classroom use? Repair or discard them when they become dirty or begin to disintegrate. Make sure information presented in classroom materials is accurate and timely. "They're just for young children" is not an excuse for misinformation or unfounded ideas.

As you manage the materials, you want to rotate them regularly so that children have opportunities to explore many types of items, particularly if these are materials that are not likely to be in many homes. For example, most preschoolers will not have a large set of blocks at home, and although all children should have access to a good library, some do not. Many children will have a limited supply of books that they can call their own, but a classroom should have dozens and dozens of books. Home art materials may be limited. At school, children should have access to a wide variety of art and music experiences, and they should be encouraged to learn about the people who have created various types of art and music.

When you are well prepared for the day, you'll be able to focus on children's learning rather than on finding the book you had intended to read. Children will be able to create a collage without waiting for the assistant teacher to go to the storeroom for glue, and you won't find your class in the middle of preparing ingredients for soup when you suddenly realize that you forgot to notify the cook that you'd be bringing the soup down to the kitchen to simmer.

The expectations set for teachers are high. They come from administrators, parents, and children. Perhaps your own expectations are even higher. Your advance preparation will help you meet most challenges, and your ability to seek and use resources will continue to help you grow as a teacher.

Help Children Understand Expectations

Most children who understand what is expected will try to respond appropriately. Therefore, teachers must be sure that their expectations are reasonable and correspond with their beliefs about children's development and learning. A teacher who professes to focus on the development of children's independence while insisting that they follow dozens of detailed rules is inconsistent. In contrast, the teacher who expects children to be responsible and works with them to develop an understanding of responsibility is more likely to find children who enjoy being in school and take pride in being responsible.

No matter what the child's age, having fun is not the goal of school, nor is keeping busy. Children attend school to learn. Sometimes they will be quite busy, and sometimes they will have fun. Most of the time they will be working, and some of the time they will not enjoy the work that is required. However, children are more likely to be engaged in their work when they are participating in a program based on constructivist theory since choice, decision making, and authentic tasks are emphasized.

When teachers decide in advance what will be expected of children, they will be able to express those expectations to children. Many of these expectations are related to routines of the school day, such as what children do when they arrive, need supplies, finish assigned work, have to go to the bathroom, or aren't sure how to complete an assignment. These expectations should be designed so that children can take care of their own needs generally without asking the teacher. At the beginning of a school year, when a new child is enrolled, and after vacations, teachers have to teach children the routines. When children forget or decide not to follow expectations, teachers who talk privately with the child or children are more likely to determine what their needs are and how to meet the child's needs while maintaining a well-functioning classroom. In situations that are beyond the expertise of classroom teachers, a different type of professional help must be provided, and it is essential that the parents are adequately apprised of the developing situation in a timely manner.

Focus on Independent Thinking

Teachers who use a constructivist approach may find that the children need support in understanding their roles. This is the case particularly when children have had previous experiences with traditional teachers who expected children to listen to adults and quietly do whatever they were told. All teachers agree that there are times when children must listen to adults and follow their directions. Nonetheless, if children understand that obeying is their only role, they often try to create ways to circumvent the teacher's power. For example, some children will throw paper wads, make faces behind the teacher's back, or challenge the teacher's authority by disrupting the class. Others will try to behave perfectly at all times and at all costs. Using an authoritarian or didactic style in response does not meet children's real needs.

When children first encounter opportunities to think for themselves, they may not believe that thinking is what is really expected. As a result, they may repeatedly test their teachers to determine whether the expectation is real and continuing. Teachers can prevent at least part of this testing by explaining in detail what is expected and why. Following their explanations, they can provide children with opportunities for a variety of types of input.

When controversy arises as part of class work, the teacher is responsible for ensuring that arguments and counterarguments are presented and that children learn the need for reliable sources. In teaching social studies, teachers have an opportunity to help children consider their beliefs and attitudes. Although they will surely not be making the same choices that adults do, children do make choices every day about friendships and responses to others. They are establishing ideas of fairness, dependability, and consideration for others. Keep in mind that someday these same children will be adults making far-reaching decisions based in part on the foundations their early childhood teachers helped them establish.

Provide Continuous Support

Teachers in constructivist classrooms **scaffold** children's learning rather than telling them exactly what to do or what the answer is. Constructivist teachers often have children work in small groups because they understand that sharing ideas helps children reconsider notions that they have previously held to be true. Even the child who is offering an explanation may revise her thinking as she speaks.

When teachers decide to have their children work in small groups, they are providing an opportunity for children to learn content without continued direct supervision by the adult. They are also providing more time for each child to be actively involved and helping children develop teamwork skills. Although putting children in groups and giving them an assignment to complete may seem simple on the surface, in fact teachers have significant planning and monitoring to accomplish.

You'll need to ensure that children know how to listen to each other and how to disagree appropriately (Cohen, 1994). When children spend all of the group-work time arguing, they obviously aren't addressing content. Once they have developed listening and disagreeing skills, they can learn to monitor the group behavior themselves and to remind each other of what is expected. Even preschoolers can develop the ability to help other children work through problems together. The following Curriculum Strategies provides guidelines for facilitating group work with children.

CURRICULUM STRATEGIES: FACILITATING GROUP WORK

- Teach children skills for working in a group.
- Create an appropriate group work task.
- Design a time frame during which groups will be able to work and a time when the assignment must be completed.

- Decide which children will be in each group or whether to allow children to decide.
- Plan how the work will be assessed.
- Teach expectations related to the assignment

You will learn to explain to children general procedures for group work, such as where each group will work, whether roles will be assigned by the teacher or chosen by the group members, and what the expectations for ending a session will be. Will you assign groups, thus ensuring that all children are included without embarrassment and perhaps providing a mixture of abilities, or will the groups form based on children's preferences, allowing the children to constitute their groups independently?

You also must learn to design assignments that require higher-level thinking rather than just getting a correct answer. For example, practicing spelling words would not be a worthwhile group activity; creating a group story using these spelling words might be effective. Checking answers on worksheets would not be valid math group work, but working together to solve real problems involving math would be. For example, being a line leader is important to many young children. They may be asked to figure out how many times each child will get to be leader if there are 180 days of school—how many times each child will be a line leader for one day at a time, and how many times each child gets another turn after everyone in the class has already had a turn.

Children must know from the beginning when they are expected to have an assignment completed. Kindergartners might work together for 15 minutes and then share their findings, while third graders might work on an issue for several weeks. However, even preschoolers, when engaged in projects of interest to them, can sustain involvement over an extended period.

Children also need to know at the outset what the criteria for a good product are. The product may be a decision about a problem, such as what to do about litter on the school playground, or it might involve finding information that will enable the group to produce a written report or present to the class orally, perhaps in the form of a skit.

Once you have the group work plans in place and the groups in operation, you must ensure that the children remain focused on content. As you move from group to group, listen to the discussions and ask children if they are following expectations, such as allowing everyone time to speak. Help the group focus children who are daydreaming, chatting about other topics, or not contributing to the group work. If at all possible, allow the group members to maintain autonomy rather than moving into the group and enforcing rules.

When one or more groups seem unable to manage effectively, you may need to review with the children the skills needed to participate in a group. Perhaps if group social skills are undeveloped, you should create a shorter and less complex assignment the next time so that the children can balance group skills and exploration of content.

Multiple Perspectives: From the Classroom

When Ronice Johnson was a second-grade teacher, she incorporated constructivist principles in her classroom. We asked Ms. Johnson to tell us how she helped children understand what is expected of them and how she helped them stay focused. Here is what she told us:

When I began to move toward a constructivist approach, I realized right away that even though the children were only in second grade, they had already learned to do what the teachers said. Many of them had moved from school to school right in our city as their families coped with poverty, eviction, poor housing and urban redevelopment.

The children didn't believe I wanted them to come up with their own ideas. When I told them they could write about whatever they wanted to write at journal time or choose which book they wanted to read next, some of them were immobilized. "Is this okay, Ms. Johnson? Can I write about a bird—'cause I found a dead bird in the street?" I had to spend a lot of time reassuring them. Some children may have wanted to test me and see if I really meant what I said. One boy wrote that he wants to have a gold chain and a big car and lots of beautiful girls. I had to admit to myself that he was writing about what he knew. I responded as I do with all the children, asking him to explain something I didn't understand, suggesting ways to help the reader know more about his thinking. Over time he moved away from that topic and began to write about how his momma helps him, about football, and even about how our city government should clean up the streets around our school.

Gradually children began to trust that I meant what I said. However, I did face the challenge presented by some children who carried making their own decisions to extremes and decided that their choice was to draw all day, talk to their friends, and in one case, go to sleep in a cozy area I had set up for individual reading. I learned that freedom doesn't mean license. Perhaps I should say, I learned that I had to help the children understand that freedom doesn't mean license. I also learned that the living conditions of some of my students were so crowded that sleeping for awhile at school may be exactly what they needed to do in order to be able to work productively the rest of the day.

Because my children, like all writers, wrote what they knew about, I decided to work toward extending their horizons. I inventoried where the children had been. Most had gone to the zoo, the fire station and a pumpkin farm with their classes. All had visited relatives, including a few whose families had driven to other states. They had been in cars, trucks, and buses, but no one had encountered trains, planes, or boats. No one had been to the center of the city, except perhaps to drive through it. No one had walked in the woods, jumped in a pile of autumn leaves, or explored a creek. I thought back to the classroom in which I had done my student teaching. Two of the children had been to Europe. Many others had flown to distant states for vacations, and all of them had yards with lots of trees.

Obviously, I couldn't take my class on a plane trip to a distant state, but maybe we could go to an airport and board a plane. Or perhaps we could go on a short train ride. Maybe riding a horse would be even more intriguing. I was quite energized at the thought of the curricular ramifications of such projects, and I was undaunted by the red tape I'd have to go through to accomplish them.

While the children strengthened their belief that I really was going to continue to let them have quite a bit of choice regarding their learning activities, I made plans, including them and their ideas as soon as I knew we really could go as a group to a camp with child-friendly horses and their handlers. As day-to-day work and planning for our one-day trip continued, I made copious notes. I wanted to be sure I could document the learning goals and how they related to the standards I was expected to ensure that children would meet.

At the end of each day for the first few weeks, we gathered in a circle just before dismissal to talk about what we had learned that day. Before long, children were so busy working that we delayed this discussion until every Friday afternoon. One Friday, Linda announced, "Last week I learned how big a horse is because we measured how big the book said, but this week I got to get on the horse and I really learned how big a horse is."

That and so many other insights the children shared, both directly and indirectly, helped me know that the children were beginning to understand the constructivist learning process and they certainly were learning. They were focused, at least much of the time, and they were learning content.

CONSTRUCTIONS

Analysis

Reread the previous Multiple Perspectives section on Ms. Johnson and her class. List the strategies she used to help children learn. Explain which strategies you think were appropriate and why, and which you think were inappropriate and why. Bring your analysis to class (or post on the class discussion board) to discuss with a classmate.

Introduce a Constructivist Approach Gradually

Let's look in on the teachers' study group meeting at Parul's infant center.

Sheila: Well, maybe group work is doable in primary grades, but preschoolers just couldn't handle it. I mean, they do play together, and sometimes they build some great buildings together. I hear them making plans and debating about how to make windows and doors—but if I try to turn my program into a constructivist way, well, I just know it won't work.

Kenisha: Wait a minute, Sheila. It sounds like you might have more of a constructivist approach than the rest of us. At least you have a good start. Children are following their interests, they're solving problems, and they're interacting. They're obviously thinking about what's going on—and you mentioned that sometimes they'll work on a building project for several days.

Jennifer: Okay, okay. So it works in preschool. But I've got third grade with all those standards, and there is no way that I'm going to throw out my textbooks and worksheets and have kids start constructing something.

Matt: It sounds pretty wild to me too, Jen, but I'm thinking of starting with just one thing at a time. What we talked about earlier gave me a pretty good idea of how to help children begin a new approach, say, at journal time. Does anybody have ideas for working with journals?

We'll leave the group now and turn to consideration of ways to get started as a constructivist.

When teachers, whether beginners or seasoned, decide to use a constructivist approach, they are usually quite energized at the thought of all the learning that will occur. They look forward to a positive climate in which their children focus on thinking and problem solving rather than on rote memorization and drill and practice. All teachers recognize that there are indeed facts to be memorized and skills to be practiced, but constructivist teachers focus first on helping children develop understanding.

New teachers who have studied constructivist learning and may even have had the opportunity to work with a constructivist teacher during student teaching or internship may feel that they are ready to implement a totally constructivist classroom right away. Experienced teachers who have begun to question their traditional approaches to teaching may want to discard all their current practices and start over with their newfound understanding. Other teachers have found that a balanced approach is more realistic.

As teachers think about organizing a curriculum based on constructivism, they must plan for the time and energy required to develop a deep understanding of the needs of each individual child and to plan for those needs. They must also be prepared to assess how well each child is progressing and how effectively they are serving each child. Because of time constraints, it is not unreasonable to retain some traditional practices while engaging in the development of more opportunities for children to construct their own knowledge.

For example, one teacher may elect to begin with a project approach to social studies while continuing other teaching with little change. As she develops that approach and helps children learn how to work within those boundaries yet with more freedom, she is able to understand where her strengths lie and to improve on an aspect of a constructivist curriculum that had previously eluded her. Perhaps she is just beginning to accept the idea that children can create wonderful and worthwhile ideas. Perhaps she must focus primarily on relating the projects to the required curriculum. She may be stymied by lack of materials in a school system that allocates all its funds for textbooks and workbooks. All of these issues and many others can be overcome. Many of them have been discussed in previous chapters.

Once you have some of these basic issues worked out, and your children have become comfortable with what for many of them is a radically different approach to learning, then you can adjust other areas of the curriculum or parts of the day to application of constructivist principles.

Elicit Ideas From Children

As you listen to children, whether informally or through their contributions at group time or in their writing, you will often be able to pick up on a topic that would probably be of interest to the entire class. A discussion with your children will help you decide whether the topic is one that can be explored by the class, a segment of the class, or an individual child. Sometimes, a conversation with the child will suffice, satisfying her that you are interested in her idea. You may discover that she is already pursuing the topic independently, something you certainly want to support, or you may discern that she doesn't have the depth of interest you may have perceived initially.

Sometimes you'll elicit ideas by observing a child, building on his or her interests, and then working to extend them. Imagine a preschooler who loves to build with unit blocks and participates in this activity almost daily. A teacher can help that child learn about simple machines by putting a ramp in the block area one week. Perhaps a little later, a pulley system could be set up. Going to a construction site or watching a video of construction machines at work may extend construction play. Children's museums often have activities involving simple machines that children can operate. Sometimes a group of children is required in order to see results from the activity.

The following Curriculum Strategies demonstrates the set of strategies for developing a topic.

CURRICULUM STRATEGIES: DEVELOPING A TOPIC

1. Generate an idea.
2. Explore the idea with children.

    a.   Make a web.

    b.   List the children's questions.

    c.   Ask them to consider the topic and discuss it further the next day.

3. Gather materials for your background information.
4. Engage children in obtaining and using materials.
5. Plan ways to integrate curricular areas and standards.
6. Work with the children to document their work and progress.
7. Plan for regular reporting in class meetings.
8. Develop a concluding experience with children.

In a first-grade classroom, a child reports at group time, "Here's a picture of my dad when he was 1 year old. He's standing next to a tree my grandpa planted because he was so happy when my dad was born." As is the practice in many classrooms, the other children are invited to ask the speaker, Coulter, questions. During that questioning, they learn that Coulter went to visit his grandparents over spring break and saw the tree, which is now much taller than his dad is. Picking up on this, the teacher begins to explore further. Do they know how tall trees get? What are determining factors? How can you tell how old a tree is? What kinds of trees grow in our area? The children respond with all kinds of ideas—some correct and some erroneous. The teacher writes the questions and ideas on a chart and promises to find out more. At the same time, she asks them to begin to look for information about trees. They decide they can talk to their families, look at trees in their neighborhoods, and find out if they have any materials at home related to trees.

That afternoon, the teacher checks with the resource center at her school and with the local public library online and finds a wealth of materials at the children's level. She continues on the Internet and looks for other resources. There she enters a teacher chat room and requests ideas for their study of trees. The response from other teachers overwhelms her. Great ideas, some activities that she considers inappropriate, a few that might even be unsafe, pictures of children engaged in studying trees—all come to her right at her classroom computer. She prints some of the resources and turns to her school district's standards book to work on aligning the possible project activities with the standards.

The next day, many of the children bring in books, magazines, leaves, pictures, and ideas. One child reports that his father told him that people are cutting down lots of trees, and birds and animals won't have a place to live any longer. Another child says that we could look around and find out that lots of things in our houses are made from trees. Nature magazines, both child and adult oriented, have articles about forests, logging, traveling to see autumn leaves, and trees that produce crops for human consumption.

The teacher lists all their questions, and the children vote on the ones they are most interested in learning about by writing down the numbers of their two top choices. A group of children volunteer to tabulate the results and find a way to bring the information to the group by the next afternoon.

In this example, one child's sharing has led to a major worthwhile project that promises to lend itself to a wide range of learning goals for children with diverse abilities. The teacher has already begun to integrate reading, writing, math, science, social studies, and oral and written conversation. The children's art may be included during the project. Songs, instrumental music, and the sounds of trees in the wind and leaves being crunched underfoot may also be explored.

CONSTRUCTIONS

Journal Entry

In your journal, write your reaction to the tree project. Did Coulter's teacher make a sound professional decision when she decided to involve the children in a study of trees? If you had been Coulter's teacher, what might you have done? Suppose only one or two other children expressed interest in trees. What might you have done in that case?

In introducing a new topic, teachers usually begin by finding out what their children already know and what they would like to know about the topic. For example, in one urban area where a Freedom Center related to the history of slavery is being built, a number of children had heard conversations about the center. Some children may have a general idea about slavery, but few, if any, will understand the personal, cultural, economic, ethical, and political ramifications. Some children may come to school with strong beliefs based on family attitudes. In fact, teachers will have their own beliefs and attitudes. When working in a classroom, teachers must not impose their biases but must help children examine, insofar as they are able, what happened and what people living in the twenty-first century can do. Teachers must not give cursory treatment to a topic to avoid addressing fairly those issues with which their constituents may not agree. Even preschoolers are quite aware of current events, many of them controversial. Although they are just beginning to take the perspectives of others, they are often eager to discuss issues of fairness in the classroom and the community. These types of discussions are important regardless of the makeup of the class in terms of socioeconomic status, racial and ethnic backgrounds, disabilities, and differences in developmental levels.

Helping Children Develop Investigations

In one third-grade class, the teacher, Mr. Childs, posted a large sheet of paper on the wall during the first week of school. He asked the children to list on the paper anything they were interested in (see Box 8.1). Mr. Childs explained that he would leave the paper up for five days. The following Monday, the class would discuss the topics and find out whether any of their classmates were also interested. If so, they could form an investigation team.

BOX 8.1 WHAT CHILDREN IN OUR CLASS ARE INTERESTED IN

Baseball
Why we have to go to school
Not having homework
Soccer
Who is the coolest singer
Harry Potter
Who takes care of the aquarium in the library
Lions (the local high school football team)
Why people are homeless
What to do when someone is mean to you
My dog—he's a German Shepherd
Field trips
Infinity

Each team would write a proposal to the teacher explaining what they wanted to explore and why. The teacher would meet with the team to help them develop an investigation plan. Time for investigating would be set aside each afternoon. The teacher would also choose an investigation for children who didn't create their own. When the children and teacher felt that the investigation was complete, that team would make a presentation to the class. By the following Monday, the class had listed a few fascinating ideas—many that one would not expect.

Throughout the exploration period, the teacher and teams met periodically to consider progress. Mr. Childs reviewed the journal each team kept of their daily work and findings. Early in the year, investigations were rather brief. One team wanted to know whether everybody in the class was on a soccer team. The teacher helped them develop a hypothesis and create the exact question to which they wanted an answer. The two team members each copied down the names of half the children in the class and then asked the question of each child. They created a computer-generated graph to show their results. One team wanted to know why there were snails in the aquarium located in the school library. They found out that the sixth-grade science teacher was the caretaker for the aquarium. She answered the team's questions during a free period, and the librarian helped the children find print materials they could read. Mr. Childs helped them find an Internet site, enabling them to print two colored pictures. Later in the year, the explorations became more extensive and occasionally included adult visitors who were knowledgeable in the area being investigated.

CONSTRUCTIONS

Journal Entry

Reread the description of the third graders' introduction to learning in Mr. Childs's constructivist classroom. Write in your journal your thoughts about what the teacher did and why. How did the teacher's role affect what the children did over time? What do you think Mr. Childs would do if a child didn't participate, even when given a topic to investigate?

In previous chapters, you have read numerous examples of how and why to include choice, decision making, and other constructivist principles. The key is to consider the principle, create curriculum that encourages you and the children to apply that principle, and make clear to children what the principle means. When you use the terminology in context and provide appropriate opportunities for decision making, most children will begin to understand. For example, you might say, "Would you like to make a decision about what to call our new hamster?" In this way, you have provided an opportunity to make a legitimate choice and to use a decision-making process. Read the example provided in Box 8.2 to see how this might lead to an investigation and additional decision making.

Use Established Constructivist Strategies

As you begin to introduce a constructivist approach in your classroom, you will find that you do not have to create a new way of doing things by yourself. Other teachers have created practices that have proven effective and are based on constructivist theory. These practices can serve as templates for you. You will insert your own topics and modify the approaches to meet the needs of children in your classes.

Margo Sampson made the chart in Box 8.2 with sentences contributed by members of her kindergarten class.

BOX 8.2 TEACHERS DOCUMENT CHILDREN'S THINKING ABOUT A TOPIC

Our Hamster
We chose to name our hamster Tiny.
There were 12 votes for Tiny.
There were 9 votes for Wiggly.
Twelve is more so 12 won.
Mrs. Sampson read us a book about hamsters.
We decided what to feed him.
(Two days later the class added the following sentences.)
We want to investigate what hamsters like.
We will watch Tiny.
Sougay and Monique will ask Mr. Wong's class about their hamster.

Projects

You have read about projects in previous chapters. One example is a quilting project, which can be an effective means for integrating all aspects of the curriculum, connecting home and school, and providing an opportunity for exploring ways in which this long-standing tradition has been used across cultures (Helm, Huebner, & Long, 2000). The authors also offer lists of related children's books, how-to books, and Web sites. Teachers of preschooler through third grade can involve their children in a quilting project. Perhaps the whole school and community could participate.

Multiple Perspectives: From the Classroom

Hilda Stegbauer, who was a preschool teacher, enjoys quilting. One day she brought her work to show her four-year-old class. Many children were intrigued, leading Hilda to plan ways to involve them in quilt making. Her children each chose a colored burlap square.

Using large needles, yarn, beads, and sequins, each child created a unique design on his or her square. Hilda sewed the squares together and hung the quilt for children and visitors to enjoy. The following year, each class member took a square home so that each family could decide together what they would put on their square.

Hilda pointed out that a project such as this usually lasts several weeks in preschool. Children are free to work on it if and when they choose to do so. However, Hilda encourages each child to participate so that there are no disappointments when the quilt is finally hung.

When one of Hilda's student teachers began teaching in an urban primary multi-age classroom, the children were studying families. Each child brought in one or two favorite items from home—a worn teddy bear, or perhaps a plastic bracelet, a baby shoe, or a book. One child brought a photograph of her grandmother with a quilt that the family had brought to the city from Appalachia. Aware that this child's grandmother lived with her, the teacher phoned her to tell her how much she had enjoyed seeing the photograph. The grandmother, who was quite pleased, offered to bring the quilt to school. When they saw it, the children asked if they could make a quilt, and a quilting project was soon underway. Students investigated quilts and quilting bees. Students decided how big their quilt should be, how big each child's piece would be, and what they would put on the pieces. This was to be a quilt similar to Grandma's they decided. (Everyone in the school now called her Grandma.) With much trial and error, children worked out patterns, measured, calculated, and only then cut into the beautiful cloth scraps that volunteers had provided. They learned about batting, backing, and binding and were especially challenged when trying to determine how much thread they would need.

A related project arose when a small group said they would like to make a book of stories about people who had made quilts. Some children interviewed relatives and gave oral reports on their findings. Another group explored other household practices during early periods of American history.

CONSTRUCTIONS

Analysis

Review the description of the quilting projects. Record in your journal which areas of the curriculum were integrated and in what ways.

When faced with children's wonderful ideas, you will have to decide whether a feasible plan can be worked out and whether you can find realistic ways to weave standards-based content into the study. You will also have to consider what else is occurring. For instance, if in three weeks your school will have a holiday pageant, and your class has been assigned to play a key role, this is not the time to start a new project. You may want to bring the idea up after winter break, or you may help children think of ways they could explore the topic independently.

Shared Reading

When the teacher uses a shared reading strategy (Justic & Kaderavek, 2002; Holdaway, 1986, 1999), the children read to a partner a passage from a book they are both enjoying. Then the partner reads a passage to the first reader. In some cases, one child is able to help the other if he or she has difficulty with a word or concept. Children may become interested in the book that a peer has shared and decide to read it for themselves. Alternatively, two children may sit next to each other at their table or even on a comfortable stack of pillows in a sunny corner of the classroom. They will take turns reading a page from the same book. Afterward, they may make an entry in their literature log.

Literature Log

A literature log is a running record of the stories or books the child has read and his or her commentary on that. At first, the comments may be quite brief, but with encouragement from the teacher, children gradually write more extensive entries. Periodically, the teacher reads each log and responds to the writer, often with questions or comments designed to encourage the child to extend his or her thinking about that and future books.

Classroom Library

Providing a variety of books in the early childhood classroom makes reading more tempting, even for children who have difficulty learning to read. Although some schools have excellent library collections and many more are available at public libraries, having a wealth of books at hand encourages children to read throughout the day. Also, the teacher can readily locate the perfect book when an unexpected learning opportunity arises.

Many teachers purchase paperback books for their personal classroom collections. Some families donate books their children have outgrown. Teachers also obtain plastic bins for storage, labeling each book with a category name, such as Animal Stories, Stories About Children, Books About Nature, Poetry, and Chapter Books. When the bins are the right size (about half the height of the books), there should be enough room for children to flip through each one to find a book that appeals to them. At the beginning of the year, the number of books should be limited to avoid overwhelming children. As the year progresses, add new books regularly.

In your classroom, you'll want to focus on the many worthwhile books that are available—those with accurate facts, well-written text, and beautiful illustrations. But occasionally a child will be on a reading jag that you would not have chosen. For example, one first grader learned to read by focusing on figuring out what was printed on his Pokémon cards. Of course, you will have to use common sense and follow school policies. Some schools list certain trade books to be read at certain grade levels. Others create reading lists in response to parental expectations, children's interests, and classroom activities.

Reading Parties

Some teachers arrange reading parties as a regular part of the school day. The teacher calls four or five children together, asking them to bring the book or books they are currently reading. If the children have all been assigned to read the same book, each can choose a favorite passage to read or report on. Alternatively, the group may have a discussion about the content, the characters, or the writer's style. When each child brings a different book to the reading party, the teacher asks the child to read a favorite part. During this time, she makes notes about the child's reading and about which book each child has chosen. She may limit the choice of books to a particular genre, difficulty level, or topic, depending on her goals for the children. During a reading party, the teacher may instruct the group on an aspect of writing or grammar. For example, she may explain the use of quotation marks. She may also discuss agreement of subject and verb. Her instruction may be in response to a child's question or comment or may be the result of her observations of children's reading or writing. Teachers who are familiar with a wide range of children's books conduct the most successful reading parties.

Journal Writing

Many teachers expect their children to write in journals daily. Some encourage children to write about whatever they choose and to develop the piece through several drafts, including reading it to other children for feedback and participating in a writer's conference with the teacher. At such a conference, the teacher provides coaching and instruction as needed, helping the child learn punctuation and grammar, as well as taking into consideration the intended audience. Since young children still have some difficulty taking the perspective of another, they may write only from their own perspective, leaving the reader to wonder what actually transpired.

This method (Taylor, Branscombe, Burcham, & Land, 2011) uses class discussion as a starting point for journal writing. Often, children have a topic that they are interested in sharing. The teacher asks children to share their idea for a story with the class and records the child's name and topic on chart paper or a white board. Usually, two or three children have something they want to share with the class. As each story is told, other children may ask the speaker questions about it. A chart might list the following ideas for the day:

Megan's grandmother came to visit from Arkansas.
Tamika got a cut finger.
Ramundo's dog died.

When the whole class is somewhat familiar with the topics, the children then vote on which story they will all write about. As they do this writing, they begin to recognize that they can try to take another person's point of view. However, they will also be presenting their own perspectives. The original storyteller will be able to hear her or his story through many other voices.

Games Created by Children or Teachers

Another constructivist teaching strategy is the use of games. A wide range of games is available commercially, and many of them focus on objectives that teachers are trying to help children reach. When a suitable game is not available or is too costly, teachers often make their own. Although game creation is time-consuming and can become expensive, the teacher's games can be designed to target very specific situations. (See Kamii & Joseph, 2004.)

When preparing to use games in the classroom, teachers must focus on the content to be explored. When you provide a range of games, children who are working at different levels of understanding can participate. For example, in a preschool classroom, you might provide a simple grid game for children who are just beginning to understand one-to-one correspondence, while a long-path game may also be available for children who are already working with two dice and perhaps have even constructed the idea of adding the two quantities of dots to determine where to move their markers.

Games may also be played using a variety of technological tools. In choosing software, the teacher must be sure to review the content and the way in which it is presented. Software should contain appropriate content and be well illustrated. While admittedly it is often easier to use animated animals and objects rather than create art with a multicultural representation of real children, it must seem confusing to children to observe that it is usually bears and talking trucks that are able to solve problems. The National Association for the

Education of Young Children (2012) has published a position statement on the use of technology with young children that will provide you with guidelines and standards for using technology in your classroom.

Working With Curriculum Mandates

In some cases the school district or center director mandates the curriculum. For example, third graders may be required to study their state's history. Most children at this age are just developing concepts of time and space. They are not sure of the physical relationships among cities, states, and countries, and if they are asked to draw a map of their state and show on their map where their city is, they may draw a small circle for their city next to, rather than within, the larger circle representing their state. In terms of time, children may think their parents were born long ago before TV and computers were invented.

Barton and Levstik (2004, 1996) interviewed children from kindergarten through sixth grade. Each child was shown nine pictures depicting various times in history, such as a family and a covered wagon on the prairie and a family reading and sewing at home circa 1930. They found that even kindergartners could divide the pictures into two groups: long ago and now. Some could make even finer distinctions. Teachers who are familiar with ways in which children organize sticks of varying lengths in a seriation task (Piaget, 1941/1965) may relate these two types of research. Piaget's work showed that children begin by grouping large sticks and small sticks without making any finer distinctions. As they develop understanding of the task, they can put each stick in order by length by comparing a stick with the one to the left and the one to the right in the sequence, and then determining whether the spot that they have chosen is accurate.

In the historical pictures study, the criterion was time rather than length of sticks, but the results were similar. Constructivist teachers take the children's ability to construct particular kinds of knowledge into account and look for ways to make required topics as meaningful as possible to children.

Stay Focused on Content

You have just read about the importance of providing opportunities for children to express their opinions and to learn to gather accurate data. Information and understanding go hand in hand, and it is the teacher's responsibility to see that children learn that discussion must be based on content. You will guide children to form ideas around experiences, information from a variety of sources, and their growing ability to think independently.

When teachers encourage children to make many choices and to design and implement projects, it is sometimes difficult to retain the focus on the curriculum standards. The following Curriculum Strategies lists several approaches you can use to ensure that the content does remain paramount and that the standards are addressed.

When teachers organize their daily plans, they juxtapose the standards they are expected to follow and the activities they and the children have chosen to carry out. Some teachers begin this process before school starts by photocopying the lists of required and selected standards. The Curriculum Strategies feature lists strategies some teachers find helpful in demonstrating that they are working with standards.

CURRICULUM STRATEGIES: STAYING FOCUSED

- Engage in detailed planning.
- Note standards addressed on your weekly plan.
- Cross-reference standards (local, state, and national).
- Post a daily agenda for yourself and the children.
- Support children doing group work.
- Use questions to help children focus.
- Relate required content to children's interests.

Multiple Perspectives: How One Teacher Uses Standards

Mrs. Wittenberg, a veteran teacher in a Cincinnati-area district, was provided a set of standards for each curricular area by the district. The district standards are aligned with the state's standards but are more detailed than those of the state. She is also particularly interested in and concerned about children's performance in mathematics. She uses her copy of the National Council of Teachers of Mathematics Standards (2000) to ensure that she is addressing the recommendations presented in the pre-K through second-grade strand.

Mrs. Wittenberg makes a copy of all the standards and cuts them apart so that she can group them and see where the similarities and differences occur. At this point, she can work out a plan, listing the basic order in which she will address the topics and the approximate amount of time she will allocate for each. As she does this, Mrs. Wittenberg realizes that she may revise her plan based on children's needs and that there will inevitably be interruptions, such as weather-related delays or postponements of school, outbreaks of flu or other illness that keep children and teachers home, and even scheduled events such as picture-taking day. See the following Curriculum Strategies for information related to integrating standards.

Mrs. Wittenberg works out a plan for the week and then for each day. She lists the learning goals for the children, what she will expect them to do, what she will do, and the materials they will need. Each day she will reassess what has happened that day and modify the next day's plans as needed. She may need to work with an individual or a small group, providing a simpler version of what she had presented the previous day. For example, if the class has been solving double-column addition problems, she may notice several children who are not yet working with 10. She may then provide them with single-digit problems and listen to their methods for solving them. She may also provide games that give children opportunities to compose 10, using various combinations (Kamii & Joseph, 2004).

CURRICULUM STRATEGIES: INTEGRATING STANDARDS

1. Assemble copies of all standards that your children are expected to meet. (For infants through preschool years, you may want to consider developmental milestones.)
2. Copy the standards and cut them apart so you can group them. For example, state and district standards probably overlap with Common Core standards to some extent.
3. Look for ways to integrate the standards. For example, measurement standards involve math and science and may also apply to social studies, literature, and art.
4. Create a plan indicating the general order of broad topics for the year and approximately how much time will be devoted to each. Keep in mind that you want your children to be involved in decision making, but you can't decide not to address multiplication if that is part of the third-grade curriculum.
5. Talk with special educators and other faculty (art, music, physical education, library) who will work with your children. Share goals, align requirements, and integrate plans if possible.
6. Work out a detailed plan for at least the first week, listing what you will do, what you expect children to do, and what materials you will need. Add code numbers or letters to denote standards addressed.
7. Develop a plan for documenting individual children's progress toward the level of proficiency accompanying some standards.
8. At the end of each day, modify plans as needed.
9. Set aside a specific time each week for planning for the next week.

CONSTRUCTIONS

Research

Locate a copy of the Common Core standards for your state for pre-K through third grade. Find out how these standards were created and who was involved in creating them. Next, locate a copy of your school district's standards; find out how they were created and who was involved. Finally, locate a copy of the standards published by a professional organization for one of the content areas such as science or language arts. Find out how these standards were created and who was involved. Then compare and contrast the three sets of standards.

Consider the Needs of Each Child

Back at the teachers' study group, in the midst of discussing ways to get started, Ron interrupted:

Ron: It sounds like every one of you has perfect classes with well-behaved children just waiting to see what's next. Now, in my class …

Jennifer: Wait a minute, Ron. Come to my class. Watch the children who speak no English and are completely bewildered at first, the three with identified special needs who struggle every day and are learning, and the little guy whose mom was handcuffed by the police and taken away in a squad car while he watched. I think almost everybody has an inclusive class. I know I do.

Sheila: My class is inclusive too. My challenge is administrators and parents and sometimes even other teachers. Everyone wants to tell me what to do. I'm being pulled in so many directions.

Parul: Maybe we should talk about some of the ways we can meet the needs of children *and* adults.

Many classrooms today consist of children from a diversity of backgrounds. At the same time, the prevailing pool of teachers of young children consists primarily of white women. This situation presents several challenges. One challenge is that teachers must learn to go beyond their own culture and do the work of learning about other cultures. A second challenge is that many children are usually taught by people from cultures other than their own. Unless teachers are also working to learn to communicate across cultures, these children are left with the difficult task of learning content in the context of an unfamiliar culture.

Teachers' Responsibility in a Diverse World

As you have been studying constructivist theory, you have developed a beginning understanding of the premise that each of us sees the world based on our experiences and the sense we have made of those experiences. "One of the most difficult tasks we face as human beings is communicating meaning across our individual differences, a task confounded immeasurably when we attempt to communicate across social lines, racial lines, cultural lines, or lines of unequal power" (Delpit, 1995, p. 66). Therefore, when the majority of teachers are from any one group, it is essential that all of them consider their attitudes toward people from other groups. Often, people think of racial differences as the major challenge. However, differences in gender, ethnicity, disabilities, and income level also present challenges. When teachers honestly examine their beliefs about others, they may uncover some feelings that had previously remained unexplored. Such findings provide opportunities for growth through reading, discussion, study groups, and seminars. The work of several authors can help interested teachers find ways to work effectively with all children (see Delpit, 1995, 2012; Derman-Sparks & Edwards, 2010; Kostelnik, Soderman, & Whiren, 2011; Ramsey, 1998).

At the same time, Shirley Chisholm, the first black woman to serve in the U.S. House of Representatives, pointed out, "We should not assume that all members of a particular group are going to see things and act the same way" (Association for Supervision and Curriculum Development [ASCD], 2001, p. 8). She also negated the idea of indicating lack of prejudice by maintaining that all children are the same. To do so would indicate ignoring an essential part of each child, and she encouraged us to obtain direct knowledge of a family's culture by talking with family members. Even if some teachers find themselves teaching entire classes of children from a culture that is basically that of the teacher (an unlikely event), each teacher is still responsible for helping those children learn about multiculturalism.

Learning to appreciate and build on each child's strengths is a primary component of becoming a good teacher. Recognizing and working with each child's understanding is at the heart of constructivist educational practice.

Children's Needs in a Multicultural World

Young children's development, coupled with the spoken or unspoken biases of the adults in their lives, makes it imperative that teachers specifically address diversity. Because children are still sorting out who they are and how they are alike and different relative to others, it is obvious that they are aware of differences. Constructivist teachers value children's ability to consider similarities and differences as they construct knowledge of their world. The people who children meet are a very real part of that world. Imagine the confusion that is engendered when teachers eagerly embrace children's questions and comments about objects and events but brush off questions about human differences, perhaps because the teachers themselves have not considered multiculturalism to any extent.

CONSTRUCTIONS

Reflection

Have you ever encountered a child staring at a person in a wheelchair and seen the adult seemingly embarrassed at the child's behavior hurry the child along? The adult becomes even more upset if the child says in an audible voice, "Why is that man in that chair?" If you were the adult, what would you do? Write your response in your journal.

Guide All Children's Learning

The types of challenges to effective group work that we have described are fairly common to a wide range of children. However, some children face more specific challenges:

- The expectations of their culture may be in conflict with the teacher's expectations. For example, in some cultures, children are expected to look to adults for knowledge, and so it would be inappropriate for them to question the teacher. They expect that the teacher knows the right answer and that it is inappropriate to discuss other possible approaches.

- The children may not have had the previous experiences with which you expect them to be familiar. A kindergarten child may never have used scissors since her mother was worried that she would get hurt. A preschooler may not have had opportunities to listen to a story being read. A second grader's entire world may have been the block on which he lives. Going downtown, to a farm, or to another neighborhood may have been unknown to him, while other children in the class may have been to other states, to museums, or to a factory to see how cars are produced or glass is blown.

- They may be in poor health. The illness may be temporary or chronic. A child with a cold that seems relatively minor may have trouble concentrating, and a child who is facing surgery may be coping with a wide range of problems. A child with asthma may be able to function normally but when an attack occurs may be frightened. When parents have been unable to obtain the proper medications, children's conditions may worsen, and school work may be a low priority.

- The children may be hungry. Children whose families do not or cannot provide proper nourishment are at a disadvantage. A hungry child focuses on her hunger. A child whose food intake consists of sodas and chips quickly loses energy and often develops health problems.

- They may feel threatened by other children. Bullying is a chronic problem in many schools. Children may be worried by threats to take their lunch money or to get others to beat them up. They may be afraid to report these incidents to school personnel or to parents due to potential reprisals. They may also have witnessed bullying where reports were made and no actions were taken.

- They may feel threatened by an assignment. When a child does not understand the math or grammar involved in an assignment or when the assignment seems so large that she can't comprehend what is expected, such a child may fail to produce anything, dawdle, act out, or feign illness.

- They may be isolated from other children. When a child is perceived as different by classmates who ostracize him, the child will certainly find it difficult to participate in school work. The concerns about what others think of him may take precedence over any interest in the assignment.

As a teacher, you must be alert to the variety of situations discussed here and others too. Observe your class and the individual children, looking for patterns of behavior. Be sure to keep good **anecdotal records,** which can provide you with clues to classroom situations. For example, Billy never seems to say anything during group discussions. Martina puts her head down on her table and falls asleep almost every day. Raymond spends a long time at the snack table daily and devours large quantities of crackers and juice.

Even in schools that assign children to homogeneous classes, no class is truly homogeneous. Perhaps a teacher will encounter a group of 25 children, all at a similar achievement level in a number of curricular areas. Nonetheless, personalities, experiences, gender, culture, and many other factors make each child unique. Constructivist teachers interview children, observe them in the classroom, and focus on what they write about and what they contribute during sharing or circle time. The teachers use these kinds of information to help them design activities that will blend the basic curriculum and the child's interests and current understandings.

When you make an effort to get to know children and their families, it will be easier for you to understand some of the situations you encounter. Of course, prying in a family's business is unprofessional but demonstrating genuine interest may help you get insight in ways to work with a particular child. However, since many circumstances will be beyond your control, it is essential that you use the resources available to you. If your school or center has a nurse, counselor, social worker, psychologist, or family advocate, you may be able to get help for the child. Be sure to investigate the legal and professional issues first.

When is it appropriate to talk to one of these support staff members about a particular child without first obtaining parental permission? Often a good starting point is to ask that staff member or consultant to observe in your room and to provide you advice in working with your class. Keep in mind, too, that few schools have many support staff. Many schools feel fortunate if even one person is assigned on a part-time basis rather than not at all. You also have a responsibility to learn about community services. Keeping a file of these will allow you to tell parents about them.

Keep your suggestions in the context of the observations you have made about that parent's child. For example, you might discuss with a parent the fact that her child never seems to respond to directions given to the entire class but does well when you go to him individually and repeat the assignment. It is beyond your professional expertise to diagnose this child as having a hearing loss, and he may not. But you can inform his parent of his behaviors as objectively as possible and suggest that she check with the pediatrician. Many factors may be leading to the child's behavior. Ruling out one potentially serious issue may lead to other possibilities. Learning that a hearing loss has occurred and that assistance can be provided may help the child improve his ability to work effectively in the classroom.

Your job is to help children learn. To do that, you must consider all the factors that can affect learning, work to eliminate roadblocks, and check your own behaviors and plans to ensure that you are doing everything possible to support each child appropriately.

Although there are pockets of single-culture families in schools in the United States, the likelihood that children will meet, work, and play with children of other cultures is strong. And even children who miss this aspect of childhood will eventually have the opportunity to meet, work, and play with people of a wide range of cultures.

In order to participate in a multicultural society, children need to begin to develop the characteristics that will enable them to be contributors rather than detractors. Derman-Sparks and Ramsey (2006) and Ramsey (1998) put forward the idea that children need to develop a strong identity as well as the ability to be critical thinkers. As critical thinkers, teachers can support them by encouraging them to ask questions. Children also need to be problem solvers and to gain the academic background to make a difference. When these goals are reached in the context of an inclusive classroom in which all children are respected, it is more likely that children will be able to grow to respect others whom they meet and to use the knowledge and ability they have begun to develop very early. The characteristics described here can be effectively developed in a constructivist classroom. However, when children are not supported in developing critical thinking skills, questioning, and problem solving, they may be less open to considering the ideas and perspectives of others.

Collaboration With Other Adults

Although you may have your own classroom and your own group of children, you will still find that collaborating with other adults is a regular occurrence. You can expect to work with other teachers, specialists, administrators, and parents.

Working With Other Staff

Today, many teachers work in teams. Teaming may mean one or more of the following:

- Two teachers working simultaneously with a group of children
- A teacher and an assistant
- A classroom teacher and a special educator
- Teachers who work with a group of children at different times, such as morning versus afternoon, or for different purposes, such as language arts with one teacher and math and science with a different teacher
- A group of teachers of different age or grade levels who meet to plan common themes and to discuss issues related to teaching

Children often remain with the same team even though they have a new teacher each year.

An advantage of working with other teachers is the ability to obtain support and the opportunity to discuss educational issues. Although some adults prefer to work independently, it is unlikely that the option will be available. Meeting the needs of each child requires diverse approaches. When adults work together, they are more likely to create workable plans or to find the particular adult who is best suited to supporting a particular child.

When teachers begin to work together, they often face the same challenges discussed earlier relative to children and group work. Communication is the key. Teachers who have developed the ability to be critical thinkers and problem solvers work well in groups.

Multiple Perspectives: From the Classroom

Juanita Sanchez was a first-grade teacher who reported that she had a difficult time during her first year of teaching:

I was so comfortable with constructivism that I began right away with my first graders. Most of the parents supported me because they are Hispanic, and I speak Spanish fluently. But it was the other teachers who presented a challenge.

Many times, I grabbed a quick lunch in my classroom because I was busy being positive that everything would be ready when the children returned from lunch. In retrospect, I believe that was a mistake. It may have led the other teachers to believe I thought I was better than they were. When I did join them for faculty meetings or see them in the hallway, they would often comment that I was working too hard. Later one teacher asked if I was trying to make the rest of them look bad. I was stunned.

Gradually, however, I noticed that a couple of teachers would come to my doorway and ask if I had any rubber bands or staples or some other ordinary question. I was aware that they were peering around the room. Finally, one teacher did accept my invitation to come on in and look around. She wanted to know how I kept them from using all the interesting games and materials before they finished their work. I pointed out that this is their work. She came back a few more times and began asking questions. I was so happy to be able to share ideas with someone, but the best part was the following year when she decided to try the constructivist approach. The year after that, we asked the principal if my first graders could go as a group to her second-grade class. Both of us had worked hard to keep him informed, so it was with only slight hesitation that he agreed.

Communicate Your Approach to Administrators

Whether you are a new teacher or have just decided to begin to focus on constructivist tenets, communicating with your administrator is imperative. You may feel that it would be preferable to keep quiet about it, especially if you aren't sure what kind of response you will receive.

Sometimes administrators question using a constructivist approach. They may have been taught a more behaviorist model and may have taught for a number of years using that approach. They may also be aware that the taxpayers in their districts are rather conservative. Therefore, when teachers come with plans that differ significantly from what is familiar, it may seem easier and safer to direct them to a more traditional approach. Teachers have found that they must be proactive in approaching administrators. They must be prepared to advocate for their thinking in advance rather than wait to defend it after their theory has been disparaged by a member of the community, a teacher, or the principal.

You can begin by taking a positive approach. You can prepare to demonstrate to administrators ways in which you will help children meet district and Common Core standards. At the same time, you can emphasize the many opportunities children will have to think and solve problems. It is imperative to let the administrator know that classroom management will be different and that children will have freedom within limits. You must convey your understanding that school rules will be met. At the same time, you must communicate your own thoughtfulness in designing a forward-looking plan.

You might bring a sample letter that will be sent to parents as the school year begins. You may want to review your teacher Web site about the constructivist approach before uploading it. Often, providing the administrator with an interesting article on the constructivist approach will prove useful, but a large stack of reading material is not what any school administrator needs. Early childhood education teachers should be familiar with research and position statements provided by the National Association of Elementary School Principals (http://www.naesp.org).

Certainly, an invitation to administrators to visit and to observe the children at work will demonstrate your openness and allow for constructive feedback. As the year gets underway, occasional notes from students to the administrator can also be an opportunity to encourage a visit.

Keep in mind that most administrators welcome innovation that moves the school forward and enhances its reputation. It is unfair and unwise to expect an administrator to find out what is going on in the school building by hearing about your project from someone outside the school. Making sure that administrators, particularly principals and directors, are well informed is the responsibility of the classroom teacher.

Discuss Your Approach With Families

Many families whose children are in early childhood education today experienced a rather structured schooling. That is what they are familiar with and what they expect their children to experience. If Johnny or Trinice does not bring home the type of homework parents expect and if instead the children talk about the wonderful time they are having learning about whales, or construction of a building, or a painting by Monet, parents may feel that their children are being shortchanged. Four-year-olds in a child-care center may be learning about pendulums and how they work, while their parents are wondering what happened to teaching the alphabet and numbers.

Families who have not been exposed to constructivist theory will want an explanation, and teachers must be prepared to give such an explanation without talking down to parents (who may in fact be far more knowledgeable than the teacher about constructivism or other topics). Teachers must also avoid using jargon such as *socially transmitted knowledge*. Effective communication between parents and teachers demands respect in both directions, opportunities to raise questions, and time to express differing perspectives. When given a clear explanation, most parents will be pleased that their children are learning with such an insightful teacher. When given a clear explanation of issues and concerns, most teachers will be delighted that they will have the opportunity to work with such interested and caring parents. Such a combination can lead to excellent teamwork and enhanced opportunities for children.

Families can keep abreast of their children's progress through conversations with the teacher and the exchange of notes, e-mail messages, work samples, newsletters, conferences, and periodic reports. Parents who are available and have been invited may exceed teachers' expectations for support. Occasionally, a few parents may feel so strongly about a more traditional approach that a compromise may have to be reached. For example, the teacher could suggest activities to be done at home that may be more satisfying to the parent. Perhaps the teacher would write a rather detailed account along with an annotated video clip of what the child is learning that week so that parents will have an opportunity to see the progress that their child is making. In any case, teachers who take a positive, professional approach will be able to work more effectively with parents. It should not be surprising that parents want the best education possible for their children. Together, parents and teachers can find ways to make that happen.

CONSTRUCTIONS

Practice

With a partner, develop a role play demonstrating a parent-teacher conference. Enact the role play demonstrating an irate parent and a defensive teacher. Then reenact the role play demonstrating an irate parent and a teacher who listens to the parent and works out a plan for meeting each of their goals. Ask your classmates about their response to the teacher in each case.

SUMMARY

- Teachers can help others understand their approach to learning and teaching even if others don't agree with them.
- Children at first may not understand a constructivist approach because they have been socialized to a different way of learning.
- It is important to meet standards imposed by school districts, governmental bodies, and professional organizations while focusing on the needs of individual children.

- Teachers should focus on teaching children as well as content.
- Teachers should be able to explain their role in facilitating learning.

CONSTRUCTIONS

1. OBSERVATION

With a partner, observe a teacher who uses a project approach. After a brief period of observing, each of you choose one child and keep a running record of what that child does for 10 minutes. Follow this observation with a brief rest period for yourself; then continue your running record for three more 10-minute writing-rest periods. Compare your notes with those of your partner. What do you think the child you observed may have been learning? Did the teacher interact with the child during your observation? If so, what did the teacher say or do?

2. CURRICULUM DESIGN

Design a project for an early childhood class. State the age or grade level for which you are planning and the goal of the project. Recognize that in a real situation your plans would be tentative and would change as the children explored the topic. Design an outline or web for what could be a workable project plan.

3. INTERVIEW

Interview a principal. Find out how the principal feels about using a constructivist approach in the classroom. Ask what he or she sees as the pros and cons. Keep in mind that you are interviewing to learn what the principal thinks and why, rather than to try to convince the principal of your own opinion.

4. RESEARCH

Examine four software packages designed for use in an early childhood classroom. Evaluate them based on what you have learned as a result of having read this chapter. You may also add other criteria, such as these:

Is the art aesthetically pleasing?
Are users provided with information about what they are expected to do?
Are users able to provide a complete answer before the program evaluates it?
Is the information in the program accurate?

Is the information geared to the approximate age or grade level indicated in the instructions?
Is the child able to manage the program independently?

5. RESEARCH

Using a topic that interests you, make a list of all the ways you could find out more about that topic. Imagine that you mentioned the topic in your early childhood classroom. What might the children want to learn about it?

6. DISCUSSION

Organize or join a group of your classmates to discuss how children should learn content during the early childhood years.

7. INTERVIEW

Interview a parent or guardian of a child who is in an early childhood education program. Remember that the child may be between birth and age 8, or third grade. Find out from the parent or guardian what content he or she expects the child to be learning. Compare your findings with those of your classmates.

Resources

Books

Adams, J., Jr. (2000). *Taking charge of curriculum: Teacher networks and curriculum implementation.* New York, NY: Teachers College Press.

Part of a series on school reform, this book emphasizes the importance of teachers working together in order to begin to make changes in curriculum. The author provides examples of variations in implementation.

Duckworth, E.R. (2006). *The having of wonderful ideas and other essays on teaching and learning* (3rd ed.). New York, NY: Teachers College Press.
Duckworth, E.R. (2001). *Tell me more: Listening to learners explain.* New York, NY: Teachers College Press.
Duckworth, E.R. & the Experienced Teachers Group. (1997). *Teacher to teacher: Learning from each other.* New York, NY: Teachers College Press.

Ever a supporter of teacher growth and development, Duckworth shows how it can be done. She and her students document the process of learning together.

Eisner, E. (2003). *Cognition and curriculum reconsidered* (2nd ed.). New York, NY: Teachers College Press.

Eisner posits that education should address the creation of mind. He views the senses as playing a strong role in the formation of concepts and encourages teachers to consider the culture of their classrooms that supports or impedes children's opportunities to approach education.

Fortson, L., & Reiff, J. (1995). *Early childhood curriculum: Open structures for integrative learning.* Boston, MA: Allyn & Bacon.

Teachers struggling with understanding curriculum integration will find this book to be a source of explanation and ideas. The authors focus on preprimary and primary education, and although they address each curriculum area separately, they carefully demonstrate ways in which integration can occur.

Franklin, B. (Ed.). (2000). *Curriculum and consequence: Herbert M. Kliebard and the promise of schooling.* New York, NY: Teachers College Press.

This book of essays in honor of the noted curriculum historian Herbert M. Klie bard addresses a range of issues of historical importance. Readers receive thoughtful perspectives on major issues related to curriculum that may be overlooked by teachers in the day-to-day press of developing and implementing curriculum.

Hillocks, G., Jr. (1999). *Ways of thinking, ways of teaching.* New York, NY: Teachers College Press.

Before passing over the book because it is based on research about teachers of English, early childhood educators might reflect on the parallels between their teaching and what is described here. Hillocks's findings on the source of teacher knowledge based on what actually happened in classrooms provide an important model for future research related to teaching young children.

Web Sites

Community Learning Network K–12, British Columbia www.cln.org/cln/html

Designed to help K–12 teachers integrate technology into the classroom. Many linkages are provided, some of which offer programs for sale.

Franklin Institute Science Museum http://www2.fi.edu

This website provides a myriad of resources, programs, virtual field trips, and information.

National Research Council http://www.nationalacademies.org/nrc. *National Science Education Standards.* Washington, DC: National Academy Press.

This Web site provides an example of the various sets of curriculum standards available to support learning by all students. Readers will find standards for teaching, professional development, assessment, and programs.

UNESCO World Heritage List www.cco.caltech.edu/~salmon/world.heritage.html

Contains over 700 sites worldwide. Users can select a country and explore one of the many high points in that area through pictures and text.

Early Childhood Investigations http://www.earlychildhoodwebinars.com/webinar-resources

This Web site provides free webinars, resources, and blogs. Users can easily learn more about various topics on the use of technology in the early childhood classroom.

Technology Tools for Educators http://www.techandyoungchildren.org/educators.html

NAEYC provides a series of articles on technology at this Web site. It categorizes the articles by age range.

Erikson Tech Center http://teccenter.erikson.edu

This is an interactive Web site that hopes to assist early childhood educators as we attempt to use technology in a culturally and appropriate manner.

Bright Hub Education http://www.brighthubeducation.com/teaching-methods-tips/125444-guide-to-effective-communication-with-parents

This is a Web site that offers helpful hints to teachers as they communicate with parents.

Videos

Kamii, C., & Joseph, L. (1989). *Double-column addition: A teacher uses Piaget's theory.* New York, NY: Teachers College Press.
Kamii, C., & Housman, B. L. (2000). *Young children reinvent arithmetic: Implications of Piaget's Theory* (2nd ed.). New York, NY: Teachers College.

9

CONSTRUCTIVIST MODELS OF INSTRUCTION

Chapter 4 describes several constructivist educational models that have been used in both preschool and primary school settings. The purpose of introducing you to these models is to help you see how others have designed constructivist curriculum, which you are probably beginning to think is too complex to try. Furthermore, models help you visualize an approach to curriculum.

After reading this chapter, you will have a better understanding of

- the purpose of educational models;
- the components of a constructivist model;
- the role of Piagetian theory in a constructivist model; and
- examples of constructivist models and emerging models.

Introduction

The teachers are chatting as they wait for others to arrive. Some of them wonder whether constructivism is limited to universities' early childhood education programs. Others struggle with wanting to see a constructivist model so that they can imitate that model.

Jennifer: I wonder whether people in other parts of the country use this constructivist approach when they are teaching. Sometimes I think it is something professors think up for their universities' programs in early childhood education. If I can see something or someone using an approach, I can understand it better.

Kenisha: With educators' new focus on national standards in math, science, language arts, social studies, and other areas of the curriculum and the core curriculum, I think teachers could use a constructivist approach, but I'm not sure what states use it and what states don't.

Sheila: I remember in my graduate course on the history of early childhood, the professor talked about constructivist preschool models in

	the 1960s. I don't think those models were used in kindergarten or the early grades.
Kenisha:	But that's in the Sixties: flower children, LSD, and all of that stuff. What good would it do us today?
Ron:	I know that there are several educational models that have been based on constructivism. I remember studying them in my Program Models course as an undergraduate.
Jennifer:	I'm not talking about some undergraduate program and some historical look at preschools. I want to know if anyone is using this constructivist approach today other than the teachers who have graduated from our university! I want to know if anyone is using it with special needs children.
Sheila:	We all know about High Scope. I had training in the High Scope model. Most people don't realize that the High Scope curriculum is designed for the early primary grades as well as preschool.
Parul:	I suggest that each of us try to find what we think is a good model that attempts to apply and interpret constructivist theory before we meet again.
Kenisha:	I don't have time to spend hours in the library.
Parul:	You won't have to do that. Just search the Internet, and see what you can find.

Educational researchers, teacher educators, and classroom teachers have made many successful attempts at applying their interpretation of constructivist theory. Those attempts have been studied, researched, and applied in preschool settings, primary grade settings, children's museums, and children's discovery centers. As a result, some of them have become known as constructivist models of education. A few of the well-known constructivist, educational models are High Scope (Roopnarine & Johnson, 2012; Schweinhart & Weikart, 2010; Weikart, Rogers, Adcock, & McClelland, 1971), the Kamii and DeVries approaches (Kamii & DeVries, 1980, 1993), Educating the Young Thinker (Sigel & Olmsted, 1970), the Ausubelian model (Ausubel, 1963; Ausubel, Novak, & Hanesian, 1978), the Reggio Emilia model (Edwards, Gandini, & Forman, 2011), constructionism through the use of computers and interactive technology (Clements, 1999; Papert, 1980a, 1993; Resnick, 1998, 2012; Kafai & Resnick, 2011/1996), and Project Construct (http://www.projectconstruct.org). Constructivist models and applications have been attempted for over 40 years.

What Are Educational Models?

Educational models are mental representations that educators create to make sense of very complex educational problems. Some of the models are based on research and others on belief. As we stated earlier, models help educators visualize the educational approach. They also help educators understand the structure, organization, and limits of that approach. By organizing and structuring an approach, the designers are imposing their reality or ideas about education on others. We could say that they have specific intentions when they create a model. Thus, an educational model is a conceptual framework for a specific theory, belief, or philosophy. The conceptual framework allows educators and researchers to make informed decisions. Some of the decisions that must be made include setting up procedures for the administration of the program, the budget, educational practices, educational materials and equipment, and evaluation of the program. Educational models also help teachers and researchers identify the elements within a specific model that allow it to represent a certain theory (Goffin & Wilson, 2001).

You will discuss educational models and theories in your educational psychology courses, but for now, we want you to have enough of an understanding of them so that you can see where and how constructivism has been used. Furthermore, we hope that this chapter will help you develop your own constructivist curriculum. After all, constructivists are leaders who create curriculum, not mindless followers who want a model to imitate.

Four lines of thought that generated educational models are metacognition, learning theory, the academic disciplines, and developmental studies of the human intellect. Box 9.1 describes all of these sources and identifies leading theorists.

BOX 9.1 SOURCES OF THOUGHT FOR EDUCATIONAL MODELS

- *Metacognition*—a theory of thinking about thought (inductive and deductive reasoning) and how thinking functions. Howard Gardner, who identified seven kinds of intelligence and designed a curriculum for his theory, is widely considered a leader in metacognition.

- *Learning theories*—theories that have students use their previously learned information to make sense of incoming information. They provide strategies for changing someone's thinking processes. Jerome Bruner is considered to be a learning theorist.

- *Academic disciplines*—theories that view students as learning through mastering the processes, ideas, and concepts of a specific discipline (such as biology or American literature). As a result of learning through the processes of the discipline, students will behave differently. Joseph Schwab worked with the academic disciplines model. He and his associates developed the Biological Science Curriculum.

- *Developmental studies of human intellect*—studies of the processes of the intellect. Theorists and researchers provide ideas of how the intellect develops. Piaget's work with intellectual development is a foundation for this group. Although Piaget never developed a model for educating children, many others, including Kamii, DeVries, Seigel, and Weikart, have applied Piagetian principles to their models.

Many educational models were developed in the 1960s because of the federal government's interest in early intervention programs, the advent of Head Start, the availability of federal funding to develop educational approaches, and Project Follow Through (Goffin & Wilson, 2001; Osborn, 1991). Most of these models were designed for preschool-age children and have since been expanded to include the primary grades. For example, the Bank Street Developmental-Interaction Approach model, the Direct Instruction Model, and many of the constructivist models are now used in both preschool and primary grade settings.

CONSTRUCTIONS

Research

Find additional information about the federal government's interest in early intervention programs and Head Start in the 1960s. Answer the following questions and then share those answers with three classmates.

1. What was the interest of U.S. President Lyndon B. Johnson in early intervention and early childhood?
2. Why did he push the federal agencies to establish early intervention programs?
3. What were some of the early intervention programs? Where were they located?
4. Who were their leaders?

What Is a Constructivist Model?

A constructivist model is an interpretation of constructivist research, theory, and curriculum. As you may remember, Piaget's theory is not a theory of teaching but rather a theory of knowing and of how knowledge develops. Piagetian theory is based on a large body of scientific research that continues to expand.

Because Piagetian theory and research are based on how knowledge develops rather than how to teach children, teachers must apply their understandings of that theory and research through their practice. Several have articulated their understandings to the point that their approach to curriculum is recognized as a constructivist model. As DeVries (1987, 2002) pointed out, teachers are concerned with the implications of Piagetian theory rather than its direct application to educational settings. Box 9.2 lists the major components of a constructivist model.

BOX 9.2 COMPONENTS OF A CONSTRUCTIVIST MODEL

- The model is based on Piagetian and constructivist theory and research. The leading thinkers are Piaget, Sinclair, Inhelder, Furth, and Ackerman.
- The research and writings of some of the leading constructivist researchers and educators—among them Fosnot, Steffe, Kamii, DeVries, Gruber and Voneche, Gagnon and Collay, Forman, and Papert—guide the designers.
- Certain epistemological assumptions are at the heart of the model: (1) Knowledge is constructed through active engagement with the environment, which provides choice (many possibilities) and authenticity. (2) Children learn by making relationships, acting on objects, and interacting with others. (3) Children symbolically represent what they know to others. (4) Children use hypothesis making, experimentation or hypothesis testing, and interpretation of their findings to try to explain things that they don't completely understand (that is, they problem solve).
- The model views the classroom as a learning environment for the child. Opportunities for authentic tasks, problem solving, questioning, reflections, acting on objects, use of what they've done, and documenting or representing what they know are provided for the children.
- Play is valued and viewed as the child's means of interacting with the environment.
- Children are valued and respected for what they know. They aren't viewed as little adults whose thinking is considered as amusing or in need of correction so that it matches the adult way of thinking.
- The model encourages the creation of a classroom community that fosters autonomy and a sociomoral learning environment.
- The model views the teacher and parents as collaborators who act as colearners, guides, memory prompters (e.g., "Remember that you used a straw to help stabilize the propeller when you built the plane"), and questioners.

- The materials are authentic and safe, allow for transformations, and allow for interaction. For example, children use child-sized tools rather than pretend tools.
- The model views documentation as a way to record the child's learning. In addition to documentation, authentic assessment (i.e., portfolios) is used rather than traditional means of assessment (i.e., standardized tests).

As you explore the programs we have selected for discussion, consider the questions listed in Box 9.3. You may want to adapt these questions for future use with other educational approaches and models.

CONSTRUCTIONS

1. Reflection

As you reflect on the questions, which ones help you identify a constructivist program. Write a blog describing how important each component of the set of questions is for you as you think about your own teaching.

2. Research

Read two articles about constructivist teaching models. Revisit each article's teaching model by using the questions to help you decide how the article's models represent constructivist thinking.

A Close Look at Selected Constructivist Models

BOX 9.3 QUESTIONS TO HELP IDENTIFY CONSTRUCTIVIST MODELS

- How are Piagetian and constructivist theories viewed in this model? What aspects of constructivist theory are emphasized? How is Piagetian theory being applied?
- Does the model base curriculum on the Piagetian ages and stages approach to development, or is it based on the three kinds of knowledge (physical, logico-mathematical, and social conventional)?
- How does this model coordinate constructivist theory with Piagetian theory? With other theories?

- What are the aims and objectives of this model?
- How does the teacher view the child in this model? As a small adult? As an active learner who is developing?
- What does this model mean by "active" learner?
- What is the teacher's role? The family's role?
- What is the role of play?
- What are the roles of autonomy and development? How are they nurtured?
- How are physical space, equipment, and materials set up in this model? How are assessment, documentation, and evaluation carried out in this model?

The teachers have discussed their own approaches to their own classrooms and now shift their discussion to thoughts about constructivist models of education. They consider the questions to help them identify a constructivist model as they talk (see Box 9.3).

Kenisha: If we apply the questions we've raised to educational models, I bet none of them will be Piagetian. Constructivist. Whatever!

Matt: I think your confusion about constructivism and Piagetian theory is important to discuss. I really think many of the educational models looked at Piagetian theory and educators' attempts to apply that.

Sheila: Well, what about constructivist theory? Where does it fit into educational models?

Parul: I think that constructivist theory includes more than Piagetian theory. For example, I think it would include the Reggio Emilia approach.

Matt: Oh, yes! That is that Italian approach everyone loves! I didn't think it was constructivist.

Parul: I think it is constructivist but not totally Piagetian. I think the questions we have generated will help us as we discuss these models.

Kenisha: Well, are all constructivist models examples of best practices?

Parul: I don't think so. Lavatelli tried to teach children how to get the right answer with the Piagetian tasks. Her work is an example of what not to do. We want to avoid trying to teach the children how to do the Piagetian tasks so that they get the "right" answers.

Ron: DeVries's, Kamii's, and Papert's approaches are all examples of approaches that are educationally sound and Piagetian.

We have selected three models to discuss. Remember that our purpose for offering constructivist models is to help you visualize what a constructivist model looks like and to provide guides for you as you design your own components of a constructivist curriculum. We don't expect you to imitate the model in your classroom. We do want you to think about the way the designers thought about constructivist education.

One of the models we discuss in this chapter was designed during the 1960s, but the other two are current approaches that are becoming known as constructivist models. We did this because we knew that many of you would have an interest in how Piagetian theory had been applied in a variety of settings. We will examine High Scope, Kamii and DeVries's approaches, and Resnick's work with the MIT Media lab that is an outgrowth of Papert's earlier work with the Massachusetts Institute of Technology Epistemology and Learning Group.

High Scope Model

David Weikart and Constance Kamii collaborated in the early 1960s with the Perry Preschool Project, an intervention program for 3- and 4-year-olds. Weikart was the director of the project, and Kamii was the research associate. In 1966 Kamii accepted a postdoctoral fellowship to study with Piaget. Weikart continued to work with the project by revising and extending the curriculum and then establishing the High Scope Educational Research Foundation.

Weikart's High Scope model is an eclectic or open approach based on Piaget's theory of cognitive development, the child development tradition, and ideas that Weikart's group felt were missing from the Piagetian theory. It is designed to improve disadvantaged children's chances for academic success.

Three essential High Scope elements are the teacher-child ratio, teachers' work in teams, and parent involvement. The teacher-child ratio is low (no more than 10 children per staff member and group sizes no greater than 20). Because of the low ratio, teachers have time to interact with children on an individual basis. A second element is teamwork. Teachers work in teams to plan, implement, and evaluate each of the day's activities in their classrooms, observe the individual children, and do inservice training. A third element is parent involvement. High Scope views parents as partners. Although High Scope doesn't require home visits, the teachers and other staff members have regular discussions with parents so that the parents know about their child's progress (Weikart & Schweinhart, 20013).

In the early years of Weikart's work with the High Scope model, he and his colleagues attempted to use Piaget's work as the objectives for their curriculum. They claimed that their curriculum would teach "Piagetian skills" through sequencing content-area skills from simple to complex or concrete to abstract.

Weikart and his team never claimed that children became operational thinkers because of their curriculum.

They have revised the High Scope curriculum and model at least four times and extended it from a preschool program to an international program for preschool and primary grades. Each revision added a new component that the staff thought was important. For example, in the late 1970s, Weikart and his group revised their curriculum so that its objectives, called Key Experiences of Cognitive Development, included topics such as active learning, language, classification, seriation, number, spatial relations, time, and experiences and representing. In a later revision, they emphasized the importance of active learning and added socioemotional objectives. These objectives, though not necessarily from a Piagetian framework, included autonomy and mutual respect (DeVries, 1987). They also pointed out that the role of dispositions and attitudes in active learning was the key to school readiness (Goffin & Wilson, 2001).

Because Weikart maintained that children are active learners, he developed his curriculum so that the children could use the cycle of plan-do-review with activities of their own. For example, the teacher meets with children and asks them what they have planned for that day's work or play. When the conference has been completed, each child begins the doing phase, that is, carrying out the plan. At certain points during the day, the teacher meets with each child and reviews the plan and the child's learning.

In the High Scope curriculum, the adults create areas of interest that serve as contexts for learning, observe the children within those contexts, support and extend their play through questioning, interact with the children, and document their learning. Unlike many other curriculum models, High Scope does not require that children use special materials or equipment. It does require that teachers create learning environments that are developmentally appropriate. It also requires that a daily classroom routine be established and maintained. This daily routine is organized around High Scope's Key Experiences (see Box 9.4) and uses the plan-do-review sequence for children's activities. It includes planning time, work time, cleanup time, recall time, small-group time, large-group time, and outdoor play (Weikart & Schweinhart, 2013).

BOX 9.4 HIGH SCOPE KEY EXPERIENCES FOR PRESCHOOL

Creative representation
Language and literacy
Initiative and social relations
Movement
Music

Classification
Seriation
Number
Space
Time

_____

Source: D.P. Weikart & L.J. Schweinhart. (2013). The High Scope curriculum for early childhood care and education. In J.L. Roopnarine & J.E. Johnson (Eds.), *Approaches to early childhood education* (6th ed., pp. 227–293). New York, NY: Pearson.

A clear understanding of the key experiences and the categories within each of those experiences is necessary to understand the High Scope curriculum. The accompanying boxes list the key experiences for High Scope's curriculum and the categories for the key experiences in movement (see Box 9.5).

BOX 9.5 HIGH SCOPE KEY EXPERIENCES IN MOVEMENT

Act on movement directions.
Describe movement.
Move the body in nonlocomotor ways.
Move the body in locomotor ways.
Move with objects.
Express creativity in movement.
Feel and express a steady beat.
Move in sequences to a common beat.

_____

Source: D.P. Weikart & L.J. Schweinhart. (2013). The High Scope curriculum for early childhood care and education. In J.L. Weikart & J.E. Johnson (Eds.), *Approaches to early childhood education* (6th ed., pp. 227–293). New York, NY: Pearson.

For assessment, Weikart and his team have developed a hierarchical system that uses instruments to assess how the child does with broad experiences as well as discrete aspects of development. For example, there are broad key experiences as well as 10 categories within each of the broad experiences. In addition, items from the Child Observation Record (COR) are used to assess each child's development throughout the year. Teachers use a team approach when they administer the COR. The COR measures the children's development and assesses the outcomes of their work with the key experiences. For the first few months, teachers use written accounts of their observations of the children's behavior in the following areas of development: initiative, social relations, creative representation, music and movement, language and literacy, and logic and mathematics. Once this phase has been completed, teachers classify the children's behaviors based on 30 five-level COR items in each of the areas (Epstein, 2006; Weikart & Schweinhart, 2013). Box 9.6 illustrates this process for one item within the general area of initiative.

BOX 9.6 EXPRESSING CHOICE LEVELS IN HIGH SCOPE: AN EXAMPLE

The classifications are in order from the lowest to the highest.

- Child does not yet express to others.
- Child indicates a desired activity or place of activity by pointing or saying a word.
- Child indicates a desired activity, place of activity, materials, or playmates with a short sentence.
- Child indicates with a short sentence how plans will be carried out ("I want to drive the truck on the road").
- Child presents detailed descriptions of intended actions ("I want to make a road out of blocks with Sara and drive the truck on it").

Source: D. P. Weikart & L. J. Schweinhart. (2013). The High Scope curriculum for early childhood care and education. In J. L. Roopnarine & J. E. Johnson (Eds.), *Approaches to early childhood education* (6th ed., pp. 227–293). New York, NY: Pearson.

The High Scope model and its curriculum is one of the most researched models in educational history. Research validates the model's use of child-initiated learning activities. It suggests that the curriculum provides children with long-lasting benefits because it empowers them through the child-initiated activities, empowers parents by involving them as full partners who help teachers support their child's development, and empowers teachers through inservice training and an effective curriculum (Weikart & Schweinhart, 2013).

Most communities have preschool and primary school programs that use the High Scope model. Many Head Start programs use either a modified version of High Scope or the actual model, and thousands of children attend

High Scope programs each day (Epstein, 2006). Additional information about High Scope can be found on the High Scope Web site (www.highscope.org). In addition to the general information about the High Scope program that you will find on the Web site, High Scope has aligned its curriculum with the various states' standards and has included the Common Core in that alignment. Information can be found at http://www.highscope.org/content.asp?contentid=268.

As you reflect on the High Scope model, you may wonder why we asked you to study it. We hope that as you read, you thought about your own classroom and curriculum. You reflected on whether you wanted to follow a specific constructivist model and receive additional training in that model. In addition, you considered the components of your curriculum. You wondered what you would do if those components needed to be revised. High Scope can serve as a model for revision because its designers have revised and revised. Finally, many constructivists maintain that although High Scope is based on Piagetian theory, it has become an eclectic model. You might want to consider how you would attempt to link your practice with your understandings of the theory. Studying models really helps you begin to realize that you can take a complex issue like constructivist education and understand how to use it.

CONSTRUCTIONS

Research

Visit the High Scope Web site, www.highscope.org and YouTube video clips like http://www.youtube.com/user/HighScopePreschool. Write a journal entry or blog that compares the work High Scope is doing at home and internationally.

Multiple Perspectives: From a Teacher of 1-Year-Olds

When Linda F. Anderson was interviewed, she was a lead teacher in the classroom for 1-year-olds at the Child and Family Study Center at the University of Wisconsin–Stout. She taught and served as an assistant director in preschool and child-care settings for the past 18 years. Linda's first position was as an assistant director and educational coordinator for the Oneida Tribe of Indians of Wisconsin Early Childhood Department in the Green Bay area. While serving as assistant director, Linda was introduced to the High Scope program model.

Although my foster parents, who came from Belgium, raised me, I am of the Oneida tribe. When I came to Stout, I became interested in my heritage and began to study and learn about people of color and the Oneida culture. Because I was raised as an Anglo and then learned about my heritage and culture, I can really help teachers because I can see both perspectives. I value the importance of culture and having culture play an important role in childcare.

At Stout, I do not recall learning about the High Scope curriculum; we learned about a hands-on approach, and it really helped the children learn quite a bit about recognizing their names and other early literacy practices. When I think back on my education, I remember Dr. Hanson, one of my professors, who taught me about teaching children about literature and being the best I could be for the children. I guess I'd say that my Early Childhood Program training was like a whole collection of values and all of the different ways of teaching those values.

I was introduced to the High Scope model when I was the assistant director and educational coordinator for the Early Childhood Program, which included Head Start and child care. I also really learned all about my culture in that position. The teachers there had been using High Scope for years and years. They also taught the Oneida culture in their curriculum. I was in an unusual position as assistant director because I observed the teachers using the High Scope model but never really had any formal training in it and I had not taught using that approach.

The High Scope model expects that the teachers do certain things in their curriculum. They use centers and themes. They use limits with the children and set up those limits like giving the children choices. The teachers I worked with really did the theme work and the plan-do-review. They planned with the children and then watched to see what the children did. They also had to talk to the children about what the children did during their play. It was like reviewing with the children. They had lots of years of working on that part. They valued that and really did a good job with it. I really liked that. There's lots of paperwork that shows what teachers are observing.

I remember one thing that happened when I first started working with the High Scope teachers. When I got there, I ordered the preschool-sized pencils for the children—you know, the kind that are big and chunky. That really created lots of controversy! The teachers were so concerned about the details of the High Scope model that they were confused and even afraid they were doing the wrong thing. For example, they were worried about how much writing should be done in a High Scope classroom. They were afraid of how much direct instruction they could do. I wanted the children to see their names in print and be able to write their names, but the teachers thought they had to use the High Scope way with symbols. They were really afraid that they would do the wrong thing and lose their jobs.

To understand this fear, you need to think about the makings of tribal communities. This will help you understand the fear the teachers had if they did it wrong. If a parent questioned what the teacher was doing, then that parent would pass it on. They may write a complaint to the tribal council person, and then it would need official follow-through in a lengthy process. The process could end back at the director's desk, or it could go on into a legal type of investigation. Everyone is connected. Some parent might tell the tribal elder, and then that would be bad. The teachers didn't want complaints and didn't want to lose their jobs, so they wanted to do the program right!

You see, the tribe hires the teachers. Most tribes have a human resources [HR] department. Our tribe had a huge organization and hired thousands of people. The director or assistant director, an elder, an HR person, sometimes a program coordinator would come with you—usually a team of about seven people—and it was set up very well and very organized. Everyone is hired this way. So, the teachers are very proud of their jobs and want to do their best.

I think I had some really good teachers who really understood what they were doing. Then I had some new teachers just starting their careers and their classes at the university. They were the ones who really were fearful! When I found out how fearful the teachers were, I invited a High Scope trainer to come and teach us about early literacy. She made it clear that the materials I thought we needed in our classrooms for literacy were okay. However, she didn't want the teachers to force literacy or writing on the children. She wanted it to be more natural. She really helped, and then we were all on the same page.

Before coming back to Stout as the lead teacher for one-year-olds, I taught in the local Head Start program. This program allowed the teachers to decide the curriculum needs in conjunction with a parent input form we did with parents on our first home visit. It was called a cultural form. I really stressed culture and having something in the child's life that that child and family valued. We really made that fit into the curriculum. For example, if a father really liked fishing, I would invite him to come in to teach the children how to fish. I really learned lots from the families. We all learned that by celebrating culture, we could ensure that parents have a part in the curriculum and the classroom.

I remember that at Head Start when we planned curriculum at the beginning of the year, we would work in small groups. Our Head Start guidelines had a component for culture. One year when we got to that part of the curriculum, some of the teachers just didn't want to do anything with it. Of course, I'm a person of color, so that was one of my favorite parts and, I felt, one of the most important parts of the curriculum. It should involve more than just reading a book. I would suggest to the curriculum coordinator to talk about this because we really needed to do more. She responded by making culture a monthly part of the agenda at our teacher meetings. We could all share how we facilitated the cultural component in our classrooms. It helped to discuss culture on an ongoing basis. Once she brought in laminated pictures of Indian dancers and asked us to tell how we would use them. At the close of the meeting, she gave them to us as resources for the month.

I can really see the advantage of High Scope. I think helping them review what they did really helps the child remember what was learned. I don't believe that teachers will do the plan-do-review process unless you tell them it's required to follow the program. I don't believe that teachers will do all of the extra paperwork that a model like High Scope expects unless they know they have to follow the program. I think High Scope made the program for the children better.

With program models, it helps the teacher think more deeply about curriculum and children. It helps the teacher think about the child and what you want that child to learn. Our student teachers do their lessons and get their themes turned in, but some are not thinking deeply about the child. Maybe it just takes years of teaching that gets you to a place where you start looking at the child … seeing the child … like really seeing the child's creativity … and how the child fits into the flow of the lesson plans and how they fit into the whole program … the whole curriculum.

I think the High Scope model helps the children know what they did during the day—you know, when they do the review part. In some programs, the children just play and go home, but with High Scope, they have to think about and review what their play. I see good in that stopping and thinking. If I were teaching preschool here, I would use the High Scope approaches but with the one-year-olds, it's totally improbable. There's curriculum, for the ones, and High Scope's principles guide me with my curriculum planning but I don't do the formal High Scope model

Kamii and DeVries's Approaches

After Constance Kamii returned from her postdoctoral study, she began to look at the educational implications of Piaget's theory. This led her to shift her ideas from the stages of cognitive development to the types of knowledge and the constructivist processes that advanced knowledge and to attempt to provide a constructivist perspective for the teaching of number and arithmetic. From 1967 to 1970, she worked on a program that was similar to the Perry Preschool Project. Kamii changed her direction to a more constructivist approach in 1969 when she met with Dr. Hermina Sinclair, a colleague of Piaget. Sinclair pointed out that Piaget never intended for his tasks to be used for instructional purposes. She also pointed out the distinction between physical knowledge and logico-mathematical knowledge. Finally, Sinclair suggested that Kamii study the functional aspects of Piaget's theory as well as the structural aspects. That meeting profoundly changed Kamii's approach to the educational applications of Piagetian theory. After her visit with Sinclair, Kamii begin studying the nature of matter, the child's construction of knowledge, and physical knowledge activities (DeVries & Kohlberg, 1987).

In the 1970s Kamii began collaborating with Rheta DeVries at the University of Illinois. DeVries had studied under Piaget just as Kamii had. Both were interested in children's sociomoral development, constructions of number and arithmetic, and understandings of reading and writing. Because of their interest in Piagetian theory, research, and educational implications, Kamii and DeVries began developing their approaches to constructivism. They based their ideas on the Piagetian implications for children's moral, social, affective, and cognitive development (Goffin & Wilson, 2001) rather than direct teaching of Piagetian tasks as if those were activities. For example, Kamii and DeVries viewed the teacher's role as providing situations that would allow children to pursue their own interests or objectives. The children could expand their use of classification schemes within those situations so that they could meet their own objectives. Their interest (rather than the teacher's instruction) would cause them to advance their thinking. The following case study demonstrates this perspective:

"Things That Move" was the theme in a kindergarten classroom. Three kindergarten children looked for ramps in their room that they could use to study the movement of objects. They decided to make ramps with hollow blocks. Once they had several ramps that varied in height and width, the children began finding objects to roll down the ramps. Two found hollow plastic balls and a plastic truck. One found a solid rubber ball, a metal truck, and a cube. As they rolled the objects down their ramps, they began to pose questions about the objects as well as to categorize their answers. For example, they discussed the speed of the object as it rolled down the ramp, the distance the object rolled, and the mobility of the object. Their actions on those objects and their discussion helped them advance their understandings of spatial and logico-mathematical relationships.

The first two educational approaches Kamii and DeVries developed were the use of physical knowledge activities and group games. Within the area of physical knowledge activities, they categorized three types of activities: those that involved the movement of objects, those that involved changes in objects, and those that fell between those two (see the discussion of physical knowledge in Chapter 3). Within the area of group games, they stressed the opportunity for children to construct physical knowledge and logico-mathematical knowledge. They also wanted the children to coordinate perspectives as they decided on rules and the procedures for the games (see Boxes 9.7 and 9.8).

BOX 9.7 PHYSICAL KNOWLEDGE ACTIVITIES: AN APPROACH TO CURRICULUM

Activities that involve the movement of objects: Balancing, blowing, dropping, kicking, jumping, pulling, pushing, rolling, sucking, swinging, throwing, twirling

Activities that involve the changing of objects: Cooking, mixing paints, making candles, melting wax, freezing, and thawing—in other words, activities that allow for transformations

Activities that fall between moving of objects and changing of objects: Sinking and floating activities, sifting activities, playing with mirrors, shadow play, producing sounds such as echoes, looking through a magnifying glass

---

Source: C. Kamii & R. DeVries (1993). *Physical knowledge in preschool education: Implications of Piaget's theory.* (Reissued with a new introduction.) New York, NY: Teachers College Press.

BOX 9.8 GROUP GAMES: AN APPROACH TO CURRICULUM

Aiming: Target ball, ring toss, marbles, a safe dart game

Racing and chasing: Duck, Duck, Goose; musical chairs; tag

Hiding: Hide and seek (hide objects in the classroom); sleight of hand games (e.g., hide a nut under one of three shells, rotate the shells, and find the nut)

Guessing: Guess the card, I spy, charades

Card games: War, Concentration, and Fives

Board games: Hi-Ho! Cherry-O; Candyland; Chutes and Ladders

Games with verbal commands: Simon Says, May I?

Source: C. Kamii & R. DeVries (1980). *Group games in early childhood education: Implications of Piaget's theory.* Washington, DC: National Association for the Education of Young Children.

At that time, Kamii and DeVries were studying the child's understandings of physical knowledge and selecting their physical knowledge activities. They were not as interested in the content areas of traditional schooling as they were in how young children construct knowledge and become more autonomous. As they designed curriculum approaches, they began to study what good teachers who based their practice on their intuitions were doing in the field. Kamii and DeVries realized that Piagetian theory could serve as a framework for existing curricula (curricula from the intuitive teachers) and could help modify certain practices or aspects of a practice that was not constructivist (DeVries & Kohlberg, 1987). Because of this realization, they redefined the teacher's role so that it reflected what intuitive teachers were currently doing. Box 9.9 lists the responsibilities that Kamii and DeVries decided on as they observed good teachers.

BOX 9.9 THE CONSTRUCTIVIST TEACHER'S ROLE IN THE CLASSROOM

- To create an environment and atmosphere conducive to learning
- To provide materials, suggest activities, and assess what is going on inside the child's head from moment to moment

- To respond to children in terms of the kind of knowledge involved
- To help the child extend his ideas

Source: R. DeVries & L. Kohlberg (1987). *Constructivist early education: Overview and comparison with other programs.* Washington, DC: NAEYC.

After their work on physical knowledge activities and group games, both Kamii and DeVries began to study traditional school curricula and look for ways to apply constructivist perspectives to it. Kamii developed approaches through daily living routines (voting, handing out materials, dividing snack), card games (War, Double War), and group games (board games) for addressing the child's knowledge of number (Kato, Honda, & Kamii, 2006). They based those approaches on the fact that Piaget and his colleagues had found that the "knowledge of number is a single system of logical classes and relations that includes conservation of number, class inclusion and seriation" (Goffin & Wilson, 2001, p. 147). Because of Kamii's interest in arithmetic and number, she extended her ideas for application and research through the fourth grade.

DeVries and Kamii have also researched reading and writing in the preschool and primary grades. Both have based their work on Ferreiro and Teberosky's research (Vernon & Ferreiro, 2005; Ferreiro & Teberosky, 1982). Ferreiro, a student of Piaget's and Sinclair's, maintained that children learn to read and write by actively constructing and then testing their hypotheses about print. DeVries focused her work on ways children learn to read through group games, cooking experiences and reading the recipes, and symbolic play. Kamii worked with Manning and Manning as they studied young children's writing.

Both DeVries and Kamii maintained that in order to teach children content areas or subject matter, the teacher must study how children understand and think about the content of that area (Goffin & Wilson, 2001). Because of this premise, both maintained that observation and documentation of children's thinking were essential tasks for the classroom teacher. Such documentation could serve as a guide for teachers as they made decisions about curriculum.

Just as Weikart and his group researched the High Scope model, Kamii, DeVries, and their followers have done extensive research on their approaches. Unlike High Scope, which focuses its research on the academic success of children from High Scope programs, Kamii and DeVries focus their research on young children's thinking. Kamii continues to research young children's mathematical thinking, and before her death, DeVries was researching the socio-moral climate of constructivist classrooms.

The Kamii and DeVries approach is just that: an approach. Many researchers view their work as an emerging constructivist model because they organize their approach around the three kinds of knowledge (logico-mathematical, physical, and social; see Chapter 3 for a discussion of each one) and focus on intellectual development. Because their approach is constructivist, they view assessment as documenting the intellectual development of the child. For example, Kamii suggests that the teacher play a card game with the child so that the teacher can understand what the child knows by his or her choice of strategies for playing the game (Kato, Honda, & Kamii, 2006). Furthermore, because their approach is a study of intellectual development, they do not address issues such as teacher-child ratio and staff development. However, Kamii does inservice workshops, teaches university courses (at the University of Alabama–Birmingham), and offers workshops for teachers who are interested in attending. Zan, DeVries's colleague, and other members of DeVries's team, continue her work at the University of Northern Iowa's Regents Center and Freeburg School. More information about her programs can be found at http://www. uni.edu/coe/special-programs/regents-center-early-developmental-education and www.uni.edu/coe/regentsctr.

The Kamii and DeVries approach offers an opportunity to see how constructivist theory helps teachers link theory to practice. It also offers a study in intellectual development. As you reflect on their approach, you may want to think about ways to structure your curriculum. You might decide to use the three kinds of knowledge, or you might use the academic disciplines (language arts, math, science) and attempt to apply constructivist practices within those disciplines. Some of you will attend one of the courses or inservice workshops that Kamii and DeVries offer.

CONSTRUCTIONS

Research

Visit DeVries's Web site (www.uni.edu/coe/regentsctr) and write down one approach from the site that you might use as you develop your own ideas about teaching.

Resnick's and Papert's Approaches

Seymour Papert was considered by many to be the world's foremost expert on new ways of knowing. He and his followers from the Massachusetts Institute of Technology's Epistemology and Learning Group maintained that they had broken away from today's constructivist approach and models and created a theory of teaching and learning they named **constructionism**. Papert saw this as necessary because he believed that we need a theory to understand the role of technologies in our society (Papert, 1990). Like the constructivist theory, Papert's theory is based on Piagetian theory and research.

Many of you might question including Papert's theory because of his claims that it is not constructivist. We decided to include it for two reasons. The first reason is that his followers are doing some of the most exciting and futuristic work with computational tools and young children. They are redefining learning environments and education through the role of technology. A quote from the Lifelong Kindergarten Web site sums up their efforts:

> The Lifelong Kindergarten group at the MIT Media Lab aims to re-invent learning and education in a digital society. We develop new technologies that, in the spirit of blocks and finger-paint of kindergarten, expand the range of what people design and create—and what they learn in the process. Our ultimate goal is a world of playfully creative people, who are constantly inventing new possibilities for themselves and their communities. (www.llk.media.mit.edu)

We wanted you to know about their work and think about it as you plan your curriculum and the role technology can play in it.

The second reason is that there are several interpretations of constructivism because of its popularity with researchers and educators. Some interpretations focus on one aspect (perhaps ages and stages of development) of the theory, while others focus on other aspects (e.g., three kinds of knowledge). However, all interpretations share an interest in understanding knowing and the intellectual development of the young child. Papert's seminal work is such an example.

Papert's study of knowing began in the 1960s when he created Logo programming language and the Logo turtle, which provided a means for children to use computers as instruments for learning and elaborating creativity. His book *Mindstorms* is a landmark for educational reform. After Papert's work with Logo programming language, he continued to research, design, and write about the role of computational tools in young children's learning.

Papert collaborated with Piaget for many years. His respect for Piaget's work is summed up in this quote: "Jean Piaget, the world's most influential authority on intellectual development, sees regularities as the results of general laws that govern the growth of intelligence, laws of epistemology rather than of biology" (1980b). Papert based his research with computers on Piagetian theory.

As Papert's work with computational tools for young children grew, he organized the Massachusetts Institute of Technology Epistemology and Learning Group. As he worked with that group, they began to elaborate their theory of constructionism and develop their approaches to curriculum. For example, Papert pointed out that the difference in the two theories is that the constructivist focus is on knowing, and constructionism focuses on doing and building (Forman & Landry, 2000).

Papert and the Technology Epistemology and Learning Group viewed the learner as actively constructing something external or shareable, such as a computer program, sand castle, or book (Forman & Landry, 2000), that is meaningful and fulfills the learner's sense of self. For example, Harel (1990) had fourth graders design their own instructional software to teach fractions to other children. The fourth graders not only understood fractions better because of teaching others and designing the software, but they also knew how to explain what they knew with regard to their designs of the software, their use of the computer, and their understanding of fractions.

Papert and his followers maintain that the child is the maker, producer, and designer, as was the case with the fourth graders. In his view, children should program their own games rather than play computer games designed by adults. Furthermore, they should make three-dimensional physical things (such as robots) rather than just use the computer. As a result of being designers, makers, and producers, the children will have a deeper understanding of various concepts and will be able to explain that understanding (Forman & Landry, 2000).

Papert (1990) summed up one of his principles in "A Critique of Technocentrism in Thinking About the School of the Future" in the following way:

I visited a school [in Sofia, Bulgaria] in which children were using computers and making programs. At the end, they said they had questions and wanted to interview me. One of the questions was, "Do children anywhere else have such a great teacher?"

I was so moved, I didn't know what to say and I said something very clumsy and awkward. But I thought, "Isn't that wonderful?" There was something about the kind of work they were doing that made them feel this way about their teacher. Of course their teacher is a wonderful person, but we can create educational environments that bring out the love for the teacher and the love for everyone else there.

Above all, even beyond the love for the knowledge, is this principle: If you love what you learn, you'll get to love yourself more. And that has to be the goal of education, that each individual will come out with a sense of personal self-respect, empowerment, and love for oneself, because from that grow all the other loves: for people, for knowledge, for the society in which you live.

Under the leadership of Mitchel Resnick, Papert's dream of developing a theory of learning and teaching that will reform society rather than serve purely as a theory of knowledge continues to evolve. Rather than academic disciplines and commercial, computer software programs, the MIT group use computational tools and technology as the core for developing their learning environments. The children design their own curriculum within those learning environments. To Papert and the rest of the MIT group, the teacher's role is to be a partner who asks leading questions, provides technical assistance, and helps children document their learning. In their minds, teachers do not need a better way of teaching; rather, they need to create more opportunities for learners to construct, do, produce, make, and design (Resnick, 2012).

Constructivists' Approaches to Children With Intellectual Disabilities

Because of constructivists' theories on learning and development, the authors have not offered separate models for children with intellectual disabilities and modifications for teaching them. For example, Chapter 3 on learning and the three kinds of knowledge does not provide information that describes the child with intellectual disabilities at the various stages. Constructivists base much of our knowing on the research and writings of Piaget and his colleagues (e.g., Inhelder, Furth). We also include Vygotsky's research as essential to our understanding of and work with children with intellectual disabilities. The following paragraphs offer a brief look at the basis for how constructivists would address intellectual disabilities in their work with young children.

Constructivists who adhere to the work of Piaget, Inhelder, and social constructivists such as Vygotsky focus on development—not behavior. As a result, Piaget and his colleagues explicitly defined and described sequences of development (e.g., classification, seriation, conservation) in various domains in children. They focused on the processes within development, which caused them to study what individuals were thinking and what thought processes were involved, or the basis of that particular thought or action. As a result of their approach, they found that children with intellectual disabilities proceed in the identical order as individuals with average intelligence (Marchand, 2000).

Inhelder, one of Piaget's leading researchers in the area of intellectual disabilities, also found that even though children with intellectual disabilities had the same sequences of development, the actual functioning of those sequences was incomplete (Marchand, 2000; Inhelder, 1943/1969). She noted that these children experienced sudden bursts of activity and then stagnation. They also experience a gradual diminishing of development. For example, they may learn a concept in one lesson but not know it in the next. This causes the child to become confined in a "false equilibrium characterized by a certain genetic viscosity" (Marchand, 2000). For example, as the child was learning a higher-order concept, a lower-order concept would seep in and interfere. Although this thinking may seem chaotic, it's not. It has structure, but within that structure the thinking operates in an incomplete manner. Inhelder labeled this genetic viscosity.

Piaget and Inhelder's research and writing on intellectual disabilities remains influential today. The results of their work are that researchers and educators have a much more defined and diverse way to look at intellectual disabilities. In addition, Piaget and Inhelder's work has caused educators to use the same models for children with intellectual disabilities. The modifications that educators make relate to issues of physical challenges and/or their own understanding of the child's developmental processes.

Like Piaget, Inhelder, and other Piagetian researchers, Vygotsky viewed intellectual disabilities from a developmental perspective. His theory, called a theory of *disontogenesis*, is based on primary defects (the biological cause of a defect), secondary defects (the child's psychological functioning), and their interactions (the result of the interaction of the two). He focused his work on the higher-order psychological functioning that he felt could compensate for the defect. Vygotsky noted that different tools (e.g., Braille, computer-enhanced keyboards) were positive approaches to assist the child in developing those higher-order psychological functioning abilities. In addition, he attempted to identify the ability that the child had and was using (actual developmental level) as well as the ability the child was capable of using (collaboration in the problem solving with adult or more capable peers). This work became known as the *zone of proximal development*. Just as Piaget and Inhelder focused on the processes that the child with intellectual disabilities used, Vygotsky focused on inclusion, education, understanding of culture, and the positive capacities of the child (Dixon & Verenikina, 2007; Gindis, 1995).

Teachers must make decisions—considering what they know about teaching and learning as well as any mandates with which they must work—about building their own models of curriculum that are appropriate and consistent with what research has shown about how children construct knowledge. See the following Curriculum Strategies for information related to building from established models of curriculum.

CURRICULUM STRATEGIES: BUILDING FROM MODELS OF CURRICULUM

- Consider whether you want to use an established constructivist model or create your own based on your reading, research, and practice.
- If you want to teach from a model, consider obtaining additional training from experts in the actual model. For example, attend High Scope workshops.
- As you construct your own model for teaching, use the questions in this chapter to guide your design of the model.
- Remember the importance of active learning, the child's voice, authentic tasks, play, and choice as you design your model.
- Make sure your educational model is based on theory and research.
- Remember that classroom research or teacher inquiry is essential for constructivist models.

CONSTRUCTIONS

1. Research

Use the Internet to find out more about the Lifelong Kindergarten Web site. As you study the site, think about ways you could use technology in your own teaching. Write several of those ideas in your journal. Compare them to others in your class.

2. Research and Practice

If you have access to the materials necessary to carry out a project similar to one you find on the Lifelong Kindergarten Web site, then try to do it. As you attempt to modify the project for your needs and materials, keep journal entries so that you can revisit your process at a later date.

SUMMARY

- Constructivist models of education have been in existence for over 30 years.
- Educational models help you make sense of an educational approach.
- Most of the educational models that were developed in the 1960s were for preschool-age children.
- Teachers use their interpretations of Piagetian theory to guide them in designing curriculum.

- Piaget never intended for his tasks to be used for instructional purposes.
- High Scope is one of the most researched programs in educational history. It is designed to improve disadvantaged children's chances for academic success.
- Kamii and DeVries were interested in how young children construct knowledge and become more autonomous.
- Papert designs computational tools and technological learning environments for the young child.
- Piaget, Inhelder, and Vygotsky's research and writing about children with intellectual disabilities focused on development and developmental processes, not behavior.

CONSTRUCTIONS

1. RESEARCH AND ANALYSIS

Select three constructivist models that we did not include in this chapter. Use a matrix similar to the one provided here and address the questions we listed earlier in the chapter to guide you through that model.

Table 9.1 **Sources of Thought for Educational Models**

	Ausubelian Model, David Ausubel	*Educating the Young Thinker Model, Irving Sigel*	*Reggio Emilia Model, L. Malaguzzi and L. Gandini*
Question 1			
Question 2			
Question 3			
Question 4			
Question 5			
Question 6			
Question 7			
Question 8			
Question 9			

Resources

Books

Goffin, S.G., & Wilson, C.S. (2001). *Curriculum models and early childhood education: Appraising the relationship* (2nd ed.). Upper Saddle River, NJ: Merrill.

A comprehensive discussion of curriculum models in early childhood education. It uses a sociohistorical approach to examine various curriculum models.

Roopnarine, J.L., & Johnson, J.E. (Eds.). (2012). *Approaches to early childhood education* (6th ed.). New York, NY: Pearson.

Each chapter in this comprehensive book is written by an author with expertise in a specific model, approach, and issue in early childhood education. Teachers and students find the book helpful and easy to understand.

Weikart, D.P., & Schweinhart, L.J. (2013). The High Scope curriculum for early childhood care and education. In J.L. Roopnarine & J.E. Johnson (Eds.), *Approaches to early childhood education* (6th ed., pp. 277–293). New York, NY: Pearson.

Web Sites

High Scope www.highscope.org

This Web site provides comprehensive information about the High Scope curriculum. In addition, it provides links to various aspects of the model.

High Scope http://www.highscope.org/content.asp?contentid=268

This High Scope Web page provides information about High Scope's alignment with the state standards that include the Common Core.

Lifelong Kindergarten http://llk.media.mit.edu

This is the official Web site for new technologies that are being used in educational settings. It is an exciting Web site that provides opportunities to interact with lab researchers, use various projects that the team is developing, and learn more about using technology in the classroom. The lab advances the work of Papert.

Regents Center for Early Developmental Education
http://www.uni.edu/coe/special-programs/regents-center-early-developmental-education

This is the official Web site for the Regents Center for Early Developmental Education at the University of Northern Iowa's College of Education. This excellent Web site provides links, lesson plan ideas, research articles, and information about constructivist teaching.

Regents Center for Early Developmental Education http://www.uni.edu/coe/regentsctr/freeburg.html

This is the official Web site for a model early childhood education program that the University of Northern Iowa's Regents' Center for Early Developmental Education and the Waterloo Community Schools developed. It is an excellent Web site that provides links, lesson plan ideas, research articles, and information about constructivist teaching in a public school setting.

10

CONSTRUCTIVIST EVALUATION: ASSESSMENT AND DOCUMENTATION

Assessment and documentation are processes used to gather data necessary to evaluate how children have grown and what they have learned. They can also be used to gather data to evaluate how your teaching practice and the curriculum content contributed to that development and learning. In Chapter 1 you learned about the aims of a constructivist curriculum, and in Chapters 4 through 6 you learned about the major components essential to a good constructivist curriculum, such as play, authentic tasks, and problem solving. This chapter extends your learning by providing a rationale for the use of assessments and documentation consistent with those goals and methods to evaluate your curriculum components. This chapter also provides information about assessment and evaluation methods that are consistent with a constructivist perspective. Through an understanding of the role of evaluation, you can become an advocate against the inappropriate use of assessment and evaluation. After reading this chapter, you will have a better understanding of

- the differences among assessment, documentation, and evaluation;
- the purposes of evaluation and assessment in early childhood education;
- the different kinds of assessment used in early childhood education;
- the meaning of authentic assessment;
- the use of documentation as a form of authentic assessment of student learning; and
- the use of documentation as a means to inform practice, provide evidence of the quality of a constructivist program, and communicate to parents and the larger community.

Introduction

The teachers are discussing how testing and evaluation are affecting their efforts to apply constructivist principles to their curriculum.

Jennifer: I really didn't want to come today because I didn't want to tell you what I've been doing these past few weeks. But then I decided it was best to come so that you could help me figure out what to do.

Matt: Well, I think you did the right thing. If you're doing something that goes against the grain, then you need to get it off your chest. Sometimes it helps just to say how you're feeling.

Jennifer: Thanks, Matt, but let's check with the others. It may be that they have other priorities for today.

Kenisha: Go on, Jen. Let's talk about it. After all, that's what this group is for.

Jennifer: Okay, here's the scoop. In two more weeks, my kids are going to have to take the state's achievement test. Their scores will be used to determine if they pass to the fourth grade or stay in third. I really feel uncomfortable with that idea, especially since my kids don't do well on those kinds of tests. But the worst part is that the test scores will also determine which schools pass and which will have to be put on alert.

Parul: So what does "being put on alert" mean?

Jennifer: It means that your school is graded in terms of the children's achievement, and you have to bring the scores up by the next year or the state may take over the school. You have to meet adequate yearly progress goals each year.

Ron: I don't think that's how those tests were intended to be used, is it?

Jennifer: I don't know about that. All I know is that's how they are being used, and I've spent the last two weeks getting the kids ready.

Sheila: We do all kinds of assessment in the Head Start program, but it isn't done with tests like that.

Kenisha: Well, I hope Jennifer is not getting them ready by teaching them the test items, because then the test is not a valid indication of what they have learned.

Jennifer: Look, I just want the kids to look good on the test, and I want to look good too!

Evaluation is the process by which we use the data gathered through assessment and/or documentation to draw conclusions and make informed decisions or judgments regarding any or all of the components of an early childhood program. For example, the National Academy of Early Childhood Programs assesses independent early childhood centers and makes a judgment regarding whether each center meets the standards necessary for National Association for the Education of Young Children (NAEYC) accreditation. Teachers evaluate children's achievement and make judgments about their learning or about the quality of the curriculum. Administrators evaluate teachers' practices and make judgments about the quality of their instruction. Evaluation may cause teachers, parents, and children much stress and anxiety, but it is necessary for determining and maintaining the quality of the educational curriculum. Although there has been considerable debate regarding the role of assessment and evaluation in early childhood education, most early childhood educators recognize the need for gathering information related to the quality of all curriculum components and for making informed decisions based on that information. However, there are also some strong differences about the kinds of instruments that should be used for this assessment and the purposes for which they should be used.

According to Gullo (1994), it "is essential that professionals who work with young children understand the constructs underlying assessment and evaluation" (p. 5). Two major constructs related to evaluation, assessment, and documentation are discussed in this chapter.

Assessment

Assessment refers to the measurement of three components central to the early childhood curriculum: the children's educational achievement, developmental abilities, readiness, and/or need for special services; the teacher's competence; and the quality of the curriculum content. It is the process of gathering data by means of a testing instrument, screening measure, or controlled observation to determine what has been accomplished or needs to be accomplished at a certain point.

Purposes of Assessment

Many professional organizations concerned with providing developmentally appropriate early childhood programs and services have acknowledged that assessment is important and potentially beneficial. To ensure that assessments are developed, implemented, and used in appropriate ways, these organizations have developed basic principles and guidelines related to assessing young children. Many of these grew from early childhood educators' concerns about how Goal 1, put forth in 1990 by the National Education Goals Panel (NEGP), would be measured. Goal 1 required that "by the year 2000, all children in America will start school ready to learn." Others have developed documents that expanded and extended these recommendations. Two of these documents are

- *Early Childhood Curriculum, Assessment, and Program Evaluation* (and an accompanying extension for English language learners), a position statement developed by the National Association for the Education of Young Children (NAEYC) and the National Association of Early Childhood Specialists in State Departments of Education (NAECS) (2003).
- *Promoting Positive Outcomes for Children with Disabilities: Recommendations for Curriculum, Assessment, and Program Evaluation* from the Division for Early Childhood (DEC) (2007).

These principles and recommendations were designed to guide the policies and practices related to the assessment of young children. The principles, put forth by Snow and Van Hemel (2008), that should guide the assessment of young children include the following:

1. Assessments should benefit children: NEGP, NAEYC, DEC;
2. Assessments should meet professional, legal, and ethical standards: NAEYC, DEC;
3. Assessments should be designed for a specific purpose and be shown to be psychometrically sound for that purpose: NEGP, NAEYC, DEC;
4. Assessments should be age appropriate or developmentally/individually appropriate: NEGP, NAEYC, DEC;
5. Parents/family should be involved in assessment when possible: NEGP, NAEYC, DEC;
6. Assessments should be linguistically and culturally appropriate/responsive: NEGP, NAEYC, DEC; and
7. Assessments should assess developmentally/educationally significant content: NEGP (in narrative), NAEYC, DEC.

In addition, the National Early Childhood Assessments Resource Group developed and explained four basic purposes for early childhood assessment. These purposes, and the assessment instruments that are used to meet them, are described in Table 10.1. In 2006 Congress requested that the National Research Council conduct a study of developmental outcomes and appropriate assessment of young children. The council identified two key principles to support effective assessment: (1) The purpose of an assessment should guide assessment decisions; (2) assessments should be conducted within a coherent system of health, educational, and support services that promote optimal development for all children (National Research Council, 2008). If assessment practices do not conform to all of these principles, then they are not appropriate for young children.

Assessment Instruments

There are a variety of assessment instruments used to gather data on which to base informed curriculum decisions. These instruments can be grouped into one of two major categories: standardized tests and alternative assessment instruments.

Standardized Tests

A standardized test is one that has been administered to large numbers of people in the intended population in order to derive **norms,** or scores for the

Table 10.1 Appropriate Uses and Technical Accuracy of Assessments Change Across the Early Childhood Age Continuum (Birth to Age 8)

Birth	1	2	3	4	Kindergarten 5	First Grade 6	Second Grade 7	Third Grade 8	Beyond Age 8

Purpose 1. Assessing to promote children's learning and development

Birth	1	2	3	4	Kindergarten 5	First Grade 6	Second Grade 7	Third Grade 8	Beyond Age 8
Parents and caregivers observe and respond as children develop language and physical skills.			Parents, caregivers, and preschool teachers use direct measures, including observations of what children are learning, to decide what to teach next.		Teachers use both formal and informal assessments to plan and guide instruction.				

Purpose 2. Identifying children for health and special services

Birth	1	2	3	4	Kindergarten 5	First Grade 6	Second Grade 7	Third Grade 8	Beyond Age 8
All children should be screened regularly for health needs, including hearing and vision checks, as part of routine health care services.			Children entering Head Start and other preschool programs should be screened for health needs, including hearing and vision checks.		All children should be screened at school entry for vision and hearing needs and checked for immunizations.				
Many serious cognitive and physical disabilities are evident at birth or soon thereafter. As soon as developmental delays or potential disabilities are suspected, parents and physicians should seek in-depth assessments.			Individual children with possible developmental delays should be referred for in-depth assessment.		Some mild disabilities may only become apparent in the school context. Districts and states must by law have sound teacher and parent referral policies so that children with potential disabilities are referred for in-depth assessment.				

(Continued)

Table 10.1 (*Continued*)

Birth	1	2	3	4	Kindergarten 5	First Grade 6	Second Grade 7	Third Grade 8	Beyond Age 8
Purpose 3. Monitoring trends and evaluating programs and services									
Because direct measures of children's language and cognitive functioning are difficult to aggregate accurately for ages from birth to 2, state reporting systems should focus on living and social conditions that affect learning and the adequacy of services.			Assessments, including direct and indirect measures of children's physical, social, emotional, and cognitive development, could be constructed and used to evaluate prekindergarten programs, but such measures would not be accurate enough to make high-stakes decisions about individual children.		Beginning at age 5, it is possible to use direct measures, including measures of children's early learning, as part of a comprehensive early childhood assessment for monitoring trends. Matrix sampling should be used to ensure technical accuracy and to provide safeguards for individual children. Because of the cost of such an assessment, states or the nation should pick one grade level for monitoring trends in early childhood, most likely kindergarten or first grade.				
Purpose 4. Assessing academic achievement to hold individual students, teachers, and schools accountable									
								Before age 8, standardized achievement measures are not sufficiently accurate to be used for high-stakes decisions about individual children and schools. Therefore, high-stakes assessments intended for accountability purposes should be delayed until the end of third grade (or preferably fourth grade).	

Source: National Education Goals Panel, www.negp.gov.

population being measured, so that each individual's score can be compared to these group norms. Standardized tests are designed to measure a specific concept, such as achievement, intelligence, or aptitude. They are administered in the same way to all subjects being measured, and they are scored following the same procedure for all subjects. Specific directions on how to interpret the scores are given in the test manuals. Some standardized tests are administered to groups, and others have to be individually administered. Information regarding the specific procedures to follow in the administration of the tests, as well as the population for whom the test is intended, is given in the test manuals.

Standardized developmental **screening tests** are **aptitude tests** used to identify children who may need special services or a special plan within the classroom setting (Gullo, 1994). One example of these standardized screening tests is the Denver Developmental Screening Test II, a 20-minute test that screens for major developmental delays in infants. Others are the ELM (Early Language Milestone) scale for children 0–3 years of age; AGS Early Screening Profiles, which are used to screen children ages 2 through 6 in all development areas; and the Battelle Developmental Inventory, which screens children from birth through age 8.

Standardized **achievement tests** are organized around large domains of knowledge, such as mathematics, science, or reading. Because it would be impossible to examine everything taught or learned within each domain, achievement tests are designed with items that are thought to sample content within the domain. Thus, the test item $1 + 6 = ?$ could be used to sample the child's ability to compute sums between 1 and 10. One example of a standardized achievement test is the Iowa Test of Basic Skills, Levels 5–8. This test is designed to assess the achievement of children from 5 to 8 years of age in four major subject areas: language and literacy, math, social studies, and science. Another popular achievement test, the Stanford Achievement Test, is designed to measure the curriculum content taught in grades one through nine. The Stanford Early School Achievement Test is designed to assess children in kindergarten and first grade. The purpose of the test is to determine what the child has achieved each year.

Standardized **intelligence tests** designed to assess the intelligence of young children are used to determine the child's need for special services. They differ from screening assessments in that they do not identify developmental delays per se, but rather identify the child's cognitive ability. These tests usually require administration by a trained psychometrist or psychologist. One example of this kind of standardized assessment is the Wechsler Preschool and Primary Scale of Intelligence–Revised. This battery of tests is designed to indicate the general intellectual functioning of children from 3 to 7 years of age. These tests can suggest the range of intellectual function according to stated norms. Another example of a standardized intelligence test is the Stanford-Binet Intelligence Scale. This test is designed to assess the intelligence and cognitive abilities of people beginning at age 2. Like the Wechsler, this test is used to identify those who may benefit from a special program.

Alternative Assessments

Alternative assessment is a term for informal assessment instruments that are used in the classroom (McAfee & Leong, 2011). Teachers of young children use a number of informal strategies to determine children's progress, achievement, development, and disposition for learning.

One of the most basic assessment strategies that early childhood teachers use is observation. All teachers observe their children daily and use the information gained to comment on a child's new shirt or to comfort a crying child. These informal observations can provide valuable information if they are recorded. There are two major strategies for recording observations: informal notes and anecdotal records. Teachers can plan for informal note taking of spontaneous events that emerge in the classroom. One method is to keep an **observation notebook** with an entry sheet for each child in a convenient and consistent place. New observations can then be quickly noted and dated. This notebook serves as a memory prompt so that the details of the event can be recorded later.

Anecdotal records are written records of carefully planned and focused observations of a specific child or a specific event, such as working in the block center. These records are designed to be objective descriptions of what happened, when it happened, and where it happened. Teachers should avoid making judgmental comments when writing these records. Statements such as "Jack was very naughty" are inappropriate in an anecdotal record. Goodwin and Driscoll (1980) suggest five characteristics for anecdotal records; they are listed in Box 10.1.

BOX 10.1 CHARACTERISTICS OF ANECDOTAL RECORDS

1. The anecdotal record is the result of direct observation.
2. The anecdotal record is a prompt, accurate, and specific account of an event.
3. The anecdotal record includes the context of the behavior.
4. Interpretations of the incident are recorded separately from the incident.
5. The anecdotal record focuses on behavior that is either typical or unusual for the child being observed.

Source: Goodwin & Driscoll (1980). *Handbook for measurement and evaluation in early childhood education.* San Francisco, CA: Jossey-Bass.

Other kinds of alternative assessments include teacher-made tests, chapter tests from curriculum texts, developmental and curriculum checklists, and rating scales. Teacher-made tests and chapter tests from curriculum texts are used to determine how well the children have learned the content taught. Teacher-made tests for young children generally ask children to circle or put an X on a picture or other artifact being tested. The teacher reads the directions aloud. As children grow in their ability to read, they are expected to read the directions and complete the test independently.

Checklists and rating scales are similar in nature but address different kinds of information. **Checklists** are used to determine if a particular skill has been mastered or not. Topics on the checklist usually refer to a skill or ability that is required of the child within a grade level or to move from one grade level to another. Items on the checklist are checked only when they have been mastered. For example, an item on an early literacy checklist might be "Can name all of the letters of the alphabet." **Rating scales** are used to make judgments about the child's progress. Rating scales use letters or numbers to indicate how a particular trait is developing. Popular rating scales in early childhood, such as the one in Table 10.2, use the letters "E" to indicate that the trait is emerging, "P" to indicate the trait is being practiced, and "A" to indicate that the trait is being applied.

Table 10.2 **Example Rating Scale**

Name_____ *Date(s)*_____

Problem Solving and Reasoning

E = Emerging   P = Practicing   A = Applying

E	*P*	*A*	*Description of Strategies or Context*
			Discusses problem
			Listens to partner(s)
			Demonstrates willingness to try
			Organizes information
			Develops and applies strategies
			Tries different strategies
			Perseveres in problem solving
			Draws diagrams/pictures
			Uses resources to solve problems
			Uses trial and error
			Explains answer/reasoning
			Invents mathematical problems

CONSTRUCTIONS

1. Observation

Visit a preschool and a primary grade setting and talk with a teacher in each to gather information about the kinds of standardized and alternative assessment procedures they use.

2. Research

Analyze the findings from these interviews to determine similarities and differences in the purposes for the assessments, in the kinds that are used, and in the teachers' feelings about their use.

Assessment Issues

There are a number of significant issues related to the assessment of young children in early childhood education. Over the past few years, the use of assessments has increased in order to address issues of school and teacher accountability. While early childhood educators are aware of the need for quality assessment in early childhood programs, they are also keenly aware of the detrimental effects that occur when testing results are misused. The majority of these issues relate to the use and interpretation of standardized achievement tests but can also be applied to teacher-made tests.

One of the major issues related to assessment in early childhood education is the developmental nature of the test subject. Young children, by nature, are developmentally different from each other and from older children. For example, a test that asks a child to mark the picture of a bank might be easy for children who live in a city environment and have visited a bank but baffling for children who live in a rural environment and fish on the bank of the river but have never been to a bank building. Another example is a test item that shows a picture on the left-hand side of the page and requires the child to mark the bubble in the appropriate answer in that row. Children who have not used ruled paper may mark the appropriate picture in a different row. According to Gullo (1994), "Young children are not reliable test takers." He suggests that the younger the child, the less reliable the test results are. In other words, a child's score on any given day is likely to vary greatly from the score the same child would obtain if tested on a different day. If the test results cannot be trusted, then making informed decisions about the child's progress or placement is not possible. As a result of this lack of reliability, young children may be inappropriately labeled or placed.

A related issue is the political misuse of assessment measures. The use of standardized tests to document school accountability has become big business. Every year, public and private school systems spend massive amounts of money to administer state or locally mandated tests. According to Kamii and Rosen-blum (1990), the results of these testing campaigns are being used by well-meaning adults who do not realize the damage they are doing. Many suggest that these tests are harmful to young children and are being used politically to help elected officials get votes, help schools and school districts look good, and help school administrators keep their jobs (Meire & Wood, 2004; Kohn, 2000).

When test results are used to make high-stakes decisions about children, teachers, or schools, the scope of the curriculum is narrowed to fit the tests. Teachers and administrators are so focused on helping children get high scores that they teach the material on the test. Since test items represent only a sample of a domain of knowledge, focusing only on test content greatly narrows the curriculum. Additionally, in many schools, teachers spend weeks preparing children for the tests and then spend considerable time administering the tests. This results in a significant loss of valuable learning time. Another issue related to assessment is the misuse of the testing results in ways that are harmful to children. Some of these decisions involve delaying entrance to kindergarten, placing children in pre-K programs, or retaining children in kindergarten. This misuse of assessment results leads to adding at least 1 year to the child's school-ing and makes many children start school thinking of themselves as failures. This self-image can have a strong impact on the child's sense of self, and many children develop test anxiety.

A final issue related to the use of standardized tests is the difficulty of de-veloping a test that is not culturally biased. When tests are used with children of differing cultural backgrounds, the results may be systematically biased. An example is asking a child whose family includes two daddies and a brother to circle "family" when the test does not include a picture of that family structure. The results of the test of these children must be carefully interpreted. McAfee and Leong (2011) suggest that we must be as objective as possible and work to understand and be sensitive to how diversity impacts assessment. Because of all these potential problems with testing, all early childhood teachers must become advocates for determining what children know in developmentally ap-propriate ways and for using that information in ways that are beneficial to chil-dren. A number of early childhood professional organizations have developed position papers on the harmful effects of using tests to determine retention, promotion, school entrance, and placement of children in special education. Two of those organizations are the Council for Exceptional Children and the NAEYC.

Authentic Assessment in the Early Childhood Curriculum

Authentic assessment refers to assessment that is related directly to the learning that is going on in the classroom at the time of the assessment. It is a process that involves careful observation, note taking, and recording to provide evidence of what children can do and how they do it. Puckett and Black (2008) have characterized authentic assessment as shown in Box 10.2.

BOX 10.2 CHARACTERISTICS OF AUTHENTIC ASSESSMENT

Authentic assessment celebrates development and learning.

Authentic assessment emphasizes emerging development.

Authentic assessment capitalizes on the strengths of the learner.

Authentic assessment is based on real-life events.

Authentic assessment is performance based.

Authentic assessment is related to instruction.

Authentic assessment focuses on purposeful learning.

Authentic assessment is ongoing in all contexts.

Authentic assessment provides a broad and general picture of student learning capabilities.

Authentic assessment is collaborative among teachers, students, and other professional persons as needed.

Source: Puckett & Black (2008). *Meaningful assessments of the young child: Celebrating development and learning* (3rd ed.). Upper Saddle River, NJ: Pearson.

Authentic assessment is the kind of assessment that is most compatible with a constructivist curriculum. Children construct knowledge as they attempt to make sense of their environment. Their intellectual and social development is dependent on interaction among children. The classroom climate should promote an atmosphere where thinking and problem solving are natural and necessary and where the exchange of ideas and reasoning is encouraged. Therefore, evaluation should reflect these goals. Additionally, evaluation should focus on process as well as product. For these reasons, the following authentic assessment strategies are recommended.

The Running Reading Record

Clay designed the running reading record as a way to assess a child's ability to read while the child reads aloud. According to Clay (2000), "If running records are taken in a systematic way they provide evidence of how well children are directing their knowledge of letters, sounds and words to understanding the messages in the text" (p. 3). A running record can be used to inform teaching about what the learner needs to know, identify the child's progress, and determine the difficulty of the text the child should be reading. It allows the teacher to determine which reading strategies the child is using to make sense of the text and provides information on how the child is developing a self-regulating reading ability. The purposes of the running record include these:

1. Help in the placement of children
2. Inform decisions on what text is the appropriate instructional level for an individual
3. Capture reading behavior that can be analyzed later
4. Keep a record of change over time
5. Determine the level of difficulty of a particular book
6. Help in making critical decisions about an individual
7. Assess children for research purposes
8. Provide information for teacher leaders in the training of teachers
9. Provide information to parents and other teachers

Learning to do a running reading record is very similar to learning to text: with practice, you become more efficient. Clay outlines how to use running records in her book *Running Records for Classroom Teachers*. The running record is most beneficial when used at the kindergarten, first-, and second-grade levels. Figure 10.1 shows a teacher's running reading record of a kindergarten child reading *Under Water* by Rebel Williams. This teacher has not been formally trained in how to take or analyze a running record. She has studied the Clay book and employed what she has learned to the assessment of the children in her classroom. She makes a check for every word the child reads correctly on each line of the text and records the incorrect substitutions for the words read incorrectly, the words omitted, and the words added. She uses "Rs" with arrows to indicate that the child reread that portion of the text, and the letters "sc (self-correction)" to indicate that the child corrected the error without help. Analyzing the errors and self-corrections made helps the teacher identify the kinds of information the child uses to figure out unknown words and the meaningfulness of the reading. Notice in the figure that the teacher has identified that the child is using pictures and his knowledge of the structure of his language to guide his thinking about the text. Notice that he added a word to sentence seven. He has used information from the picture and a sentence structure with which he is familiar. This teacher has also noted that he has corrected one of three of the errors made. She considers this good because self-corrections seem to indicate that the child is attempting to get at the meaning of what he is reading.

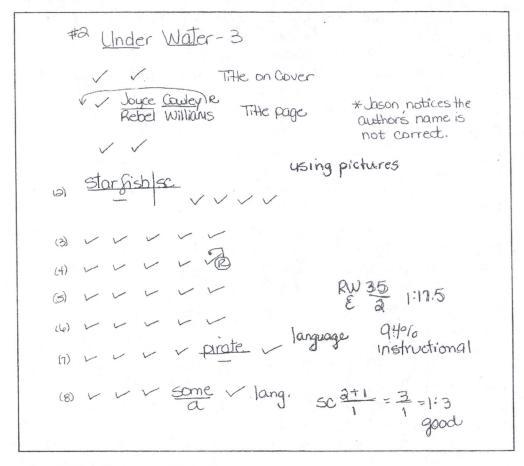

Figure 10.1 **Running Reading Record.**

An Analysis of Writing Samples

The analysis of writing samples was designed for teachers to use as they analyze and evaluate the purposeful writing of the students in the classroom (Taylor, Branscombe, & Gunnels, 2000, p. 208). Many teachers feel unsure about how to evaluate writing, particularly the writing of young children. Consequently, they focus on details such as letter formation and punctuation and don't give much attention to the compositional qualities of the writing. The purpose of the analysis of writing samples is to provide teachers with a set of questions to use when analyzing and conferencing with students about their writing. It starts with questions about the literary qualities of the writing and follows with questions about organizational qualities. This analysis can be used for the evaluation of poetry, prose, journalistic reports, and essays. The analysis of writing samples form is presented in Box 10.3.

Box 10.4 demonstrates how one teacher used the analysis of writing form to evaluate a child's journal entry.

BOX 10.3 AN ANALYSIS OF WRITING SAMPLES

Purposes: To get "inside the student's head" to determine what the student means and the strategies the student has available to communicate that meaning in writing. To use what the student knows as the instructional starting point.

What to look for in a child's writing:

1. Literary Qualities

Meaning–what is the content, story, or purpose for the writing?

Does the piece move you in some way? Make you laugh? Cry? Chuckle? Evoke a memory?

Is there a use of literary conventions such as figurative language, metaphor, or pun?

Does the piece demonstrate a specific genre?

Does the writer use an individual voice?

2. Organizational Qualities

Does the writer speak with authority?

Does the piece hold together? Does the writer use cohesive strategies related to genre?

Does the piece have an opening, middle, and end?

Does the piece use unusual organizational strategies, such as foreshadowing or flashbacks?

Does the piece develop? Is it focused, complete, and does it have structure?

3. Language Qualities

Does the writer use clear, simple, and effective phrasing?

Does the writer make effective use of sentence combining?

Does the writer select effective vocabulary?

Does the use of language clarify and simplify the content, and not draw attention to itself?

4. Writing Conventions

Does the writer use genre-specific conventions, such as he and she said dialogues in stories, first person in essays?

After editing, is the piece conventionally punctuated?

After editing, is the piece conventionally spelled?

After editing, is the handwriting acceptable?

5. Writing Attitudes

Does the writer like the piece?

Does the writer take risks and experiment with the writing?

Does the writer take pride in reading the piece?

Does the writer compare the piece to other writings?

Box 10.4 demonstrates how one teacher used the analysis of writing form to evaluate a child's journal entry.

BOX 10.4

WILD Horse
ATTack
One day Elisabeth went to her grandmother's house with her friend. They went thier neigborore's horse. They got a new horse it was not trained. "Can I ride it?" I guess they said. So Elisabeth got on it. She kicked the horse very hard. It started kicking and then bucking and then running and wouldn't stop. She pulled back on the raine and shouted "Wo! Stop!" It jumped the fence and ran across the road. Elisabeth's grandfather got in his truck and slowed it down. Jessie stood in front of the horse and stopped it. "Would you like to ride it again?" Asked Jessie. "Are you crazy!" screamed Elisabeth.

By: Beth

Illistated By: Beth

General Statement: Based on this writing sample, it is evident that Beth has a good grasp of a number of writing concepts. These include the following:

1. Literary Qualities

Content	Elisabeth's ride on a horse at her grandparents' house
	Recounts an event in the life of a classmate
Affective	Piece moves from excitement to humor
	Piece makes you chuckle and evokes memories of your childhood
Literary Conventions	"One day" as opening
	End of story and end of quote for closing
	Exaggeration
Genre	Narrative
Voice	Evidence of the beginnings of Voice

2. Organizational Qualities

The writer speaks with authority through the details of the story and the language chosen (i.e., horse not trained; thus it bucked)

Story made sense (i.e., had a beginning, middle, and end; anchored the reader in terms of setting)

Cohesion   Chronological order
Use of pronouns
Use of "and," "so," and "and then"
Use of spatial markers ("in front of")
Piece develops through the events and dialogue

3. Language Qualities

Each sentence conveys a logical thought that is complete, even though Beth is ready for some help with the punctuation of direct quotations

Some evidence of sentence combining—could use more

Effective vocabulary (i.e. "kicking and then bucking … screamed")

Uses language to tell the story and not draw attention to vocabulary words used

Also uses language to show degrees of action (i.e., "kicking and bucking")

4. Writing Conventions

Writes according to convention (indents: left to right and top to bottom; uses title)

Writer uses dialogue and all-knowing third-person point of view

Correctly punctuated 13 sentences

Average sentence length: 7 words

Conventionally spelled 105/110 words (might want to address homo-
phones in a mini-lesson)

Conventional use of quotation marks

5. Writing Attitudes

Beth seemed to enjoy working with this piece.

Beth evidences pride in the piece (signing of name for authorship and
illustrations).

She experiments with dialogue and representing the action within the
events through language.

Understanding Children's Reasoning Through Observation

Observation is the best way to identify children's ability to think mathemati-
cally (Kamii & Rosenblum, 1990). Teachers can keep track of how logico-
mathematical knowledge develops by collecting different kinds of information
for different audiences. For example, teachers need specific information about
how each child thinks. Teachers use this kind of specific information to make
teaching decisions. Systematic observations of daily living situations, group
games, and oral group discussions can provide considerable information about
the thinking of the children, as can written solutions to story problems with explanations of those solutions. Individual interviews related to content appropriate
to the child's age and ranges of abilities also yield valuable information. Teachers
use progress sheets to record the progress children have made during each grad-
ing period of the year. These kinds of summary data can be used to discuss the
child's progress with the child and his or her parents and can then be quantified
for reporting the overall performance of the class to the administrators.

Portfolios

Portfolios are organized collections of children's work and sometimes teachers'
informal assessments that are used to provide evidence of a child's development
over time. Portfolio contents vary according to the purpose they serve: assessment, reflection, or reporting progress (Seitz & Bartholomew, 2008; Wortham,
2001). The portfolio allows students the opportunity to visit, revisit, and reflect
on their work and to take ownership of their progress by assessing and selecting work that best represents their current level of thinking. The portfolio enhances communication between parents, teachers, and children and heightens

parents' understanding of their child's development. Portfolios can contain a variety of documentation including, but not limited to, the examples shown in the following Documentation in Portfolios.

DOCUMENTATION IN PORTFOLIOS

Evidence of Achievement	Evidence of Progress	Evidence of Individuality
Work samples	Observational records	Student's self-reflections
Self-evaluation narratives	Anecdotal records	Self-selected products
Products	Checklists	Journal entries
Project work	Teacher-made tests	Favorite books read
Parent evaluation	Interviews	Portfolio design

Advocacy for Developmentally Appropriate Assessment

Assessing young children is an important and necessary process that provides the kind of information necessary to make informed decisions. The three main purposes for developmentally appropriate assessment in early childhood are to promote children's learning, identify children who need special services, and evaluate the quality of the programs that serve children. Many have expressed that all assessments should be appropriate and directly linked with the assessment's purpose; additionally, no high-stakes accountability testing should be conducted with children before the end of third grade (Shepard, Kagan, & Wurtz, 1998; Snow & Van Hemel, 2008). Teachers should be willing to speak out about the misuses of assessments such as standardized tests and to be advocates for appropriate ways to document children's learning. Teachers can use a variety of informal, authentic kinds of measures to meet

---

CONSTRUCTIONS

Research

Collect a writing sample from a child in the first or second grade. Analyze the sample and assess the child's writing ability. What literary qualities did you find? What surprised you about the writing? Have other classmates assess the same sample. How did your assessments agree? Interview and tape children who are 5 and 7 years old. Ask them, "Can you tell a good story? What makes a good story? Can you write that story on paper?" Compare their responses.

the necessary purposes for assessment. These measures take into account the cultural and developmental diversity found in most classrooms today.

Documentation

The six teachers have come to Parul's child-care center after the public schools have been dismissed. They are sitting in the teachers' planning room so that they can be somewhat removed from the sounds of the children at play. Parul was particularly interested in having them come to her center so that she could share what she has learned about documentation.

Parul: I'm so excited about what I learned from my recent trip to visit the city-run preschools in Pistoia, Italy, and I wanted you to see how I'm using it with the infants. I think you might be able to use it in your classrooms too!

Matt: Yes, and I was really eager to come because I've read many articles about the preschools in Reggio Emilia, and I was hoping that what you observed in Pistoia was similar.

Parul: From what I understand, they are very similar. Both are based on the theories of Piaget and Vygotsky, both seem to use the same kind of teaching projects, and both use documentation as a form of evaluation.

Kenisha: So do you think that what you learned about documentation will be of value to us as constructivist educators?

Parul: I would think so, but I'll let you be the judge of that!

Matt: Hey, Parul! You're beginning to sound like a constructivist.

Jennifer: Well, if what you learned can replace having to be judged by how well your kids do on those standardized achievement tests, I'm ready to learn.

Ron: But will it be applicable in the United States? You know how difficult it is to implement methods that seem good in other countries because the cultures are different.

Parul: Yes, but I understand that the documentation process is being used successfully in many places in the United States, and not just in preschools.

Sheila: So go ahead, Parul, and show us what you're doing.

Parul: Well, I'm using all sorts of ways to show what the infants are learning. For example, I take pictures of special events like the first time the infant rolls over. Then I write a little narrative about what I observed to use with the photo. Sometimes I use videotapes and audiotapes to capture the special events. I use all of these kinds of evidence to create a book that documents the learning experiences of the child, as well as his physical, intellectual, social, and linguistic development over the first 3 years of his life. At the end of the third year, I will send the book home for the parents.

Sheila: Wow! Isn't that a lot of work?

Parul: Yes, it is time consuming, but I saw how much it meant to those parents to see all that their child is learning. And you should have seen the books I saw in Pistoia! They were absolutely magnificent!

Jennifer: Let's look at what you've documented so far.

Documentation, as defined by Forman and Fyfe (1998), is "any activity that renders a performance record with sufficient detail to help others understand the behavior recorded" (p. 241). According to this definition, one drawing or piece of writing by itself would not be considered documentation. However, an "edited videotape of the child creating a drawing or a set of redrawn portions to plot the development of the final drawing would be considered documentation" (p. 241).

Documentation is an integrated form of assessment and evaluation that originated in the municipally supported Italian preschools of Reggio Emilia and Pistoia (Edwards, Gandini, & Forman, 2011). It is a collaborative process in which teachers and children use many different media, such as photographs, audiotapes and videotapes, field notes, work samples, and reflections, to gather evidence of their accomplishments and revisit their learning experiences (Gandini & Kaminsky, 2004; Rinaldi, 2004). It has developed from a mere gathering of evidence into an "analysis of the processes of learning and the interconnections between children's different ideas, activities, and representations" (Vecchi, 1998, p. 141).

Effective documentation always includes many documents that allow for individual and group reflection and interpretation of the learning experience. Katz (1998) suggests that documentation "provides four fundamental and equally important improvements to early childhood education" (p. 38). First, it adds to and enriches children's learning by heightening their curiosity, interest, and confidence as they think about what they have accomplished. Second, it provides a way for parents to understand the learning experiences of the school. Third, as a reciprocal process between teachers and children, it allows teachers to learn from each other and from the children and their parents. This continuous interactive look at their practice helps teachers research and modify their practice. Finally, documentation provides visible evidence of children's learning that cannot be identified through other forms of assessment, such as standardized tests or checklists of skills mastered. Talking with others about the documentation helps create common meanings about learning between teachers, parents, and children. The main purpose of documentation is to explain rather than to display.

Documentation to Support Student Learning

When children engage in documentation activities, their learning becomes more meaningful to them because the documentation is directly related to their learning experiences. They become more confident when they are able to interact with teachers, parents, and other children in meaningful ways about their learning (Rinaldi, 2004). Their curiosity is provoked when they revisit an earlier learning experience with new questions. There are several documentation strategies that teachers can use to support student learning. They are described in Box 10.5.

BOX 10.5 DOCUMENTATION STRATEGIES TO SUPPORT STUDENT LEARNING

Webbing: Developing a concept web allows children to make a record of what they already know. As they continue in their work, they are able to add new understandings to the web. These webs can be group or individual.

Negotiation: Reviewing multiple forms of documentation together gives children opportunities to examine the work from others' perspectives. This often leads to negotiation when mutual plans need to be made for revising or continuing the work. Negotiation can be used to find solutions to problems that arise during the project work.

Reflection: Revisiting photos, narratives, and the products of their earlier experiences allows children to think about what they learned and what they still want to know.

Interpretation: Revisiting photos, narratives, and products of their earlier experiences helps children construct meaning.

Provocation: Thinking about their experiences through the evidence that documentation provides often gives rise to new questions that extend children's thinking.

An example of a concept web can be seen in Figure 10.2. Here, groups of children returned from a walk in the meadow and added what they observed to the original web (Helm, Beneke, & Steinheimer, 1998b).

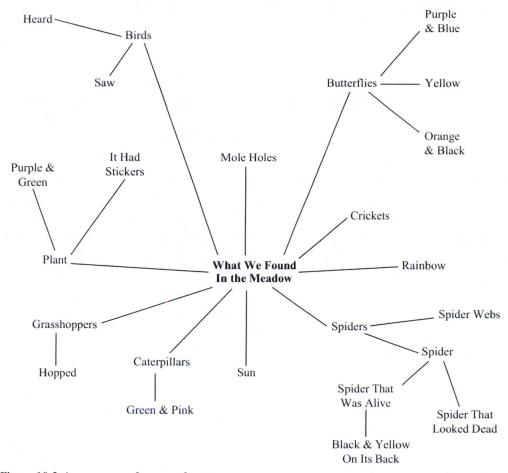

Figure 10.2 **A concept web example.**

Photographs, audio and video recordings, samples of work, and written narratives that are assembled also support student learning in that they provide children with a real and observable memory of what they said and did. In this way, documentation serves as a memory prompt for what they have learned. This kind of direct observation gives children opportunities to self-evaluate and sometimes self-correct their thinking.

Documentation can serve as a starting point for the next steps in the learning process. It provides opportunities for group association, which can give rise to conflicting ideas that promote discussion. Because collaboration is an essential component of the documentation process, it provides opportunities for children to make comparisons with other children to support or negate their hypotheses and interpretations. This kind of social interaction is one of the essential components of a constructivist curriculum.

Documentation for Informing Practice

Documentation extends the usefulness of observations and listening by making them more visible to the child, other children, the teacher, and other teachers. Rinaldi (2004, p. 3) describes documentation as "visible listening" where children can share their theories about the world through their representations. Documentation requires that teachers continuously see what the children are doing and hear what the children are saying. It requires that these observations be recorded in some fashion so that they can be revisited, interpreted, and shared with the children and other teachers. Sharing documentation with others allows the teacher to return to the classroom prepared with new insights and responses to the children's work.

Documentation provides a history of the teacher's teaching and allows teachers opportunities to revisit their own development and transformations of teaching practice. This revisiting helps them develop common meanings and values. According to Forman and Fyfe (1998), documentation "presents the wisdom of the teachers who write the explanations and provocations, but documentation, by itself, is not a systematic evaluation" (p. 246). Because the purpose of documentation is to explain, an array of children's pictures would not be considered documentation. The teacher's narrative is necessary to show the data as a representation of some principle that can be applied in new contexts. Documentation is used to heighten talk rather than to provide a record of past experiences. Its purpose is to raise questions about children's thinking and teachers' teaching, not to mark the progress of all children.

Multiple Perspectives: Documentation in the Kindergarten

Angela Carr, a kindergarten teacher, uses documentation to inform her practice and to ensure parents and administrators that her integrated project approach meets state and national standards. The project "Peter, Peter Pumpkin Eater" arose from a study of nursery rhymes the teacher was using as a way to incorporate required standards within a meaningful context for her students. In addition to learning the rhymes, the children participated in making words activities using the words from the rhyme. Through these kinds of activities, the teacher was able to meet a range of diverse needs of her students.

As a part of the study, Mrs. Carr and her students decided to carve a pumpkin shell to make their own "pumpkin house." To document this process, Mrs. Carr took photos of

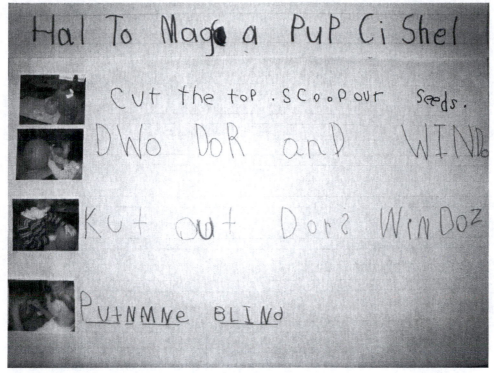

Figure 10.3 **Documentation from pumpkin project.**

each step, then the students sequenced the photos and wrote out the steps on a chart to display in the classroom (see Figure 10.3).

The chart reads as follows:

"How To Make a Pumpkin Shell"
"Cut the top. Scoop out seeds."
"Draw door and window."
"Cut out doors, windows."
"Put in mini-blinds."

The children used the photos provided to provoke their memories of the sequence of steps; then, they used their understandings of written and spoken language to develop the documentation of their process.

After carving their pumpkin, the students began to discuss Peter's wife (from the nursery rhyme) actually living in the house. Because some children had previous experiences with carved pumpkins, they knew that the pumpkin wouldn't last forever. In their discussions, they asked the question, "How long could Peter's wife have lived in the pumpkin shell?" Mrs. Carr used this as an opportunity to propose the children document their observations of the pumpkin shell each day so that they would have a record and attempt to answer their question. So, a chart for documentation was developed, and the children recorded their daily observations (see Figure 10.4).

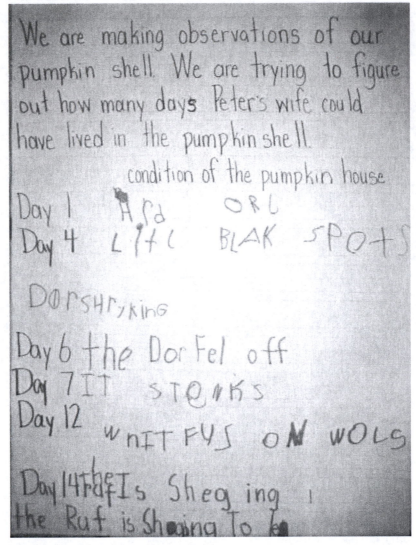

Figure 10.4 **Documentation: Observation chart.**

The translation of the children's writing on the Observation Chart reads as follows:

Day 1   "Hard" "Orange"
Day 4   "Little black spots"
        "Door shrinking"
Day 6   "The door fell off"
Day 7   "It stinks"
Day 12 "White fuzz on walls"
Day 14 "The roof is sagging"
        "The roof is starting to lean"

The children were participating as scientists as they carefully observed the changes in the physical object over time and documented those observations on the chart.

All of this work led to the question, "Could we make a pumpkin big enough for Peter's wife?" The students decided that a pumpkin shell that was large enough for their student teacher to fit in would be large enough for Peter's wife. So they began by measuring the student teacher's height. They used their foot rulers and determined that a height of 5 feet would be big enough. They then began to discuss what materials they could use to construct a 5-foot-tall pumpkin. They began with materials from their classroom such as blocks. They quickly discovered that creating a large round object out of rectangular blocks was not an easy task. After making a round structure, they wrote about why they thought that the blocks were not a good choice for this project (see Figure 10.5).

Figure 10.5 **Documentation of investigation of blocks as a material to build the pumpkin. (a) The final "round" structure using blocks; (b) documentation of the reasons the blocks are not a good choice.**

The children determined that the blocks were not a good choice for this project because "They don't stick together," they weren't strong enough to support the roof, and "the blocks are straight. The pumpkin has curves." The children were participating in the scientific process and trying out their ideas, then drawing conclusions based on the results.

The experimentation continued as the children developed models using other materials. They experimented with Playdough (it was too soft and "squishy") and Unifix cubes (these wouldn't make rounded sides); finally, they made models out of art supplies such as pipe cleaners, scrap paper, tape, paper plates, and so on. After each child made a model, the class examined all of the models and developed a list of criteria for the pumpkin shell (see Figure 10.6a). The criteria included "1. Curves, bends; 2. Something to put it on that is hard and strong." They felt this was important to assist in selecting the most appropriate model. They then sorted the models based on the criteria and selected the one they felt best fit their criteria. Next, they developed a supply list based on the criteria so that Mrs. Carr would know what to purchase at the building supply store for them to begin construction (see Figure 10.6b). The supply list included "wire, bendy stuff, wood, nails, bendy pipe, hard plastic."

Mrs. Carr supplied the requested materials (e.g., PVC pipes with connectors, chicken wire, paper). The students worked with the PVC pipes to construct the frame of the pumpkin shell. They covered the frame with chicken wire. They then used their foot rulers to measure paper that would fit around the pumpkin shell. They used primary colors of paint to mix just the right shade of orange paint, and they painted the paper. They then cut the paper and stapled it together to form the ribs they observed on the pumpkin. Finally, they attached the paper to the frame to complete their pumpkin that was big enough for Peter's wife to fit inside. After a final discussion and vote, the children chose to put books inside their pumpkin shell and use it as their classroom library.

Mrs. Carr was able to take advantage of her students' interests and allowed a study of a nursery rhyme to extend into a much larger and engaging project. Throughout the study, she used documentation to provide evidence that she and her students were, indeed, meeting all of the required standards and learning in a highly engaging and meaningful manner.

Documentation for Communication

Documentation makes the learning process and product visible, which in turn makes it easier for teachers to communicate student learning to parents. Documentation panels are organized displays of students' work used for this purpose. They explain the kind of learning that is going on at the school. Some panels are very large and complex, while others are more narrowly focused. They use a variety of different kinds of information to portray the learning that is taking place. Box 10.6 describes some of the features of documentation panels that make them more meaningful than bulletin boards.

(a)

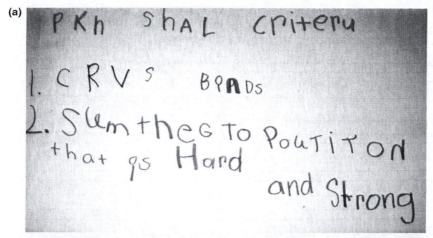

(b)

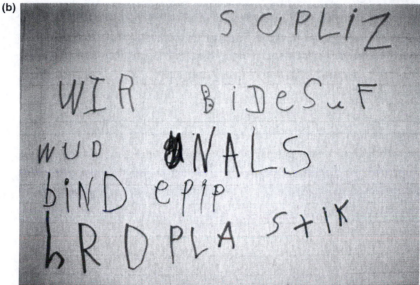

Figure 10.6 Documentation of pumpkin criteria and supplies. (a) Documentation and criteria; (b) documentation of supplies.

BOX 10.6 FEATURES OF DOCUMENTATION PANELS

Webbing or Mind Mapping: Webbing or mind mapping before the learning experience, during the experience, and after the experience documents growth in concepts and understanding of the relationship between concepts. It also documents vocabulary growth.

Time one, time two representations: Drawings become more detailed as students learn more about the objects they are studying. Other forms of representation are paintings, constructions such as block structures, play environments, songs, or dictated stories. Older students' representations include drawings, essays, plays, books, or constructed models.

Narratives of a learning experience: Step-by-step explanations of what happened in a learning experience show what students thought, what they tried, and what happened.

Window on a child's development: This method shares one child's experiences and how that child developed new knowledge or skills or how that child's disposition or attitudes toward learning changed through the project experience.

Lists of concepts or words: Lists of words and concepts that the children have learned are added to as the project progresses.

Explanation of relevance of project for curriculum and assessment system: Knowledge, skills, and dispositions (often stated in standards) that are part of a curriculum and monitored by an assessment system are displayed.

Teacher self-reflection: Teachers' thoughts about teaching strategies, discoveries about the effectiveness of various experiences, and ways that individual differences were accommodated are highlighted in a Teacher Self-Reflection or speech bubble. Consistent use of the bubble shape enables parents and other viewers to immediately recognize teachers' thoughts.

Source: J. H. Helm (1998). *Experiencing documentation: The turtle project.* http://ceep.crc.uiuc.edu/eecearchive/books/projcat2/helm2.html

Time one, time two representations (described further on in Box 10.7) are an excellent way to document a child's growth over time. Children may revisit the same work at another time using a different medium or a newly learned technique, so that their later representation reflects the advanced learning. Rinaldi (1998) suggests sharing documentation that explains what the children are doing, as well as how and why they are doing it, as this allows parents to understand the meaning this learning has for their children. Brown-DuPaul, Keyes, and Segatti (2001) suggest that the interactive format of documentation panels makes them more effective in drawing reticent parents to the classroom than many other means often used. They advise that the use of these panels "supports home-school communication more readily than does reading a newsletter at home" (p. 210). Helm and Helm (2006) explain that documentation can also be used to build support for your school with all stakeholders, including parents and the community.

Documentation is often shared with the community through exhibits of children's work on the walls of the school and in other special exhibitions.

Documentation panels validate children's learning for the community. They provide the authentic detailed evidence necessary to show that the community's interest in the school's quality of instruction is satisfied. Through these exhibits of children's work, teachers can enlist the community's reaction and support (Helm & Helm, 2006). Teachers frequently use other methods of documentation to communicate what the children have learned. Some develop portfolios that can be used for parent-teacher conferences and planning and evaluation conferences with administrators. Figure 10.7 shows a page of the documentation from one teacher's portfolio. Notice how carefully the teacher explains what the children are doing and how they are doing it. Additionally, she provides the learning principles on which the work is based so that others will understand what the children are learning and why.

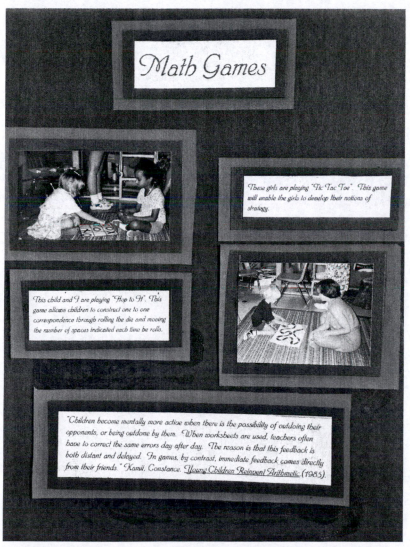

Figure 10.7 **Documentation of Children's Learning in a Teacher's Portfolio.**

Other teachers invite parents to the classroom when some of the project work has been completed. Here again, the teacher portfolio can be on display. Some teachers plan open house activities that encourage parent-child interaction as they look at the results of the children's work documented in the classroom and in the commons areas. Box 10.7 illustrates a handout one teacher used to allow the children to share what they learned throughout their project on the ocean. This kind of documentation helps parents and the community better understand what the children are learning, and its use can help educate the public about how schools are accountable for quality instruction.

BOX 10.7   HELPING PARENTS TALK WITH CHILDREN ABOUT WHAT THEY HAVE LEARNED

Ocean Celebration
Mr. Smith's Class
March 8, 2002
Tour Agenda

You will be guided to various exhibits that you will discuss with your tour guide. Most exhibits will require your participation. Please feel free to ask any questions. If you experience a less than talkative tour guide, some good sample questions are provided for each exhibit. If you cannot find an exhibit, please feel free to ask the manager (Mr. Smith) where it is located. Remind your tour guide to mark each exhibit off the list as you move to a new exhibit. The order in which you view the exhibits is unimportant. I hope you all enjoy your tour!

____**Gallery Art Work Display**   **(Main Hallway)**
Which piece is yours?
Can you tell me about your artwork?
Which piece is your favorite? Why?

____**Whale Shark Exhibit**   **(Pink Pod Commons Area)**
How old is this whale shark?
What does a whale shark eat?
Do whale sharks have teeth? How many?
Do they eat people?

____**Rhyming Work Posters/Books**   **(Toy Center Wall)**
Can you find two words/pictures that rhyme?
Can you think of a word that rhymes with *hop? Mad? Shark? Fish?*

____**Homemade Books Display**   **(Big Book Stand)**

Can you read these books with me?

Can you read these books to me?

Which pictures did you do?

____**Blends Display**   **(Group Time Wall)**

Can you tell me a word that starts with *Gr? Cr? Sp? Cr? Bl?*

____**Octopus Display**   **(Behind Bookstand)**

How many legs does an octopus have?

What are his legs called?

How does he catch his food?

What else can you tell me about the octopus?

____**Journal Reading Area**   **(Reading Center)**

Have the children flip through their journal with you and read a few selections. If you need some help interpreting, please contact the on-staff interpreter (Mr. Smith).

____**Starfish Exhibit**   **(Hanging from Ceiling by Reading Corner)**

How did you make the starfish?

Do all starfish have the same number of arms?

What happens if one arm falls off?

What else can you tell me about starfish?

____**Jellyfish Display**   **(Hanging from Ceiling Near Art Shelf)**

What color are jellyfish?

How do they get food?

How big can a jellyfish grow?

What else do you know about jellyfish?

____**Fact Book Reading Area**   **(Reading Center or Other Comfortable Spot)**

Have the children flip through their fact book with you and read a few selections. If you need some help interpreting, please contact the staff interpreter (Mr. Smith).

____**Digraphs Display** *(Sh, Ch, Th, Wh)*   **(Home Living Center Window)**

Can you tell me a word that begins with the letters *Sh? Ch?Th? Wh?*

_____**Sea Urchin Display**   (**Home Living Center Window**)

How do sea urchins move?

Why do they have spikes?

_____**Seascape Painting**   (**Over the Chalkboard**)

This is going to be used as the backdrop of a book we are writing to submit
   to a contest. Scholastic Books will publish the winning entry. Please
   sign the forms for your child to participate.

_____**Sea Anemone Exhibit**   (**Top of Block Shelf**)

What are the wavy things on the top?

What do they use them for?

What kind of animal lives in the tentacles?

How do they move? (There are two answers.)

_____**Coral Exhibit**   (**On Blue Box in Middle of Room**)

What does coral look like?

What color is coral?

What else can you tell me about coral?

_____**Squid Exhibit**   (**Cabinet Door**)

Did you like dissecting the squid?

What was your favorite/least favorite part of dissecting the squid?

What can you tell me about squid? (Should be able to get 3 to 6 responses.)

_____**Anything Else Your Tour Guide Feels Is Important**

_____**Refreshments**

THANK YOU FOR COMING!

I HOPE YOU ENJOYED YOUR TOUR!

PLEASE PAY YOUR TOUR GUIDE A HUG BEFORE LEAVING!

SUMMARY

- Assessment and documentation are important parts of the evaluation process. They are necessary in determining the quality of the teaching methods, the children's achievement, the children's growth and development, and how the curriculum reflects the goals of the school.
- Constructivist teachers can evaluate those same components in ways that are consistent with their goals and are developmentally appropriate.
- There are many different ways to evaluate curriculum.

- Many different kinds of standardized tests assess intelligence, aptitude, and achievement.
- The use of standardized tests to determine promotion and retention is developmentally inappropriate.
- Evaluation is necessary to inform instruction, identify children's needs for special services, and determine the quality of the early childhood curriculum
- There are many kinds of informal assessments used in early childhood education, such as checklists, rating scales, and anecdotal records.
- Authentic assessment is consistent with a constructivist perspective.
- Documentation is an integrated form of authentic assessment and evaluation.
- Documentation informs practice and provides evidence of the quality of the curriculum.
- Documentation communicates to parents and the larger community about how the school functions and how and what the children learn.

CONSTRUCTIONS

1. OBSERVATION

In teams of two or three, attend a meeting where teachers are learning about the use of documentation to examine their teaching practices. Take notes on what you observe, and compare and contrast those notes with those of classmates. Identify the significant things you learned from this observation, and be prepared to share them with the class.

2. RESEARCH

Select one child you are teaching to observe carefully for one week. Use multiple ways to document what you see and hear the child doing during that week. Spend some time analyzing and interpreting data you have collected. Then share the data with a partner; have the partner analyze and interpret the data also. Then get together and share your thinking. Determine how each of you arrived at similar and dissimilar interpretations.

Resources

Books and Articles

Gandini, L. & Kaminsky, J. A. (2004). Reflections on the relationship between documentation and assessment in the American context: An interview with Brenda Fyfe. *Innovations in Early Education: The International Reggio Exchange, 11*(1), 5–17.

Gredler, G. R. (1992). *School readiness: Assessment and educational issues*. Brandon, VT: Clinical Psychology.

Greenspan, S. I., & Meisels, S. J. (1996). Toward a new vision for the developmental assessment of infants and young children. In S. J. Meisels & E. Fenichel (Eds.), *New visions for the developmental assessment of infants and young children*. Washington, DC: Zero to Three: The National Center for Infants, Toddlers, and Families.

Helm, J. & Helm, A. (2006). Building support for your school: How to use children's work to show learning. New York, NY: Teachers College Press.

Kohn, A. (2000). *The case against standardized testing: Raising the scores, ruining the schools*. Portsmouth, NH: Heinemann.

McAfee, O. & Leong, D. J. (2011). *Assessing and guiding young children's development and learning* (5th ed.). Upper Saddle River, NJ: Pearson.

Meier, D. & Wood, G. (2004). *Many children left behind: How the No Child Left Behind Act is damaging our children and our schools*. Boston, MA: Beacon Press.

Meisels, S. J. (1994). Designing meaningful measurements for early childhood. In B. L. Mallory & R. S. New (Eds.), *Diversity in early childhood education: A call for more inclusive theory, practice, and policy* (pp. 205–225). New York, NY: Teachers College Press.

Meisels, S. J. (1987). Uses and abuses of developmental screening and school readiness testing. *Young Children 42*(2) 4–6, 68–73.

Meisels, S. J. (1989). High-stakes testing in kindergarten. *Educational Leadership 46*(7), 16–22.

National Association for the Education of Young Children. (1988). NAEYC position statement on standardized testing of young children 3–8 years of age. *Young Children 43*(3), 42–47.

National Association for the Education of Young Children and National Association of Early Childhood Specialists in State Departments of Education. (1991). Guidelines for appropriate curriculum content and assessment in programs serving children ages 3 through 8. *Young Children 46*(1), 21–38.

Perrone, V. (1991). On standardized testing: A position paper of the Association for Childhood Education International. *Childhood Education 67*(3), 131–142.

Puckett, M. B., & Black, J. K. (1994). *Authentic assessment of the young child: Celebrating development and learning*. New York, NY: Merrill.

Rinaldi, C. (2004). The relationship between documentation and assessment. *Innovations in Early Education: The International Reggio Exchange, 11*(1), 1–4.

Shepard, L.A. (1991). The influence of standardized tests on the early child-hood curriculum, teachers, and children. In B. Spodek & . . Saracho (Eds.) *Yearbook in early childhood education* (Vol. 2). New York, NY: Teachers College Press.

Shepard, L.A. (1994). The challenges of assessing young children appropri-ately. *Phi Delta Kappan, 76*(3), 206–213.

Shepard, L.A. (1997). Children not ready to learn? The invalidity of school readiness testing. *Psychology in the Schools, 34*(2), 85–97.

Web Sites

Experiencing Documentation by Judy Harris Helm http://ceep.crc.uiuc.edu/eecearchive/books/projcat2/helm2.html

   The National Education Goals Panel, (1998). *Principles and Recommendations for Early Childhood Assessments* govinfo.library.unt.edu/negp/reports/prinrec.pdf

Videos

National Association for the Education of Young Children. *Voices: Child Assess-ment* (DVD). http://www.naeyc.org/store/node/17197

GLOSSARY

ACCOMMODATION—Occurs when a child is confronted with new information and has no existing scheme in which it fits. The child does one of two things: creates a new scheme for the information or modifies the existing scheme so that the information fits it.

ACHIEVEMENT TESTS—Measurements that determine how much learning a child has achieved over a particular period of time, for example, a school year.

ACTION—Mental as well as physical activity.

ACTIVE METHODS—Methods where the child is not only physically active and involved in manipulating objects, experimenting with things, or interacting with others, but also is mentally involved through active reflection on his or her actions and the result of those actions.

ANECDOTAL RECORDS—A written record of a specific child that describes the setting, the event, the child's behavior during this event, and the date and time of the observation.

APTITUDE TESTS—Measurements that predict the potential or ability the individual has to accomplish a certain kind or level of learning.

ASSESSMENT—A process of gathering evidence to measure the abilities of children, usually through the use of tests and observations.

ASSIMILATION—Filtering or modification of input through one of the structures that the child has created.

AUTHENTIC ASSESSMENT—Assessment that is conducted in the classroom as the children are learning and is based on the child's products, processes, and performances.

AUTHENTIC PURPOSE—The real reason for learning the school content, or what the teacher is required to teach, as opposed to getting a good grade or pleasing the teacher, the societal use to which the content will be put.

AUTHENTIC TASKS—Tasks that children have a genuine need to accomplish.

AUTONOMY—(1) Self-regulation. (2) The ability to make decisions about right or wrong while considering relevant variables including the perspectives of others. (3) The ability to create rules.

CHECKLISTS—An informal assessment measure that teachers use to record when skills and abilities have been mastered.

COGNITIVE CONFLICT—Internal conflict that comes about because children want to understand, figure out, or resolve something so that they can reconcile their internal conflict.

COMMUNITY—Experiences of belonging to a group, feelings of unity with those in the group, and commitment to the functioning of the group.

CONSTRUCTIONISM—A view of knowledge as something you build in your head. The way to do that is to build something tangible, outside of your head that is personally meaningful.

CONSTRUCTIONS PLAY—For the purpose of making products that represent objects in the real world.

CONSTRUCTIVIST THEORY—A well-researched theory that provides documentation about how knowledge is constructed.

CONTENT—The topics about which the child is constructing knowledge.

COOPERATE—To act in coordination with another's perspective for the mutual benefit of those concerned.

CRITICAL EXPLORATION—A method of questioning children in order to provoke their thinking further about a topic or idea.

CURRICULUM INTEGRATION—Various areas of curriculum (e.g., mathematics, literacy, science, social studies, expressive arts) are connected in theme or project work.

DECENTER—The ability to consider multiple perspectives or viewpoints of others simultaneously with your own viewpoint.

DISEQUILIBRATION—A mental sense of imbalance that occurs when incoming information does not fit into the individual's existing cognitive structures.

DISEQUILIBRIUM—Discord or lack of harmony in relationships.

DISTRIBUTIVE JUSTICE—Justice through equality for all.

EDUCATIONAL MODELS—Mental representations that educators create to make sense of very complex educational problems. Some of the models are based on research, and others are based on belief.

EGOCENTRISM—The inability to take another's point of view or to decenter.

EMPIRICAL ABSTRACTION—As a young child acts on an object, he or she will focus on one property, such as color, and ignore the other properties, such as size and weight.

EPISTEMOLOGIST—A person who studies how knowledge develops.

EQUILIBRATION—(1) The process of continuous balance between assimilation and accommodation. If an organism experiences disequilibration, it experiences a form of cognitive conflict or cognitive imbalance that results in a new process of balance or equilibration. Assimilation and accommodation are the mechanisms that control equilibration. (2) A sense of continuous balance between incoming information and existing cognitive structures; a mental state that all individuals strive to attain.

EQUILIBRIUM—A state of harmony or balance.

ETHIC OF AUTHORITY—Unilateral respect shown by obedience to the adult, parent, or other authority.

ETHIC OF MUTUAL RESPECT—Mutual respect shown by obedience to mutually agreed-on rules.

EVALUATION—Making decisions or judgments about the merit or value of an educational program.

FUNCTION—An aspect of constructivist theory that refers to two major ideas: organization and adaptation.

GAMES WITH RULES—Play that is governed by established rules.

HETERONOMY—Morality through external regulation that is based on rewards and punishments.

HYPOTHESIS—An assumption or proposition that provides an explanation that guides investigation.

INFER—The cognitive process of interpreting the meaning of an observation.

INQUIRY—Activities and thoughts that individuals use as they seek information and knowledge.

INTELLIGENCE TESTS—Measurements that assess the mental age of the individual—the level at which an individual is able to function intellectually.

INVENTION PHASE—The period of time when children, working collaboratively, create hypotheses.

KNOWLEDGE—The result of interaction between a subject (the child) and an object (a toy, a trip to the park, a playmate).

LOGICO-MATHEMATICAL KNOWLEDGE—An understanding of internal relationships and the coordination of those relationships—for example, the relationships of some/different, some/all, and part/whole.

MENTAL STRUCTURES—Allow a child or adult to create or construct new knowledge or to modify previously constructed knowledge and to modify and construct new structures.

METACOGNITION—The act of thinking about one's own thoughts and thinking.

NEGOTIATION—A strategy used to resolve tension or conflict in interactions.

NORMS—Scores that have been determined by averaging the scores of large numbers of people at different ages or grade levels in school so that an individual's score can be compared to the average score of the individual's age or grade level.

OBSERVATION NOTEBOOK—Usually a two- or three-ring loose-leaf notebook with a tabbed section of paper for each child in the classroom for recording and dating informal observations.

OPERATIONS—Actions that can be internalized or thought about and are mentally reversible.

PERSPECTIVE TAKING—The ability to see or understand another's viewpoint. The ability to decenter from one's perspective.

PERTURBATION—Occurs when something unexpected happens and the individual realizes, "This is not what I thought it was."

PHYSICAL KNOWLEDGE—Acquired as we touch, move, and physically investigate objects in our environment through our actions on them. A child explores the texture and weight of an object by handling, feeling, and even tasting it.

PLAY—An action done for sheer enjoyment or pleasure; assimilation of reality.

PRACTICE PLAY—Repetition of structures or behaviors for pleasure or skill practice.

PREOPERATIONAL STAGE—One of the stages of development Piaget identified. In this period, children can represent thought but continue to use perception rather than logic.

PROBLEM POSING—Action taken to define, investigate, or reformulate a question of interest.

PROBLEM SOLVING— Cognitive activities inherent in inquiry and investigation.

PROJECTS—Sustained, in-depth activities initiated by children or children and teachers for the purpose of studying a topic deeply.

RATING SCALES—Measurement devices that allow the evaluator to describe the degree to which a skill or trait has been acquired and used. Rating scales are used to measure academic abilities such as knowing the letters of the alphabet and social behaviors such as conduct and problem solving.

RECIPROCAL CONSEQUENCES—Consequences that are the result of a misdeed (for example, if you lie to me, then I can't believe you).

RECIPROCITY—Two-way exchange in interactions; give-and-take with another.

REFLECTION—Analyzing our actions, decisions, or products through contemplation and linking thoughts to previous or subsequent experiences.

REFLECTIVE ABSTRACTION—The child coordinates what he or she believed to be the case with what was surprising.

REGGIO EMILIA APPROACH—A northern Italian approach to teaching preschool children that focuses on helping children understand perspective taking, building community, and aesthetics through questioning and challenging their assumptions.

REPRESENTATIONAL THOUGHT—Different from logico-mathematical thought because it is influenced by the quantity, quality, and nature of the sign systems a learner experiences.

RETRIBUTIVE JUSTICE—Justice through the use of punishment that penalizes the guilty.

SANCTIONS BY RECIPROCITY—Restrictions imposed on children to help them learn the effects of their actions.

SCAFFOLD—Temporary aid provided by one person to encourage, support, and assist a lesser-skilled person in carrying out a task. These skills are gradually transferred to the learner.

SCHEME—A thought or an action used to identify or process incoming information.

SCREENING TESTS—Aptitude tests that assess the child's need for special services.

SEMIOTICS—The sign-symbol system that humans use to make and provide meaning to self and others.

SHARED EXPERIENCES—Interactions characterized by pleasant feelings when there is no tension or conflict to resolve.

SOCIAL KNOWLEDGE—Arbitrary truth agreed on by groups of people. It is knowledge passed or transmitted from one person to another, usually through language.

STRUCTURES—The internal organizational properties or schemata that children have that explain their capacity for thought at given ages.

SYMBOLIC PLAY—Play characterized by make-believe and representation of an absent object.

THEORY—An explanation of a phenomenon, usually consisting of linked hypotheses.

VERIFICATION PHASE—The period of time when children seek to prove their thinking, often resulting in disagreements among group members.

WORK—Goal-directed activity.

REFERENCES

Alexander, K. K. (1999, November). Playtime is canceled. *Parents*, 114–118.

Almon, J. & Miller, E. (2011). *The crisis in early education: A research-based case for more play and less pressure*. College Park, MD: Alliance for Childhood.

Almy, M. (1984). A child's right to play. *Young Children, 39*(4), 80.

American Academy of Pediatrics [AAP]. (2011). The importance of play to promoting healthy child development and maintaining strong parent-child bonds [Clinical Report]. www.pediatrics.org.

Association for Supervision and Curriculum Development [ASCD]. (2001, March). The diverse challenges of multiculturalism. In *ASCD Update*. Alexandria, VA: Author.

Ausubel, D. P. (1963). *The psychology of meaningful verbal learning*. New York, NY: Grune & Stratton.

Ausubel, D. P., Novak, J. D., & Hanesian, H. (1978). *Educational psychology: A cognitive view* (2nd ed.). New York, NY: Holt, Rinehart, & Winston.

Awakening Seed School. (2000, October). Statement from a Seed graduate. *The Seed*, p. 2.

Barton, K. C., & Levstik, L. (1996). Back when God was around and everything: Elementary children's understanding of historical time. *American Educational Research Journal, 33*, 419–454.

Barton, K. C., & Levstik, L. S. (2004). *Teaching history for the common good*. New York, NY: Routledge.

Baylor, B. (1994). *The table where rich people sit*. New York, NY: Charles Scribner's Sons.

Bergen, D. (Ed.). (1987). *Play as a medium for learning*. Portsmouth, NH: Heinemann.

Beyer, B. K. (1987). *Practical strategies for the teaching of thinking*. Boston, MA: Allyn & Bacon.

Bodrova, E., & Leong, D. J. (2007). *Tools of the mind: The Vygotskian approach to early childhood education*. Upper Saddle River, NJ: Prentice Hall.

Bongiorno, L. (2012). *Preschool parents' perceptions of learning through play* (Doctoral dissertation). Walden University. Retrieved from http://gradworks.umi.com/35/18/3518497.html

Branscombe, N. A., Castle, K., Dorsey, A. G., Surbeck, E., & Taylor, J. (2000). *Early childhood education: A constructivist perspective*. Boston, MA: Houghton Mifflin.

Bredekamp, S., & Rosegrant, T. (Eds.). (1995). *Reaching potentials: Transforming early childhood curriculum and assessment* (Vol. 2). Washington, DC: National Association for the Education of Young Children.

Bringuier, J. C. (1980). *Conversations with Jean Piaget*. Chicago, IL: University of Chicago Press.

Britton, J. (1982). Spectator role and the beginnings of writing. In G. Pradl (Ed.), *Prospect and retrospect: Selected essays of James Britton* (pp. 46–67). London, England: Heinemann.

Brosterman, N. (1997). *Inventing kindergarten*. New York, NY: Abrams.

Brown, F., & Patte, M. (2012). From the streets of Wellington to the Ivy League: Reflecting on a lifetime of play. An interview with Brian Sutton-Smith. *International Journal of Play, 1*(1), 6–15.

Brown, S., & Walter, M. (1993). *Problem posing: Reflections and applications.* Hillsdale: NJ: Erlbaum.

Brown-DuPaul, J., Keyes, T., & Segatti, L. (2001). Using documentation panels to communicate with families. *Childhood Education, 77*(4), 209–213.

Bruner, J. (1985). On teaching thinking: An afterthought. In S.F. Chipman, J.W. Segan, & R. Glasser (Eds.), *Thinking and learning skills* (Vol. 1, pp. 603–605). Hillsdale, NJ: Erlbaum.

Burk, D. (1996). Understanding friendship and social interaction. *Childhood Education, 72*(5), 282–285.

Carter, M., Cividanes, W., Curtis, D., & Lebo, D. (2010). *Becoming a reflective teacher* [Teaching Young Children Staff Development Guide]. Retrieved from http://www.naeyc.org/files/tyc/file/TYC_V3N4_Reflectiveteacherexpanded.pdf

Castle, K. (1990). Children's invented games. *Childhood Education, 67,* 82–85.

Castle, K. (1998). Children's rule knowledge in invented games. *Journal of Research in Childhood Education, 12*(2), 197–209.

Castle, K. (2012). *Early childhood teacher research.* New York, NY: Routledge.

Castle, K., & Richards, H.C. (1979). Adult/peer interactions and role-taking ability among preschool children. *Journal of Genetic Psychology, 135,* 71–79.

Castle, K., & Rogers, K. (1993–1994). Rule-creating in a constructivist classroom community. *Childhood Education, 70*(2), 77–80.

Caulkins, L.E. (1994). *The art of teaching writing.* Portsmouth, NH: Heinemann.

Chaille, C. (2008). *Constructivism across the curriculum in early childhood classrooms: Big ideas as inspiration.* Boston, MA: Pearson and Allyn and Bacon.

Chaille, C., & Britain, L. (1996). *The young child as scientist: A constructivist approach to early childhood science education* (2nd ed.). New York, NY: Longman.

Chaille, C., & Britain, L. (2002). *The young child as scientist: A constructivist approach to early childhood science education* (3rd ed.) New York, MY: Longman.

Chaille, C., & Silvern, S.B. (1996). Understanding through play. *Childhood Education, 72*(5), 274–277.

Clay, M. (2000). *Running records for classroom teachers.* Portsmouth, NH: Heinemann.

Clements, D. (1999, October). Computers and young children. *Early Childhood Today,* 44–47.

Cohen, E.G. (1994). *Designing groupwork: Strategies for the heterogeneous classroom* (2nd ed.). New York, NY: Teachers College Press.

Cohen, M. (1967). *Will I have a friend?* New York, NY: Collier Books.

Cooney, M.H., Gupton, P., & O'Laughlin, M. (2000). Blurring the lines of play and work to create blended classroom learning experiences. *Early Childhood Education Journal, 27*(3), 165–171.

Copple, C., & Bredekamp, S. (2009). *Developmentally appropriate practice in early childhood programs serving children from birth through age 8* (3rd ed.). Washington, DC: National Association for the Education of Young Children.

Delpit, L. (1995). *Other people's children: Cultural conflict in the classroom.* New York, NY: New Press.

Delpit, L. (2012). *"Multiplication is for white people": Raising expectations for other people's children.* New York, NY: New Press.

Derman-Sparks, L., & Edwards, J.O. (2010). *Anti-bias education for young children and ourselves.* Washington, DC: NAEYC.

Derman-Sparks, L., & Ramsey, P.G. (2006). *What if all the kids are white?: Anti-bias multicultural education with young children and families.* New York, NY: Teachers College Press.

DeVries, R. (1969). Constancy of generic identity in the years three to six. *Monographs of the Society for Research in Child Development, 34*(3), Serial No. 127.

DeVries, R. (1987). *Programs of early education: The constructivist view.* New York, NY: Longman.

DeVries, R. (1997). Piaget's social theory. *Educational Researcher, 26*(2), 4–17.

DeVries, R. (2002, June). What does research on constructivist education tell us about effective schooling? *The Iowa Academy of Education Occasional Research Paper #5.* Retrieved from http://www.education.uiowa.edu/html/iae

DeVries, R., Haney, J., & Zan, B. (1991). Sociomoral atmosphere in direct-instruction, eclectic, and constructivist kindergartens: A study of teachers' enacted interpersonal understanding. *Early Childhood Research Quarterly, 6,* 449–471.

DeVries, R., & Kohlberg, L. (1987). *Constructivist early education: Overview and comparison with other programs.* Washington, DC: NAEYC.

DeVries, R., Reese-Learned, H., & Morgan, P. (1991). Sociomoral development in direct-instruction, eclectic, and constructivist kindergartens: A study of children's enacted interpersonal understanding. *Early Childhood Research Quarterly, 6,* 473–517.

DeVries, R., & Zan, B. (2012). *Moral classrooms, moral children: Creating a constructivist atmosphere in early education* (2nd ed.). New York, NY: Teachers College Press.

DeVries, R., Zan, B., Hildebrandt, C., Edmiaston, R., & Sales, C. (2002).

Division for Early Childhood [DEC]. (2007). *Promoting positive outcomes for children with disabilities: Recommendations for curriculum, assessment, and program evaluation.* Missoula, MT: Author.

Dixon, R.M., & Verenikina, I. (2007). Towards inclusive school: An examination of Socio-cultural theory and inclusive practices and policy in New South Wales DET schools, *Learning and Socio-cultural theory: Exploring Modern Vygotskian perspectives International Workshop 2007, I(1), 2007.* Retrieved from http://ro.uow.edu.au/llrg

Duckworth, E.R (1973). The having of wonderful ideas. In M. Schwebel & J. Raph (Eds.), *Piaget in the classroom* (pp. 132–154). New York: Basic Books.

Edwards, C., Gandini, L., & Forman, G. (Eds.) (1993/1998). *The hundred languages of children: The Reggio Emilia approach to early childhood education.* Norwood, NJ: Ablex.

Edwards, C., Gandini, L., & Forman, G. (Eds.) (2011). *The hundred languages of children: The Reggio Emilia experience in transformation* (3rd ed.). Santa Barbara, CA: Praeger.

English, L.D. (1997, November). Promoting a problem-posing classroom. *Teaching Children Mathematics, 4,* 172–179.

Epstein, A. (2006, Spring). High/Scope and Head Start: A good fit. *High/Scope ReSource.* www.highscope.org

Epstein, A. (2007). *The intentional teacher. Choosing the best strategies for young children's learning.* Washington, DC: NAEYC.

Feeney, S., Freeman, N.K., with Pizzdongo, P.J. (2012). *Ethics and the early childhood educator: Using the NAEYC code* (2nd ed.). Washington DC: NAEYC.

Ferguson, C. (1999). Building literacy with child-centered sociodramatic play centers. *Dimensions of Early Childhood, 27*(3), 23–29.

Ferreiro, E. (1990). Literacy development: Psychogenesis. In Y.M. Goodman (Ed.), *How children construct literacy* (pp. 12–25). Newark, DE: International Reading Association.

Ferreiro E., & Teberosky, A. (1982). *Literacy before schooling.* Portsmouth, NH: Heinemann.

Forman, G. (1996). *Jed draws his bicycle: A case of drawing-to-learn.* Amherst, MA: Videatives. Retrieved from https://www.videatives.com/store/node/1859

Forman, G., & Fyfe, B. (1998). Negotiated learning through design, documentation, and discourse. In C. Edwards, L. Gandini, & G. Forman (Eds.), *The hundred languages of children* (2nd ed., pp. 239–260). Norwood, NJ: Ablex.

Forman, E.A., & Kraker, M.J. (1985). The social origins of logic: The contributions of Piaget and Vygotsky. In M.W. Berkowitz (Ed.), *Peer conflict and psychological growth* (pp. 23–40). San Francisco, CA: Jossey-Bass.

Forman, G.E., & Kuschner, D.S. (1983). *The child's construction of knowledge: Piaget for teaching children.* Washington, DC: NAEYC.

Forman, G., & Landry, C. (2000). The constructivist perspective on early education: Applications to children's museums. In J.L. Roopnarine & J.E. Johnson (Eds.), *Approaches to early childhood education* (3rd ed., pp. 149–174). Upper Saddle River, NJ: Merrill.

Fox, M. (1989a). *Feathers and fools.* New York, NY: Harcourt Brace.

Fox, M. (1989b). *Koala Lou.* New York, NY: Voyager Books.

Fromberg, D.P. (1990). Play issues in early childhood education. In C. Seefeldt (Ed.), *Continuing issues in early childhood education* (pp. 223–243). Columbus, OH: Merrill.

Fromberg, D.F. (2002). *Play and meaning in early childhood education.* Boston, MA: Allyn and Bacon.

Fromberg, D.F. (2012). *The all-day kindergarten and pre-k curriculum: A dynamic themes approach.* New York, NY: Routledge.

Frost, J.L., Wortham, S.C., & Reifel, S. (2012). *Play and child development* (4th ed.). Boston, MA: Pearson.

Fuqua, B. (1999). Young children's decisions about naughtiness and punishment in constructivist classrooms. *Dissertation Abstracts International, 60*(02), 328P. (University Microfilms No. AAT99–20203)

Furth, H.G. (1969). *Piaget and knowledge: Theoretical foundations.* Englewood Cliffs, NJ: Prentice Hall.

Gallagher, J., & Reid, D. (1981). *The learning theory of Piaget and Inhelder.* Monterey, CA: Brooks-Cole.

Gallagher, J.M., & Reid, K. (2002). *The learning theory of Piaget and Inhelder.* Lincoln, NE: Authors Choice Press.

Gallas, K. (1994). *The language of learning: How children talk, write, dance, draw, and sing their understanding of the world.* New York, NY: Teachers College Press.

Gallas, K. (1995). *Talking their way into science: Hearing children's questions and theories, responding with curricula.* New York, NY: Teachers College Press.

Gandini, L., & Kaminsky, J.A. (2004). Reflections on the relationship between documentation and assessment in the American context: An interview with Brenda Fyfe. *Innovations in Early Education: The International Reggio Exchange, 11*(1), 5–17.

Gardner, H. (2007). *Five minds for the future.* Boston, MA: Harvard Business School.

Garvey, C. (1977). *Play.* Cambridge, MA: Harvard University Press.

Gilligan, C. (1982). *In a different voice: Psychological theory and women's development.* Cambridge, MA: Harvard University Press.

Gindis, B. (1995). The social/cultural implication of disability: Vygotsky's paradigm for special education. *Educational psychologist, 30*(2), pp. 77–81.

Glover, M. (1999). Charlie's ticket to literacy. New York: Scholastic.

Goffin, S.G., & Wilson, C.S. (2001). *Curriculum models and early childhood education: Appraising the relationship* (2nd ed.). Upper Saddle River, NJ: Merrill.

Gonzalez-Mena, J. (2001). *Multicultural issues in child care* (3rd ed.). Mountain View, CA: Mayfield.

Goodwin, W., & Driscoll, L. (1980). *Handbook for measurement and evaluation in early childhood education.* San Francisco, CA: Jossey-Bass.

Goolsby, L., & DeVries, R. (1994a). *When a friend refuses to share.* Cedar Falls, IA: Regent's Center for Early Developmental Education.

Goolsby, L., & DeVries, R. (1994b). *When a friend eats more than her share.* Cedar Falls, IA: Regent's Center for Early Developmental Education.

Goolsby, L., & DeVries, R. (1994c). *When a friend steals.* Cedar Falls, IA: Regent's Center for Early Developmental Education.

Gopnik, A. (2012 September). Scientific thinking in young children: Theoretical advances, empirical research, and policy implications. *Science, 28,* 337. Retrieved from www.sciencemag.org

Gopnik, A., & Tenenbaum, J. B. (2007). *Bayesian networks, Bayesian learning and cognitive development,* Developmental Science, *10,* 281–287.

Gronlund, G., & Stewart, K. (2011). Intentionality in action: A strategy that benefits preschoolers and teachers. *Young Children, 66*(6), 28–33.

Gruber, H. (1973). Courage and cognitive growth. In M. Schwebel & J. Raph (Eds.), *Piaget in the classroom* (pp. 73–108). New York, NY: Basic Books.

Gruber, H., & Voneche, J. (1995). *The essential Piaget: An interpretive reference and guide.* Northvale, NJ: Jason Aronson.

Gullo, D. (1994). *Understanding assessment and evaluation in early childhood education.* New York, NY: Teachers College Press.

Harel, I. (Ed.). (1990). *Constructionist learning.* Cambridge, MA: MIT Media Laboratory.

Harper, S., Platt, A., & Pelletier, J. (2011). Unique effects of a family literacy program on the early reading development of English language learners. *Early Education and Development, 22*(4), 989–1008.

Heine, H. (1986). *Friends.* New York, NY: Aladdin Books.

Helm. J.H. (1998). *Experiencing documentation: The turtle project.* Retrieved from http://ceep.crc.uiuc.edu/eecearchive/books/projcat2/helm2.html

Helm, J., & Beneke, S. (2003). *The power of projects.* New York, NY: Teachers College Press and Washington, DC: NAEYC.

Helm, J., Beneke, S., & Steinheimer, K. (1998a). *Teacher materials for documenting young children's work.* New York, NY: Teachers College Press.

Helm, J., Beneke, S., & Steinheiner, K. (1998b). *Windows on learning: Documenting young children's work.* New York, NY: Teachers College Press.

Helm, J. & Helm, A. (2006). Building support for your school: How to use children's work to show learning. New York, NY: Teachers College Press.

Helm, J., Huebner, A., & Long, B. (2000, May). Quiltmaking: A perfect project for preschool and primary. *Young Children, 55,* 44–49.

Henderson, J.G. (1992). *Reflective teaching: Becoming an inquiring educator.* New York, NY: Macmillan.

Hirsch, E.S. (Ed.). (1996). *The block book.* Washington, DC: NAEYC.

Holdaway, D. (1986). The structure of natural learning as a basis for literacy instruction. In M.R. Sampson (Ed.), *The pursuit of literacy: Early reading and writing* (pp. 56–72). Dubuque, IA: Kendall/Hunt.

Holdaway, D. (1999). *The foundations of literacy.* New York, NY: Scholastic. (Original work published in 1979)

Hyson, M., & Taylor, J.L. (2011). Caring about caring: What adults can do to promote young children's prosocial skills. *Young Children, 66*(4), 74–83.

Inhelder, B. (1943/1969). *Le diagnostic du raisonnement chez les debiles mentaux.* Neuchatel, Paris: Dalachaux et Niestle.

Inhelder, B., Sinclair, H., & Bovet, M. (1974). *Learning and the development of cognition* (S. Wedgwood, Trans.). Cambridge, MA: Harvard University Press.

Isenberg, J.P., & Jalongo, M.R. (2006). *Creative expression and play in early childhood* (4th ed.). Upper Saddle River NJ: Prentice Hall.

Isenberg, J., & Quisenberry, N. (1988). *Play: A necessity for all children.* Wheaton, MD: Association for Childhood Education International.

Jalongo, M., & Isenberg, J. (2000). *Exploring your role: A practitioner's introduction to early childhood education.* Upper Saddle River, NJ: Merrill.

Jessee, P.O., Wilson, H., & Morgan, D. (2000). Medical play for young children. *Childhood Education, 76*(4), 215–218.

Jukes, I., McCain, T., & Crockett, L. (2010/2011). Education and the role of the educator in the future. *Phi Delta Kappan, 92*(4), 15–21.

Justic, L. M., & Kaderavek, J. (2002). Using shared storybook reading to promote emergent literacy. *Teaching Exceptional Children, 34*(4), 8–13.

Kafai, Y. B., & Resnick, M. (2011). *Constructivism in practice: Designing, thinking, and learning in a digital world.* New York, NY: Routledge.

Kamii, C. (1982). *Number in preschool and kindergarten: Educational implications of Piagetian theory.* Washington, DC: NAEYC.

Kamii, C. (1989). *Young children continue to reinvent arithmetic, 2nd grade: Implications of Piaget's theory.* New York, NY: Teachers College Press.

Kamii, C. (2000). *Young children reinvent arithmetic: Implications for Piaget's theory* (2nd ed.). New York, NY: Teachers College Press.

Kamii, C., & DeVries, R. (1980). *Group games in early childhood education: Implications of Piaget's theory.* Washington, DC: NAEYC.

Kamii, C., & DeVries, R. (1993). *Physical knowledge in preschool education: Implications of Piaget's theory* (Reissued with a new introduction). New York, NY: Teachers College Press.

Kamii, C., with Housman, L. (2000). *Young children reinvent arithmetic: Implications of Piaget's theory* (2nd ed.). New York, NY: Teachers College Press.

Kamii, C., with Joseph, L. (2004). *Young children continue to reinvent arithmetic, 2nd grade* (2nd ed.). New York, NY: Teachers College Press.

Kamii, C., & Livingston, S. J. (1994). *Young children continue to reinvent arithmetic: Third grade.* New York, NY: Teachers College Press.

Kamii, C., Miyakawa, Y., & Kato, T. (2007). Trying to make a lever work at ages 1 to 4: The development of "functions" (logicomathematical thinking). *Early Education and Development, 18*(1), 145–161.

Kamii, C., & Rosenblum, V. (1990). An approach to assessment in mathematics. In C. Kamii (Ed.), *Achievement testing in the early grades: The games grown-ups play* (pp. 119–132). Washington, DC: NAEYC.

Kangas, S., Maata, K., & Uusiautti, S. (2012). Alone and in a group: Ethnographic research on autistic children's play. *International Journal of Play, 1*(1), 37–50.

Kato, Y., Honda, M., & Kamii, C. (2006, July). Lining up the 5s: A card game to encourage logico-mathematical thinking. *Beyond the Journal: Young Children on the Web.* Washington, DC: NAEYC. Retrieved from www.naeyc.org/files/yc/file/200607/Kamii706BTJ.pdf

Katz, L. G. (1998). What can we learn from Reggio Emilia? In C. Edwards, L. Gandini, & G. Forman (Eds.), *The hundred languages of children* (2nd ed., pp. 27–48). Norwood, NJ: Ablex.

Katz, L. G., & Chard, S. C. (2000). *Engaging children's minds: The project approach* (2nd ed.). Norwood, NJ: Ablex.

Killion, J., & Todnem, G. (1991). A process for personal theory building. *Educational Leadership, 48*(6), 14–15.

Kohlberg, L. (1984). *The psychology of moral development.* New York, NY: Harper & Row.

Kohlberg, L., & Lickona, T. (1987). Moral discussion and the class meeting. In R. DeVries & L. Kohlberg (Eds.), *Programs of early education* (pp. 143–181). New York: Longman.

Kohn, A. (1998). *What to look for in a classroom.* San Francisco, CA: Jossey-Bass.

Kohn, A. (1999). *The schools our children deserve.* Boston, MA: Houghton Mifflin.

Kohn, A. (2000). *The case against standardized testing: Raising the scores, ruining the schools.* Portsmouth, NH: Heinemann.

Kostelnik, M. J., Soderman, A. K., & Whiren, A. P. (2011). *Developmentally appropriate curriculum. Best practices in early childhood education.* Washington, DC: NAEYC.

Krauss, R. (1945/1989). *The carrot seed.* New York, NY: Harper & Row.

Kriete, R. (2002). *The morning meeting book.* Greenfield, MA: Northeast Foundation for Children.

Labinowicz, E. (1980). *The Piaget primer: Thinking, learning, teaching.* Menlo Park, CA: Addison-Wesley.

Leong, D. J., & Bodrova, E. (January 2012). Assessing and scaffolding make-believe play. *Young Children, 67*(1), 28–34.

Lickey, D. C., & Powers, D. J. (2011). *Starting with their strengths: Using the Project Approach in special education.* New York, NY: Teachers College Press.

Lieberman, E. (1977). *Constancy of human identity and the pre-operational child* (Unpublished master's thesis). Tempe: Arizona State University.

Lindfors, J. (1999). *Children's inquiry: Using language to make sense of the world.* New York, NY: Teachers College Press.

Lionni, L. (1968). *Swimmy.* New York, NY: Pantheon Books.

Lionni, L. (1970). *Fish is fish.* New York, NY: Pantheon Books.

Maccoby, E. E., & Jacklin, C. N. (1987). Gender segregation in childhood. In E. H. Reese (Ed.), *Advances in child development and behavior* (Vol. 20, pp. 239–287). New York, NY: Academic Press.

Marchand, H. (2000). From the diagnostics of reasoning in the mentally disabled to the microgenetic study of the processes of discovery: Barbel Inhelder's contribution toward a global understanding of the subject. *Genetic Epistemologist* (28:4). Annual Newsletter of the Jean Piaget Society. Retrieved from http://www.piaget.org/GE/GE-ToC.html

Martin, C. L., & Fabes, C. A. (2001). The stability and consequences of young children's same-sex peer interactions. *Developmental Psychology, 37,* 431–446.

Mayer, R. E. (1992). *Thinking, problem solving, cognition* (2nd ed.). New York, NY: Freeman.

McAfee, O., & Leong, D. J. (2011). *Assessing and guiding young children's development and learning* (5th ed.). Upper Saddle River, NJ: Pearson.

McGuffee, M. (1996). *The day the Earth was silent.* Bloomington, IN: Inquiring Voices Press.

Meek, A. (1991). On thinking about teaching: A conversation with Eleanor Duckworth. *Educational Leadership, 48*(6), 30–34.

Meier, D., & Wood, G. (2004). Many children left behind: How the No Child Left Behind Act is damaging our children and our schools. Boston, MA: Beacon Press.

Messner, K. (2011). *Sea monster's first day.* San Francisco, CA: Chronicle Books.

Miller, E., & Almon, J. (2009). *Crisis in the kindergarten: Why children need to play in school.* College Park, MD: Alliance for Childhood.

Miyakawa, Y., Kamii, C., & Nagahiro, M. (2005). The development of logico-mathematical thinking at ages 1–3 in play with blocks and an incline. *Journal of Research in Childhood Education, 19*(4), 292–301.

Monighan-Nourot, P. (1992). Play, the role of, in development. In L. R. Williams & D. P. Fromberg (Eds.), *Encyclopedia of early childhood education* (pp. 229–230). New York, NY: Garland.

Montessori, M. (1965). *Spontaneous activity in education.* New York, NY: Schocken Books.

Moses, B., Bjork, E., & Goldenberg, E. (1993). Beyond problem solving: Problem posing. In T. J. Cooney & C. R. Hirsch (Eds.), *Teaching and learning mathematics in the 1990s: 1990 Yearbook* (pp. 82–91). Reston, VA: National Council of Teachers of Mathematics.

National Association for the Education of Young Children (NAEYC). (1998/2011). *Code of ethical conduct and statement of commitment.* Washington, DC: Author.

National Association for the Education of Young Children (NAEYC). (2012). *Technology and interactive media as tools in early childhood programs serving children from birth through age 8.* Washington, DC: Author.

National Association for the Education of Young Children & National Association of Early Childhood Specialists in State Departments of Education. (2003). *Early childhood curriculum, assessment, and program evaluation.* Washington, DC: NAEYC.

National Board for Professional Teaching Standards [NBPTS]. (2012). *Early childhood generalist standards* (3rd ed.). Arlington, VA. Retrieved from www.nbpts.org

National Council of Teachers of Mathematics [NCTM]. (1991/1995). *Professional standards for school mathematics.* Reston, VA: Author.

National Council of Teachers of Mathematics [NCTM]. (2000). *Principles and standards for school mathematics.* Reston, VA: Author.

National Research Council. (2008). *Early childhood assessment: Why, what, and how?* Washington, DC: National Academies Press.

National Research Council. (2013). *Next generation science standards.* Washington, DC: National Academy Press.

Nelsen, J., Lott, L., & Glenn, H. S. (2000). *Positive discipline in the classroom: How to effectively use class meetings and other positive discipline strategies* (3rd ed.). Rocklin, CA: Prima Publishing.

Noddings, N. (2005). *The challenge to care in schools* (2nd ed.). New York, NY: Teachers College Press.

Norton, D. E. (1997). *The effective teaching of language arts* (5th ed.). Upper Saddle River, NJ: Prentice Hall.

Novack, A. (1964). Scientific inquiry. *Bioscience, 14,* 25–28.

Oldland, N. (2011). *The busy beaver.* Tonawanda, NY: Kids Can Press.

Osborn, D. K. (1991). *Early childhood education in historical perspective.* Athens, GA: Daye Press.

Owocki, G. (1999). *Literacy through play.* Portsmouth, NH: Heinemann.

Paley, V. G. (1981). *Wally's stories.* Cambridge, MA: Harvard University Press.

Paley, V. G. (1999). *The kindness of children.* Cambridge, MA: Harvard University Press.

Papert, S. (1980a). *Mindstorms: Children, computers and powerful ideas.* New York, NY: Basic Books.

Papert, S. (1980b). *Redefining childhood: The computer presence as an experiment in developmental psychology.* Tokyo, Japan: International Federation for Information Processing World Conference. Retrieved from http://www.papert.org/articles/RedefiningChildhood.html

Papert, S. (1990). *A critique of technocentrism in thinking about the school of the future* (Epistemology and Learning Memo No. 2). Cambridge, MA: MIT Media Lab. Retrieved from http://www.papert.org/articles/ACritiqueofTechnocentrism.html

Papert, S. (1993). *The children's machine: Rethinking school in the age of the computer.* New York, NY: Basic Books.

Park, B., Chae, J., & Boyd, B. F. (2008). Young children's block play and mathematical learning. *Journal of Research in Childhood Education, 23*(2), 157–162.

Parten, M. (1932). Social participation among preschool children. *Journal of Abnormal and Social Psychology, 27,* 243–262.

Patton, M. M., & Mercer, J. (Fall 1996). "Hey! Where's the toys?" Play and literacy in 1st grade. *Childhood Education, 73*(1), 10–16.

Piaget, J. (1932/1965). *The moral judgment of the child.* New York, NY: Free Press.

Piaget, J. (1941/1965). *The child's conception of time.* New York, NY: Ballantine Books.

Piaget, J. (1948/1972). *To understand is to invent.* New York, NY: Grossman Publishers.

Piaget, J. (1955). *The elaboration of the universe: The construction of reality in the child.* London, England: Routledge.

Piaget, J. (1962). *Play, dreams and imitation in childhood.* New York, NY: Norton.

Piaget, J. (1965/1995). *Sociological studies.* New York, NY: Routledge.

Piaget, J. (1967/1971). *Biology and knowledge.* Chicago, IL: University of Chicago Press.

Piaget, J. (1970). *Science of education and the psychology of the child* (Derek Coltman, Trans.). New York, NY: Orion Press.

Piaget, J. (1972). *Science of education and the psychology of the child.* New York, NY: Viking Press.

Piaget, J. (1973). *Psychology of intelligence.* Totowa, NJ: Littlefield, Adams.

Piaget J. (1987). *Possibility and necessity: Vol. 1. The role of possibility in cognitive development* (Helga Feider, Trans.). Minneapolis: University of Minnesota Press. (Original work published 1981)

Piaget, J. (1995). Science of education and the psychology of the child. In H. E. Gruber & J. Voneche (Eds.), *The essential Piaget: An interpretive reference and guide* (pp. 695–725). Northvale, NJ: Jason Aronson.

Piaget, J. (1997). *The moral judgment of the child.* New York, NY: Simon & Schuster.

Piaget, J. (2001). *Studies in reflecting abstraction* (R. L. Campbell, Trans.). In J. Piaget, *Sociological studies* (L. Smith, Ed., pp. 158–183). London: Routledge. (Original work "Les relations entre la morale et le droit," published in J. Piaget, *Etudes sociologiques*, Geneva, Switzerland: Droz, 1977)

Piaget, J., & Duckworth, E. (1973, October). Piaget takes a teacher's look. *Learning*, pp. 22–27.

Piaget, J., & Garcia, R. (1974). *Understanding causality.* New York, NY: Norton.

Piaget, J., & Inhelder, B. (2002). *The Psychology of the Child* (2nd ed.). New York, NY: Basic Books.

Ponciano, L., & Shabazian, A. (2012). Interculturalism: Addressing diversity in early childhood. *Dimensions of Early Childhood, 40*(1), 23–29.

Puckett, M., & Black, J. (2008). *Meaningful assessments of the young child: Celebrating development and learning* (3rd ed.). Upper Saddle River, NJ: Pearson.

Ramsey, P. (1998). *Teaching and learning in a diverse world: Multicultural education for young children.* New York, NY: Teachers College Press.

Ranz-Smith, D. J. (2012). Explicating the place of play: Resolving dilemmas of research-to-practice. *Journal of Early Childhood Teacher Education, 33*(1), 85–101.

Resnick, M. (1998). Technologies for lifelong kindergarten. *Educational Technology Research and Development, 46*(4), 43–55.

Resnick, M. (2012, July–August). Reviving Papert's dream. *Educational Technology, 52*(4), 42–46.

Rinaldi, C. (1998). Projected curriculum constructed through documentation—Progettazione: An interview with Lella Gandini. In C. Edwards, L. Gandini, & G. Forman (Eds.), *The hundred languages of children* (2nd ed., pp. 113–126). Norwood, NJ: Ablex.

Rinaldi, C. (2004). The relationship between documentation and assessment. *Innovations in Early Education: The International Reggio Exchange, 11*(1), 1–4.

Rogers, K. (1999). *The essence of care in the classroom* (Unpublished doctoral dissertation). Oklahoma State University, Norman.

Romero, H. (2000, October 5). Third grade fired up by football math. *Arizona Republic* (Chandler Community ed.), p. Bl.

Roopnarine, J. L., & Johnson, J. E. (Eds.). (2012). *Approaches to early childhood education* (6th ed.). New York, NY: Pearson.

Rubin, K. H., & Ross, H. S. (1982). *Peer relationships and social skills in childhood.* New York, NY: Springer-Verlag.

Saracho, O. N. (2012). *An integrated play-based curriculum for young children.* New York, NY: Routledge.

Schön, D. (1983). *The reflective practitioner.* New York, NY: Basic Books.

Schön, D. (1987). *Educating the reflective practitioner.* San Francisco, CA: Jossey-Bass.

Schwebel, M., & Raph, J. (1973). *Piaget in the classroom.* New York, NY: Basic Books.

Schweinhart, L. J., & Weikart, D. P. (2010). The High Scope model of early childhood education. High Scope Educational Research Foundation, Ypsilanti, MI. Retrieved from http://bfi.uchicago.edu/humcap/wp/papers/TheHighScopeModelofEarlyChildhood Education6thEdition.pdf

Scott, A. H. (1967). *Sam.* New York, NY: McGraw-Hill.

Seitz, H., & Bartholomew, C. (2008). Powerful portfolios for young children. *Early Childhood Education Journal, 36*(1), 63–68.

Selman, R. L. (1980). *Promoting the social development of young children.* Mountain View, CA: Mayfield.

Selman, R. L., & Schultz, L. H. (1990). *Making a friend in youth.* Chicago, IL: University of Chicago Press.

Seuss, Dr. (1984). *The butter battle book.* New York, NY: Random House.

Shepard, L., Kagan, L., & Wurtz, E. (Eds.). (1998). *Principles and recommendations for early childhood assessments.* Washington, DC: National Education Goals Panel.

Sherwood, S., & Reifel, S. (2010). The multiple meanings of play: Exploring preservice teachers' beliefs about a central element of early childhood education. *Journal of Early Childhood Teacher Education, 31,* 322–343.

Sigel, I. E., & Olmsted, P. (1970). The development of classification and representational competence. In A.J. Biemiller (Ed.), *Problems in the teaching of young children* (pp. 49–67). Ontario, Canada; Ontario Institute of Studies in Education.

Silver, E. (1994). On mathematical problem posing. *Learning of Mathematics, 14,* 19–28.

Simpson, N. (1994). Getting it all together: A study of the human body. *Talking Points, 6*(2), 25–27.

Sinclair, H. (1970). The transition from sensory-motor behaviour to symbolic activity. *Interchange, 1*(3), 119–126.

Sinclair, H. (1994). Early cognitive development and the contribution of peer interaction: A Piagetian view. In *Developmental follow-up: Concepts, domains, and methods* (pp. 129–138). San Diego, CA: Academic Press.

Smyth, J. (1989). Developing and sustaining critical reflection in teacher education. *Journal of Teacher Education, 40*(2), 2–9.

Snow, C.E., & Van Hemel, S.B. (Eds.). (2008). *Early childhood assessment: Why, what, and how.* Atlanta, GA: National Academies Press.

Spodek, B., & Saracho, O.N. (1994). *Right from the start: Teaching children ages three to eight.* Boston, MA: Allyn and Bacon.

Stanton-Chapman, T.L., & Hadden, D.S. (2011). Encouraging peer interactions in preschool classrooms: The role of the teacher. *Young Exceptional Children, 14*(1), 17–28.

Steiner, S. Scribner, & E. Souberman (Eds. & Trans.), Cambridge, MA: Harvard University Press.

Stroud, M. (1993). *Reaching the children: In celebration of the rights of the child.* New York, NY: United States Committee for UNICEF.

Surbeck, E., & Glover, M. (1992). Seal revenge: Ecology games invented by children. *Childhood Education, 68*(5), 275–281.

Surbeck, E., Han, E., & Moyer, J. (1991). Assessing reflective responses in journals. *Educational Leadership, 48*(6), 25–27.

Taunton, M., & Colbert, C. (2000). Art in the early childhood classroom: Authentic experiences and extended dialogues. In N.J. Yelland (Ed.), *Promoting meaningful learning: Innovations in educating early childhood professionals* (pp. 67–76). Washington, DC: NAEYC.

Taylor, J. (1991). Implementing whole language: The new basal? *Virginia English Bulletin, 41*(1), 5–12.

Taylor, J., Branscombe, N., & Gunnels, J. (November, 2000). Writing that matters: Developing children's writing. Unpublished paper presented at the National Association for the Education of Young Children, Atlanta, Georgia.

Taylor, J.B., Branscombe, N.A., Burcham, J.G., & Land, L. (2011). *Beyond early literacy: A balanced approach to developing the whole child.* New York, NY: Routledge.

Tom, A. (1985). Inquiring into inquiry-oriented teacher education. *Journal of Teacher Education, 36*(5), 35–44.

Tribe, C. (1982). *Profile of three theories.* Dubuque, IA: Kendall/Hunt.

Tryphon, A. and Voneche, J. (2001). *Working with Piaget: Essays in honour of Barbel Inhelder.* East Sussex, UK. London, England: Psychology Press.

Vecchi, V. (1998). The role of the Atelierista: An interview with Lella Gandini. In C. Edwards, L. Gandini, & G. Forman (Eds.), *The hundred languages of children: The Reggio Emilia Approach to Early Childhood Education* (2nd ed., pp. 139–148). Norwood, NJ: Ablex.

Verba, M., & Musatti, T. (1989). Minor phenomena and major processes of interaction with objects and peers in day care centres. *European Journal of Psychology of Education, 4*(2), 215–227.

Vernon, S.A., & Ferreiro, E. (1999, Winter). Writing development: A neglected variable in the consideration of phonological awareness. *Harvard Educational Review, 69*, 395–415. Retrieved from http://www.hepg.org

Vernon, S.A., & Ferreiro, E. (2005). Early literacy content and supporting research. *Growing Readers*. High Scope Educational Research Foundation. Retrieved from http://www.highscope.org/file/EducationalPrograms/ReadingInstitute/grc_research_support.pdf

von Glasersfeld, E. (1995). Sensory experience, abstraction, and teaching. In L.P. Steffe & J. Gale (Eds.), *Constructivism in education* (pp. 369–383). Hillsdale, NJ: Erlbaum.

Vuyk, R. (1981). *Overview and critique of Piaget's genetic epistemology 1965–1980*, Vol.1. London, England: Academic Press.

Vygotsky, L.S. (1930–1935/1978). *Mind in society: The development of higher mental processes.* V. John-Steiner, S. Scribner, & E. Souberman (Eds. & Trans.) Cambridge, MA: Harvard University Press.

Vygotsky, L.S. (1976). Play and its role in the mental development of the child. In J.S. Bruner, A. Jolly, & K. Sylva (Eds.), *Play—Its role in development and evolution* (pp. 537–554). New York, NY: Basic Books.

Wadsworth, B. (1978). *Piaget for the classroom teacher.* New York, NY: Longman.

Wadsworth, B.J. (2003). *Piaget's theory of cognitive and affective development* (5th ed.). New York, NY: Longman.

Wasserman, S. (1992). Serious play in the classroom. *Childhood Education, 68*(3), 133–139.

Wasserman, S., & Ivany, J. (1988). *Teaching elementary science: Who's afraid of spiders?* New York, NY: Harper & Row.

Weikart, D.P., Rogers, L., Adcock, C., & McClelland, D. (1971). *The cognitively oriented curriculum: A framework for preschool teachers.* Urbana, IL: University of Illinois Press.

Weikart, D.P., & Schweinhart, L.J. (2013). The High Scope curriculum for early childhood care and education. In J.L. Roopnarine & J.E. Johnson (Eds.), *Approaches to early childhood education* (6th ed., pp. 227–293). New York: Pearson.

Williams, C., & Kamii, C. (1986, November). How do children learn by handling objects? *Young Children*, pp. 22–26.

Wilson, J., & Jan, L. (1993). *Thinking for themselves: Developing strategies for reflective learning.* Portsmouth, NH: Heinemann.

Wohlwend, K.E. (2011). *Playing their way into literacies.* New York, NY: Teachers College Press.

Wortham, S. (2001). *Assessment in early childhood education* (3rd ed.). Upper Saddle River, NJ: Prentice Hall.

Wright, F.L. (1943). *An autobiography.* New York, NY: Duell, Sloan, & Pearce.

Zan, B. (1996). Interpersonal understanding among friends: A case-study of two young boys playing checkers. *Journal of Research in Childhood Education, 10*(2), 114–122.

INDEX

Page numbers followed by *b* and *t* indicate a box and table, respectively.

agreements 121–2; role of teacher in
enlivening 38

Bank Street Developmental-Interaction
Approach model 281
Barton, K. C. 262
board game/game making strategies of
children 176–9, 177*b*, 178*t*
Bodrova, E. 145
Bongiorno, L. 154
Boyd, B. F. 150
Bringuier, Jean-Claude 56
Britain, L. 71
Brown, C. P. 175
Bruner, J. 144
building a constructivist curriculum. *see*
constructivist curriculum building

caring communities: emotional comfort
in 214–15; emotional safety in 214;
intellectual safety and comfort in 215;
physical comfort in 212; physical safety in
210–11; *see also* community
The Carrot Seed (Krauss) 15
Chae, J. 150
Chaille, C. 71, 145
Charlie's Ticket to Literacy (Glover) 184–5
children: active learning needs of 18–19;
activities for representing what they know
40–2; choosing authentic tasks by 30–5;
cognitive conflict reconciliation by 37;
English as a second language learning
strategy 21; game creation by 261–2;
interactions with objects, others 35–7;
investigations development of 255–6;
knowledge construction in 18; learning
from others 42–3; learning to read
process 15; mental structures of 52, 55,
101, 345; movement from heteronomy
21; needs of, in a multicultural world
266–7; occasional dangers of autonomy
16; preparing in constructivist classrooms
35; refinement, coordination of thinking
process 39–40; and reflection 191–3;
representation of what they know by
40–2; revision of thinking by 10; struggles
in constructivist classroom 20–21; teacher
consideration of learning processes
14–15; teacher elicitation of ideas from
252–5
The Child's Conception of Space (Piaget) 52*b*
The Child's Conception of Time (Piaget) 52*b*
choice 110–19; acceptance of responsibility
fostered by 112–13; addition (in first-

grade) fostered by 118–19; authentic
choice 116; in the integrated curriculum
117; limited choice 115; physical
knowledge in preschool fostered by
118; purposeful choice 116; reading in
literature discussion groups fostered by
117–18; role of, in the classroom 110–11;
thinking of alternatives fostered by
111–12; use of, in the classroom 116*b*–17
b; wise decision making fostered by 112
classroom authenticity. *see* authentic tasks
classroom environment: authentic
environment, planning for 30*b*, 31, 45;
creating support for children 6; desk
arrangement in 35; impact on children
10, 27, 53; learning through interactions
with 13, 15, 51, 53; mental structures and
52; objects for inclusion in 53
*Code of Ethical Conduct and Statement of
Commitment* (NAEYC) 242–3
cognitive, social and moral development
134–6
cognitive balance 10, 88
cognitive conflict 37, 39, 174, 343
cognitive decentering 6, 134–5, 149, 344
cognitive development: approach of
High Scope model 285–92; choice and
promotion of 111; constructivist theory
description of 58–60, 88; development of
interests and 170; meaning creation and
56; moral development relation to 134–6;
play and imitation as avenues of 98,
144–5, 149, 182; project work and 39–40;
role of teacher 6*b*, 22, 31, 37–8; social
development relation to 134–6; testing
and 194–5
cognitive structure 55–6
collaborative projects 142, 229–30
Common Core Standards xiv, 8, 32,
264*b*–5*b*, 271
Common Core State Standards (CCSS) 8
community 201–32; absence and presence
of 208–9; adaptations for special needs
children 225–6; caring communities
206–8; children's books for promotion of
218; classroom communities 32–3, 137–8;
classroom discussions 222; classroom
environment planning 222–4; creation of
classroom communities 205–9; creation
of safe classroom communities 210–15;
curriculum strategies in infant-toddler
classroom 209*b*–10*b*; definition 201,
203–4; extending community beyond
the classroom 226–32; friendships,

social actions and 138–41; Kristi Dickey's second-grade classroom community 205; learning as community activity 11–12, 24; planning the classroom environment 222–6; problem posing and 175; reflection on shared experiences 217; Reggio Emilia approach in building 37–8; rule creation 220–1; shared decision making for creating 218–19; sharing bonds, forming bonds 216–22, 226–32; spontaneous, planned shared experiences 216–17; stories as tool for creation of 217–18; values inclusion by teachers 18, 23; *see also* caring communities

computers/interactive technologies instructional model 279

concrete operations stage of development (Piaget) 59

constructionism (of Papert and Resnick) 297

constructions play 146, 344

constructivism: defined 9–14; importance of, in appreciating children's understanding 89; individual responsibility for learning 13; interpretations of 297; learners supporting learners 13; learning as community activity 11–12; *see also* constructivist assumptions; constructivist theory

constructivist assumptions: activities for refining, coordinating old ways of thinking 39–40; activities for representation of what children know 40–2; communication, learning through social knowledge 42–3; graduate student perspective on 43–5; instructions for using 30*b*; learning through interactions with objects, others 35–7; use of surprise, and intrigue 37–8; vs. principles 28–9

constructivist classrooms: children interactions with objects, others 35–7; complexity of, teacher dislike for 34; conferences, workshops related to 29; matching the use of state-mandated content in 169; preparation of children in 35; problem solving activities 176–9, 177*b*, 178*t*; problem solving focus in 169; role of reflection in 190–1; teaching objectives in 6*b*; use of objects for children 35

constructivist curriculum 14–19; active teacher involvement 18; autonomy development focus 21–3; building, from children's questions 186–7;

building, from children's thinking 184; building, from teachers' interests 188–9; building and balancing 189; choice component 110–19; construction of 15–19; constructivist teaching objectives 6*b*; context considerations 18–19; development as shared enterprise 6; keeping children focused on content 262–4; organization of materials 17; physical knowledge activities 293*b*; problem posing and solving 179–84; for special needs children 299–300; strategies for community creation in infant-toddler classroom 209*b*–10*b*; strategies for projects 157*b*–8*b*; strategies for supporting play 155*b*; teacher consideration of children's learning processes 14–15; teacher planning of 5–6; use of children's cognitive, emotional growth 31; *see also* constructivist curriculum building; integrated curriculum

constructivist curriculum building 241–73; classroom library 259–60; collaboration with other adults 270–3; consideration of needs of each child 265–70; ethical behavior of teachers 242–3; game creation, by children and teachers 261–2; gradual introduction of constructivist approach 250–62; helping children understand expectations 245–9; journal writing 191, 260–1; knowledge about policies and procedures 244; knowledge related to content 243–4; literature log 259; organizing furniture, materials 244–5; reading parties 260; shared reading 44–5, 259; working with curriculum mandates 262–4

constructivist evaluation. *see* assessment; documentation

constructivist models of instruction 278–301; academic discipline sources for 280*b*; for children with intellectual disabilities 299–300; components of 282*b*–283*b*; defined 279–83; development studies of human intellect sources for 281*b*; of DeVries and Kamii 279, 292–6; examples of 279, 281; High Scope model 279, 285–9; learning theory sources for 280*b*; metacognition sources for 280*b*; questions to help identify 283*b*–284*b*; of Resnick and Papert 296–9; sources of thought for 302*t*

constructivist teachers: active involvement vs. desk work 18; being informed about